International and Development Education

The *International and Development Education Series* focuses on the complementary areas of comparative, international, and development education. Books emphasize a number of topics ranging from key international education issues, trends, and reforms to examinations of national education systems, social theories, and development education initiatives. Local, national, regional, and global volumes (single authored and edited collections) constitute the breadth of the series and offer potential contributors a great deal of latitude based on interests and cutting edge research. The series is supported by a strong network of international scholars and development professionals who serve on the International and Development Education Advisory Board and participate in the selection and review process for manuscript development.

SERIES EDITORS
John N. Hawkins
Professor Emeritus, University of California, Los Angeles
Senior Consultant, IFE 2020 East West Center

W. James Jacob
Assistant Professor, University of Pittsburgh
Director, Institute for International Studies in Education

PRODUCTION EDITOR
Heejin Park
Project Associate, Institute for International Studies in Education

INTERNATIONAL EDITORIAL ADVISORY BOARD
Clementina Acedo, *UNESCO's International Bureau of Education, Switzerland*
Philip G. Altbach, *Boston University, USA*
Carlos E. Blanco, *Universidad Central de Venezuela*
Sheng Yao Cheng, *National Chung Cheng University, Taiwan*
Ruth Hayhoe, *University of Toronto, Canada*
Wanhua Ma, *Peking University, China*
Ka-Ho Mok, *University of Hong Kong, China*
Christine Musselin, *Sciences Po, France*
Yusuf K. Nsubuga, *Ministry of Education and Sports, Uganda*
Namgi Park, *Gwangju National University of Education, Republic of Korea*
Val D. Rust, *University of California, Los Angeles, USA*
Suparno, *State University of Malang, Indonesia*
John C. Weidman, *University of Pittsburgh, USA*
Husam Zaman, *Taibah University, Saudi Arabia*

Institute for International Studies in Education
School of Education, University of Pittsburgh
5714 Wesley W. Posvar Hall, Pittsburgh, PA 15260 USA

Center for International and Development Education
Graduate School of Education & Information Studies, University of California, Los Angeles
Box 951521, Moore Hall, Los Angeles, CA 90095 USA

Titles:

Higher Education in Asia/Pacific: Quality and the Public Good
Edited by Terance W. Bigalke and Deane E. Neubauer

Affirmative Action in China and the U.S.: A Dialogue on Inequality and Minority Education
Edited by Minglang Zhou and Ann Maxwell Hill

Critical Approaches to Comparative Education: Vertical Case Studies from Africa, Europe, the Middle East, and the Americas
Edited by Frances Vavrus and Lesley Bartlett

Curriculum Studies in South Africa: Intellectual Histories & Present Circumstances
Edited by William F. Pinar

Higher Education, Policy, and the Global Competition Phenomenon
Edited by Laura M. Portnoi, Val D. Rust, and Sylvia S. Bagley

The Search for New Governance of Higher Education in Asia
Edited by Ka-Ho Mok

International Students and Global Mobility in Higher Education: National Trends and New Directions
Edited by Rajika Bhandari and Peggy Blumenthal

Curriculum Studies in Brazil: Intellectual Histories, Present Circumstances
Edited by William F. Pinar

Access, Equity, and Capacity in Asia Pacific Higher Education
Edited by Deane Neubauer and Yoshiro Tanaka

Policy Debates in Comparative, International, and Development Education
Edited by John N. Hawkins and W. James Jacob

Increasing Effectiveness of the Community College Financial Model: A Global Perspective for the Global Economy
Edited by Stewart E. Sutin, Daniel Derrico, Rosalind Latiner Raby, and Edward J. Valeau

Curriculum Studies in Mexico: Intellectual Histories, Present Circumstances
William F. Pinar

Forthcoming titles:

Taiwan Education at the Crossroad: When Globalization Meets Localization
Chuing Prudence Chou and Gregory Ching

Internationalization of East Asian Higher Education: Globalization's Impact
John D. Palmer

Curriculum Studies in Mexico

Intellectual Histories, Present Circumstances

Edited by
William F. Pinar

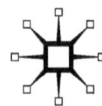

CURRICULUM STUDIES IN MEXICO
Copyright © William F. Pinar, 2011.
Softcover reprint of the hardcover 1st edition 2011 978-0-230-11480-7

All rights reserved.

First published in 2011 by
PALGRAVE MACMILLAN®
in the United States—a division of St. Martin's Press LLC,
175 Fifth Avenue, New York, NY 10010.

Where this book is distributed in the UK, Europe and the rest of the world, this is by Palgrave Macmillan, a division of Macmillan Publishers Limited, registered in England, company number 785998, of Houndmills, Basingstoke, Hampshire RG21 6XS.

Palgrave Macmillan is the global academic imprint of the above companies and has companies and representatives throughout the world.

Palgrave® and Macmillan® are registered trademarks in the United States, the United Kingdom, Europe and other countries.

ISBN 978-1-349-29612-5   ISBN 978-0-230-33788-6 (eBook)
DOI 10.1057/9780230337886

Library of Congress Cataloging-in-Publication Data

Pinar, William.
    Curriculum Studies in Mexico : intellectual histories, present circumstances / William F. Pinar.
        p. cm.—(International & development education)

    1. Curriculum planning—Mexico. 2. Education and state—Mexico. I. Title.

LB1564.M6P56 2011
375'.0010972—dc22   2011010884

A catalogue record of the book is available from the British Library.

Design by Newgen Imaging Systems (P) Ltd., Chennai, India.

First edition: October 2011

Contents

Series Editors' Introduction   vii

Acknowledgments   xi

List of Acronyms   xiii

Introduction   1
William F. Pinar

1. Curriculum Studies in Mexico: An Overview   29
   Ashwani Kumar

2. Footprints and Marks on the Intellectual History of Curriculum Studies in Mexico: Looking toward the Second Decade of the Twenty-First Century   49
   Alicia de Alba

3. Curriculum Studies in Mexico: History and Current Circumstances   75
   Frida Díaz Barriga Arceo

4. Curriculum Studies in Mexico: Origin, Evolution, and Current Tendencies   91
   Ángel Díaz Barriga

5. Curriculum Studies in Mexico: Key Scholars   111
   Alfredo Furlán

6. Acculturation, Hybridity, Cosmopolitanism in Ibero-American Curriculum Studies   137
   José María García Garduño

7. Revisiting Curriculum Studies   165
   Raquel Glazman-Nowalski

8 Professional Education in Mexico at the Beginning
   of the Twenty-First Century   181
   María Concepción Barrón Tirado

9 Curriculum Studies in Mexico: The Exchanges,
   the Concepts, the Practices   207
   William F. Pinar

Epilogue: The Final Word
Alicia de Alba   249
Frida Díaz Barriga Arceo   251
José María García Garduño   252

Contributors   257

Index   261

Series Editors' Introduction

We are pleased to welcome a third contribution to the International and Development Education Book Series by University of British Columbia professor William F. Pinar. His previous two volumes examined country case studies of curriculum studies in South Africa and Brazil. Now from a third continental perspective, Pinar assembles an equally stellar cadre of curriculum scholars in *Curriculum Studies in Mexico: Intellectual Histories, Present Circumstances*. This latest contribution delves into the thorny issue of curriculum in a setting that is both complex and diverse. The historical context and current development of curriculum in and about Mexico is brilliantly analyzed by the nine contributing scholars. And it is not just a story of Mexico but also involves the complex relationship of two societies bound together in significant ways. The authors of this volume explore these issues in a variety of ways, but it is in the context of *thinking* about curriculum that much of value is added. Going back to Ivan Illich and other progressive thinkers, this study puts curriculum into a context that is essential for an informed understanding of how it works on both sides of the United States–Mexico border. In much the same way as a dominant paradigm has come to define what we mean by schooling, formal schools became the best institutions in which learning should occur, with a planned curriculum, disciplines, units of study, graded classrooms, testing, and evaluation.

The curriculum in particular became a pillar of support for the dominant paradigm. The role of the formal and informal curriculum within the dominant paradigm was an essential part of the substructure that prevented alternative ways of viewing "education." Suffice it to say that course identification, organization, presentation, content, and prioritization came to be identified with and support the goals and objectives of the dominant paradigm and itself to become impervious to change. The perennial concerns as to what knowledge is worthwhile, the appropriateness of teaching patterns, and assessment have been argued over the years (from Dewey to Apple), yet fundamental patterns of curriculum at both precollegiate and collegiate levels are readily recognized worldwide, with little or no debate or discussion. It is these issues and others that this volume urges one to think on. The intellectual history of curriculum in Mexico, its evolutionary development, and its various forms are all discussed in-depth, thus providing the reader with a first-rate social history and analytical argument about this problematic. Thus, this study will be of value not only to those interested in curriculum per se but also to those interested in the educational intellectual history of transborder relations between Mexico and the United States.

This volume highlights the dominant influence the United States has on countries in the Western Hemisphere and especially on its southern neighbor, Mexico, including the dominant influence it has had on Mexican history and education. This influence leads some critical curricularists to argue that it is one way the United States maintains its ideologic hegemony through education on Mexico. Over the past 170 years the histories of the two countries are often shared, and—despite the Mexican-American War from 1846–1848—migrations from both countries have interwoven a geographic tapestry that in many ways binds the two together in terms of cultures, ethnicities, languages, and education. This shared history remains a vibrant part of the current curricular context of both countries as we enter the second decade of the twenty-first century, especially with so many millions of Mexicans who currently reside within the United States legally and illegally.

The current status of curriculum studies in Mexico is too diverse to box into a single definition, according to Frida Díaz Barriga Arceo in chapter 3. Several authors signal the influence of globalization on Mexican curriculum studies and argue that the Mexican context cannot be fully understood without first understanding Mexico's relationship with other countries. In chapter 6, José María García Garduño emphasizes the need to position Mexican curriculum studies from an Ibero-American perspective and the unique circumstances wherein curriculum studies arose in Argentina, Brazil, Mexico, and Spain. Curriculum studies in each of these four countries have undergone three phases according to Garduño: acculturation, hybridity, and cosmopolitanism. Each of these phases emphasize the dynamic nature of cultural studies in general and how diversity in curriculum studies is part of the complex national context that underpins Mexican education today.

Just as he did with his other two books on South Africa and Brazil, Pinar includes both local and international perspectives on the historical and current status of curriculum studies in this present volume. The entire process in writing this volume is somewhat unique, in that Pinar provided an opportunity for dialogue between the contributors and gives the "final word" to Alicia de Alba, Frida Díaz Barriga Arceo, and José María García

Garduño of Mexico. This approach also provides each contributor to serve both as an object and as a subject of curriculum studies. The volume represents a category of conversation, providing a venue for discussion, debate, and understanding. And it is Pinar's unique category of conversation approach on curriculum studies that serves as what de Alba terms the "nodal point" for this volume. This book represents a major milestone in documenting the historical evolution, current status, and projected trends of curriculum studies in Mexico. It is a must-read for scholars, policy makers, and educators at all levels with an interest in Mexican education.

JOHN N. HAWKINS
University of California, Los Angeles

W. JAMES JACOB
University of Pittsburgh

References

Pinar, William F., ed. 2010. *Curriculum Studies in South Africa*. New York: Palgrave Macmillan.

Pinar, William F., ed. 2011. *Curriculum Studies in Brazil*. New York: Palgrave Macmillan.

Acknowledgments

I thank Palgrave Macmillan's Burke Gerstenschlager, and Professors W. James Jacob and John Hawkins for their support of this project.

I thank Ashwani Kumar, my graduate assistant—who helped in ways large and small—and whose synoptic essay on curriculum studies in Mexico appears here as chapter 1.

I thank Carole Wallace for continuing to make possible my daily life at University of British Columbia (UBC).

I am grateful to Professor Frida Díaz Barriga Arceo for her generous help from beginning to end of the project.

Without the support of the Social Sciences and Humanities Research Council of Canada, this project could not have been undertaken.

Without the generosity of my Mexican colleagues, this project could not have occurred. To each of you—Alicia de Alba, Frida Díaz Barriga Arceo, Ángel Díaz Barriga, Alfredo Furlán, José María García Garduño, Raquel Glazman-Nowalski, María Concepción Barrón Tirado—I express my gratitude.

Acronyms

ABP	problem-based learning
AERA	American Educational Research Association
AID	International Agency for Development
ANUIES	Asociación Nacional de Universidades e Instituciones de Educación Superior
CCEC	Fields of Structural Curricular Arrangement
CCH	College of Sciences and Humanities
CEE	Centre for Educative Studies
CEG	generalized structural crisis
CESU	Centre of Studies on Universities
CIDE	Centro de Investigación y Documentación Educativa
CIDOC	Center for Intercultural Documentation
CINVESTAV	Centre for Research and Advanced Studies
CISE	Center of Investigations and Educative Services
CNME	Commission for New Teaching Methods
COMIE	Mexican Counsel of Educative Investigation
CONACYT	National Council of Science and Technology
CONALEP	Educational Modernization Program
CONAPO	Census of the National Population Council
CONOCER	Council for Standardization and Certification of Labor Proficiency
CREFAL	Regional Center for Basic Education for Latin America
DIE	Department of Educative Research
ENEP	National School of Professional Studies
EXANI	National Income Examinations
FFyL	Faculty of Philosophy and Liberal Arts
FTA	Free Trade Agreement
HEIs	higher education institutions
IAACS	International Association for the Advancement of Curriculum Studies
IISUE	Research Institute for Universities and Education

ILO	International Labour Organization
INEE	National Institution of Educational Evaluation
IPN	National Polytechnic Institute
ITESM	Monterrey Institute of Technology and Higher Education
LBP	Learning-based problem solving
NAFTA	North American Free Trade Agreement
OAS	Organization of American States
OECD	Organisation for Economic Co-operation and Development
PIB	Gross Internal Product
PMETYC	Project for Modernization of Technical Education and Training
PRI	Institutional Revolutionary Party
SEP	Ministry of Public Education of Spain
SNCT	National System for Training for Work of Spain
SNI	National System of Researchers
TIC	information or communication technologies
TLC	Free Trade Agreements
UAM	Autonomous Metropolitan University
UAM-X	University-Xochimilco
UAN	University of Nayarit
UAN	Autonomous University of Nayarit
UBC	University of British Columbia
UFRHEA	Unit of Human Resources Formation and Academic Evaluation
UNAM	National Autonomous University of Mexico
UNDP	United Nations Development Programme
USAID	United States Agency for International Development

Introduction
William F. Pinar

> There are two Mexicos: one within the border of the republic and one in the US
>
> José David Saldívar (2006, 145)

How many US curriculum studies professors know either? While the brute facts of US-Mexico history are familiar to many, even these tend to remain contextualized in US history. At the time of this writing (summer 2010), Mexicans working illegally in the US are so contextualized, converted into pretexts for domestic political wrangling. Drug wars, kidnappings, and violence in general: these horrific facts of contemporary Mexican life provide provocation for a paranoid patriotism in the United States, intensified by a mass media industry that acts as if only sensationalism sells. Even in the ordinarily restrained *New York Times* the July 2010 election was first reported in patronizing terms, as assurance that "amid all the violence Mexico's democracy, flawed as it may be, endures" (Lacey 2010, A4). One day afterward a more sober and subtle commentary did appear—from Mexico City (see Krauze 2010, A19).

Such relentless recontextualization also occurs in the US scholarly literature, wherein even achieving Mexican American students are often represented as struggling (Pope 2001, 51) and as out-of-sync with school (Tyack and Hansot 1990, 246). In US conflations of the two Mexicos, the "deficit model" seems dominant (Garcia 1997, 147; Miller 1996, 81), even though critical questions concerning representation—broadly cultural and specifically curricular—have been raised by many (Hoberman 1989, 188; Quintanar-Sarellana 1997, 50; Curtis 2001, 131; Rodriguez and Kitchen 2004). Too often, however, the two Mexicos dissolve into figments of the "Anglo" imagination.

For many Americans "Mexico" has never been "there," except as (in the nineteenth century) an obstacle to imperial expansion, and (in the twentieth century) as a source of drugs, labor, a holiday or retirement destination, and, more seriously, a site of self-conferred exile and self-rejuvenation. Serious scrutiny of the Mexican nation[1]—including by curriculum studies scholars, whose professional obligation includes having an at least introductory knowledge of curriculum scholarship worldwide—remains a casualty of a pervasive US culture of narcissism (Lasch 1978). In self-defense, English translations of Mexican curriculum scholarship are infrequently available. In the *International Handbook of Curriculum Research*, summaries became available (see Díaz Barriga, A. 2003; Díaz Barriga, F. 2003). In this collection we gain an individuated and in-depth insight.

For generations US intellectuals have traveled to Mexico, sometimes to learn about Mexico, often to escape the United States. Molly Mullin (1995, 170) references Stuart Chase's 1931 *Mexico: A Study of Two Americas* (a book illustrated by Diego Rivera) as one example in which a comparative study found life in the US wanting. Like other US intellectuals and academicians, Mullin tells us (1995, 170), Chase was "especially attracted" to indigenous Mexican cultural productions because they seemed to him to be instances of "nonalienated labor, a merging of the utilitarian and the creative, art and community, undivided by class and the distinctions of taste ensuing from mass consumption." Chase was hardly alone in discerning in Mexico progressive possibilities foreclosed in the United States.

For many US curriculum studies scholars, it was Ivan Illich and his Center for Intercultural Documentation that expressed such progressive possibility. In his chapter, Ángel Díaz Barriga references the Center, as does Joel Spring (2006, 3) in his invaluable study of the "educational security state." Spring (2006, 139) recalls that Paulo Freire came to "rely on Erich Fromm's [Freire met Fromm at Cuernavaca] work to explain Guevara's admonishment that revolution would be a revolution of love." In 1970 Spring himself visited the Center where he met Freire (Spring 2006, 142).[2]

Cuernavaca was where the African American poet Audre Lorde experienced an "epiphany,"[3] that changed and deepened her ideas about poetry" (De Veaux 2004, 51).[4] De Veaux (2004, 51) tells us,

> One day, while walking down a hill at dawn on her way to the square for the bus that would take her to the *Cuidad Universitaria*, she realized there was a connection between the "a quality of light" in Mexico, what she felt deeply, and words. For the first time in her life, she "had an insight into what poetry could be." Where once she'd thought of her poems as "love for the blind beauty of words," she now saw in them the possibility to "*re*-create" a feeling, like the one she was having on that hill, rather than the dreamlike imitation of feeling she felt so much of her writing had been.

Poetry can recreate feeling, but for whom? Can only she or he who underwent the feeling then recognize the feeling recreated poetically?

As this very brief and subjective sampling of Mexico in one American mind implies, these questions about poetry and the recreation of feeling problematize this study of curriculum studies in Mexico. Is the Mexico that the Mexican scholars reference in their chapters visible to us "on the outside"? Or does our position as inheritors of the imperial past consign us to incomprehension? If we went to Mexico, could we see what the Mexican scholars have seen? The visual verb is itself misleading, because what the scholar-participants—whom I shall introduce momentarily—are describing can be "seen" (e.g., experienced) only from the "inside," from having lived and worked as they have in a Mexico that they themselves would not claim to have fully seen but have nonetheless experienced through the singularity of their subjectivities and life histories.

My reconstruction of the scholar-participants' interviews, essays, and exchanges as "complicated conversation"—not only with me and the panel members, but also with their own experience in the field in which they have worked—further fades this "inside," as inevitably I recontextualize it into conversations I have had and am now having with other scholars in other countries—including South Africa (Pinar 2010) and Brazil (Pinar 2011a)—and within myself. Has, then, Mexico once again disappeared into an American imagination? Was I able—in Chapter 9—to grasp the distinctive realities the scholar-participants described, even while translating these into terms I know "from the inside"? This challenge—it is the challenge of internationalization[5]—becomes evident in our capacity to grasp the distinctive Mexican inflections of common curriculum concepts, among them "activity."

In Mexico, the concept of "activity" is not associated with Franklin Bobbitt (1918, 18, 19, 35) or W. W. Charters and "activity analysis" (Thirty Schools 1943, 119; Pinar et al. 1995, 101; Ravitch 2000, 166–168), wherein the content of the curriculum is derived from adult activities that school students are then to learn. In contrast, in Mexican curriculum studies the concept of "activity" is construed as a social practice, not in instrumental terms reminiscent of US-style social efficiency (Pinar et al. 1996, 91) but, instead, evoking Marxist echoes of political practice, derived specifically from the work of Louis Althusser (Díaz Barriga, A. 2003, 450). Althusser's notion of interpellation denotes a theory of socialization that is structured politically as well as socially and subjectively (for a lucid discussion, see Butler 1997).

Accordingly, then, instead of US-style "preparation" (as in teacher "preparation" or "training"), one finds in the chapters that follow references to "formation," a considerably more complex concept that recalls European conceptions of education, including *Didaktik* and *Bildung* (Westbury et al. 2000; Pinar 2006a). In contrast to the predominance of psychologism, which in the United States has advanced a conception of individualism linked with capital accumulation and consumption and always focused on "behavior," "formation" is a much more expansive and changing concept that integrates (but does not conflate) subjectivity and sociality.[6]

To study such "formation," I juxtaposed the scholar-participants' life histories with their intellectual histories of the field and analyses of present circumstances, a strategy informed by *currere*, the lived experience of curriculum (Pinar et al. 1995, 518). Such an autobiographically inflected strategy enables us outside Mexico to grasp the specificity of nationally distinctive curriculum concepts—such as "activity" and "formation"—as it reiterates the historicity of the curriculum and of the field that attempts to understand it. Such a juxtaposition underlines as well the subjectivity of historicity, as it is individual scholars whose "activity" engages the legacies bequeathed to them—sometimes forcibly, as we will see—as well as the professional obligations incurred by present circumstances. Individual intellectual life histories, then, inform present circumstances as these restructure disciplinary histories according to opportunities simultaneously bared and barred by the present moment. The concepts of "genealogy" and "archeology" specify what is at stake in such a conception of disciplinarity, wherein the field's intellectual advancement depends upon studying its intellectual histories and present circumstances.

Intellectual Histories, Present Circumstances

Genealogies are historical studies whose purpose is to produce critical effects in the present.

John S. Ransom (1997, 79)

"Genealogy," David Roberts (1995, 61) points out, was Nietzsche's term for analyzing that which has "somehow come into being," what has happened between the beginning of something (in our case, curriculum studies in Mexico) and the present.[7] In Nietzsche's practice of genealogy, David Owen (1995) explains, three related interests, posed interrogatively, come into play: (1) "What are we?"; (2) "How have we become what we are?"; and (3) "Given what we are, what can we become?" (Nietzsche, quoted in Owen 1995, 40). Despite the straightforward even commonsensical character of these questions, Nietzsche emphasizes "the conflictual elements of this history and, second, its psychological dimensions" (Ransom 1997, 5). These two dimensions—historicity and subjectivity—intersect in the formation of curriculum studies.

Genealogy is, as we also see in these chapters, a form of cultural and political critique. It elaborates regenerative possibilities immanent within current practices by contesting regressive (if dominant) ones. It requires, Nietzsche insisted, heroic individuals[8] who "do not carry forward any kind of process but live contemporaneously with each other" (quoted in Roberts 1995, 61). These individuals—the scholar-participants in the present case—engage in rigorous and sustained dialogue across history. "The goal of genealogy," Joshua Dienstag (1997, 78) underscores, "is not just recovery of the past, but the redemption of that past through the use of it in the creation of the future." In these genealogical terms, then, intellectual histories restructure present circumstances, providing passages to futures that the present appears only to foreclose.

It is from Nietzsche, Ransom (1997, 79) reminds, that Foucault "acquired his ideas on genealogy as a method of historical inquiry." Although derived from Nietzsche, the concept of genealogy in Foucault, Martin Jay (1993, 409 n. 100) asserts, "reversed the distancing, contemplative gaze of traditional historical analysis." Foucault may have rejected traditional scholarly pretensions to apolitical neutrality, but other students of Foucault point out that distancing is prerequisite to the genealogical undertaking. Ransom (1997, 80, emphasis added), for instance, emphasizes that "the first critical task of genealogy, then, involves *distancing* oneself from the institution, morality, or worldview that is investigated." Such distancing—one potential of internationalization—leads to no transcendental apolitical detachment, but it can constitute a "nonplace...in between," wherein Foucault imagined "divergence and marginal elements" can emerge (quoted in Roberts 1995, 219). The "objectivity" that "traditional historical analysis" promised may be one casualty of Foucault's engaged analysis, but distancing creates openness to the contingent and provisional truth of lived experience in History. In such a "nonplace" the repressed returns.

What returns are archeological disclosures of power in ever-changing formation, in our time trumpeted as educational "reforms" and "innovations." "By genealogy," Ransom (1997, 78) specifies, "Foucault refers to the historical investigation of the origins and rationality of specific power formations." In this definition we glimpse the reciprocity of distance and engagement. "Genealogy," Ransom (1997, 5) affirms, "works to uncover the battles that gave birth to the world we accept as natural, to make it questionable again, and to make it possible to fight over it once more." In this sense genealogy parallels psychoanalysis, as both are focused on the recovery of insight and agency through memory and its articulation in relationship with others. In this "activity" of reconstructing one's "formation," the symbolic and the psychic reconfigure each other, as implied in Kögler's (1999, 175) distinction between genealogy and archeology: "Whereas the archaeological analysis lays bare symbolic structures, the genealogical investigation focuses on individual- and group-directed techniques of normalization, control, and exploitation." Without the subjective agency the concept of "formation" preserves, normalization means *only* control and exploitation. As these chapters demonstrate, however, educational "activity"—simultaneously a social practice and a subjective formation—reconstructs present circumstances through the study of intellectual history (e.g., through memory and the historicity memory supports).

Nietzsche's concept of genealogy works in two ways, Owen (1995) suggests. First, it seeks to articulate an overcoming of nihilism—in our era a pervasive sense of victimization—by articulating our experience of defeat. Only after being rendered intelligible does our defeat in the present become something we can surpass intellectually and psychologically. Second, Nietzsche's genealogical activity articulates an overcoming of decadence[9] by communicating those affective dispositions—such as heroism and irony—he deemed necessary to mobilize our volitional resources for undertaking cultural renewal. (In the method of *currere*, synthesis is the moment of mobilization [Pinar et al. 1995, 521]). For Owen (1995), Nietzsche's conception of genealogy represents an eroticized conception of truth, reason, and human freedom that I might summarize as "worldliness" (Pinar 2009a).

Beginning in 2006, Alicia de Alba, Frida Díaz Barriga Arceo, Ángel Díaz Barriga, Alfredo Furlán, José María García Garduño, Raquel Glazman-Nowalski, and María Concepción Barrón Tirado participated in such a genealogical undertaking. In the first phase of the project, these scholars generously allowed me to pose questions concerning their intellectual life histories, asking them how Mexican national history and culture as well as globalization structured their own intellectual-professional formation. From these interviews and with their permission I have drawn the sketches of introduction that follow. In the second phase, the scholar-participants composed essays concerning the intellectual histories and present circumstances of curriculum studies in Mexico; these essays were then studied by two members of an international panel: Professor Alice Casimiro Lopes of Brazil and Professor Yuzhen Xu of China. In the third phase of the project, I studied the exchanges between the scholar-participants and the panel members, summarizing them in Chapter 9. As in the previous studies (2010, 2011), Ashwani Kumar provides an overview.

The Mexican Scholars

The process of understanding moves back and forth, between idea and context, or between myself and the other I seek to understand.

David D. Roberts (1995, 35)

Alicia de Alba

Reflecting on her intellectual formation, Alicia de Alba testified to her parents' influence. As a young man, her father had been a member of the Communist Party; at the same time he was faithful to his conservative Catholic wife's wish for their children to be educated in the Catholic faith, "a promise," de Alba confides, "that is incomprehensible to me even to this day." However, by primary school de Alba's skepticism had started, supported by her paternal grandmother, an anthropologist and archaeologist, who provided de Alba with "another view of being a woman." "An exceptional woman," de Alba recalls, "she was a very important influence in my life, as much in intellectual aspects as in other aspects." With these conflicting influences, "my profound social and intellectual interest began."

Alicia de Alba's father taught in the Faculty of Economics of the National Autonomous University of Mexico (UNAM).[10] When he returned from campus each evening there were often "several cars waiting for him. He always had time for his students." She recalls, "I was fascinated with these dialogues, with the discussions, with the debates." Among the memories that remain is her father's prescient prediction that China would play an increasingly prominent role in the world economic system. He was a key figure in her formation, de Alba acknowledges: "I am the desire of my father."

Combining social commitment with academic study, de Alba became interested in the children who came to the houses in her neighborhood asking for bread. A primary-school student herself at this time, de Alba interviewed these children, asking about their specific circumstances, discovering that several had been sent out by "small organized mafias." Others were looking for work: "I remember one girl who started to work by cleaning bird cages and later she went back to school."

"I belong to the generation of 1968," de Alba acknowledges. As in France, the United States, and elsewhere, in Mexico too there was a strong student movement. On October 2, 1968, ten days before the Summer Olympics, the military "assassinated a great number of students." De Alba reports, "I was not at the meeting but the events of 1968 marked me, like they marked the majority of those of us who were students at that time."

On June 10, 1971, "we suffered another violent repression of the student movement. That day there was another slaughter. On this occasion I was at the meeting and it is one of the strongest memories I have of my life as a student."

De Alba's began her undergraduate career studying architecture. On "Red Sundays" UNAM architecture students volunteered to work in the revolutionary community "Ruben Jaramillo." While helping in the construction of houses, de Alba found herself also attending to the social problems of the community, specifically the educational problems. This was, she recalls, a "strong experience" that persuaded her to leave architecture to study in the social sciences, specifically in education.

De Alba's introduction to curriculum studies occurred in the Unit of Human Resources Formation and Academic Evaluation (UFRHEA) in the National School of Professional Studies in Zaragoza (ENEP-Zaragoza) of the UNAM. She had studied the work of Raquel Glazman and María Ibarrola concerning "study plan[11] designs," guided by María Esther Aguirre Lora, her baccalaureate thesis director. "In an artisanal way and following in her footsteps," de Alba recalls, "I learned the occupation of investigating." Adriana Puiggros has proven a "constant light during my entire academic career."

In January 1982, studying at the Center of Investigations and Educative Services (CISE) at UNAM, Ángel Díaz Barriga acknowledged an article de Alba had written: "This gesture from Ángel was incommensurable and constitutive for me." Almost a decade later, de Alba worked with Ángel Díaz Barriga and with Edgar González Gaudiano, resulting in an anthology entitled *The Field of the Curriculum*. Engagement with educational politics and curricular projects has proved "imperative" to the research de Alba has undertaken. The radical disparities across the world in incomes and standards of living constitute an ongoing curriculum concern for de Alba, as are matters of citizenship, environment, gender, identity, and diversity.

Frida Díaz Barriga Arceo

Since 2007, in collaboration with Ángel Díaz Barriga and María Concepción Barrón Tirado, Frida Díaz Barriga Arceo has been engaged in a historical investigation entitled "Educative Models and Their Impact on Curricular Projects and Practices." The central question concerns how the curriculum reform of the past two decades has "transformed the educative practices and the role of the actors, principally professors and their students." In particular, Díaz Barriga Arceo studies how "attitudes, conceptions and practices" are changing in response to these programs and politics. Thus far "we found, as would be expected, contradicting visions and experiences." Although for those "functionaries" working in university administrations these programs and politics have been "favorable," for many others they have not been so, as they express "the neo-liberal spirit of the era." A self-aggrandizing system of individualism and competitiveness in obtaining funding, coupled with an "exaggerated efficiency" that breaks down the social network of the universities, results in poor conditions for collaborative, especially long-term, research. Educational institutions are funded inequitably, penalizing those smaller institutions located in poorer sections of Mexico. The natural sciences are favored over the social sciences and the humanities. The overall effect is the effacement of particular histories of relationships between educational institutions and the communities in which they reside. Have these developments and preoccupations influenced Díaz Barriga Arceo's professional trajectory? "The answer is a resounding yes." She pointed out,

> We cannot remove ourselves from the zeitgeist or the spirit of the era that we have lived through, from the generation that we belong to; however, at the same time, as social actors, we make decisions and we construct our own life projects. This has been my case.

To illustrate, Díaz Barriga Arceo recounted key moments in her professional self-formation.

The first occurred during her secondary school experience in the 1970s, when she was a student in "an innovative curricular project of the era." Inspired by Leftist thinking, this project construed education as anti-authoritarian as it promoted critical thinking. The experience committed Díaz Barriga Arceo to social change through education. During her undergraduate studies, despite the strong influence of behaviorism in the Faculty of Psychology of the UNAM, Díaz Barriga Arceo studied cognitive psychology, specifically constructivism and critical pedagogy. At the beginning of the 1990s, Ángel Díaz Barriga—the Latin American scholar "most recognized in the area of curriculum studies"—invited her to join him and his colleagues in an ongoing curricular investigation supported by the Mexican Counsel of Educative Investigation (COMIE). For fifteen years, Díaz Barriga Arceo participated in this interdisciplinary community of Mexican investigators committed to curriculum research. She attributes her own and the field's intellectual advancement to this collective concentration of effort.

During the 1970s, a decade when there was public support for "social transformation" and "the awakening of conscience," Díaz Barriga Arceo participated in various educational projects. During the 1980s, the hegemony of behaviorism in academic psychology was challenged, enabling the emergence of constructivism, cognitive psychology, humanism, and critical pedagogy. During this period, she continues, four "great" tendencies formed within curriculum studies: (1) the systemic-technological; (2) the critical-reconceptualist; (3) the psycho-pedagogical or cognitive-constructivism orientation; and (4) the interpretive. During the 1990s, neoliberalism arrived, and with it, the so-called flexible curricula defined by the logic of competencies focused on the learning of students. "But above all," Díaz Barriga Arceo reflects, "the reforms lack a deep reflection about the sense and repercussions that they caused, failing to take into consideration the ethical, cultural and human costs of neoliberal reform."

Curriculum studies in Mexico is now "polysemous," characterized by a range of theoretical perspectives—styles of work and intellectual interests that are sometimes shared but also sometimes conflict with each other. "Therefore," Díaz Barriga Arceo concludes, "the choice of a personal point of view ... necessarily implicates ruptures, turns and exclusions." Rather than "an exclusive dedication to the topic," curriculum research in Mexico is typified by "incursions in different fields and study objectives that are related to the phenomena" under investigation, as her own professional history suggests:

> I have worked around curriculum studies, teaching, evaluation and teacher formation. And of course, in my work agenda, there is a strong link and a concern for a series of problems and social demands of the country and of the Latin American region.

Indeed, Díaz Barriga Arceo regards the researcher's commitment to the community as primary, and detachment from social reality as epistemologically problematic. Such commitment does not mean coinciding with the government's agenda or with the agenda of funding agencies; indeed, she notes, "a series of tensions and conflicts arise." At the institutional level, she reports, faculty felt "the pressure of the international organizations and of certain national institutions and agencies with respect to the what and how of development and of investigation relating to the topics of education and curriculum." The free trade agreements in which Mexico participates, moreover, coupled with the politics of industrial reconversion (involving the standardization of certification of technical and professional studies), and above all those policies that placed conditions on the funding that the universities and academic investigators receive, have all structured contemporary curriculum studies in Mexico.

Mexican curriculum discourses are increasingly focused on competencies, curricular flexibility, quality, re-engineering, strategic planning, and institutional analysis. In one sense, Díaz Barriga Arceo notes, this development represents an intensification of corporate or business thought that can be traced back to the mid-1970s. Even more so than its antecedents, however, contemporary versions—rationalized by economic globalization and cultural cosmopolitanism—prioritize "efficiency, evaluation and quality certification in the search for excellence, the formation of highly competent and competitive human capital, judged not only by national but global standards." Neoliberalism predominates, undermining concerns for understanding and theoretical reflection. In Díaz Barriga Arceo's specialization—university curriculum development—there is a continuing failure to respond to those "social needs" that had characterized the formation of professionals in public universities in the 1970s (and even into the mid-1980s). Now informationalism, not social ethics, provides the rationale for professionalism. The latter has devolved into continuous evaluation, the impact of which Díaz Barriga Arceo has been investigating.

Frida Díaz Barriga Arceo characterizes her own contribution to the curriculum field as "psycho-pedagogical." This contribution adds to the intellectual advancement of curriculum studies in Mexico by providing alternatives to "the transmissible-reproductive vision of knowledge and a critical view to the behavioral focus of learning and its applications to curriculum and teaching." In the three decades she has worked with these curricular themes, Díaz Barriga Arceo has formulated specific curricular forms of socio-constructivism. The classic questions of the curriculum—"the what, how, why and for whom"—require, she argues, psychological, didactic, and socio-educative knowledge of school scenarios. In her most recent research, Díaz Barriga Arceo has focused on "the subjective meanings and in the personal experiences" of "educational actors," especially professors and students as they grapple with present circumstances (e.g., "the demands of these new curricular models"), specifically, the hegemony of evaluation. In this way, Díaz Barriga Arceo aspires to contribute to understanding curriculum, particularly from the perspectives of educational actors.

Frida Díaz Barriga Arceo regards globalization primarily negatively,[12], judging its impacts in the spheres of education, culture, and the quality of life of human beings in general. Globalization, she underscores, is to "the detriment of all that is national and local." She acknowledges instances of resistance to globalization, and it is in these social movements that she looks for "change" and "alternative thought." Within education, globalization has meant the uncritical importation of models from so-called developed nations—models that were, however, destined to accept "a naturalization card in Mexico; in other words, they have suffered multiple local adaptations, idiosyncrasies." She finds similar recontextualizations in Brazil, Chile, Argentina, and Venezuela.

Neoliberalism has not succeeded in improving the quality of education in Latin America. Nor has it contributed to the promotion of equity or of sustainable social development. Instead, Díaz Barriga Arceo judges, neoliberal policies constitute "mechanisms of regulation, control and centralized coordination" through various governmental agencies. The result has been a relative loss of autonomy for academics working in educational institutions. Specifically inappropriate to Mexico are those "rational-technocratic" discourses that are copied from "business thought" and reflecting a "corporate vision." Translated into large-scale projects of "reform," these discourses reflect "the so-called demands of the information society and of globalization, without a profound reflection as to what this implies," for example, its "consequences: very little is known about the results in practice." Ignored is the history of present circumstances. It is this ongoing catastrophe that Frida Díaz Barriga Arceo addresses in her research.

Ángel Díaz Barriga

Ángel Díaz Barriga's investigation began with the problems professors encountered when working with the university curriculum. His intellectual formation was informed by Didactics, influential during the early 1960s. The student movement of 1968 left its mark: "We stopped seeing education as a technical, didactic (in its classical version) or primarily psycho-pedagogical problem. We always looked for the social sense in education." Not only in Mexico but across Latin America in general, he reports, the 1970s was a decade of "struggle" and "searching." The Cuban revolution had inspired many to believe that the achievement of a just society was politically possible. Díaz Barriga began to combine Didactics with studies of Latin America, specifically Argentina, a nation traumatically altered by the "*coup d'etat*" of 1976. At this time, technicist US curriculum theory (Benjamin Bloom, Robert Mager, James Popham, Eva Baker, Ralph Tyler, Hilda Taba,) had been imported, followed by French theory that challenged technicism, for example, Pierre Bourdieu, Michel Lobrot (his initial work on institutional pedagogy), Rene Lourau, and Louis Althusser.

The military dictatorship meant the migration of Argentineans to Mexico; they brought with them psychoanalytic studies of education. Also arriving in Mexico at this time was the work of Paulo Freire, challenging social domination by teaching students to enact freedom through education. Contradicting these intellectual events was the federal government's embrace of technical approaches from the United States, converting the Mexican educational systems into one "big laboratory" in order to test them. The Alliance for Progress distributed books by Robert Mager, Benjamin Bloom, and James Popham to educational authorities all over Latin America. Despite this heavy-handed intervention in the intellectual life of the nation, Mexican scholars sought progressive educational experiments. However, when an experiment became "radical," like the one introduced in the Autonomous University of Nayarit (UAN) during 1974–1976, the government acted, on that occasion occupying the campus with the military. Inspired by the hope of improving life for all, the UAN experiment involved students' traveling to rural communities where they worked in multidisciplinary groups to help the community resolve health problems (helped by doctors and nurses), social problems (with the assistance of economists and sociologists), and legal problems (aided by lawyers). Public health workers at the Autonomous Metropolitan University-Xochimilco (UAM-X) adopted conceptions of medical practice associated with the OPS (Pan-American Health Organization). Instead of using a Needs Diagnosis, UAM-X faculty and students constructed Professional Reference Frameworks analyzed from perspectives associated with the dominant and the dominated sectors of society. Replacing Bloom's taxonomy, this analysis of "decadent, dominant and emerging practices" enabled the construction of study plans focused on specific learning problems. These plans included students' relocation to marginalized communities where they labored to resolve problems that local residents identified.

In the 1990s with the ascendancy of technocratic bureaucrats, educated in the "Chicago School" of economics, neoliberalism arrived in full force. Díaz Barriga focused on the displacement of curriculum theory by evaluation that was enforced by the state, and not devised and conducted by professional societies. As in the United States (see Taubman 2009), private business profits from such state-enforced evaluation. Under "pay-per-merit" schemes, university professors augment their nominal salaries of US$1,500 to US$4,500 if they "participate" in these state-generated evaluation programs. Under such circumstances, academic labor in general and curriculum research in particular become modified; the challenge Díaz Barriga has undertaken is the documentation of this "modification."

Curriculum studies in Mexico has focused on postsecondary education. In the universities, curriculum development is ongoing and specific to courses and programs. Until the mid-1980s, curriculum studies in Mexico was associated with the formulation of study plans and programs. With the importation of scholarship from the United States and the United Kingdom, the focus of curriculum studies began to broaden.

Indeed, in Díaz Barriga's view, curriculum studies suffers from "too many themes." No longer restricted to study plans and programs, curriculum studies incorporates even ethnographic methods, on occasion without sufficient conceptual foundations. Displacing Didactics, curriculum studies became conflated with analyses of power and the reproduction of the dominant culture, a fate threatening the United States as well (Pinar 2009b). Constructivism became influential, and the influence of the Spanish curriculum scholar César Coll focused researchers' attention on the classroom.

Dedicated to helping teachers understand the circumstances of their daily labor, Ángel Díaz Barriga's research confronts inequities in society, including the federal government's complicity in social inequality. With intellectual dispositions provided by Didactics and curriculum studies, Díaz Barriga studies the roles of standardized examinations in the reproduction of such inequality. The results of these evaluations become linked to public financing of educational institutions, rationalizing the government's redistribution of resources away from states with greater social needs (e.g., Guerrero, Oaxaca, Chiapas). Díaz Barriga found that universities in these states were assigned less than 10 percent of what was allocated to universities located in states with greater social, cultural, and economic development.

Critical of recommendations made by the World Bank and the Inter-American Bank of Development, Díaz Barriga has also criticized those colleagues who provide technical support to these institutions. Despite these efforts to influence public policy, Ángel Díaz Barriga's "fundamental interest has always been the teachers." He notes that this interest positions him as "reactive" in his investigations, forcing him to conclude, "My future in this field is not very clear to me. What I see is that since the decade of the nineties, I have put myself in reactive investigations." Ignoring, for instance, "competency-based" proposals proffered 25 years ago, he refused to confer upon these schemes the respect that the attention it attracted implied. Now Díaz Barriga feels forced to critique them as he continues to work "on the side of the teachers." I am reminded of Pier Paolo Pasolini's declaration (quoted in Greene 1990, 138): "As for me, I am on the side of victims."

Alfredo Furlán

Alfredo Furlán has studied problems of discipline and violence in schools, problems, he argues, interrelated with the curriculum. Especially when the curriculum does not engage students, discipline problems, even violence, follow. Violence, substance abuse and other addictions are now so common that as topics they have been included in the teacher education curriculum. At the time of this interview (2008) Furlán was studying a governmental program—"Safe School"—dedicated to "schools free of addiction and violence." Furlán studies problems of "those who suffer social exclusion." He also cites "deterioration" in what he calls the "cultural credibility" of schools, a problem he ascribes to traditional models of pedagogy.

Furlán's ongoing inquiry represents an "expression of my biography which was almost always marked by political events and by cultural changes that happened in Mexico." His inquiry began in Argentina, at the National University of Cordoba where he studied the Educational Sciences. Prepared to be a teacher of Physical Education, he worked for four years as a teacher in secondary schools. Furlán moved first to the city of Rio Cuarto, then to La Pampa, where he enjoyed the opportunities "to work with a group of very outstanding professors" who "shaped my way of working." Realizing he was under military surveillance, Furlán fled Argentina in 1975, just before the *coup d'etat* of March 1976. Exile, Furlán reports, was an imprinting influence in his intellectual formation. In Mexico, he believes, he has enjoyed opportunities that he would not have enjoyed in Argentina, among these studying in Paris for his doctorate.

Although Furlán enjoys "absolute freedom" in choosing his research projects, that freedom is structured by widening circles of influence. Every ten years the Mexican Council for Educative Investigation (COMIE) sets research guidelines derived from its judgments concerning the state of the art of various academic disciplines, including curriculum studies. Like other countries, Mexico suffers, Furlán judges, from the "globalization of educative politics." Since the 1990s, Mexico has emphasized a "curriculum of 'competencies,' standardized tests as parameters of 'quality,' and constructivism [as] the theory of learning." This localization of global neoliberalism has, in Furlán's judgment, "provoked a collapse of the capacity to think, which has been noticed in all the fields, including curriculum studies." Although neoliberalism is no longer unquestioned and, indeed, is losing its popular support, it remains in place as Mexican state policy.

In his research Furlán has focused on "curricular practices and processes" as well as on the "conceptualization of the curricular sphere." Like the great Canadian theorist Ted Aoki (2005, 159–160), Furlán has distinguished between the curriculum as "thought" and the curriculum as "lived." In doing so, he has dwelled on the differences between US and Mexican conceptions of curriculum as study plans, the latter derived from the *Ratio Studiorum* (the plan of Jesuit studies, dating from 1599) and the German *Lehrplan* (also curriculum as study plans). From this research Furlán has focused on "pedagogical management," including questions of school discipline and violence as well as of corporate efforts to profit from these problems. From this research, Furlán suggests, understanding of curriculum issues may achieve "a greater magnitude, increasing the geographic scope to Latin America, that is, a greater sharing of perspectives developed by specialists in the entire region." Furlán's is a socially situated, politically committed curriculum research that addresses the particularities of place, personified in the problems students and teachers face in schools deformed as businesses.

José María E. García Garduño

José María E. García Garduño's began his career as an elementary school teacher teaching third and fourth graders in a "marginal" neighborhood in Mexico City. At that time, Garduño reports, teacher preparation was academically equivalent to senior high school (now it has been placed at the bachelor's degree level). While working as teacher he completed a *licenciatura* (equivalent to a bachelor's degree, but more professionally oriented) in clinical psychology at a Jesuit university (*Universidad Iberoamericana*). Despite this concentration, his commitment to social service persuaded Garduño to choose teaching over attending to middle and upper class patients as a psychotherapist. His father was also an influence: he had served as an rural elementary schoolteacher in the 1930s and 1940s.

After graduate study, Garduño joined a team evaluating a national curricular reform of the first and second years of elementary education. By chance he met Patricio Daowz, a Mexican engineering major who had pursued graduate studies in education in France. At the time working at the Ministry of Education, Daowz advocated an approach to curriculum development he termed *curricular reticulation*, a concept widely used in urban planning that emphasized the concept of network. In this scheme, curriculum would be developed not by objectives but by direct attention to subject matter, a view I too endorse (2006b). Daowz argued that if networks of stakeholders are constructed, curriculum deliberation (even agreement) could follow.

In 1983 at the *Universidad Pedagógica Nacional* Garduño met the Argentinean scholar Eduardo Remedí. Resettled in Mexico, Remedí understood curriculum in psychoanalytic terms. Having read curriculum scholarship from Brazil, the United States, and the United Kingdom, and having completed his doctorate at Ohio University, Garduño's intellectual formation is decidedly international. While a student of US curriculum history, Garduño has also been influenced by Ángel Díaz Barriga's commitment to formulating a specifically Mexican curriculum theory. After working in teaching evaluation, Garduño became engaged in a network of curriculum scholars led by Ángel Díaz Barriga that undertook the intellectual consolidation of Mexican curriculum studies. Today, he reports, "my main concern is the advancement of curriculum theory in Mexico by analyzing curriculum theory and history, specially US and Latin American histories of their respective fields." In my judgment, the intellectual advancement of our respective fields depends in large part upon such research.

Raquel Glazman-Nowalski

The research of Raquel Glazman-Nowalski follows from her teaching. It was while teaching that Glazman-Nowalski observed weakness in her students' analytical capacities, including in their capacities for critique and argumentation. Evident not only in their academic work, this weakness is also discernible in students' incapacity to critique politics in the public domain. These two interrelated domains—public politics and academic capacities—stimulate and focus Glazman-Nowalski's research. As is the case in Brazil, research teams structure and focus curriculum research in Mexico. For ten years, Glazman-Nowalski has worked with María de Ibarrola and five others in formulating a methodology for designing national study plans. During the 1970s, this work was influenced by US curriculum studies (e.g., Tyler, Taba, Bloom, Bruner) and by Mexican scholars such as Pablo Latapí as well. Coauthored with María de Ibarrola and first published in 1980, this research enjoyed considerable influence until 2000.

During the 1980s and 1990s curriculum studies scholars focused their research on conditions specific to Mexico in particular and Latin America in general. During the last decade, scholars have criticized neoliberalism and globalization as these are reflected in the government's curricular demands. Within this critical scholarship, there is "a current" Glazman-Nowalski characterizes as "testimonial." Such research contributes to the clarification of curriculum, including the role of "formation" in building the pedagogical capacity of instructors, the influence of ideological currents within a school or university faculty, the impact of the different procedures (those conditions prerequisite to curriculum change), and the consequences of the diffusion of "innovations." This research has clarified the local as well as global sources of the educational realities specific to Mexico.

For meaningful progress in curriculum research to occur, Glazman-Nowalski endorses additional research on the learning process, specifically research focused on the relations among disciplinary, interdisciplinary, and transdisciplinary currents across the academic disciplines as these are influenced by specific national and international policies. Also urgent, she asserts, is an ongoing analysis of the educational necessities of the Third World as these are determined, in Glazman-Nowalski's view, by well-known and ongoing social, ethical, and ecological emergencies. In such research the local and the global intersect.

María Concepción Barrón Tirado

María Concepción Barrón Tirado took her BA in pedagogy from UNAM in 1975, having studied in the Faculty of Philosophy and Liberal Arts. She recalls that the majority of her professors were very young: "We worked on educative technology, objective tests, and models of didactic planning," at the same time, "we looked through texts from Paulo Freire and liberating education." As well Barrón Tirado studied psychology (Skinner, Piaget, Freud, and the Gestaltists) and sociology (primarily the functionalists) but, she notes, "there were professors who sympathized with historic materialism." She also studied with faculty who had fled *coups d'etat* in South America. The primacy of educational technology was contrasted with various "philosophical-anthropological positions," among them existentialism (including Nietzsche), the Frankfurt school, liberation theology, and psychoanalysis, among others. Juxtaposed to these sophisticated intellectual traditions were simplistic models of curriculum development imported from the United States: "The models of curriculum we studied derived from Tyler and Taba, emphasizing the different steps needed to design a study plan." In such models, the design of study plans is a "technical" and "objective" process.

In contrast, she continues, the notions of pedagogy "we studied derived from an idealistic conception and study plans were constructed from this point of view." In Mexico, Barrón Tirado explains, teaching—Didactics—has predominated curriculum and "education in a fuller sense." She summarizes: "From this perspective, pedagogy is a discipline which is integrated by theoretical and technical knowledge. Therefore, in the first semester an emphasis was made on subjects of the theoretical type and later students worked on problems of the technical type." Two currents characterized curriculum thought in Mexico: (1) the philosophical-idealistic tendency, linked to the teacher (as he or she preserves certain ethical values) and associated with philosophy, history, anthropology, and the other social sciences, and not necessarily emphasizing "concrete instruments that support the immediate resolution of problems;" and (2) the scientific-technical perspective, dominated by instrumental reason that defines the work of pedagogues as technicians who can conduct specific and determined tasks, for example, educational planning, making study plans and programs, elaborating evaluation strategies, and conducting in-service education for noneducational workers who require specific forms of training. This second tendency emphasized professional "formation" that forefronted "concrete, useful and efficient solutions according to the market demands." Persons became converted into "human capital," and education became a mere calculation in investments for future profitability.

As did her colleagues, Barrón Tirado acknowledged the student movement of 1968, noting that university students "openly denounced the authoritarian tendencies of the political regime" and "produced a critique of the economic model." This movement ended with its suppression; this "marked the end of the period of consensus between the Universities and the State." Following was "an era of transition" wherein an intensified incorporation of science in the curriculum of higher (superior) education converged with a vulgar pragmatism, requiring universities to adopt models of social modernization associated with industrial development. Empirical investigation must be calibrated to the solution of specific problems, foreshadowing the domination of the demand to know "what works."

The students of 1968, Barrón Tirado recalls, were influenced by Marxist ideas (especially those thinkers associated with the Frankfurt School such as Herbert Marcuse and Erich Fromm, and those associated with Soviet and Cuban socialism). "These influenced me," Barrón Tirado recalls, "and I began to consider education from the political-ideological perspective and to recognize the lack of neutrality in the formation of students, of schools and of study plans." Her doctoral dissertation research focused on bachelor's degrees in pedagogy offered in the private universities of metropolitan Mexico City. Each of the institutions she studied designed their curricula according to the cultural values they promoted. Barrón Tirado found that the various curricular codes and symbols that these educational institutions emphasized were related to different classes in an unequal society. She concluded:

> The selection, organization, distribution and evaluation of knowledge that is selected in scholarly institutions alludes to a type of cultural capital that is intentionally promoted. The collection of symbols and ideas that denote the beliefs, values and principles that different groups sustain are distributed selectively, thereby contributing to social inequality.

The demands of academic employment required Barrón Tirado to suspend additional research in favor of "technical rationality," at one point developing study plans for nursing programs structured by objectives and aligned with Bloom's taxonomy.

In 1982 Barrón Tirado moved to another campus of the UNAM, called the National School of Professional Studies Aragon (ENEP Aragon), where Ángel Díaz Barriga became the head of the department. He proposed that faculty consult students when evaluating study plans for the bachelor's degree in pedagogy, enabling Barrón Tirado to resume her doctoral dissertation research. She participated in the elaboration and application of evaluation instruments, in the analysis of her research results and in the composition of the final report. "This was a pioneer investigation in Mexico," she remembers, "incorporating qualitative considerations like student opinion in the evaluation of study plans." Ángel Díaz Barriga and Barrón Tirado reported the results in *The Study Plans of the Bachelors Degree in Pedagogy: An Exploratory Study from the Students' Perspectives* (1984).

History's Effects

> *Capricious though our history has been, it has resulted in something in particular, in this and not that.*
>
> David D. Roberts (1995, 61)

These intersecting particularities of individual lives and national histories converge in this genealogical study of curriculum studies in Mexico. There is no conflation of these two, however, as these individual scholars specified—in their interviews with me, essays (chapters 2–8), and exchanges with Professor Lopes and Xu—how the historical promise of Mexican curriculum studies has been fractured by globalization, for example, subsumed in a totalizing logic of economism[13] in which the workplace and not social reconstruction becomes the reason of education. Mexican scholars have not been fooled, as they remain wide awake,[14] their gaze steady on the present idolatry, informed by historical knowledge and subjective memory, and ennobled by the understanding that education is in the service of humanization (Freire 1970, 27) not capital accumulation (Nussbaum 2010, 3, 127, 141).

Understanding the specificity of History and its effects (our present circumstances, materialized in our social and subjective "formation") through dialogical encounter with oneself and others, we labor through scholarly and pedagogical "activity" to provide passages to futures that do not betray the past. Although "genealogy" may enable us to testify to this past, doing so, as Dienstag (1997, 120) reminds us, cannot unravel history's effects. We move among them now, as we read these histories of curriculum studies in Mexico.

Notes

1. Mexico is not the only US neighbor about which Americans generally, and curriculum studies scholars specifically, are largely ignorant. I have been engaged in a long-term project of referencing Canadian curriculum studies in my US publications, first in *Understanding Curriculum*, and more recently (1) by editing—with Rita L. Irwin—the collected works of the great Canadian curriculum theorist Ted Aoki (Pinar and Irwin 2005); (2) with the republication of George Tomkins' legendary history of Canadian curriculum (2008); (3) in a study of Canadian identity in Canadian curriculum studies (Pinar 2011b), and (4) by increasing Canadian content in the second edition of *What Is Curriculum Theory?* (Pinar 2012).
2. Spring (2006, 146) describes the Center succinctly:
   > Ivan Illich's Center for Intercultural Documentation (CIDOC) in Cuernavaca, Mexico, helped to spread both liberation theology and Freirean educational ideas. Liberation theologists, such as Gustavo Gutiérrez, and North and South American educators, including Paulo Freire, John Holt, and Clarence Karier, gathered at CIDOC to exchange ideas on radical change and education.... I was one of those who carried his ideas back to North America. At CIDOC, I coedited a book with liberation theologist Father Jordan Bishop, *Formative Undercurrents in Compulsory Knowledge,* and with Clarence Karier and Paul Violas, *Roots of Crisis.* These books contributed to discussions of radical school reform in the United States.

   Here Spring is being customarily modest about his role: his scholarship did more than "contribute," it not only revolutionized educational history in the United States but also animated efforts to understand curriculum as historical and political text (see Spring 1972; Pinar et al. 1995, Chapters 2, 3, and 5).
3. Not all drugs move *from* Mexico *to* the United States. There is also a history of many going to Mexico to experience drug-induced epiphanies, most famously (in the United States, that is) Peruvian-born American anthropologist Carlos Castaneda (1925–1998) who, in *The Teachings of Don Juan*, reported his experiences with a Yaqui shaman named Don Juan Matus. There are European accounts of epiphanies as well, including those by Antonin Artaud, who, Derrida reports, wondered if Mexican drugs could contribute to
   > the emancipation of the subject; provide an end to that subjection which from birth had somehow expropriated the subject; and most of all, provide an end to the very concept of subject. ... Indeed, at stake in this experience was a desire to be done with the judgment of God. (quoted in Derrida 1993, 8)

Derrida (1993) comments that it was Artaud's commitment to challenge especially those prohibitions associated with European culture (especially those associated with European religion) that had led him to Mexican drugs. Audre Lorde also used drugs—evidently amphetamines (De Veaux 2004, 89)—in order to stay alert during her "hectic schedule," not to facilitate subjective reconstruction.

4. It was not only Lorde's sense of poetry that was deepened in Cuernavaca. There she met a lover—Eudora Garrett—a journalist twenty-seven years older than she. It was Garret who "totally engaged" (Lorde in De Veaux 2004, 52) Lorde "in the erotic, psychic, and physical aspects of lesbian loving for the first time, embodying Audre's deepest desires for a sister-confidante-teacher-lover-mother figure" (De Veaux 2004, 52). Lorde was not the only important African American poet to spend time in Mexico. So did Langston Hughes (Hughes 1995/1996, 66).

5. In contrast to globalization (which implies standardization), internationalization denotes dialogical encounter across national differences devoted to understanding national and regional specificities within curriculum studies worldwide. The current project is, I propose, one micro-moment of such internationalization.

6. In his exchange with Yuzhen Xu and Alice Casimiro Lopes, Ángel Díaz Barriga contrasted US educational "science" with European pedagogical philosophy, a contrast evident in contemporary tensions between vocational education (preparing students for the world of work) and citizenship education (preparing students to become democratic agents), between US-style social efficiency (linking objectives with evaluation through instruction) and European humanism. Within the United States, Ángel Díaz Barriga notes, technicism—which he traces to Bobbitt (pointing out that in Chapter 6 of *The Curriculum* [1918] Bobbitt recommends that employers be consulted in curriculum construction)—triumphed over child-centered humanism (which he traces to Dewey's 1902 *The Child and the Curriculum*). Ángel Díaz Barriga adds that in the 1920 translation of Dewey's book into Spanish "program," not "curriculum," was the term employed: this is in contrast to Dewey's original usage. It was a substitution repeated (he points out) in 1970s translations of US technicism. I wonder whether the Mexican tendency to associate curriculum with study plans—rather than with educational experience broadly defined—can be traced to this tradition of translation.

7. It seems that the concept of rhizome precludes genealogy, as Deleuze and Guattari (1987, 12–13) explain: "the rhizome is … a map and not a tracing.… A map has multiple entryways, as opposed to the tracing, which always comes back 'to the same.' The map has to do with performance, whereas the tracing always involves an alleged 'competence.'" As I employ it, "genealogy" (tracing intellectual histories, simultaneously individual, national, and disciplinary) informs the "mapping" of the present circumstances of the field. There are multiple (indeed, individuated) entrances to such a project, but it recursively returns to the realities of national history, politics, and culture (however elusive those realities inevitably may be). In Brazil, Amorim (2011, 55-69) embraces Deleuze in his articulation of curriculum as a plane of sensation.

8. Despite its defamation by popular usage, the notion of "heroic" conveys courage in confronting the actuality of History. Such actuality (always "conflictual") includes the alterity of lived experience itself, made vivid (even lacerating) by imprinting events, among them the crushing of the 1968 student movement. In this sense genealogy emphasizes, Roberts (1995, 187) notes, "not continuity but discontinuity, which is to be true to the singularity of the single event, 'the singular randomness of events'."
9. Here decadence means defeat, not self-indulgent resistance to dominant cultural (in the West derivatively Christian) scripts of self-deprivation. In his *Vie Nuove* "dialogue" of July 9, 1960 regarding Pasternak, Pier Paolo Pasolini asserted that Marxism's "great mistake" was in conflating irrationality with late nineteenth-century European decadence. In insisting on "rationality above all," Pasolini judged that the Left had fallen into prudery, rejecting all fantasy and imagination as "reactionary." Rethinking the role of *decadentismo* as a historical movement might, he suggested, free Marxism in general (and Italian Communism in particular) from hypocrisy and intolerance (quoted passages in Schwartz 1992, 369). Pasolini's contemporary Fellini, Deleuze (1989, 6) notes, embraced "even that decadence which means that one loves only in dreams or in recollection, sympathizes with those kinds of love, as an accomplice of decadence, and even to provoke it, in order to save something, perhaps, as far as is possible." Closer to Nietzsche's meaning was Sorel's association of decadence with pessimism (Sternhell 1994, 71), not with love or sexual libertinism.
10. Ángel Díaz Barriga points out (in his exchange with Lopes and Xu) that the National Autonomous University of Mexico (UNAM) has been and continues to be the most influential in Mexico. It is also the oldest university on the American continent, founded in 1551, more than eight years before Harvard (Cusset 2008, 299). As ancient (in North American terms) as UNAM is, it is not the oldest educational institution in Mexico. Some 20 years earlier, in 1529, the first secondary school for Indians was established in Mexico City (Reyhner and Eder 2004, 18).
11. The concept of "study plans" has a more expansive meaning than the English phrase implies, José María García Garduño points out. It means, he writes, "curriculum programs, course of study or written curriculum. I suggest you use any of the latter words."
12. Díaz Barriga Arceo (2010) writes, "The impact [of globalization] has been mainly negative, although some benefits can also be found, such as the possibility of sharing these critical views of society, the economy and the culture with groups and individuals from other places. Groups and movements have also emerged as a product of globalization that promote for substantial changes for the benefit of society, fairness, the ecology, human rights, etc."
13. While the hegemony of economistic thinking is relatively recent, even US "progressives" contributed to its triumph by emphasizing the use-value of thinking (Simpson 2002, 98). The great Canadian political economist and communications theorist Harold Innis (as Arthur Kroker [1984, 104–105] reminds) quoted Nietzsche regularly, including this insight regarding utility: "In the long run,

utility, like everything else, is simply a figment of our imagination and may well be the fatal stupidity by which we shall one day perish." Reforming education after business is, indeed, proving to be a "fatal stupidity."

14. In the United States, the philosopher of education Maxine Greene is famously associated with this metaphor of wide-awakeness. "Through the awareness," Greene (2001, 11, emphasis added) has argued, "through the *wide-awakeness* brought about by aesthetic education (or by authentic teaching conducted to that end), our students will in some sense be free to find their own voices, as they find their eyes and ears." Perhaps Greene derived the concept from John Dewey (1910, 57, emphasis added) who asserted that "the word logical is synonymous with *wide-awake*, thorough, and careful reflection—thought in its best sense. Reflection is turning a topic over in various aspects and in various lights so that nothing significant about it shall be overlooked—almost as one might turn a stone over to see what its hidden side is like or what is covered by it." It seems to me that such reflection characterizes curriculum studies in Mexico, at least as we glimpse the field in this collection.

References

Amorim, Antonio Carlos 2011. Curriculum Disfiguration. In Curriculum Studies in Brazil: Intellectual Histories, Present Circumstances, ed. William F. Pinar, 55-69. New York: Palgrave Macmillan.

Aoki, Ted. 2005. "Teaching as Indwelling between Two Curriculum Worlds." In *Curriculum in a New Key: The Collected Works of Ted T. Aoki*, ed. William F. Pinar and Rita L. Irwin, 159–165. Mahwah, NJ: Lawrence Erlbaum.

Arceo, Frida Díaz Barriga, 2010. Email Communication from the author, Vancouver, Canada to Mexico City, September 17, 2010.

Bobbitt, Franklin. 1918. *The Curriculum*. New York: Houghton Mifflin.

Butler, Judith. 1997. *The Psychic Life of Power: Theories in Subjection*. Palo Alto, CA: Stanford University Press.

Castaneda, Carlos. 1971. *A Separate Reality: Further Conversations with Don Juan*. New York: Pocket Books.

Curtis, Kimberley. 2001. "Multicultural Education and Arendtian Conservatism: On Memory, Historical Injury, and Our Sense of the Common." In *Hannah Arendt and Education: Renewing our Common World*, ed. Mordechai Gordon, 127–152. Boulder, CO: Westview.

Cusset, François. 2008. *French Theory: How Foucault, Derrida, Deleuze, & Co. Transformed the Intellectual Life of the United States*. Trans. Jeff Fort. Minneapolis: University of Minnesota Press.

Deleuze, Gilles. 1989. *Cinema 2. The Time-Image*. Trans. Hugh Tomlinson and Robert Galeta. Minneapolis: University of Minnesota Press.

Deleuze, Gilles, and Félix Guattari. 1987. *A Thousand Plateaus: Capitalism and Schizophrenia*. Trans. Brian Massumi. Minneapolis: University of Minnesota Press.

De Veaux, Alexis. 2004. *Warrior Poet: A Biography of Audre Lorde.* New York: Norton.
Dewey, John. 1902. *The Child and the Curriculum.* Chicago: University of Chicago Press.
Dewey, John. 1910. *How We Think.* Boston: D. C. Heath & Co.
Díaz Barriga, Ángel. 2003. "Curriculum Research: Evolution and Outlook in México." In *International Handbook of Curriculum Research*, ed. William F. Pinar, 443–456. Mahwah, NJ: Lawrence Erlbaum.
Díaz Barriga, Frida. 2003. "Main Trends of Curriculum Research in México." In *International Handbook of Curriculum Research*, ed. William F. Pinar, 457–469. Mahwah, NJ: Lawrence Erlbaum.
Dienstag, Joshua Foa. 1997. *"Dancing in Chains": Narrative and Memory in Political Theory.* Stanford, CA: Stanford University Press.
Freire, Paulo. 1970. *Pedagogy of the Oppressed.* [Trans. Myra Bergman Ramos] New York: Herder and Herder.
Garcia, Sara S. 1997. "Self-Narrative Inquiry in Teacher Development: Living and Working in Just Institutions." In *Preparing Teachers for Cultural Diversity*, ed. Joyce E. King, Etta R. Hollins, and Warren C. Hayman, 146–155. New York: Teachers College Press.
Garduño, José María García. 2010. Email Communication with the author, from Vancouver, Canada to Mexico City, August 19, 2010.
Greene, Maxine. 2001. *Variations on a Blue Guitar: The Lincoln Center Institute Lectures on Aesthetic Education.* New York: Teachers College Press.
Hoberman, James. 1989. "Vietnam: The Remake." In *Remaking History*, ed. Barbara Kruger and Phil Mariani, 175–196. Seattle: Bay Press.
Hughes, Langston. 1995/1996. "Father." In *Brotherman: The Odyssey of Black Men in America*, ed. Herb Boyd and Robert L. Allen, 66–72. New York: Ballantine/One World.
Jay, Martin. 1993. *Downcast Eyes: The Denigration of Vision in Twentieth-Century French Thought.* Berkeley: University of California Press.
Karier, Clarence J., Paul Violas, and Joel Spring. 1972. *Roots of Crisis: American Education in the Twentieth Century.* Chicago: Rand McNally.
Kroker, Arthur. 1984. *Technology and the Canadian Mind: Innis/McLuhan/Grant.* Montreal: NewWorld Perspectives.
Kumar, Ashwani. 2010. "A Synoptic View of Curriculum Studies in South Africa." *The Journal of the American Association for the Advancement of Curriculum Studies*, 6. Available online at: http://www.uwstout.edu.
Kumar, Ashwani. 2011. "Curriculum Studies in Brazil: An Overview." In *Curriculum Studies in Brazil*, ed. William F. Pinar, 27–42. New York: Palgrave Macmillan.
Lacey, Marc. 2010. "Even Under Siege, Democracy Endures in Mexico." *The New York Times*, July 6, CLIX (55,093), A4, A12.
Lasch, Christopher. 1978. *The Culture of Narcissism: American Life in an Age of Diminishing Expectations.* New York: Norton.
Miller, Jerome G. 1996. *Search and Destroy: African-American Males in the Criminal Justice System.* New York: Cambridge University Press.

Mullin, Molly H. 1995. "The Patronage of Difference: Making Indian Art 'Art, Not Ethnology.'" In *The Traffic in Culture: Refiguring Art and Anthropology*, ed. George E. Marcus and Fred R. Myers, 166–198. Berkeley and Los Angeles: University of California Press.

Nussbaum, Martha C. 2010. *Not for Profit: Why Democracy Needs the Humanities*. Princeton, NJ: Princeton University Press.

Owen, David. 1995. *Nietzsche, Politics, and Modernity: A Critique of Liberal Reason*. London: Sage.

Pinar, William F. 2006a. "*Bildung* and the Internationalization of Curriculum Studies." *Transnational Curriculum Inquiry* 3 (2). Available online at: http://nitinat.library.ubc.ca.

Pinar, William F. 2006b. *The Synoptic Text Today and Other Essays: Curriculum Development After the Reconceptualization*. New York: Peter Lang.

Pinar, William F. 2009a. *The Worldliness of a Cosmopolitan Education: Passionate Lives in Public Service*. New York: Routledge.

Pinar, William F. 2009b. "The Unaddressed "I" of Ideology Critique." *Power and Education* 1(2): 189–200. Available online at: http://www.wwwords.co.uk.

Pinar, William F., ed. 2010. *Curriculum Studies in South Africa*. New York: Palgrave Macmillan.

Pinar, William F., ed. 2011a. *Curriculum Studies in Brazil*. New York: Palgrave Macmillan.

Pinar, William F. 2011b. "Nationalism, Anti-Americanism, Canadian Identity." In *Curriculum in Today's World: Configuring Knowledge, Identities, Work and Politics*, ed. Lyn Yates and Madeleine Grumet, 31-43. London: Routledge.

Pinar, William F. 2012. *What Is Curriculum Theory?* [Second edition.] New York: Routledge.

Pinar, William F. In press. *The Character of Curriculum Studies: Bildung, Currere, and the Recurring Question of the Subject*. New York: Palgrave Macmillan.

Pinar, William F., and Rita L. Irwin, eds. 2005. *Curriculum in a New Key: The Collected Works of Ted T. Aoki*. Mahwah, NJ: Lawrence Erlbaum.

Pinar, William F., William M. Reynolds, Patrick Slattery, and Peter M. Taubman. 1995. *Understanding Curriculum: An Introduction to Historical and Contemporary Curriculum Discourses*. New York: Peter Lang.

Pope, Denise Clark. 2001. *Doing School: How We Are Creating a Generation of Stressed Out, Materialistic, and Miseducated Students*. New Haven: Yale University Press.

Quintanar-Sarellana, Rosalinda. 1997. "Culturally Relevant Teacher Preparation and Teachers' Perceptions of the Language and Culture of Linguistic Minority Students." In *Preparing Teachers for Cultural Diversity*, ed. Joyce E. King, Etta R. Hollins, and Warren C. Hayman, 40–52. New York: Teachers College Press.

Ransom, John S. 1997. *Foucault's Discipline: The Politics of Subjectivity*. Durham, NC: Duke University Press.

Reyhner, Jon, and Jeanne Eder. 2004. *American Indian Education: A History*. Norman: University of Oklahoma Press.

Roberts, David D. 1995. *Nothing But History: Reconstruction and Extremity After Metaphysics*. Berkeley and Los Angeles: University of California Press.
Rodriguez, Alberto J., and Richard S. Kitchen, eds. 2004. *Preparing Mathematics and Science Teachers for Diverse Classrooms*. Mahwah, NJ: Lawrence Erlbaum.
Saldívar, José David. 2006. "Border Thinking, Minoritized Studies, and Realist Interpellations: The Coloniality of Power from Gloria Anzaldua to Arundhati Roy." In *Identity Politics Reconsidered*, ed. Linda Martín Alcoff, Michael Hames-García, Satya P. Mohanty, and Paula M. L. Moya, 142–170. New York: Palgrave Macmillan.
Schwartz, Barth David. 1992. *Pasolini Requiem*. New York: Pantheon.
Simpson, David. 2002. *Situatedness, Or, Why We Keep Saying Where We're Coming From*. Durham, NC: Duke University Press.
Spring, Joel. 1972. *Education and the Rise of the Corporate State*. Boston: Beacon Press.
Spring, Joel. 2006. *Pedagogies of Globalization: The Rise of the Educational Security State*. Mahwah, NJ: Lawrence Erlbaum.
Sternhell, Zeev, Mario Sznajder, and Maia Asheri. 1994. *The Birth of Fascist Ideology: From Cultural Rebellion to Political Revolution*. Princeton, NJ: Princeton University Press.
Taubman, Peter M. 2009. *Teaching by Numbers: Deconstructing the Discourse of Standards and Accountability in Education*. New York: Routledge.
Tomkins, George S. 2008. *A Common Countenance: Stability and Change in the Canadian Curriculum*. Vancouver, Canada: Pacific Educational Press.
Tyack, David, and Elizabeth Hansot. 1990. *Learning Together: A History of Coeducation in American Schools*. New Haven, CT: Yale University Press.
Westbury, Ian, Stefan Hopmann, and Kurt Riquarts, eds. 2000. *Teaching As Reflective Practice: The German Didaktik Tradition*. Mahweh, NJ: Lawrence Erlbaum Associates, Publishers.

Chapter 1

Curriculum Studies in Mexico: An Overview

Ashwani Kumar

Introduction

In this chapter I provide a synoptic view of the evolution of the field of curriculum studies in Mexico, as portrayed in the chapters to follow. Broadly, I have organized the evolution of the Mexican field into three phases. The first phase—the decade of the 1970s—was marked by the dissemination of the Spanish translations of curriculum studies texts from the United States, primarily articulating the technicist-behavioral curriculum theory (see Frida Díaz Barriga Arceo's Chapter 3; Ángel Díaz Barriga's Chapter 4; William F. Pinar's Chapter 9[1]). During the second phase—the decade of the 1980s—Mexican field experienced its consolidation in the form of four major curriculum communities (critical theory, constructivism, interpretivism, and professional development), which posed critical challenges to the dominance of the technicist-behavioral curriculum theory of the previous decade (Chapter 3). In the third and the current phase of curriculum studies in Mexico, which began in the 1990s, the globalization of educational reforms—marked by the neoliberal notions of "innovation" and "accreditation"—has promoted an economistic vision of education, which has reduced education to vocationalism and evaluation, and latter to what can be measured through quantitative means (see Chapter 3; Chapter 4; Raquel Glazman-Nowalski's Chapter 7; Ma. Concepción Barrón Tirado's Chapter 8).

Phase I: The 1970s

> Curriculum research conducted in Mexico during the 1970s was focused on intervention: the design of study plans and programs structured by so-called technological rationality, accented by behaviorist psychology and the educational technology [imported from the United States].
>
> Frida Díaz Barriga Arceo (Chapter 3)

> Educational reform in the 1970s was based, then, on behaviorist objectives from which instructional activities would be implemented and evaluated.
>
> Ángel Díaz Barriga (Chapter 4)

> Educational imports from the United States into Mexico was an American strategy to consolidate its ideological hegemony. Such hegemony ensured continued imperialism.
>
> Ángel Díaz Barriga quoted in José María García Garduño (Chapter 6)

Import of Technicist-Behavioral Models of Curriculum Development from the United States

The student protests of the late 1960s, to which the state initially responded with repression that ended in a massacre of youth in the *Tres Culturas Plaza* (*Tlatelolco*) on October 2, 1968, compelled the new Mexican administration headed by Luis Echeverría to press for political, industrial, and educational reforms in the Mexican society (Alicia de Alba's Chapter 2; Chapters 4, 6, and 7)

Protective economic policies that restricted imports led to rapid industrial growth during the 1970s (approximately 8 percent annually), which, in turn, required the training of workers and professionals on a massive scale. In order to meet the demands of industrial modernization, the Mexican State imported technicist models of curriculum development from the United States. Several agencies associated with the US government—namely, International Agency for Development (AID), the Department of Education and Culture, and the Organization of American States (OAS)—financed Spanish translations of more than 20 US books on curriculum development including the works of "traditionalists" in US curriculum studies, namely, Eva Baker, Benjamin Bloom, Robert Gagné, James Popham, Hilda Taba, and Ralph Tyler. These models were to guide new curriculum policies and programs (Chapters 3, 4, and 9). Publishers were encouraged to print approximately 20,000 to 40,000 copies of the selected texts, which were then sold to the public as well as distributed for free in libraries throughout Latin America (Chapter 4). These translated texts were also disseminated to Ministries of Education, teacher training units, pedagogical institutes, and schools. These models achieved a significant influence in Mexican curriculum studies during the 1970s and the beginning of the 1980s (Chapter 4).

Significantly, the adoption of the aforementioned US scholars' work during the 1970s, which had been published in the United States between late 1940s and late 1960s, was also an intentional political act. It coincided with a US strategy to counteract the Cuban communist revolution, which threatened to spread throughout Latin America. This containment strategy was conducted through the Alliance for Progress, President John F. Kennedy's initiative for US "cooperation" with Latin America in the early 1960s, whereby the technological and behavioral "American pragmatist pedagogy" was enforced on Latin America (Chapters 4 and 6), an ideological undertaking that was later characterized as "satellization" or "colonization" (Chapter 3). Ángel Díaz Barriga argued that educational imports from the United States into Mexico were a US strategy to consolidate its "ideological hegemony" (Chapter 6).

The technological-behaviorist perspective, or what Frida Díaz Barriga Arceo terms the "technological-systematic tendency" (Chapter 3) that guided 1970s Mexican curricular reform was forced upon the Mexican educational system, which was (and remains today) highly centralized. Study plans for primary education, the first three years of secondary education, teacher education, and technological education were dictated by the National Ministry of Education.

The first internally generated text that marked the genesis of Mexican curriculum studies was the *Design of Study Plans* (1978) by María de Ibarrola and Raquel Glazman (see Alfredo Furlán's Chapter 5). This pioneering book inspired a number of curricular innovations in Mexico. *Design of Study Plans* became legendary; it was not only widely accepted but also generated widespread discussions and debates, which, in turn, constituted the birth of curriculum studies in Mexico (Chapter 2). María de Ibarrola and Glazman did not simply replicate Tyler's rationale or Taba's extension of it or Bloom's taxonomy; their work was hybrid, bearing some resemblance to the "conceptual-empiricist approach" described by Pinar (1975) (Chapter 6). María de Ibarrola and Raquel Glazman (now Glazman-Nowalski) consulted many works available at the time, connecting curriculum design with social needs, the worldwide student movement including the 1968 university movement in Mexico, the structure and development of knowledge, and the role of the universities, among others (Chapter 7). The other notable Mexican texts included *Programmed Teaching* (Commission of New Teaching Methods 1976); *Self-learning Packages for the Evaluation of Learning* (Fernando 1978); *Curricular Planning* (Arnaz 1981); and *Development of Descriptive Letters* (Gago 1982) (Chapters 3 and 4).

Influences from Europe and Latin America

While recontextualizing the technical rationality forcibly imported from the United States, the Mexican field also accepted theoretical and pedagogical influences from other countries in Latin America and Europe during the 1970s (Chapters 4 and 7), among them were (1) Michel Lobrot's *Institutional Pedagogy* (1980); (2) institutional analysis of Lourau and Lapassade (1974); (3) adoption of the *Letters from a Teacher* (de Barbiana 1972); (4) Freire's *Pedagogy of the Oppressed*; (5) the approaches of Everett Reimer (1971) and Ivan Illich (1972) regarding deschooling, including the work of ecclesiastical groups associated with the Second Vatican Council, accented by the CIDOC (Center for Intercultural Documentation) by Illich in Cuernavaca where the first Spanish edition of Freire's *Pedagogy as the Practice of Freedom* (1969) was printed; and (6) the Belgian version of Group Dynamics, reconstructed for Latin America by Jésus Andrés Vela (*Técnicas y Prácticas de las Relaciones Humanas*, 1972) (Chapter 4). As well, in the last years of the 1970s, with Edgar González Gaudiano as its academic leader, the Unit of Human Resources Formation and Academic Evaluation (UFRHEA) was formed at the National School of Professional Studies (ENEP) Zaragoza. This unit comprised 20 recently graduated pedagogues who worked with great enthusiasm on a series of projects (which they themselves initiated and assigned) on teacher preparation, curriculum design, and curriculum evaluation (Chapter 2).

Mexican curricular thought was also influenced by Didactics movement associated with the National University of Cordoba, Argentina. The work of Susana Barco, Azucena Rodríguez, and Gloria Edelstein, and Mirtha Antebi and Cristina Carranza characterized those theories of Didactics elaborated in and for Latin America. Specific educational projects incorporating social dimensions of professional formation were undertaken, among them were popular architecture and social or preventive medicine sponsored by the Pan-American Association of Health (Chapter 4). Both projects became fundamental references for Modular Study Plans by Transformational Objectives in the 1970s and 1980s (as we will see in Phase II in this chapter).

Diversification of Graduate Programs

The demands of industrialization, the promise of democratization, and specifically the import of technicist-behaviorist curriculum models from the United States as well as the theoretical and pedagogical influences from Europe and from within Latin America supported diversification of graduate programs in Mexico. Graduate programs began to offer a wide and diverse range of courses and workshops focused on different educational themes, among them were General Didactics, the elaboration of study plans and programs by instructional objectives, group dynamics, the evaluation of learning, and the psychology of teaching. Many of these courses reflected technical conceptions imported from the United States, whereas others reflected currents of thought from Europe and Latin America that were considered alternatives to US conceptions of curriculum. Consequently, in the same institution graduate programs could exhibit multiple, even contradictory, theoretical tendencies. In some seminars, then, curriculum content reflected Latin American concerns such as the student-teacher relationship in the classroom as a "dialogical relationship," learning as a "social process," and the importance of the "whole person" in the educational process. Other seminars reflected US technicist influences, for example, studies in educational planning, wherein academic content was reduced to observable behaviors, courses in learning understood only as a product, and curriculum comprised of mechanical relationships among objectives, teaching, and assessment (Chapter 4).

The establishment of academic research groups responsible for the formulation of study plans and academic programs, including teacher education programs, paved the way for Mexico's first generation of curriculum researchers. By the end of the 1970s, Mexican scholars began to question US technicist models inspired by both internal developments—the modular system based on the objectives of social transformation—and additional imports, among them the Spanish translation of Philip Jackson's *Life in Classrooms* (1968) in 1975. It is important to point out that while the "reconceptualization" of curriculum in the United States during the 1970s (that critiqued and dismissed technicist-behaviorist curriculum thought) and French structuralism (including the reproduction theory of Pierre Bourdieu) became known in Mexico by the end of the 1970s, a critique of the technical rationality in Mexico had also emerged locally, and not only as a critique of technicism, but also as a critical response to deep-rooted and widespread social inequality (Chapter 4).

Phase II: The 1980s

> *Curricular debate in Mexico during 1980s started giving birth to a number of concepts and developments specific to Mexican national conditions.*
>
> Ángel Díaz Barriga (Chapter 4)

> *The constitution of the curriculum field [in Mexico] is marked, then, with a strong Latin American footprint of struggle, hope and commitment.*
>
> Alicia de Alba (Chapter 2)

> *Curriculum studies in Mexico is a complex conceptual and practical construction typified [by] very diverse... communities of curriculum scholars, with shared epistemological perspectives,... work styles and interests within their groups, but groups that are frequently in conflict with the other groups.*
>
> Frida Díaz Barriga Arceo (Chapter 3)

Consolidation of Curriculum Communities

During the 1980s curriculum studies in Mexico experienced substantial growth marked by the diversification of theoretical and methodological approaches. As well, curriculum studies became "institutionalized" whereby the K-12 schools as well as the universities and other institutions of higher education established formal departments or at least faculty groups dedicated to the study of curriculum, especially the design and evaluation of study plans and programs. Simultaneously, courses in curriculum theory and practice (e.g., training workshops and courses leading to diplomas and even postgraduate degrees)—often directed toward teachers, educational planners, psychologists, and even the bureaucrats and other decision-makers in educational institutions—proliferated (Chapter 3).

The 1980s are also memorable because they saw the development of a number of curricular concepts specific to Mexican national conditions. Through the National Council of Science and Technology, the first national congress of educational research was held in 1981. This congress invited eight scholars to present state-of-the-art reports on eight research themes assessing their progress since the 1970s. Curriculum was one of the eight themes. In the report it became evident that international concepts—especially those imported from the United States—now coexisted with concepts formulated by Mexican researchers in the formulation of social perspectives focused on the complex relationships between higher education and Mexican society. Mexican curriculum studies, thus, remained in accord with a nationalist vision inherited from the legacies of the Mexican revolution (Chapter 4). For Mexican scholars, engagement with curriculum studies provided means to cultural and social struggle for radical social transformation. The constitution of the Mexican curriculum field is, therefore, marked with a strong Latin American footprint of struggle, hope, and commitment (Chapter 2).

In this phase of Mexican curriculum history, two significant books were published—*Didactics and Curriculum: Articulations in Study Programs* (Díaz Barriga 1984a) and *Essays on the Problem of Curriculum* (Díaz Barriga 1984b)—influencing curriculum studies throughout Latin America (Chapters 2, 4, and 6). Ángel Díaz Barriga and his associates—among them young Argentinean scholars (who fled from Argentina to escape military coup d'etat) Roberto Follari, Alfredo Furlán, Eduardo Remedí, and Azucena Rodríguez—at Mexico's National Autonomous University conducted extensive critiques of the Tyler Rationale and of educational technology, especially of what they termed US industrial or efficiency pedagogy, thereby paving the way for the conceptual development of curriculum studies in Mexico (Chapters 3, 4, 6, and 7). The main criticisms advanced against technocratic curricular rationality include the following: (1) the technological-systemic tendency was reductionistic, rigid, and decontextualized, resulting in the "fragmentation" and "trivialization" of learning through behavioral objectives, superficial technical processing, and "atomization" of academic content; (2) the technological-systemic tendency lacked historical and social analysis of the curriculum; and (3) US models would lead to an intensification of administrative control of the academicians and school teachers. This US positivistic research tendency, thus, emphasized on "curriculum development" (characterized by studies on diagnosis, documentation, and evaluation of curricular projects) rather than on "understanding curriculum" (Chapter 3).

While many institutions continued (and still do) to work under the spell of technological rationality in their efforts to make education more "effective" through the application of "scientific" techniques (Chapter 3), this definitive critique of behavioral and positivist curriculum models gave rise to diverse curriculum communities, which promoted distinct traditions, creating "habitus" (Chapter 4), and were accented by the following events: (1) the seminars coordinated by Ángel Díaz Barriga on Bobbitt's *The Curriculum*; (2) the seminar on curricular evaluation coordinated by Alicia de Alba as well as her work at ENEP-Zaragoza; (3) the work of the ENEP-Iztacala group led by Alfredo Furlán and Eduardo Remedí; (4) the work of Glazman-Nowalski and María Ibarrola, who drew upon US and

European sources, among them the work of William Alexander, Michael Apple, David Ausubel, Basil Bernstein, Franklin Bobbitt, Jerome Bruner, John Dewey, Henry Giroux, David Hamilton, Philip Jackson, Stephen Kemmis, Peter McLaren, Anthony Penna, William Pinar, Joseph Schwab, Hilda Taba, Ralph Tyler, Carr Wilfred, Paul Willis, and Michael Young, among others; (5) the works of Susana Barco (who came to Mexico during the time of the Argentinean dictatorship); (6) the influence of Paulo Freire, who came to Mexico on various occasions and whose books have been widely read, analyzed, and put into practice by several generations of curriculum scholars; and (7) the traditions of philosophers, psychoanalysts, and sociologists, among them Louis Althusser, Pierre Bourdieu, Cornelius Castoriadis, Gilles Deleuze, Jacques Derrida, Emile Durkheim, Friedrich Engels, Michel Foucault, Sigmund Freud, Hans-Georg Gadamer, Antonio Gramsci, Jurgen Habermas, Georg Wilhelm Frederick Hegel, Martin Heidegger, Edmund Husserl, Immanuel Kant, Jacques Lacan, Ernesto Laclau, Claude Lévi-Strauss, Jean-François Lyotard, Karl Marx, Friedrich Nietzsche, Nicos Poulantzas, Leon Trotsky, and Slavoj Zizek, among others (Chapter 2). These aforementioned events, projects, and theoretical influences gave rise to four distinctive curriculum groups in Mexico: critical theory, professional development, constructivism, and interpretivism (Chapter 3).

Critical Theory

The social and student protests of the 1960s, 1970s, and 1980s led to the emergence of "popular, democratic and critical universities," distinguished by a "clear socialist orientation" in their principles and in their educational practice (Chapter 2). The major schools of critical thought include (1) The new sociology of education from the United Kingdom (primarily Michael Young's *Knowledge and Control* [1971]); (2) the "reconceptualization movement" from the United States (primarily Henry Giroux, Anthony Penna, and William Pinar's *Curriculum and Instruction* [1981] and Michael Apple's *Ideology and Curriculum* [1994/2004]); (3) neo-Marxist analysis and French theories of reproduction and resistance (primarily the works of Louis Althusser, Christian Bauldelot, Pierre Bourdieu, Roger Establet, and Jean-Claude Passeron); (4) the liberation pedagogy of Paulo Freire (Chapters 2 and 3); the Argentinean scholars in exile who were influenced by Gramsci, Mario Manacorda, and George Snyders; and (5) the Latin American sociologists' "dependency theory" (Chapter 6), according to which the world is organized into a core-periphery model where developed countries form the core while the developing world, including the Latin American region, the periphery.

Mexican scholars have made important contributions to this "critical-reconceptualist" line of thought through discussing the cultural and ideological hegemony of imperialist countries over Latin America, especially through the institutionalization of technological and scientific dependence, as discussed in Phase I. The Mexican scholars who critiqued the incorporation of US technicist curriculum models included Alicia de Alba, Ángel Díaz Barriga, Roberto Follari, Alfredo Furlán, María de Ibarrola, Porfirio Moran, Margarita Pansza, and Eduardo Remedí.

Acknowledging the political nature of school curriculum, critical-reconceptualist-inspired scholarship rejected the technical rationality imported from the United States by means of undertaking an extensive theoretical analysis, often distinguishing between the "formal" and the "actual" curriculum. Critical theories of the curriculum shared "emancipating and liberating impulses" (Silva 1999 in Chapter 3) for the transformation of education and the reconstruction of society. Despite their interest in making accessible their theoretical analyses, an important criticism of critical theory was that it was difficult to comprehend, especially for educators who did not have expertise in curriculum theory. When it did take accessible forms, it seemed to lose its critical edge (Chapter 3).

The most practical implementation of the critical theory was the curricular project at the Autonomous Metropolitan University of Xochimilco where an innovative modular system was established during the late 1970s. In contrast to curricular organization via the academic disciplines, this system required multidisciplinary integrations of academic knowledge, identifying for each profession urgent social problems, which became known as the "objectives of transformation" (Chapter 3).

Modular Study Plan by Transformational Objectives

The Modular Study Plan by Transformational Objectives was a "highly advanced" concept from the curricular point of view. Whereas the technicist model enforced the systematization of behavioral objectives by linking instructional models with evaluation schemes, the modular perspective focused on an "object of transformation": a problem of socially and economically impoverished groups that need to be studied and engaged with professionally (Chapter 4). In this modular study plan, knowledge from different disciplines was integrated according to its social significance. Instead of using a "needs diagnosis model" based on socioeconomic calculations, the specific setting wherein a profession was to be practiced was taken as the point of reference. The curricula of various professions were, then, informed by, but not necessarily aligned with, the academic disciplines. They took the forms of modules organized around professional problems, recalling Hilda Taba's conception of an "integrated curriculum" (Chapter 4).

Guided by the modular program, universities established academic programs placing students in interdisciplinary groups (agronomists, doctors, dentists, economists, sociologists etc.) that traveled to specific places, often to rural communities where they offered viable solutions to problems presented by local inhabitants themselves (Chapter 4). Education, thus, was located not only in libraries and classrooms, but also in actual communities where students, often working in collaborative groups, studied actual social problems, presented documented studies of specific problems, and researched possible actions that might be undertaken to resolve those problems.

Utopic aspirations for higher education represented by such "transformational objectives" began to fade soon after their formulation. Prominent among the factors undermining this social-action-oriented education was the economic crisis of 1982 that ended the Institutional Revolutionary Party (PRI)'s government, which had been in power since the Mexican Revolution. A party associated with the Chicago School (under the aegis of "free market" economics as advanced by Milton Friedman) came to power in 1982, imposing "Consensus Washington" that stipulated policies in return for loans from the International Monetary Fund and the World Bank. This was followed by other neoliberal policies promoting the expansion of the capitalistic market mechanisms while requiring the contraction of public sector. Consequently, the budget allocated to higher education suffered a drastic decrease, because the state was the sole provider of funds for public universities in Mexico (Chapter 4).

The end of projects based on transformational objectives was also brought about by the crisis of the academic communities that sustained them. The capacities of the participating academicians were diminished drastically due to decreased salaries as well as the intensified bureaucratization that enforced "efficiency" over social activism. Moreover, the pro-efficiency bureaucrats, in defiance of the fact that the proper functioning of the modular system required groups of no more than 20 students each, started increasing the number of students per module. The very conditions that had enabled society-oriented educational projects began to dissolve in these degraded circumstances (Chapter 4). In Phase III I will discuss the current phase of Mexican curriculum studies beset with neoliberal discourses of global capitalism, which has reduced education to the level of a commodity instead of the rich experience enabling the transformation of individuals and the society they inhabit.

Professional Development

Although professional development did not take a singular theoretical or methodological form, research was directed to determine the social practices of Mexican professionals. At first, demographic descriptive studies were conducted through surveys, several of which monitored graduates' professional trajectories. By the 1990s, professional preparation and practice studies acquired more theoretical consistency and came to be collectively designated as the "sociology of professions." Many drew upon Donald Schon's (1992) concept of "reflective practitioners." Because they were "in-house" projects of curricular change in schools and universities, many of these studies were never published. The circulation of research reports was restricted to committees responsible for these projects (Chapter 3).

Constructivism

Constructivism started as a critique of disciplinary organizations of knowledge and teacher-centered pedagogy, underscoring the significance of cognitive understanding in organizing school knowledge as well as in designing student-centered pedagogic practices. This curriculum research orientation drew heavily upon cognitive psychology. Constructivism started in the 1970s and reached its zenith in the 1980s when several curriculum research projects with public and national character drew upon the works of David Ausubel, Jerome Bruner, and Jean Piaget, among others. In the 1990s this research orientation shifted from individual/psychological constructivism to sociocultural theories of constructivism, drawing generally upon the work of Russian psychologist Lev Vygotsky and specifically upon the work of Spanish curriculum researcher César Coll (Chapter 3).

Significantly, these national curriculum planning and implementation projects, guided by constructivism, failed "on the ground." Evidently, the administrative and managerial culture of Mexican educational institutions clashed with the philosophy and operational requirements of constructivism, prominent among them was collaboration at various levels of curriculum development and implementation. Due to the hierarchical system and national politics of educational reform such collaboration was not possible. Even after almost three decades of curricular reform founded on constructivist theory and research, Mexico remains far from any actual transformation of educational practices in its classrooms, primarily because Mexican educational system has not been able to abandon a centralized, transmission-dominated, and authoritarian educational administration.

Although in theoretical terms the influence of psycho-pedagogical constructivism is strong, more research is needed to understand its meaning for various educational actors, specifically the identification of possibilities of translating constructivism into curricular designs for classroom teaching and the formation (e.g., professional preparation) of professors (Chapter 3).

Interpretivism

Interpretive studies have focused on understanding subjective and intersubjective meanings and experiences of educators and those they educate. These studies have drawn upon the multiple scholarly traditions of discourse analysis, hermeneutics, phenomenology, psychoanalysis, and sociology. The main methodological strategies employed in these studies include auto-ethnographic accounts, case studies, discourse analysis, in-depth interviews, and life histories. These studies have made significant and diverse references to gender, multicultural concerns, questions of social representation, as well as epistemological issues. Due to their breadth and diversity, interpretive studies focused less on specific curricular problems, including practical problems such as the design of curricular projects to transform educational practices (Chapter 3).

Curriculum studies in Mexico is, thus, characterized by diverse communities of scholars, with multiple, even contradictory epistemological perspectives; social, cultural, and political interests; and research orientations. The field, therefore, is "dispersed and balkanized," reflecting an intricate set of social, political, educational, legal, economic, psychological, and epistemological questions (Chapters 2, 3, 5, and 7). Since every position necessarily implies biases and exclusions, Mexican curriculum studies accommodates conceptions that are not only divergent but also antagonistic. There is little agreement regarding what the curriculum is—its meaning as an educational and social project—and what, how, and why it should be researched (Chapter 3). The "polysemic" and "multi-referential" nature of curriculum studies in Mexico is a sign of its intellectual vitality, which requires open and tolerant attitudes, wherein uncertainty and conflict combine with rigor, careful work, and imagination (Chapter 5)

This complex and diverse nature of the field became explicit in 1991 when de Alicia de Alba, Ángel Díaz Barriga, and González Gaudiano published two edited volumes. The first volume featured the works of US scholars, among them were Bobbitt, Dewey, Giroux, Taba, and Tyler. The second volume was dedicated to the history of curriculum studies in Mexico and included essays by important Mexican curriculum scholars, namely, Ángel Díaz Barriga, Frida Díaz Barriga, Glazman and Ibarrola, Guevara Niebla, Serrano and Ysunza, Guzmán, Ulloa, Aguirre Lora, Pansza, Remedí, Furlán, González Gaudiano, de Alba, Michel Cerdá, Follari and Berruezo, Kuri and Follari, Hoyos Medina, Galán Giral and Marín Méndez, Bravo Mercado, Herrera Labra, and Orozco Fuentes. This latter volume, which provided the first systematic treatment of curriculum studies in Mexico, set the stage for the state-of-the-art curriculum knowledge coordinated by Ángel Díaz Barriga (1993, 2003), authorized by the Mexican Council for Educative Research (COMIE) (Chapter 2).

Phase III: The 1990s–Present

The social commitments of the 1970s–inspired by Marxism and the student movements–have been replaced [in the 1990s] with economistic demands to align curriculum with the market...

Alicia de Alba (Chapter 2)

[Neoliberalism has] created a spirit of curricular reform in which prevails an absence of criticism, a decontextualized character, a lack of consensus and little or no consultation with [curriculum] specialists...

Raquel Glazman-Nowalski (Chapter 7)

In aligning curriculum to the market politicians [in Mexico and elsewhere] contradict the cultural and social mission of educational institutions.

Ma. Concepción Barrón Tirado (Chapter 8)

Curriculum Studies in the Era of Neoliberal Globalization

As a result of the economic crises of the 1980s international financial organizations such as the World Bank, the Inter-American Bank of Development, and UNESCO required orchestration of educational reforms aligned with the neoliberal policies of global capitalism. These international organizations and the so-called Washington Consensus prescribed structural adjustments (reduction in public finances), strict budget priorities, and the liberalization and globalization of the economy (Chapter 4). The Free Trade Agreement (FTA) with Canada and the United States required certification procedures standardizing educational programs and professions to be disseminated through the decentralization of the national educational administration (Chapter 3).

These international agencies, especially UNESCO, emphasized the institutionalization of "innovation" in higher education, specifying its teaching, research, and service functions according to its connections to the employment world, controlled by the State and patterns of public financing, stipulating its interactions with other levels and forms of education (Chapter 8). Furthermore, these international agencies argued that higher education had acquired greater "urgency" because economic development requires graduates capable of continuously updating their knowledge not only to find employment, but also to create jobs in a constantly changing and highly competitive market (Chapter 8). Educators were instructed to teach students to "learn how to learn" so that they may compete in this complex and uncertain twenty-first century. Curriculum has come to the forefront once again, not as academic knowledge structured according to educational ideals but as a means to serve the workplace demands of neoliberal global capitalism (Chapter 3).

Besieged by these neoliberal educational reforms, scholarly discussions in this period focused on (1) complying with free trade demands in educational and professional curricula; (2) developing strategies for the "innovation" of educational systems, including the implementation of accreditation schemes based on the notions of "accountability," "homologation," "study certification," and "quality control" (Chapter 3); (3) creating more "flexibility" in the organization of curricula, supported by the newest information technologies; and (4) cultivating students' intellectual skills for handling technological, economic, and cultural change (Chapter 8).

Evaluation: Accreditation and Innovation

Exploiting the discourse of "quality," international organizations have promoted a series of "reforms" focused on the "evaluation" of education based on the criteria of "accreditation" and "innovation" (Chapters 4 and 7). In Mexico such accreditation of programs is a relatively recent practice; it began with the "peer assessment model" in 1990. Since 2002 accrediting agencies have been conducting formal evaluations of educational institutions according to numerical criteria. Higher education institutions must restructure according to these criteria so that their academic programs achieve accreditation, a prerequisite for receiving funding from the State. The economistic conception of education has reduced higher education to a series of numbers: the number of doctorates in the academic faculty, the number of publications, the number of graduating students, the number of volumes in the library, the number of accredited programs, and the number of graduates working in the labor market. Only those academic programs that are evaluated favorably will receive funding. Stressing the "need" to diversify the higher education system (and thereby encourage "competition"), the State has also promoted the establishment of private universities. In this economistic conception of education whatever cannot be assigned a number is not an indicator of quality. The concept of curriculum expertise is now replaced by curriculum "engineering," aligning curriculum with accreditation criteria (Chapter 4).

The rhetoric of "innovation" has also become a key discourse in evaluation schemes since the 1990s (Chapters 3, 4, and 8). Curricular debates have been coded by new concepts, as policymakers and university administrators promote the establishment of "innovative" curricula (Chapter 4). This emphasis upon "innovation" disguises policymakers' accession to international agencies, which demands that Mexican education and society be increasingly amenable to global capitalism. These so-called curricular innovations are devoid of any deep reflection regarding the consequences of the uncritical incorporation of economic conceptions into curricular structures and classroom realities, which are culturally and nationally specific. Such "innovations" are forced on schools by the central authorities and their representatives (Chapters 3 and 4).

The rhetoric of curriculum reform is marked by apparently commonsense categories: "innovations," "competencies," "flexibility," "quality," "excellence," "student-centered pedagogy," "experiential learning," "academic tutorship," "problem-based learning," "information or communication technologies," and "curricular themes" (e.g., sustainability, values, and civic mindedness), among others (Chapter 3). Such "innovations" quickly lose their commonsense meanings—indeed, become jargon—as they are aligned with technicist standards of certification and evaluation "guaranteeing" professional quality by enforcing uniformity of the curricula not only among various institutions, but even across various countries, all justified in the name of educating for a highly competent and competitive job market (Chapter 8). Consider more carefully the concepts of "flexibility" and "competency."

"Curricular flexibility" first emerged as a concept of "innovation" in the 1990s, signifying the training of students to become "versatile professionals" by acquiring the technical, social, and communicational proficiencies prerequisite to entrepreneurship (Chapter 8). In curricular terms, "flexibility" was to provide students with several professional formation "options" during the final phases of their bachelor's degree study. In academic psychology, for instance, curriculum concentrations in educational, clinical, social, or labor psychology were available. In addition to these customary options, students were given the choice of obtaining a technical or professional degree. Another form of "flexibility" allowed students to study an optional subject in another university, or in another department of the same university. Such "options" had existed in several programs since the 1970s, but during this era of "innovations" these were paraded as examples of "curricular flexibility" renamed as "new" (Chapter 4).

After the Bologna agreements, students can, with economic support, study one semester outside Mexico. The Universitas Foundation of the Santander Bank and institutional resources supported such student mobility. Internships in business were also promoted consequent upon the agreements between institutions of higher education and employers. Through such internships students also earned academic credits. But the number of students who have access to these possibilities has not exceeded 1 percent of the total enrollment. Such "options" of "innovation" and "flexibility" were limited to students; professors have been barred from both (Chapter 4).

In Latin America, curriculum flexibility has been presented as a "new" concept that can provide specific solutions to the problems of higher education, particularly in this era of liberalization of economies, rapid mutations of technologies, new forms of work organization, population pressures, and other changes that are occurring in practically all strata of society. The concept of flexibility is not new. This scheme, promoted by the international agencies for institutions of higher learning in Latin America, had already been designed, developed, evaluated, and rethought in the European educational systems, principally in France, Germany, and England, as well as in the United States. "Flexibilities," such as the combination of short- and long-term training cycles (with the awarding of diplomas that confer recognition of proficiencies with different degrees of complexity and specialization), presented as "innovations," have, in fact, existed for many years. Besides not being the innovations they are said to be, these practices represent another round of enforced imports from Europe and the United States that efface the specificity of the Mexican situation (Chapter 8).

During the 1990s the innovation known as "competency-based education" was launched. As they did with "flexibility," administrators and policymakers enforced competency-based education. Unlike internships in business, study plans structured by competencies are accessible to everyone. Knowledge of competency-based approaches was confusing (Chapter 4); for example, there were multiple meanings of "competency" and there was no agreement regarding its implementation (Chapter 3). For some competency meant "skill" while to others the concept implied competence in unknown situations. Whatever they are, competencies are always in the process of development. One theme that unites all competency-based advocates is their antagonism toward knowledge-based teaching. What the world today needs, advocates insist, is not the classically educated persons, but "competent" and "flexible" entrepreneurs ready with skills to solve problems (Chapter 4). Constant innovation means new competencies will always be in demand, requiring new subjects, rendering some experts amateurs and some amateurs experts.

Adding to the confusion was the acknowledgment that questions of sequencing competencies remain unanswered. What is clear, however, is that competency-based study plans reinstall behavioral objectives. Professional competency is divided into multiple sub-competencies following W. W. Charters' early twentieth-century conception of "task analysis." What constitutes evidence for these sub-competencies is never obvious, and the conditions for the "execution" of various competencies tend to be highly specific, similar to those accompanying behavioral objectives. Moreover, competency-based curriculum means that teachers must constantly modify their teaching content, pedagogy, and evaluation procedures. The competency model requires, presumably, a student-centered pedagogy so as to facilitate the integration of information, but it always starts from specific problems and linking new knowledge with actual problems in real settings. Despite all the talk, teachers continue to teach the way they have been doing it for years (Chapter 4). The constructivist philosophy—particularly, student-centered pedagogy and resource-rich curriculum—that was said to form the basis of competency curriculum could not be enacted due to the over-enrollment of students and inadequate infrastructure (Chapter 9).

Implications of Neoliberal Reforms for Curriculum Studies in Mexico

The forceful imposition of neoliberal economic policy and reforms through conceptions of "accreditation" and "innovation" has had deleterious effects on the curriculum research and scholarship in Mexico. First of all, under these reforms academicians no longer enjoy autonomy over the curriculum. Evaluation mechanisms have tightened administrators' and politicians' grip over scholars and intellectuals and, thereby, greatly curbed their academic (that is to say, intellectual) freedom (Chapter 7). This has been a great setback to the curriculum scholars, especially because before the 1980s higher education in Mexico had enjoyed relative autonomy. It is intellectual autonomy—including the opportunity to compose curriculum—that has been the core of Mexican curriculum studies (Chapters 6 and 7). Curricular projects are now subjected to processes of budget negotiation and allocation that have removed curricular decisions from teachers as well as from educational institutions. Curricular design is now directed by guidelines set by national and international organizations. By the manipulation of evaluation (of programs, professors, and students), politicians and bureaucrats have installed themselves as curriculum "designers" because they specify the basic academic content, the curricular models, and the pedagogic strategies that characterize education in Mexico. Rationalized by slogans such as "learning by competencies," curriculum development decisions are now being made by governmental and nongovernmental organizations, business councils, and diverse civil associations instead of curriculum scholars and disciplinary experts (Chapter 3). The 2003 state-of-the-art assessment of curriculum knowledge registers that many scholars have abandoned the field (Chapter 2), no doubt a consequence of deteriorating conditions.

Indeed, now evaluation determines funding, and funding determines the policies and practices of educational institutions, including curriculum development (Díaz Barriga, Barron and Díaz Barriga 2008). This is the formula of neoliberalism. Not only does it undermine collaborative or long-term research, it reinstalls institutional inequalities, as there is inequality in the distribution of resources: the most prestigious educational institutions are favored over those located in the poorest states of the country. As the power and influence of organizations that accredit study plans and programs continue to grow, dictating which curricular models educators must implement, curriculum decision-making will reside completely in the hands of administrators, bureaucratic functionaries, evaluation agencies, and others external to educational institutions (Chapter 3).

These developments have intensified long-standing tensions between curriculum scholars and administrators. Curriculum scholars' consideration of theory and history, especially as these enable understanding of curricular processes locally and globally, conflict with those of the administrators who are concerned only with accountability to politicians. Because research is in the hands of curricular specialists, the academic field of curriculum studies is where one finds the openness to psychological, anthropological, and social research that is truly innovative and has international resonance. Tragically, curriculum research depends not on the priorities of the Mexican field's internal intellectual development, but on funding aligned with the accreditation of academic programs. Curriculum scholars are confronted not only by these funding priorities but also by regional, national, and international pressures, problems, and politics, which restrict the possibilities for curriculum research and educational reforms (Chapter 3). Curriculum research is, thus, prompted by variables rather than intellectual pursuits (Chapter 9). As a consequence of the neoliberal reforms research on curricular practices (the lived curriculum) has decreased considerably; studies on the hidden curriculum have simply stopped (Chapter 4). Contemporary research priorities privilege quantitative scientific production, forcing a dangerous uniformity by excluding research dissonant with government priorities (Chapters 3 and 7).

In certain respects, curriculum studies in Mexico is presently facing the same imperialism the field encountered in the 1970s. In the first decade of the new millennium, however, this technological rationality comes from the economism of neoliberal ideology. Such economism has permeated many educational systems, and not only in Mexico. The triumph of neoliberalism has led to the hegemony of standardized evaluation and accountability schemes, including the design of curricula according to the so-called competencies and evaluation centered on quality assurance and certification, always forefronting assessment of performance. Through these schemes Mexican scholars once again confront the "satellization" or "colonization" of their field (Chapter 3).

Conclusion

Over the past four decades curriculum studies has emerged as a major area of research in Mexico, as evident in the three state-of-the-art assessments of curriculum research production that the Mexican Council for Educative Research (COMIE) has commissioned since the 1980s (Chapter 5). The genesis of the Mexican field was marked by the import of behavioral-technicist approaches from the United States during the 1970s. During the 1980s, the curriculum scholars in Mexico conceptualized critique of these enforced importations that gave birth to Latin American concepts (e.g., "transformational objectives"). The consolidation of the field followed, exhibiting an internal complexity characteristic of sophisticated fields. Since the 1990s, the field has been assaulted by neoliberal educational reforms that, as historically minded critical analysis shows, represent a reinstallation of the same old industry-driven behavioral-technicist approaches, now disguised as "innovation" in the era of globalization. Despite these adverse circumstances, Mexican curriculum scholars are continuing—as this collection testifies—to do world-class curriculum research.

Note

1. All references in this chapter are to other chapters within this volume.

Chapter 2

Footprints and Marks on the Intellectual History of Curriculum Studies in Mexico: Looking toward the Second Decade of the Twenty-First Century

Alicia de Alba[1]

Today is November 1, 2008; exactly ten years ago I found myself in the house of Stephen and Maria[2] in Wivenhoe, County of Essex in England. That day I finished writing the prologue for the Spanish version of the book *Revolutionary Multiculturalism* by Peter McLaren. Concerning this paper, I had just received an answer from William Pinar. He told me that the paper he is asking for is about the intellectual history of the curriculum field in Mexico, where it would be advisable for me to incorporate elements from an Internet interview that was conducted months ago. It was a biographical type of interview where the questions led me to link elements from my personal history with the constitution, development, consolidation, and crisis of the curriculum field in Mexico.

Part I: The Constitution, Consolidation, and Crisis of Curriculum Studies in Mexico

It is interesting to note that, on this 1st of November, the writing of my biography and autobiography emerged at significant moments in my life.

Today is a special day; even a sacred day, due to the incorporation I made, about two decades ago, of the "Day of the Dead" into my own cultural practices. So today I make my offering, with much love, for my parents, my brother, my grandmother, my Tita,³ and other loved ones who have preceded me. I dedicate this day to them. I remember them; I always go to the offering site where I arrange the objects that I have put there. I remember their laughs and their joy for life; I feel that they nourish me day by day with their legacy, their energy. A part of their souls has been left in my own soul. I am in communion with them; they are a part of me. Therefore, I adopted this ancestral indigenous custom.⁴ It comforts me, cheers me, makes me human as it connects me with myself, with them, with Mexico, and with the world-worlds⁵ that we inhabit, of which we are a part, where we are inscribed and we inscribe our daily duties.

With these lines I begin this essay, a story of the footprints and marks on the intellectual history of curriculum studies in Mexico. I will concentrate on certain footprints and marks, conscious that I omit certain events, papers, and relevant authors.

To embark upon the intellectual history of the curriculum field in Mexico we must go back decades to the intertwining of multiple experiences of a diverse nature,⁶ geopolitical situations, especially in Latin America, the construction of institutional study spaces, debates and the elaboration of proposals, as well as the emergence of different lines of research. We, the majority of Mexican specialists, who have been and are part of the curriculum field in this country, belong to the generation of 1968. In the interview that I did with Pinar, in one answer I pointed out:

> I belong to the generation of 1968, like in France; in Mexico there was also a student movement that marked the generation of 1968 and the following generations. Within the framework of this movement and with the zeal of achieving successful Olympic Games, we have in our history the genocide committed by the government on 2 October 1968, where they assassinated, with impunity, a great number of students. That day…I was not at the meeting but the events of 1968 marked me, like they marked the majority of those of us who were students at that time. (de Alba 2008)

Closely linked with October 2, in the history of the student movement in Mexico, is June 10, 1971. I responded in the following way to Pinar about that day:

> On 10 June 1971, we suffered another repression of the student movement. On that day there was another slaughter, in this occasion I was at the meeting and it is one of the strongest memories I have of my life as a student.

I have a strong mental block because I cannot connect the memories with the emotions. Only once in my life, when I was writing something to my son about this passage, did I shed tears. It is very violent to watch your fellow students being shot and to see an old man in an old, moving car with a colorful, decorated handkerchief around his neck—I am running—and he points at you to shoot you and the shot stays frozen in the gaze between this man and myself, the car moves forward but the emotions have stayed frozen also for the rest of my life, even to this day. (de Alba 2008)

In this way, these intertwining, interwoven individual experiences are linked with political repression and with intense desire for struggle and transformation. Education in general and curriculum studies in particular appeared to us in the cultural and social struggle through which our generation dreamed of radical social transformation toward a better world for everyone. In this intertwining, we recognized different perspectives and conceptual paths—social, cultural, and political interests, ethical aspirations—working daily to understand our reality, in the weaving together and unweaving of educational and curricular areas.

The constitution of the curriculum field is marked, then, with a strong Latin American footprint of struggle, hope, and commitment.[7] I have chosen to discuss this moment by accenting footprints and marks from my own academic history and those of my colleagues, citing experiences, events, and key readings in the intellectual, social, academic, institutional, and political context[8] of Mexico. It is Mexico as a Latin American country, as neighbor to the United States in North America and with diverse types of intellectual relations with countries from Europe (principally with England, France, and Spain, especially in terms of curriculum history), Australia, and Canada. I will combine types of writing: in some sections I will use more of a traditional academic type of writing and in others I will use a biographical or autobiographical type.

The Emergence of the Massive University and New Curricular Proposals

During the 1970s an important expansion of university enrollment occurred; it was accompanied by the formulation of different curricular proposals in various institutions. Among these were the College of Sciences and Humanities (CCH)[9] and the National Schools of Professional Studies (ENEP's)[10] from the National Autonomous University of Mexico (UNAM),[11] where the departmental model was incorporated; the

Autonomous Metropolitan University (UAM),[12] which devised an innovative modular system, as well as the UAM—Xochimilco (recounted by Roberto Follari), the UAM—Azcapotzalco, and experimented in self-government at the Faculty of Architecture from the UNAM.[13] During the 1970s and 1980s, new universities[14] emerged, distinguished by a clear socialist orientation in their principles and in their educational practices. As a result, a multitude of university and professional services became available to those who lived close to these university centers.

I entered university life through one of these new universities: the National School for Professional Studies Zaragoza (ENEP-Zaragoza). There I started my journey into curriculum studies when I became head of the Curricular Evaluation Department. It was an intense, important, and productive experience, and, at some point of my professional life, if it were required, I could write a paper exclusively dedicated to this period. Suffice to say here that my journey into curriculum research started immediately after my time at the ENEP-Zaragoza.

The constitutive moment came in January 1982 when I obtained an academic position at the disappearing Center of Investigations and Educative Services (CISE) at UNAM. Ángel Díaz Barriga[15] came into my room and told me that he thought something I had written at the ENEP-Zaragoza was interesting. This gesture from Ángel was incommensurable and constitutive for me, initiating a strong stage of formation. In the years that followed, Ángel coordinated the seminar wherein we analyzed *The Curriculum* by Franklin Bobbitt (1918). In that seminar, I remember, important contributions were made by Azucena Rodríguez. With Ángel Díaz Barriga I started my career that coincided with the constitution of curriculum studies in Mexico.

The 1980s and 1990s were marked by many interesting experiences, reflections, and theoretical contributions. It was a time of consolidation as well. In 1985 I organized and coordinated the conference "Analysis of Curriculum Evaluation." In 1991 I wrote two books: *Curriculum Evaluation* and *Curriculum, Crisis, Myths and Perspectives*. I started an investigation entitled "The University Curriculum and the Challenges of the 21st Century." I coordinated commissions that organized meetings, special events, and conferences. I started to work from what we have previously called *Formative Investigations* wherein investigative projects underway at different state universities of Mexico were incorporated with projects at universities in other countries, and students were teamed with students from those countries. I worked with colleagues from Spain, among them were Eustaquio Martin Rodriguez, Roberto Aparici, Gimeno Sacristan, Angel Perez Gomez. Argentina: Adriana Puiggros, Roberto Marengo, Silvia Dosba de Duluc, Liliana Petrucci, Rita Guerrero, Victoria Baraldi, Dorita Alaluf, Sonia Araujo, Edith Litwin, Mariana Maggio. Those from the United States

I worked with were Michael Apple, Henry Giroux, Peter McLaren, Donaldo Macedo, Antonia Darder, and Thomas Popkewitz. During this time I was influenced by the work that was underway in England that had been initiated by Michael F. D. Young (e.g., *Knowledge and Control*), what became known there as the New Sociology of the Education and in the United States as the Reconceptualist Movement, comprised by the work of, among others, Henry Giroux, Anthony Penna, and William Pinar (1981). I read *Learning to Labour* (Willis 1977) as well as work from New Zealand (Colin Lankshear and Michael Peters), from Costa Rica (Alicia Gurdian and Leda Badilla), from Colombia (especially Mario Diaz Villa), and, of course, from Mexico (including Ángel Díaz Barriga, Raquel Glazman, María de Ibarrola, Marisa Ysunza, Lyle Figueroa de Katra, Luz Maria Nieto Caraveo, Rita Angulo Villanueva, Bertha Orozco Fuentes).

The Architects of Curriculum Studies in Mexico

Between my experience at the ENEP-Zaragoza, my entrance into the CISE at the UNAM (another constitutive moment in my trajectory), my later incorporation—along with 27 colleagues from the CISE—into the Centre of Studies of Universities (CESU)[16] at the UNAM in 1984 and my work at this Centre during the 1980s and 1990s on national issues concerned with the curriculum, several scholars and intellectuals became preoccupied with curriculum, writing essays and books that comprised the construction of the field. They became its founding architects. As I reflect on this period of constitution and consolidation, these moments emerge as memorable.

Design and Critique of Study Plans: María de Ibarrola and Raquel Glazman

The genesis of curriculum studies in Mexico was marked by the appearance of the book *Design of Study Plans* (1978) by María de Ibarrola and Raquel Glazman. A number of curricular innovations were undertaken in Mexico due to this book, which recapped, among others, the ideas of Bloom (1956), who had been translated into Spanish in the early 1970s. The Ibarrola and Glazman book became legendary. Not only was it widely accepted, it also provoked numerous discussions and debates that, in effect, constituted the birth of curriculum studies in Mexico. María de Ibarrola and Raquel Glazman are without doubt the pioneers of the field in Mexico. Almost a decade later, they conducted a self-critique of their book (1987).

The ENEP-Iztacala: Furlán and Remedí

When acknowledging the intertwining of ideas, influences, and geopolitical situations in the genesis of curriculum studies in Mexico, I am referencing those intellectual youth from South America who came to Mexico, to live in exile from the military dictatorships and authoritarian regimes in place in their countries during those years. Most conspicuous among these were Alfredo Furlán and Eduardo Remedí, who, in the late 1970s, began working at the National School of Professional Studies (ENEP)-Iztacala. Furlán and Remedí stood out due to their capacity to devise new methodological and theoretical proposals as well as to provide reflection and analysis of those curricular proposals that were then being promoted at the new UNAM School they had joined. Known as the "yellow book" (Furlán and Remedí 1979), their contribution remains memorable.

The ENEP-Zaragoza: González Gaudiano, de Alba

In the late 1970s, with Edgar González Gaudiano as its academic leader, the Unit of Human Resources Formation and Academic Evaluation (UFRHEA) was formed at the National School of Professional Studies (ENEP), Zaragoza. We were a group of 20 recently graduated pedagogues who worked with great enthusiasm on a series of projects (both initiated by and assigned to us) on teacher preparation, curriculum design, and curriculum evaluation.

The UAM-Atzcapotzalc: Follari, Villasenor, Guevara Niebla

In the late 1970s and early 1980s, a series of interesting curriculum projects were conducted by groups of scholars (among them Roberto Follari, Guillermo Villasenor, and Gilbero Guevara Niebla) from the Autonomous Metropolitan University (UAM).

Educational Technology

The 1970s and 1980s were also marked by the appearance of the "Transfer of Educational Technology" project, imported from Florida State University. In various Latin American countries courses, seminars, and other academic events and training programs were organized to implement this project. In November of 1980 the second National Congress of Technology and Education was held in Toluca, State of Mexico (Mexico). There assembled faculty and students from different ENEPs at the UNAM, from other universities—such as the UAM-Xochimilco—and from other institutions of higher education. I remember two key speakers from that event: Claudio Zaki Dib (who spoke on the implications of the Transfer project for teaching science) and the Italian Mario Manacorda (who critiqued the project). A number of us also critiqued the project, instituting upon our academic freedom and intellectual independence, declining to accept this project from the United States. *Educational Technology* (de Alba et al. 1985) expressed Mexican scholars' capacity for reflection and critique. By this time, then, curriculum studies was enjoying a distinct identity. It was a brief period of consolidation. Just a decade later, however, consolidation was eclipsed by crisis, which I will describe here.

*Didactics and Curriculum (*Díaz Barriga *1984)*

In Mexico and in Latin America in general, we spoke of study plans and not about the curriculum. This focus provoked interesting critiques and debates, among which the work of Enrique Moreno de los Arcos stands out, a well-known scholar from the College of Pedagogy at the UNAM, who argued that we did not have to incorporate the word "curriculum" to refer to specialized areas of knowledge known as study plans. Some of us contested so sharp a distinction, although acknowledging that the two did not coincide. But both incorporated the interrelation of academic knowledge and pedagogical practice. Although the book by Raquel Glazman and María de Ibarrola (1978) referenced "curriculum," detailing its conception and methodology, the title itself referred to study plans. The first book in Mexico that forefronted the curriculum was Ángel Díaz Barriga's (1984) *Didactics and Curriculum*. This work, as well as others from Díaz Barriga and other Mexican scholars (including those working in Mexico but of other nationalities), informed the emergence of curriculum studies in Argentina.

*An Anthology of Curriculum Studies in Mexico (*Díaz Barriga, González Gaudiano, *and* de Alba *1991)*

It is important to recognize the strong influence of North American and British scholarship in the construction and consolidation of the curriculum field in Mexico. For example, Giroux, Penna and Pinar's (1981) *Curriculum and Instruction* and Michael F. D. Young's (1971) *Knowledge and Control* influenced our conceptualization of curriculum studies in Mexico; they also impacted our curricular practices. This becomes evident in one of the most important works of this period, an anthology (comprised of two volumes) of curriculum essays edited by de Alba, Díaz Barriga, and González Gaudiano (1991). The first volume reflected curriculum studies in North America in general, featuring the works of Henry Giroux, Franklin Bobbitt, John Dewey, Ralph Tyler, and Hilda Taba, among others. The second volume was dedicated to the history of curriculum studies in Mexico, including works from Díaz Barriga, Glazman and Ibarrola, Guevara Niebla, Serrano and Ysunza, Guzmán, Ulloa, Aguirre Lora, Pansza, Remedí, Furlán, González Gaudiano, de Alba, Michel Cerdá, Follari and Berruezo, Kuri and Follari, Follari, Hoyos Medina, Díaz Barriga Arceo, Galán Giral and Marín Méndez, Bravo Mercado, Herrera Labra and Orozco Fuentes. This anthology—the first systematic treatment of curriculum studies in Mexico—set the stage for state-of-the-art curriculum knowledge, coordinated by Ángel Díaz Barriga (1993, 2003), authorized by the Mexican Council for Educative Research (COMIE).[17]

National Congresses of the Mexican Council for Educative Research

Starting from the second National Congress of Educative Research (1992) and with the foundation of the COMIE, the second round of disciplinary assessments—states-of-the-art-of-knowledge—was conducted in the various areas of educational research. In curriculum studies, there were two such assessments, both coordinated by Ángel Díaz Barriga (1993, 2003). It became clear in a 2003 report that many had abandoned the field in order to dedicate themselves to other areas of educational research. Even so, new generations of novice researchers and scholars with enthusiasm and seriousness have carried on the legacy that we, the builders of curriculum studies in Mexico, have left them. Although today (2009) we can speak about a crisis in the field, we witness at the same time the emergence and strengthening of new groups of curriculum researchers and scholars.

The Identity of Curriculum Studies in Mexico

What is it that ties together curriculum studies in Mexico, enabling us to speak of a certain profile or identity of this field? There are multiple curricular conceptions, positions, reflections, models, and practices. While there is great diversity in thought and practice, there is also unity in such dispersion (Foucault 1969). In articulating what I have called the marks and footprints I have sketched a kind of network of theories and practices that characterize the curriculum field in Mexico, accomplishing one of Pinar's research objectives: "Document the imbrications of local and global knowledge in the intellectual advancement of nationally distinctive fields" (Pinar 2008, 1). In the following, I identify the elements of the distinctive identity of curriculum studies in Mexico.

Working from Primary Sources: From Bobbitt and Dewey to Pinar, Penna, and Giroux

I link two events with the constitution of the field: (1) the new curricular models of the 1970s associated with CCH, ENEP, UNAM, and the Popular, Critical, and Demographic Universities and (2) the critique of the "Transfer of Educative Technology" project. Supplementing these events were groups of academic youth who were, simply, interested in the curriculum, sometimes especially the curricula of those institutions they had been and were attending. This admixture of theoretical, institutional, and spontaneous subjective interests animated the study of curriculum in Mexico. What linked them was the urgency of thinking through and acting upon the various new curricular proposals and models, requiring the reading of both historical and contemporary scholarship, not only from Latin America but from North America and Europe as well. This multiplicity of scholarly and institutional sources for the field became congealed for me in three clusters of intellectual and institutional events: (1) the seminars coordinated by Díaz Barriga on Bobbitt; the seminar on curricular evaluation coordinated by de Alba; the projects of González Gaudiano and de Alba at the ENEP-Zaragoza; the work of the ENEP-Iztacala group led by Furlán and Remedí; the work of Glazman and Ibarrola, among others, which derived from Michael Young, David Hamilton, Paul Willis, Carr Wilfred and Stephen Kemmis, Basil Bernstein, Terry Eggleston, David Ausubel, Franklin Bobbitt, John Dewey, William Alexander, Ralph Tyler, Hilda Taba, Joseph Schwab, Jerome Bruner, Philip Jackson, William Pinar, Anthony Penna, Henry Giroux, Michael Apple, and Peter McLaren, among others; (2) the almost clandestine works of Susana Barco (who came to Mexico during the time of the Argentinean dictatorship); the influence of Paulo Freire, who came to Mexico on various occasions and whose books have been widely read, analyzed, and put into practice by several generations of curriculum scholars; the work of Adriana Puiggros; (3) the work of Karl Marx, Friedrich Engels, Leon Trotsky, Antonio Gramsci, Georg Wilhelm Frederich Hegel, Immanuel Kant, Edmund Husserl, Martin Heidegger, Friedrich Nietzsche, Michel Foucault, Jacques Derrida, Gilles Deleuze, Jean-François Lyotard, Jurgen Habermas, Hans-Georg Gadamer, Sigmund Freud, Jacques Lacan, Slavoj Zizek, Ernesto Laclau, Pierre Bourdieu, Lévi-Strauss, Louis Althusser, Emile Durkheim, Nicos

Poulantzas, and Cornelius Castoriadis, among others. These three clusters of events, projects, and theoretical exposition were intertwined with very strong political, social, and institutional events, evidenced not only in bibliographies but also in the relationships of curriculum specialists with important decision makers. They also became expressed in the strong link between researchers and teachers. The now nonexistent Center of Research and Educative Services (CISE) played an important role in this regard. Also illustrating the link between past and present is the conversion of the assessor figure in curricular projects into an object of conceptual reflection and analysis (see Angulo and Orozco 2007). It is this capacity for reflection and criticism that is the throughline in curriculum studies in Mexico, from the time of its constitution in the 1970s until today, personified in Bertha Orozco Fuentes and Raquel Glazman. This capacity for reflection, critique, and self-critique is also evident in the self-critique that Glazman and Ibarrola conducted of their classic *Design of Study Plans* (1978).

The Crisis of Curriculum Studies in Mexico?

At the current moment curriculum studies can be found in a paradox. While on the one hand the field is dispersed, disintegrated, de-structuralized, even balkanized, on the other hand, less populated (as many curriculum specialists left the field) scholarly production (articles, books, magazines, etc.) grows stronger and more extensive day by day. At present there are at least two major assessments of the field, one that affirms its dissolution (Díaz Barriga 2008) and another that affirms the field's emplacement in a context of globalized tension, a generalized structural crisis (de Alba 2007). This I find is a productive tension that promotes and stimulates the imagination and animates commitment. With this second position I associate my vision of the future of curriculum studies in Mexico, a vision I now articulate.

Part II: The Internationalization of Curriculum Studies: Toward the Second Decade of the Twenty-First Century

I would like to start this last but central part of the chapter with the same words that I used to start my replies to Pinar's "Intellectual Life History Questions."

> I would like to start [our discussion about the Internationalization of Curriculum Studies] by recovering the idea of Pinar about a "complicated

conversation" with colleagues from different parts of the world. He suggests that this "complication" constitutes itself through the historical and especially national positioning of the participating colleagues. I suspect that this work in the field of curriculum, in Mexico, and in different points around the globe, affects and is changed by, the identity of the participants, especially their professional commitments, as these are aligned with the cultural, political, social, economic and ethical issues with which they are engaged as they conduct their daily activities. Not doubt the relation—possible conversation—among curriculum experts from different parts of the world, exhibits very strong levels of complexity among other issues, due to historic processes, that while related, accent their own specificity, and which are difficult to understand in the first place, as they belong to distinctive semiotic, cultural configurations of national and local realities. (de Alba 2008)

The internationalization of curriculum studies is a historical imperative linked, then, among other things, to understanding the curriculum-society relationship in a significant and productive way, forefronting the strong cultural specificity that is lived out regionally in the world. Especially in Central Europe, the United States, and England,[18] there is as well a balkanization of subjectivities and identities reflected in the curriculum field at the global, local, and "glocal" levels, illustrated not only by the complexity of communication across national borders but also by the difficulty of achieving meaningful communication between different generations within nations.

To comprehend the contemporary curriculum-society relationship, it must be apprehended from the perspective of the tension of globalization, a generalized structural crisis. In the following paragraphs I will reference in a theory of cultural contact (de Alba 2006a) that enables us to look beyond multiculturalism and interculturalism while recovering the advances of these theoretical viewpoints. In the first draft of this essay, I began to elaborate the balkanization of identities and subjectivities and their impact on the curriculum field in order to contribute to the recovery of subjectivity-identity. I began with an analysis of the interrelation between interiority and its exteriority, and I briefly underlined the importance of incorporating a generational focus in studies of the curriculum field, supplemented with environmental and gender elements. Given the length of the essay, I have decided to leave these two points for later papers, although it is worth mentioning that I have already undertaken this analysis in *Curriculum-Society: The Weight of Uncertainty, the Strength of Imagination* (2007).

The strongest pressure I experience in my work today derives from international spheres, refracted nationally and socially. *Indeed, for me, the most powerful commitment must be the ongoing study of curriculum in the framework of the tension*[19] *between a generalized structural crisis and globalization.* Such study is a complex intellectual, cultural, and political undertaking. To think and act in the field of the curriculum at the present time is to think and act in a social context structured by the strong tension between globalization and generalized structural crisis.

At present we are faced with a reality in the curriculum field that is radically different from the reality we were faced in the 1980s and 1990s. New demands are emerging, and they have arrived in Mexico from international organizations. They arrived in a social imagery—in Latin America in general and in Mexico in particular—that reflects a changed curriculum-society relationship. To identify one event, the fall of the Berlin Wall (1989) indicated a very strong break in the collective social imagery about socialism, and in the different ways that socialism had been conceived until that moment. The social commitments of the 1970s—inspired by Marxism and the student movements—have been replaced with economistic demands to align curriculum with the market (e.g., curriculum based on competencies), organized around technology (e.g., new information technology, communications, TICC knowledge), structured by measurement and evaluation, and always accelerating to keep abreast with "change." Accompanying these developments is an absence of analysis, of understanding the wide social context in terms that allow us to see the outlines that lead toward the construction of other possibilities in the world,[20] especially the emergence of new social, even utopic horizons. Indeed, of the most important challenges we face at present in 2011 is to study the wide social context so that we can see and build the curriculum in a committed, meaningful, and efficient way. It is imperative to think of this context as the tension between globalization and CEG.

Globalization

The concept of globalization alludes to many and diverse fields of meaning that have been the object of reflection, conceptualization, and debate. In this essay I would like to underscore two elements that predominate. One of these is globalization as events and actions that affect all parts of the world. One of these is the environmental crisis;[21] in this sense, it is a credible, pertinent, and truthful usage of the term. Another globalizing phenomenon is Internet use: "The year 2000 started, *without any doubt*, consolidating cyber communication which has put *all* the inhabitants of the planet online" (Bong Seo 2000; emphasis added). Enthusiasm for such globalization reflects an incapacity to comprehend the "world-worlds" we inhabit. It communicates an ill-informed common sense, but it is also a strong argument for deconstructing our own positioning.[22]

The meaning that interests me most is that which refers to the term or meaning[23] "globalization" as that which systemizes the current global disorder—order, central to the task of thinking of the complexity of the world in which we live today. The enthusiasm expressed by Bong Seo (2000) becomes understandable if we conceive it as proclaiming a new world order, acknowledging the human necessity to live according to systems and organization that protect us from the chaos of destructuralization. In this sense globalization becomes a social, cultural, and economic project, bound by an ontological-semiotic codes.[24]

Generalized Structural Crisis

In the course of the intellectual life history interview, in reply to my first set of replies, Pinar asked me "By 'structural' do you refer to 'economic' and specifically to the periodic crisis of currency exchange?" I affirm that by CEG I understand the complex interrelation of cultural, epistemic, theoretical, social, educative, religious, ethical, economic, financial structures[25] articulated by ontological-semiotic code, or by confrontations between ontological-semiotic codes. This understanding finds its roots and genealogy in post-structuralism and post-Marxism.[26]

By CEG I denote a general weakening of the elements[27] of relational systems of differential but interrelated structures that at the same time comprise a structure or system of greater significance, a process that leads to the proliferation of floating elements or meanings.[28] In our time, this crisis implies a weakening of economic, political, social, cultural, educative, cognitive, and ethical structures. A generalized structural crisis is characterized by the destructuring of structures more than by the structuring of new structures, although in its interior, complex articulation phenomena such as social structures are produced. Several theorists have referenced such structural or organic crises[29] in the sense that I have acknowledged here. At this time, however, I want to underline its "generalized" character.

By the term "generalized" I emphasize that the crisis affects the majority if not the totality of social, political, cultural, and economic systems that are interrelated in different ways. It is this interrelation that marks the generalized character of the crisis. This interrelation, although depicted as a linkage between different dimensions of the social structure, is also marked by an interrelation that shares an ontological-semiotic code or by an interrelation where different ontological-semiotic codes are confronted. From our positioning, in Mexico and Latin America, it is obligatory to note that Western culture has been erected as the ontological-semiotic dominant code, but that in the current generalized structural crisis this code or ontological-semiotic dominant system is showing[30] its limits.[31] Therefore, at the core of the current generalized structural crisis, structures that share this same Western cultural horizon are becoming dislocated as they are confronted with structures associated with different cultural horizons or ontological-semiotic codes.

Among the most important aspects of this generalized social crisis are (1) its "generalized" character, referencing the destructuring of the systemic interrelation of structures as they are confronted with diverse structural interrelations, all organized by distinct ontological-semiotic codes or systems; (2) its duration, although it is not possible to predict how long it will take to destructure the entire interrelation of structures that comprise societies; (3) its locatedness, as this destructuring of diverse structures occurs at different times varying intensities in different areas of the world and even within regions or countries, and among distinct groups or social sectors; (4) new structures arising from destructured ones, requiring that we face these in creative and committed ways; and (5) the generalized structural crisis demands new ways of thinking and acting (e.g., new sets of language and new forms of life).[32]

In their diverse dimensions, societies are always in processes of erosion and dislocation, disclosing structures that are breaking down. So the crisis of our time, while uniquely ours, can also be observed in different forms in other societies. Such structural erosion and dislocation[33] provoke the proliferation of floating elements of significance, which implies, one, the loss of empty elements of significance[34] that organize societies according to Western culture, as modernity reaches its historical limits, and as it is being reconfigured by those just now embracing and/or resisting its structures, themselves sedimented from the eighteenth, nineteenth, and twentieth centuries; and, two, the dislocation of individual lives, groups, institutions, nations, and countries that have been developed at the core of these societies, that is, those who have lived through intellectually the historical arch of modern times (the French Revolution in 1789 and the Fall of the Berlin Wall in 1989).

Such complexity makes it difficult to understand the accelerated shifts underway in Mexican society. It is unsurprising, then, to find pessimism and even catastrophic expectations shared by many, defensively reformulated by others as an unmeasured enthusiasm for progress and scientific advances and technology and an unwavering faith in the future, predicting that globalization will connect us all, if it has not already done so, in a worldwide "society of information and knowledge." For me, it is imperative to formulate a position between these two extremes, acknowledging that the tension and crisis in which we are currently living also constitutes a crucible of unedited opportunities to contribute in various ways to the task of transforming reality toward a better world. In this way the internationalization of the curriculum becomes an opportunity to contribute in the fashioning of new utopia horizons, enabling us to look in creative and committed ways toward the future.

How we can do so rests on two aspects: (1) the effort to seriously read reality, acknowledging that there is no historical, political, social project able to resist neoliberalism, but recognizing that with globalization are intertwined elements that portend new figures of the world, that is, even though they have not yet been profiled, they portend the constitution of new hegemonies; and (2) how we position ourselves in the tensions between globalization and crisis, as living through the crisis requires the solidarity of entire generations, as different generations live at different times in the historical present. Many of us will live the rest of our lives in this crisis, continually trying to articulate possibilities of new social structures and figures.

Social Structures

In the globalization of destructuring, new processes and social phenomena emerge, characteristics or elements[35] associated with destructuring as articulated moments,[36] translated into new articulations of new structures. That is, faced with floating elements of significance comprising the core of the generalized structural crisis, new articulations emerge, condensations of meaning with sedimentations, tending to result in new social structures. These articulations point toward new figures of the world, drawing us closer to understanding the moment in which we live, thereby enabling us to devise strategies, programs, and actions to make pertinent and committed interventions in this context. Such articulations are comprised of various elements or characteristics (floating elements of significances) that detach themselves from the structures where they are found as they break away and reemerge as disruptions or new elements.

These elements, characteristics, or floating elements of significance that emerge in the current context of globalization and crisis can (1) come from structures in the process of destructuring or from elements contained within these structures (rearticulating these elements into new visions and configurations and/or perpetuating current structures); (2) present themselves as disruptive characteristics, as unexpected and capable of increasing the breakage of the structure(s) (Fall of the Berlin Wall in 1989, Twin Towers New York in 2001, Obama's ascent to power in 2009). It is difficult to know whether such elements will comprise new social structures or whether they will disappear like shooting stars in nights of tension and crisis; and (3) become new, possibly disruptive unedited elements, such as the new families.[37]

Theory of Cultural Contact

Cultural contact refers to the interchange of cultural goods and interrelations among groups, sectors, or individuals from different cultures—and, therefore, with different ontological-semiotic codes, different self-management and uses of signs (e.g., means of communicating significance and meaning)—that produces changes in the distinctive subjects that participate in this process. The varieties of multiculturalism and pluralism can be considered as markers for cultural contact, representing and reconstructing identity interiority,[38] as they contain the keys of the ontological-semiotic code. One of the principal characteristics of cultural contact is that it transforms subjectivity and identity, as one is never the same after cultural contact has occurred. From my perspective, cultural contact is central to the internationalization of curriculum studies.

Cultural contact[39] is a space in which different discourses, language games, forms of life, ways of intelligibility and sensibility interact on the domains of *the different*. Cultural contact implies several processes of articulation over discursive practices of symbolic dispatches, over psychic, ontological, semiotic, and discursive practices. It is important to affirm that mainstream multiculturalism blocks cultural contact, as identity politics promotes separatism and isolation among different subcultures. In this sense, I agree with Zizek (1997) that multiculturalism is the multinational logic of capitalism. Cultural contact, in contrast, engages ontological-semiotic codes and thereby reconfigures subjectivity and identity. The constitutive elements of cultural contact are relational, historical, conflictive, unequal, and productive in themselves.[40]

To say cultural contact is *relational* is to underscore that it is discursive and negative. It implies interrelations among different cultures, *language games, forms of life*,[41] and ways of sensibility and intelligibility. As Saussure (1916) points out, the sign is arbitrary, then, when the contact occurs among those who belong to the realm of the *very form of the different*. There is nothing natural in helping to initiate contact, given that members of diverse cultures have radically different semiotic (nor semantic) codes, signs, and tropes. Each element in a given contact exhibits its ontological and semiotic background and framework, its own tropes of open and precarious relationships. This cultural encounter produces a *dislocation* of the symbolic order of each culture, an eruption of the Lacanian Real. In this sense cultural contact disrupts subjectivity and identity. Despite this difficulty, cultural contact is possible because it is relational. This is the first aspect of cultural contact and it is important to emphasize it, because at the beginning contact produces strong dislocation.

To say that cultural contact is *historical* is to underline that it occurs in time through events. Cultural contact becomes incomprehensible if severed from History. Not only do we have historical evidence of cultural contact—it can be like an earthquake or it can occur so slowly as to be imperceptible, as if it were a slow dripping. Whether fast or slow, dramatic or subtle, cultural contact draws us close to others, enabling us to understand their histories and cultures as personified in those we encounter. In these social relations sedimented histories become renegotiated.

To say that cultural contact is conflictive is to underscore the structural and semiotic difficulties in communication and relationship. If we have been deeply involved in contact our identities have suffered some kind of "*trastocación*,"[42] precipitating difficulty in the very articulation of their forms of life. In this conflicted situation *chronotope* not only helps us understand the constitutive moment of cultural contact, the concept also conveys the very character of cultural contact's constitutive dimension in itself. Indeed, there is a *chronotopic dimension* of every cultural contact and of the whole cultural contact realm. As a consequence, we can construct new spaces and new surfaces of inscription of the meanings that function as bridges and hinges among and between their diverse semiotic codes. This can occur because the tropes[43] of distinctive cultures nonetheless contain capacities to transform into different tropes in a realm of infinite possibilities.

Despite these capacities, identity necessarily reproduces its own ontological-semiotic codes, language games, forms of life, preserving the traits of its subjectivity. In that way, cultural contact is conflictive and we cannot elude this fact. Cultural contact produces strong struggles inasmuch as this struggle is constituted as a relational tension between culture as metonymy and culture as metaphor in very different rhetoric spaces. In culture as metonymy tropes act mainly in the field of time, contiguity, or juxtaposition, constructing chains of consecutive events. In culture as metaphor, tropes act with dispatches, displacements, and condensations, choosing among substitutions, producing equivalent significations, that is, contributing to create new chains of equivalence. One can say this is the compulsion of diverse signifiers to hegemonize discursive, symbolic, and cultural space, fighting for the emergence of signifiers that could assume the role of empty signifiers in new chains of equivalence.

Cultural contact is unequal. When two or more cultures come into contact they must negotiate the tension between the intent to dominate and the desire to meet the *Other*, to know who it is and how it is. It is in some sense an ontological encounter. In both cases, there is the imperative to develop mechanisms that preserve constitutive nodal traits of their subjectivities and identities. Deep encounter with the *Other* produces its own conditions of possibility insofar as the very conditions of cultural contact bring with them access to new technologies, ideas, practices, styles of sensibility and intelligibility, language games and forms of life. Productivity emanates from this situation due to relationality, its conflictive and unequal character, permitting and sometimes accelerating the dislocation of cultural identities and subjectivities. In this sense, they effect strong displacements and trope transformations and the production of new elements of significance.

Understanding cultural contact as nodal assumes the catachretical dimension of the languages, that is, the figural dimension of the languages and its possibilities of mutation and transformation. The chronotopic dimension of cultural contact allows us to play with this complex catachretic dimension, to participate in the transformation of elements of significance signs and to incorporate semiotic frameworks significations belonging to other semiotic or cultural structures with which we have been in contact. In so doing, we are performing the catachrestical dimension of language and the chronotopic dimension of cultural contact, enabling us to create new ontological alphabets.

Because multiple interpellations are produced among discourses, subjects, and groups, cultural contact is productive. Floating signifiers proliferate, traversing one to another culture, even though tropes could be incomprehensible to each other. In these complex surfaces of inscription, new traits and new constellations of meanings as well as new metaphors and metonymies are produced in a rhetoric field through mechanisms of identification. Thus, new semiotic structures and semantic elements permit not only communication among cultures but also their reciprocal transformation and, with long and intense periods of contact, the emergence of new cultures.

This productive character of cultural contact—accomplished through displacements, condensations, and dispatches of tropes in symbolic rhetoric space—articulates discontinuous and unequal elements, from those subjects located in the very form of different cultures. This productive capacity refers to the rhetoric capacity to resignify new elements of significance, formulating new tropes and new semiotic frameworks[44] and thereby traversing the globalized structural crisis of our time, in our field, accomplishing the internationalization of curriculum studies.[45]

Notes

1. Titular researcher from the Research Institute for Universities and Education (IISUE) from the National Autonomous University of Mexico (UNAM). Member of the National System of Researchers (SNI) from the National Council of Science and Technology (CONACYT) of Mexico.
2. Stephen Ford and Maria, his wife, are intimate friends who gave me shelter in many ways during 1998, the year that I did my postdoctorate in Political Philosophy with Ernesto Laclau, in the Centre for Theoretical Studies in the Humanities and Social Sciences—founded by Laclau in 1990, at the University of Essex, England. In the first semester of that year I let a flat in Wivenhoe, but in the second I was living with Stephen, Maria, and Nicolas (their son). It was an extraordinary experience.
3. My Tita, great aunt on my mother's side, was my second mother.
4. The *Day of the Dead* in Mexico is an ancestral celebration with a popular and pre-Hispanic character. "Day of the Dead [in Mexico]..., many Mexican families erect altars to the dead in their homes...Included in these altars are offerings of the favorite foods and drinks of the departed, to be enjoyed by their spirits when they return to visit their loved ones. The altar is laden with bright orange marigolds (the *zempoalxochitl*, flower of the dead)... This is a time of happy communion with the dead, not a time of sorrow." Nobel Prize winner Octavio Paz in his essay "The Labyrinth of Solitude" explores the Mexican fascination with the duality of life and death. "Our relations with death are intimate," Paz writes, "more intimate perhaps than those of any other people." In my case, as in the case of many others, it has a special meaning due to the fact that I have started doing this cultural practice as an adult woman. Reflecting on my intellectual history and my academic life is now associated with the Day of the Dead: without meaning to, I have started or ended important pieces of work with vital information that goes beyond the strictly academic and engages me in a very strong way.
5. "When I speak of world-worlds I am referring to the current social complexity and to the different existing forms of conceiving society, of naming it or formulating it. We speak of the first world, the third world, of the fall of the block or Socialist world, of developed countries, sub-developed countries or those that are developing (of poor countries and rich countries, etc.). Without a doubt, these ways of looking at the world are linked to the social space of the person who is conceiving them and to the particular way in which the person organizes the aforementioned social complexity in his/her own subjectivity" (de Alba 1993, 33).

6. From a genealogical perspective, we recognize the emergence of this intertwining in the late 1970s and the early 1980s, a time marked by (1) the dictatorships in several Latin American countries that forced valuable intellectuals into exile, many of whom came to Mexico; (2) the then still called guidelines—socialist on one hand, capitalist on the other—that people used for imagining and fighting for building a better world that they thought would reach a certain level after which everything would progress toward the future; and (3) "massive" growth of education, and of universities, particularly in some Latin American countries, specifically in Mexico.
7. My generation of scholars and researchers emerged at this moment and has had, among other things, the task of instituting and institutionalizing the curriculum field at the heart of educational research in Mexico. Groups and institutions that have been protagonists in this process, among others, have been the Centre for Educative Studies (CEE), the Department of Educative Research (DIE) from the Centre for Research and Advanced Studies (CINVESTAV), the now nonexistent Centre for Research and Educative Services (CISE), the Faculty of Philosophy and Liberal Arts (FFyL), and the Institute of Research on Universities and Education (IISUE)—until 2006 Centre of Studies on Universities (CESU)—at the National Autonomous University of Mexico (UNAM).
8. By context I mean environment as structuring and structured factors, linked with the interiority and exteriority of what occurs.
9. College of Sciences and Humanities (CCH).
10. National School of Professional Studies (ENEP).
11. National Autonomous University of Mexico (UNAM).
12. Autonomous Metropolitan University (UAM).
13. This self-government experiment was rooted in the movement of 1968; it included community projects for the people, to support them in the design and construction of houses or in other types of construction, even the design of streets or of neighborhood lots, planning the construction of houses and other buildings. In the early 1970s, I studied Architecture (which I left to continue with the Faculty of Philosophy and Liberal Arts). In this respect, I told Pinar, "*The popular and revolutionary colony 'Ruben Jaramillo':* Within the framework of architectural self-government, I lived through a strong experience. On the *Red Sundays* in the revolutionary and popular 'Ruben Jaramillo' all of us architecture students would go to help build up the colony. We would get in with our student credentials. After working on the construction of the houses, I would dedicate myself to analyzing the social problems and particularly the educational problems of the community. This is one of the reasons that I left architecture and decided to study the social sciences, particularly education. I was more interested and I dedicated more time to the social than to the architectural part." (de Alba 2008)
14. The so-called Popular, Democratic and Critical Universities.
15. Ángel Díaz Barriga is without a doubt one of the most important pillars in the curriculum field in Mexico and Latin America.
16. Center of Studies about the University.

17. Mexican Council of Educational Research (COMIE).
18. In this theory of cultural contact I forefront the United States, the United Kingdom (mainly England), and central Europe, because in a metaphoric way, they are huge human laboratories. Within their territories there are many intense intercultural contacts every day, due to historic and current migrations (de Alba 2006b).
19. "For me, the moment of tension always happens when there are two components in a relation, both necessary but nevertheless cannot be automatically adjusted." Interview of Ernesto Laclau by Alicia de Alba, November 3, 2006, The Homestead, Evanston, Illinois (Northwestern University).
20. "The basic ideas that characterize an era show the way in which the entire world is configured before man. Therefore, what we could call the 'figure of the world' is condensed. A figure of the world starts to slowly appear at the core of the aforementioned" (Villoro 1992, 8).
21. "Most of the contamination that destroys the ozone layer comes from the northern half of our planet. But the hole in the ozone on earth is found above the South Pole, not above the North Pole. Why? Recent research confirms what scientists have always suspected: gigantic atmospheric waves caused by the elevation of terrain (like the Himalayan mountains) shelter the formation of an ozone hole in the Northern hemisphere and, as a consequence, the cities in the Arctic Zone stay free from the undesirable dosage of solar ultraviolet radiation—at least for now. Researchers warn that a change in the climate could undo the work of these waves and convert the Arctic zone into an area with a greater incidence of ozone holes" (Barry and Phillips 2001).
22. In the year 2000 around 1 percent of humanity had access to the Internet. By September 30, 2008, that figure rose to 22.3 percent.
23. Used in political philosophy at the University of Essex in England, deconstruction emphasizes the arbitrary if predominant role of significants (acoustic, verbal, written, visual, architectonic forms, etc.) in a semiotic system (or ontological-semiotic).
24. The ontological-semiotic code refers to the system that constitutes and organizes the signs inside a significant configuration, system, or structure and gives it meaning. It is an ontological-semiotic code where radical differences are found, among different groups and social sectors and among historical subjects. The ontological-semiotic system is the main point upon which different elements of cultural articulation, of a cosmo-vision, of a world figure are determined and organized.
25. In no way, then, am I referring to the old Marxist conception that considered the economic dimension to be the structural dimension as the only structural dimension and, therefore, the determining one.
26. Specifically, in the position of Laclau (Cfr. Laclau and Mouffe 1985; Laclau 1990).
27. According to Laclau and Mouffe, weakening is indicated by "a completely different element that is not articulated discursively" (1985, 119).
28. By "floating" I understand elements that have different meanings in different discourses; during moments of crisis these elements of meaning tend to

dilute themselves. There is a strong relationship between floating and empty elements of significance. In a situation of generalized structural crisis, in processes of destructuring, floating elements of significance proliferate. For example, the significance of "revolution" in Mexico, from 1910, has been an element of floating significance, due to the differences in meaning that it has had for different social sectors and subjects. In this regard, it is empty. Insofar as it accomplishes the function of systemizing the variable meanings of the "Revolution," in configuring the post-revolutionary Mexican political system it exhibits a floating significance that tends to be diluted. For example, the meanings of "revolution" have changed in a notable way in Mexico since the regime of Fox (2000, 2006).

29. Cf. Laclau and Mouffe (1985), who conserved the denomination of organic crisis from Gramsci and reconceptualized it.
30. In the sense of Wittgenstein (1953).
31. In the sense of Laclau (1990).
32. I am using these notions in the sense associated with Wittgenstein (1953).
33. I am using the concept of dislocation. From Laclau (1993a) I recover three dimensions of dislocation: "(1) as a form of temporality (that marks the distance, separation, irreducible hiatus between before and after, what is represented and what is not represented, between agent and structure, opens possibilities to the undetermined); (2) as a form of possibility (different from Aristotelian possibility where a 'telos' would already be marked) which does not have a predefined future (when dislocation disorders a system it operates as a moment that is above conventional rules and relations); and (3) as a form of freedom and indetermination because if the structure is faulty, the identities that make it up are organized from a structural fault that hopes to be resolved via successive identifications. This supposes that the empty 'foundation' and constitutive exteriority are those that organize the systematic system, which does not say much. Temporality, possibility and freedom are imbued in dislocation. The event exterior to the structure, impossible to be absorbed as an internal moment of self-deployment (as Hegelian ontology would supposes)" (Burgos 2003, 83–84).
34. The function of empty significances is to represent the identity that is purely equivalent. That is, the differences are dissolved in equivalence chains and make up an identity (to go deeper into this theme consult Laclau [1994]).
35. According to Laclau and Mouffe "we will call all differences that are not discursively articulated *elements*."
36. According to Laclau and Mouffe "we will call *moments* differential positions, insofar as they appear articulated inside a discourse" (1985, 119).
37. "It is more and more common to find non-traditional families for instance, single-parent families, same-sex parents, or families after divorce and separation, now with new partners. These so-called new families [can also be] adults who educate children that aren't theirs (grandparents, adopting parents)... .. these familiar nuclei are more and more common, dismantling the concept of traditional families, and they are faced with special challenges before society and ... education" (Burgos and Ayuntamiento 2005). Also, "Sociological

research carried out in Navarra by experts from the Public University unveiled that there is a growth of up to 11 percent of single parent families, and in a more sensitive way of women who decide to undertake maternity and their children's education without establishing any type of coexistence relationship" (Javar 2004).

38. By interiority, I understand those identifying elements that have been incorporated in the individual, familiar, group, social, community, and national subjects, constituted through differential movements that tend to close, excluding those elements that threaten.
39. Among the elements of cultural contact are the following: (1) the catachrestical dimension of the language; (2) the transformative capacity of the discursive articulation; (3) the manifold possibilities of creation, transformation, mutation, and movement of the tropes from the rhetorical turn; and, (4) the possibility that the Bakhtinean chronotope helps us understand encounters and contacts amongst different cultures, that is, different chronotopic realities.
40. In comparison with multiculturalism, a logic in which difference is forefronted, but not from its unavoidable conflictive character. Indeed, multiculturalism contains conflict by positing equivalence from the cultural dominant pole, which translates the corresponding *difference* into its own code (ontological-semiotic code).
41. For *language games* and *forms of life*, see Wittgenstein (1953).
42. In Spanish *"trastocar"* means to be touched and at the same time to affect identity.
43. "A trope (...) is a particular entity either abstract or consisting of one or more concrete entities in combination with an abstraction...I propose now that entities like our fine parts or abstract components are the primary constituents of this or any possible world, the very alphabet of being" (Williams 1953).
44. In such a process we establish new conversations: "[b]y introducing ourselves in such conversation, the adherents to the traditional recognize the nature of their own understanding as historic, contingent and culturally located... what Gadamer calls his 'historic horizons.' Thus, the consequence of conversation is no 'objective' understanding of the situation, but a 'fusion of horizons'—a mutual and shared understanding, in which the inadequacies and limits of the initial understanding of each participant becomes evident and what is precious is kept within a more integrated and comprehensive understanding of the situation under research" (Car 2006) or, in our case, of the situation within cultural contact.
45. Today is February 2, 2009, another holiday in Mexico, it does not have the same importance as the Day of the Dead, but it is interesting that on this day I have been able, in general terms, to finish this essay. "*Candelaria* is celebrated on the 40th day after Christmas (February 2nd). This religious celebration marks the end of the Christmas festivities observe the birth of Christ. *Candelaria* commemorates the day when Christ was presented in the temple by his parents, following Jewish practice." Mexican families celebrate by "raising" the Christ Child figure from the nativity scene. The Christ figures and icons are then brought to the church to be blessed. Finally the nativity set

is put away until the beginning of the next season's Christmas celebrations. Available online: http://www.sanmiguelguide.com/candelaria.htm.
46. The directory of Science of the Marshall Center for Spatial flights from NASA sponsors the internet pages Science@NASA that include Ciencia@NASA. The mission of Ciencia@NASA is to help the public to understand the research stimulants carried out at NASA and to collaborate with scientists in their work of dissemination.

References

Angulo Villanueva, Rita, and Bertha Orozco Fuentes, eds. 2007. *Methodological Alternatives of Curricular Intervention in Superior Education*. Mexico City: Plaza y Valdés.
Bakhtin, Mikhail. 1981. *The Dialogic Imagination: Four Essays*, ed. Michael Holquist, Trans. Caryl Emerson and Michael Holquist. Austin, TX: University of Texas Press.
Barry, Patrick L., and Tony Phillips. 2001. "Planetary Waves Prevent the Formation of Holes in the Ozone Layer." Ciencia@NASA.[46] Available online at: http://ciencia.msfc.nasa.gov.
Bloom, Benjamin, ed. 1956. *Taxonomy of Educational Objectives*. New York: David McKay.
Bloom, Benjamín. 1956. *Taxonomy of Educational Objectives. The Classification of Educative Goals*. Trans. Marcelo Pérez Rivas. Buenos Aires: Editorial El Ateneo.
Bobbitt, Franklin. 1918. *The Curriculum*. Boston: Houghton Miffin Company.
Seo, Yoon Bong. 2000. "Two Fruits of the Cyber-Net Era: The Net Generation and the Hackers." Mexico: University of Guadalajara. Available online at: http:fuentes.csh.udg.mx.
Bruner, Jerome. 1960. *The Process of Education*. Cambridge, MA: Harvard University Press.
Buenfil Burgos, Rosa Nidia. 2003. "How Do We Position Ourselves When Looking at the Field? Tools for Political Análisis of the Discourse." In *Philosophy, Theory and Field of Education. National and Regional Perspectives*, ed. Alicia de Alba, 68–94. Mexico City: COMIE, SEP, CESU-UNAM 671.
Carr, Wilfred. 2006. "Philosophy, Methodology and Action Research." *Journal of Philosophy of Education* 40 (4): 421–435.
de Alba, Alicia. 1993. "University Curriculum Faced With the Challenges of the XXI Century: The Paradox between Post-Modernism, Absence of Utopia and Curricular Determination." In *University Curriculum Faced With the New Millennium*, 29–45. Mexico City, CESU-UNAM: Plaza y Valdés.
de Alba, Alicia. 1995. *Teacher Expectations Faced With the Problem and Challenges of University Curriculum in Mexico*. PhD diss., National University of Distance Education. Madrid, Spain.

de Alba, Alicia. 1999. "Curriculum and Society: Rethinking the Link." *International Review of Education* 45 (5/6): 479–490.

de Alba, Alicia. 2002. *University Curriculum: Academics and Future.* Mexico City: Plaza y Valdés.

de Alba, Alicia. 2006a. "Der Kulturelle Kontakt. Anknüpfung." In *Cultural Studies und Pädagogik. Kritische Artikulationen*, eds. Paul Mecheril and Monika Witsch. Bielefeld, Germany: Transcript Verlag (Pädagokik).

de Alba, Alicia. 2006b. "Cultural Contact. The Nodal Role of Trope and Chronotope." Paper presented at the Conference of Trope, Affect and Democratic Subjectivity, Northwestern University, Evanston, IL, November 2–4, 2006.

de Alba, Alicia. 2007. *Curriculum-Society: The Weight of Uncertainty, the Strength of Imagination.* IISUE-UNAM, Mexico City: Plaza y Valdés.

de Alba, Alicia. 2008. "Intellectual Life History Questions," Interview by William Pinar, June 27, 2008, via the Internet.

Dewey, John. 1902. *The Child and the School Program. My Pedagogic Creed.* 5th ed. Trans. and preliminary study by Lorenzo Luzuriaga. Buenos Aires: Losada.

Díaz Barriga, Ángel. 2008. "Conceptual Tensions. Curriculum." *Theory and Curricular Processes*, September 16. Available online at: http://teoriasyproc.blogspot.com.

Foucault, Michel. 1969. *Archeology of Knowledge.* London and New York: Routledge.

Furlán, Alfredo, and Eduardo Remedí. 1979. *Contributions to the Didactics of Superior Education.* Mexico City: Department of Pedagogy, Autonomous National University of Mexico.

Giroux, Henry, Anthony Penna, and William Pinar. 1981. *Curriculum & Instruction. Alternatives in Education.* Berkeley: McCutchan.

Giroux, Henry. 1981. "Introduction and Overview to the Curricular Field." In *Curriculum & Instruction. Alternatives in Education*, ed. Henry Giroux, Anthony Penna, and William Pinar, 1–12. Berkeley: McCutchan.

Glazman, Raquel, and María de Ibarrola. 1978. *Design of Study Plans.* Mexico City: CISE/UNAM.

Glazman, Raquel, and María de Ibarrola. 1987. "Design of Study Plans: Curricular Model and Reality." In *Study Plans. Institutional Proposals and Curricular Reality*, 251–289. Mexico City: Nueva Imagen.

HazteOir.org. 2005. Home Page. Madrid: HazteOir.org. Available online at: http://www.hazteoir.org.

Jackson, Philip W. 1981. "Curriculum and its Discontents." In *Curriclum & Instruction*, ed. Henry Giroux, Anthony Penna, and William Pinar, 367–381. Berkeley, CA: McCutchan.

Laclau, Ernesto. 1990. *New Reflections on the Revolution of Our Time.* London: Verso.

Laclau, Ernesto. 1991. *Emancipation(s).* London: Verso.

Laclau, Ernesto. 1993. "Discourse." In *A Companion to Contemporary Political Philosophy*, 431–437. Oxford: Blackwell Publishers Ltd.

Laclau, Ernesto. 1994. "Why the Empty Signifiers Matter to Politics?" In *The Lesser Evil and the Reater Good. The Theory and Politics of Social Diversity*, ed. Jeffrey Weeks, 167–178. London: Rivers Oram Press.

Laclau, Ernesto. 2001. "The Politics of Rhetoric." In *Material Events*, ed. Andrzej Warminski, Barbara Cohen, Tom Cohen, and J. Hills Miller, 229–253. Minneapolis: Minnesota University Press.

Laclau, Ernesto. 2006. "Ernesto Laclau Interview by Alicia de Alba." November 3, 2006. The Homestead, Evanston, Illinois (Northwestern University) USA.

Laclau, Ernesto, and Chantal Mouffe. 1985. *Hegemony and Socialist Strategy*: Towards a Radical Democratic Politics. London: Verso.

Lacan, Jacques. 1953–1954. *The First Seminar: Technical Writings of Freud*. Trans. Pascual Cevasco Mira and Vicente Rithe, 1986. Barcelona: Paidós

Pinar, William. 2006. "Intellectual Advancement through the Internationalization of Curriculum Studies." Project proposal submitted to the Social Sciences and Humanities Research Council of Canada.

Puiggrós, Adriana. 2005. *From Simon Rodriguez to Paulo Freire. Education for Ibero-American integration*. Bogotá DC: Andrés Bello Conference (Confluencias Collection).

Saussure, Ferdinand de. 1916. *Course in General Linguistics*. Trans. Wade Baskin, 1983. New York: McGraw-Hill.

Taba, Hilda. 1979. *Curriculum Elaboration*. 4th ed. Trans. Rosa Albert. Buenos Aires: Troquel.

Tyler, Ralph W. 1982. *Basic Principles of Curriculum*. 4th ed. Trans. Enrique Molina Vedia. Buenos Aires: Troquel.

United Nations Development Programme (UNDP). 1995. *Human Development Report 1995*. New York: UNDP. Available online at: http://www.undp.org.

UNDP. 1999. *Human Development Report*. New York: UNDP.

Villoro, Luis. 1992. *Modern Thought. Renaissance Philosophy*. Mexico City: The National College-FCE.

Williams, Donald Cary. 1953. "On the Elements of Being." *Review of Metaphysics* 7: 3–18, 171–192.

Willis, Paul. 1981. *Learning to Labour*. New York: Columbia University Press.

Wittgenstein, Ludwig. 1953. *Philosophical Investigations*. Trans. George Edward Moore, 2001. Oxford: Blackwell.

Young, Michael. 1971. *Knowledge and Control*. London: Collier-Macmillan.

Zaki Dib, Claudio. 1980 (November 22). "Transfer of Educative Technology in the Scientific Area." Paper presented at the II National Congress of Technology and Education, Toluca, State of Mexico, Mexico City.

Zizek, Slavoj. 1997. "Multiculturalism, Or, the Cultural Logic of Multinational Capitalism." *New Left Review* 225: 28–51.

Chapter 3

Curriculum Studies in Mexico: History and Current Circumstances

Frida Díaz Barriga Arceo

As is the case elsewhere, in Mexico it has been difficult to define what is understood by curriculum studies and to specify its disciplinary limits, its borders with other fields of educational research. This difficulty is understandable as there is neither a unified gaze nor a unique or hegemonic focus that allows us to delimit the range of research topics, problematic areas or situations that belong only to curriculum research. The concept of curriculum is characterized by its polysemic character, supplemented by the fact that it is a theme open to controversy. What is understood by curriculum has always been linked to diverse paradigms associated with diverse disciplines, and to politics both national and international in scope, wherein conflicting conceptions and vested interests are expressed.

Since the 1970s, at least from the viewpoints of educational and governmental officials, curriculum studies has been defined by its practicality. In other words, curriculum equals intervention plans, curriculum design and evaluation, study plans and programs. This emphasis upon practicality is understandable since its main task, from the viewpoint of educational institutions, is to propel curricular reforms. What predominates as "curriculum" are academic study plans, reflecting an emphasis on formal curricular products and structures, models and proposals, all designed to support innovations in teaching.

From the viewpoints of specialists, however, curriculum is much broader than the aims listed above. For curriculum specialists, the field is also concerned with curriculum development more broadly understood. It is concerned as well with understanding curriculum, especially those social, political, and educative processes that inform it. Therefore, in addition to specific curricular plans and models, curriculum studies in Mexico has focused on themes such as the following: the hidden curriculum as well as daily life in the classroom; formation (or preparation) of professionals; the social function of professions; the selection, organization, and distribution problems of curricular content; subjective interpretations of actors engaged with the curriculum; processes of learning and social interaction in school settings; specific curricular and didactic reforms; curriculum theory and history; gender and multicultural studies; financing; international organizations and politics and curriculum determination.

What stands out from this researcher's perspective is that the previous themes, which define a spectrum of areas related to curriculum studies, derive from diverse disciplines, such as psychology, sociology, pedagogy, didactics, and history, taking into consideration the current thought or paradigms that belong to them. As a field, then, curriculum studies in Mexico is a complex conceptual and practical construction typified by very diverse collections or communities of curriculum scholars, with shared epistemological perspectives, shared work styles and interests within their groups, but these groups are, however, frequently in conflict with the other groups. And given the fact that every position necessarily implies biases and exclusions, it is understandable that in our country, in curriculum studies we find conceptions that are not only divergent but also antagonistic, frankly debated over what the curriculum is, its meaning as an educational and social project, and what, how, and why it should be researched.

Curriculum studies are of great interest in Mexico, not only to educational researchers but to governmental authorities and institutions as well. In fact, curriculum is one of the educational themes that is most researched and published, as evidenced in the two state-of-the-art assessments of curriculum research production that the Mexican Council for Educative Research (COMIE) commissioned in the 1980s and 1990s (see A. Díaz Barriga et al. 1995, 2003).

Curriculum studies in Mexico, past and present, exhibits strong links with Mexican and Latin American social problems. Among the issues that interest curricular researchers are problems in the Mexican educational system such as the following: overcrowding and the low quality of teaching; obsolescence and rigidity in curricular plans and teaching models; social inequality (especially inequality in access to education); unequal quality of educational offerings; the incapacity of educational institutions to respond to the demands of the labor market and of the society as a whole; alleged deficiencies in academic, communicative, and scientific competencies among primary and secondary school students; deficiencies in didactic and disciplinary formation (preparation) of the professors; the absence of connections between what is learned in school and relevant learning for life; insufficient knowledge regarding what happens in Mexican classrooms and of the impact of recent curricular reforms and innovations.

Beginning in the 1990s, economic and cultural globalization has brought profound changes to all walks of life in Mexico, and not only in the economic and political spheres. In developing countries, such as Mexico, characterized by enormous socioeconomic inequality and by scientific and technological dependence, it is difficult to assess the impact of globalization. Nevertheless, many have concluded that globalization has intensified Mexico's dependence on developed economies, resulting in a deterioration in the quality of life for the majority of people, including increases in insecurity, violence, and unemployment, and decreases in government projects designed to benefit the public. The deleterious impact of globalization can also be felt in culture and education, in values and ways of life, deteriorating the national and the local.

The main consequence of globalization, driven by international organizations and national educational policies, is the adoption of logics and policies that mirror curriculum reform in developed countries. Among these are the following: the politics of accountability; models of educational quality assurance through evaluation, including the certification of educational processes, programs, and agents; linking funding to outcomes (obtained in quality and productivity evaluations of educational institutions); reformulation of study plans according to those "competencies" presumably prerequisite to performance in the global economy. Underpinning everything is standardized evaluation. Such curricular reform has been adjusted according to local circumstances and translated into curriculum. Always aligned with regulation, control, and centralized coordination, neoliberal curriculum reform has transformed the panorama of curriculum studies in Mexico.

The 1970s and 1980s

In an earlier essay (see Frida Díaz Barriga 2003), I identified the main tendencies of curricular investigation from the mid-1970s until the end of the 1980s, focusing on curriculum development. Later, I broadened this discussion to include the 1990s (see F. Díaz Barriga 2005; Díaz Barriga and Lugo 2003). These essays form a part of the state-of-the-art of curriculum knowledge commissioned by the Mexican Council for Educative Research

(COMIE) and conducted under the direction of Ángel Díaz Barriga and his team of collaborators (2003, 1995).

Curriculum research conducted in Mexico during the 1970s was focused on intervention: the design of study plans and programs structured by so-called technological rationality, accented by behaviorist psychology and the educational technology of this era. An adoption of the practical models especially of US theories was effected, not only in Mexico but across Latin America. Later this would become known as "satellization" or "colonization." This enforced adoption precipitated resistance from several Mexican scholars, for example, there appeared critiques of these US models as well as formulations of alternatives, the latter of which drawing on critical theory, sociology, and cognitive psychology. But it is not until the 1980s that we see a substantial growth in Mexico in the field of curriculum studies, in the form of a diversity of conceptual foci and methodological strategies. It was also during the 1980s that curriculum studies became "institutionalized": K-12 schools as well as universities and other institutions of higher education established formal departments or at least faculty groups dedicated to the study of curriculum, especially the design and evaluation of study plans and programs. At the same time, courses in curriculum theory and practice (as training workshops, courses leading to diplomas, and even postgraduate degrees) proliferated. These were often directed toward teachers, educational planners, psychologists, and even bureaucrats and other decision-makers in educational institutions.

Technological-Systematic Tendency

This tendency I associate with the "traditionalists" in US curriculum studies (Hilda Taba, Ralph Tyler) and teaching (Benjamin Bloom, Robert Gagné). Influential in Mexico during the 1970s and 1980s, this tendency saw the development of study plans and entire academic programs, structured by the four questions Tyler had posed: (1) What educative objectives have to be reached? (2) Which educative experiences allow us to reach them? (3) How can these experiences be efficiently organized? (4) How must we evaluate the achievement of these objectives? In Mexico, curriculum proposals for the design of academic study by objectives that were formulated by Glazman and de Ibarrola (1976) and by Arnaz (1981) were the most representative, but other proposals were influential as well (see Commission of New Teaching Methods 1976; Huerta 1981; Gago 1982).

Almost from the outset, critiques followed. In general terms, these judged this "technological-systemic" tendency as reductionistic, rigid, and decontextualized, resulting in the fragmentation and trivialization of learning through behavioral objectives, superficial technical processing, and atomization of academic content. Also decried was the lack of historical and social analysis of the curriculum. Finally, it was alleged that US models would lead to an intensification of administrative control. In sum, this research tendency represented a form of curriculum development (in contrast to research focused on understanding) characterized by studies on diagnosis, documentation, and evaluation of curricular projects. Many institutions continue to work with this technological rationality in their efforts to make education more "effective" through the application of "scientific" techniques that are frequently extrapolated from the industry.

The Critical-Reconceptualist Movement

Within the context of the social movements of the 1960s and 1970s, important critiques of society and education emerged in different countries that had important repercussions in Mexico. Among these was the appearance of a generation of Mexican scholars considered as "critical pedagogues." Within this tendency there were different currents of thought, among them the new sociology of education (M. Young) from the United Kingdom, the reconceptualization movement (William Pinar, Henry Giroux, Michael Apple, Peter McLaren) from the United States, neo-Marxist analysis and French theories of reproduction and resistance (Louis Althusser, Pierre Bourdieu, Jean-Claude Passeron, Christian Bauldelot, and Roger Establet), and, perhaps most conspicuously, the liberation pedagogy of Paulo Freire. Mexican scholars have made important contributions to this "critical-reconceptualist" line of thought, from discussing the cultural and ideological hegemony of imperialist countries over Latin America, especially through the institutionalization of technological and scientific dependence. The repercussions of such dependence for curriculum studies in Mexico were identified by Ángel Díaz Barriga, Alfredo Furlán, Eduardo Remedí, Margarita Panza, María de Ibarrola, Alicia de Alba, Roberto Follari, and Porfirio Moran. The common denominator of this work was its critical questioning of the social and political functions of education. Acknowledging the central importance of school curriculum, Mexican scholars now openly rejected the technical rationality imported earlier. The most illustrative example of this tendency was the curricular project at the Autonomous Metropolitan University of Xochimilco that established an innovative modular system. In contrast to curricular organization via the academic disciplines, this system required multidisciplinary integrations of academic knowledge, identifying a series of urgent social problems for each profession, which became known as the "objectives of transformation."

These critical pedagogues undertook extensive theoretical analysis, often distinguishing between the formal and the actual curriculum. For Silva (1999, 115), critical theories of the curriculum shared "emancipating and liberating impulses" that transcended any narrow interest in transforming education as they aspired to reconstruct society itself. Despite their interest in making accessible their theoretical analyses, an important problem of these projects was that they were difficult to comprehend, especially for educators who had not specialized in curriculum theory. Moreover, deriving practical applications from them, for instance, in the conduct of curricular development, proved problematic.

The Formation and Social Practice of Professionals

Although there was no one theoretical tendency or methodological strategy that united them, these studies can be summarized by their research objectives (e.g., determining the formation and social practice of professionals in Mexico) and by their interest in educational intervention (e.g., formulating models to contribute to the development and evaluation of the university curriculum). At the beginning of this trend, we find descriptive studies of a demographic-statistical nature that were conducted through surveys, several of which monitored graduates' professional trajectories. By the 1990s, studies of professional preparation and practice began to exhibit more theoretical consistency as they became defined as studies in the sociology of professions (see A. Díaz Barriga and Pacheco 1990; Marin 1993). Another theme in this tendency was the concept of reflective professionals, adapted from the work of Donald Schon (1992). Because many of these studies were generated during "in-house" projects of curricular change in schools and universities, they were never published. They were comprised of documents whose circulation was restricted to those internal committees dedicated to the development projects. As well, those in charge of the studies did not always exhibit sufficient expertise in curricular development processes, and even less theoretical sophistication (Jimenez 2000).

Psycho-Pedagogical Approaches to the Curriculum

This tendency emerged and was then consolidated around the implementation of new forms of knowledge organization and innovative teaching proposals designed to facilitate student learning and thereby promote significant and complex learning. Such curricular research was closely linked to the psychology of learning and development, more recently to the constructivism associated with David Ausubel, Jerome Bruner, Joseph Novak, César Coll, Phillipe Perrenoud, and Lev Vygotsky, among others. According to Posner (1998), new forms of curricular organization follow from educational psychologists' critiques that study plans that reflect disciplinary structures fail to recognize the psychological structure of knowledge and the complex processes of human learning. This psycho-pedagogical tendency parts from the time-worn premise that the curriculum should reflect the way that a person learns, emphasizing instead content analysis (concepts, procedures, attitudes) in the design of learning experiences. It is interesting to note that this perspective linked cognitive psychology and curriculum design.

Beginning in the 1970s and reaching its zenith in the 1980s were research and curricular projects, some with a public and national character that were cognitively oriented and inspired above all by Jean Piaget and his followers, although the ideas of Jerome Bruner and (especially) David Ausubel were also influential. In the 1990s these shifted toward constructivism accenting sociocultural considerations. Among these, the Spanish curriculum researcher César Coll (1987, 1990), dedicated to Spanish curricular reform in basic and secondary education, was influential. His curricular model inspired multiple curricular reforms throughout Latin America.

This tendency of developing curriculum with theories of learning represents a crossroad between curriculum studies and those studies dedicated to the theme of teaching and didactics. National curriculum planning and implementation projects rationalized by this psycho-pedagogical perspective, focused on preschool and basic education (primary and secondary), have been accompanied by different curriculum research efforts related to processes of cognitive development and learning. These psycho-pedagogical projects exhibited variable results in quality, diffusion, and impact. Why?

There were two main obstacles. The administrative and managerial culture of Mexican educational institutions clashed with the philosophy and operational requirements of constructivism. These projects were centralized and required vertical implementation, given that their curricular logic was developed by experts. They were not proposals requiring collaboration except in minor ways. The authority of these psycho-pedagogical experts was, however, undermined by the national politics of institutional reform. The casualty was the conversion of curricular constructivist principles centered on students into institutional reality, undermining any possibility of creating curricula that were flexible, situational, and dependent on teacher training both to create them and to put them into practice. After almost three decades of curricular reform founded on theory and research about processes of knowledge construction, we are far from any actual transformation of educational practices in the classroom because we have not been able to abandon a traditionally centralized, transmission-dominated authoritarian educational administration.

Interpretative Studies about the Vision of Curricular Subjects

Interpretive studies comprised a line of research focused on the study of subjective meanings of pedagogical and curricular experiences. They were mainly interested in analyzing the subjective and intersubjective meanings reported by participants in educational processes. The particular point was to discover how processes of identity construction occur. In these projects, the interest of researchers was not the curriculum in and of itself, but, rather, the subjective experience of the curriculum. There were diverse theoretical references to gender, multicultural issues, questions of social representation, as well as epistemological beliefs or values. For Silva (1999), this tendency reflected post-structuralist and post-critical conceptions of the curriculum. For him, this line of research emphasized multicultural themes, including questions of curricular representation of minorities and other vulnerable social groups. Others studied gender or feminist pedagogy, even reinterpreting the curriculum as primarily an ethnic or racialized narrative.

These studies of the subjective meanings of curriculum derived from multiple scholarly traditions, among them phenomenological hermeneutic traditions, sociology of knowledge, psychoanalysis, and discourse analysis. Methodological strategies included in-depth interviews, life histories, case studies, auto-ethnographic accounts, and discourse analysis. There was a dilemma in this line of research, as even projects that were strictly or exclusively about the curriculum lost specificity because the concept in this line of work became diffused as it reached for the totality of meanings and identities constructed by multiple and conflicting subjects. Moreover, this line of research distanced itself from all practical interest, at least from any development of curricular projects designed to transform educative practices in the classroom. Instead, its basic interest was the understanding of what happens within and among educational institutions and actors.

Each of these curricular research tendencies remains today, although they have been influenced by consequent social and cultural changes, which I will discuss hereunder.

Curricular Innovation and Global Influences: The 1990s to the Present

From the 1990s to the first years of the new millennium, important curricular reforms traversed all levels of the Mexican educational system. Educational institutions undertook various innovations that were, presumably, responsive to global forces and politics promoted (if not outrightly imposed) by international organizations. These reforms were rationalized by the arrival of a new world order, the so-called information age, the knowledge society. Now, we were informed, students must "learn how to learn," so they may compete in this complex and uncertain twenty-first century. Curriculum came to the forefront once again, not only because it expresses educational ideals but also due to its characterization as the means to form the citizens that this new world order demands.

Scholarly discussions focused on (1) specific globalization requirements due to free trade agreements and the means of complying with these demands in educational and professional curricula; (2) curricular dilemmas created by globalization and the new media and information technologies; (3) conflicting conceptions of culture and identity in multicultural curricular projects; and (4) strategies for the transformation of educative systems, including the implementation of accreditation schemes accented by accountability, homologation, study certification, educative quality control, and other requirements. New local and national organizations and associations appeared, all dedicated to promoting alignment among policy, intervention, and research.

Due to these demands, new curricular projects (especially at the technical and higher education levels) were framed by policies of economic globalization, especially international commerce agreements, mainly the Free Trade Agreement (FTA) with Canada and the United States. These required certification procedures that standardized educational programs and professions, accomplished in part by the decentralization of the national educational administration. At the same time, announcements from international agencies such as UNESCO (see Delors Report from 1996, the base document from the First Global Conference on Higher Education that was held in 1998), the Inter-American Bank of Development (see the document *Superior Education in Latin America and the Caribbean* from the year 2000), and the World Bank (through a series of documents detailing investment policies in which quality, equality, leadership, and efficiency were emphasized) resulted in the reorientation of Mexican educational systems and curricular projects (San Martin 2004).

In the *International Handbook of Curriculum Research* (Pinar 2003) one finds similarities that links curriculum studies in Mexico with that in other nations. Although there is a local and national character to curriculum studies in every country—even when the field is characterized more by its internal diversity than by its national uniqueness—there are nonetheless resonances among the nationally distinctive fields. In the first place, there are relatively few studies in curriculum theory or history, at least compared to projects dedicated to intervention in educational institutions. This was certainly the case in Mexico in the 1990s (see A. Díaz Barriga et al. 2003).

In several countries, there is acknowledgment of contradictions between the academic curriculum field and the demands of government (and nongovernment) agencies. In Mexico we can speak of the "separate agendas" of curriculum researchers and those authorities responsible for curricular reform. There has been a constant tension between "what" (critical discourses) and "how" (technical discourses) concerning the curriculum. Indeed, there remains a pervasive tension between research and intervention. Because research as knowledge construction is in the hands of curricular specialists, the academic field of curriculum studies (housed in universities) is where we find the most an openness to psychological, anthropological, and social views that are innovative and have international resonance. Nevertheless, these research developments have not extended to the daily practice of teachers and students.

In my judgment, we are faced today with substantially the same institutional logic of intervention that characterized curriculum "reform" in the 1970s. Except that, now, in the first decade of the new millennium, this technological rationality comes from "business thought" in the so-called neoliberal (end-of-ideology) era. This "business thought" seems to have permeated many educative systems, and not only in Mexico. The triumph of neoliberalism has led to the hegemony of standardized evaluations and accountability schemes in general, including the design of curricula according to so-called competencies and evaluation centered on quality assurance and certification, always forefronting evaluation of performance.

I agree with Coll's (2006) warning regarding curricular improvement conceived only in terms of "quality" and performance evaluations. Coll affirmed that we have to equip ourselves with knowledge external to official curriculum policies, as these are inevitably ideological and political. Official policies operate by accountability logics and educative systems management; necessarily they ignore pedagogical logic. Therefore, nonofficial orders of analyses and diagnoses are required, including detailed studies of curriculum in action, focused on the realities with which educative actors are faced.

For others (see A. Díaz Barriga et al. 2008), this new cult of evaluation has created competition between individuals and institutions, resulting in merit pay systems that distribute research funding according to government-determined politics and practices. These research priorities privilege quantitative scientific production, forcing a dangerous uniformity by excluding research dissonant with government priorities. Despite this system we have not seen any increase in the quality of scientific research or pedagogical practices.

Once again an uncritical adoption of practical discourses and technological models from the United States and from other so-called advanced countries is underway, reproducing "satellization" or "colonization" of Mexico. There remains resistance. Some criticize Anglo-Saxon and European curriculum theory and development as restricted to problems of instructional content, for example, knowledge distribution in educational classrooms. If the meaning of curriculum theory and research is the formulation of a vision of humanity for the future, that panoramic project has been replaced by what Hamilton (1999, 6) called "the short term question: What should students know? which is replacing the curricular question: What should students become?" In the *Handbook of Research on Curriculum*, Philip Jackson (1992) affirmed that the majority of curriculum studies in the United States were concerned with implementation and evaluation. This was a voluminous, detailed, technical production, he judged, especially when compared to curricular productions that were oriented to "the construction of general theories or principles about curriculum development or ample curriculum perspectives as a whole or its status as a field of study" (Jackson 1992, 3). The same is true in Mexico, even if we acknowledge the prolific production and diversification of the field.

The scholarly production of curricular scholars working in Mexican universities or centers of educational research has come closer to Pinar's conception (2003, 2004) of "understanding" curriculum, as the field now focuses on comprehending curriculum's historical, political, phenomenological, or identitarian elements. During the past decade critical essays have been appearing on topics such as the following: dilemmas that the curriculum faces in the globalization of a subordinated economy such as Mexico's; the problem of environmental education; the problem of multicultural diversity and identity; critiques of those strategies and policies of international organizations structuring Mexican education, specifically the curriculum. Currently, research conducted by university scholars and curriculum researchers comprehending the curriculum is emphasized, even when it is not the main current or one that generates the most voluminous written productions. This line of studies is of increasing importance, particularly with respect to the theme of identity construction through curriculum and, more generally, of educative experiences of various actors.

Since the 1990s, the term *innovation* has dominated the rhetoric of curriculum design and application, including the promotion of new prototypes and methodological strategies for teaching. This emphasis upon "innovation" disguises policymakers' accession to international demands that Mexican education support a society that is increasingly globalized. So-called curricular innovations expressed the slogans and novelties of the moment, without any deep reflection regarding their implications or any informed forecast of the consequences of their uncritical incorporation into curricular structures or classroom realities, completely overlooking educative cultures and practices prevailing in any given educative community. Unsurprisingly, these "innovations" were implemented vertically, forced down the organizational charts by central authorities and their representatives. Only in some cases was innovation understood as the need for profound change in paradigms and social and educative practices in an educative community.

Díaz Barriga and Lugo (2003) identified the following "innovations" characterizing curriculum "reforms" in Mexico:

- Curriculum by competencies
- Curricular flexibility
- Administrative foci on strategic planning, institutional analysis, or total "quality" and "excellence" applied to curriculum development and evaluation
- Curriculum centered on students, based on psycho-pedagogical constructivism and cognitive and sociocultural psychology: *learning how to learn* is the slogan
- Curriculum design focused on theory-practice integration and on professional formation through practice, service, situated, or experiential learning in real scenarios
- Proposals for tutelary guides for the student during his/her professional preparation and formation, based on so-called empowerment or entitlement approaches, expressed in the models of academic tutorship and designed to prevent students from failing or even falling behind in their studies
- Teaching and curricular program design centered on problem-solving approaches, so-called problem-based learning (ABP) and case analysis, particularly in disciplines such as mathematics, medicine, health sciences, architecture, and experimental sciences
- The incorporation of new themes or fields of knowledge in the development of curricular projects, particularly denominated as curricular themes or transversal axes. In this area, works published throughout

the decade on the curriculum and environmental education stand out, particularly from the perspective of sustainable ecological development. Other emerging themes are related to human rights in the curriculum; education on values, civic mindedness, and ethics; education and gender; curriculum and new technologies, and, to a lesser degree, curriculum and multi- or inter-cultural communication.
- The incorporation of information or communication technologies (TIC) into the curriculum and teaching.

It is important to emphasize that we do not find any unified vision in these so-called curricular "innovations." The curricular discourses that thematize these different models of innovation derive from diverse disciplinary and theoretical references, and their expression in concrete projects is likewise diverse. Only in a few cases do we have any knowledge of their implementation and eventual success. Above all, in the case of curriculum by competencies and characterized by flexibility, we find multiple meanings and ways of understanding these concepts, and there is no agreement concerning implementation. Theoretically, the influence of psycho-pedagogical constructivism is undeniable. More research is pending, however, if we are to understand the meanings of these approaches for various educational actors, including the identification of possibilities of translating constructivism into curricular designs for classroom teaching and the formation (professional preparation) of professors.

Conclusion

After participating in two state-of-the-art assessments of curriculum knowledge in Mexico and based on my experience at several private and public educational institutions, I conclude that, in the majority of cases, curriculum development continues according to technocratic rationality. As an academic field, curriculum studies remains organized around the development of formal documents, focused on planning and without achieving articulation between classroom work and professors' preparation (or formation). Satisfactory solutions to basic educational problems in Mexico have not been offered or achieved. Authoritarian educational practices continue, as does the psycho-pedagogical demand for structuring academic content according to the characteristics of students, and as per the most pressing social needs. This is the pending agenda for curriculum development in Mexico.

In the 1990s, educational institutions, especially at the superior or higher-education level, enjoyed autonomy over the curriculum. This is no longer the case, as curricular projects are now subjected to processes of budget negotiation and allocation that relocate curricular decisions from teachers and even from educational institutions. Curricular design is now directed by politics, especially interests and guidelines set by national and international organizations. Acting through the manipulation of evaluation (of programs, professors, or students), politicians and bureaucrats have been promoted into curriculum "designers," as now they specify the basic academic content that must be taught and the curricular models that must be implemented. Through the promotion of program evaluation, accreditation, and certification systems, rationalized by slogans such as "learning by competencies," curriculum development decisions are now being made by governmental and nongovernmental organizations, business councils, and very diverse civil associations (Valle 2003). Now curriculum development is no longer the domain of academic specialists.

Although we do not yet know what impact this calamity will have on education in Mexico, we have studies at our disposal that specify what is at stake. In one study that we conducted concerning the impact of evaluation systems and their respective policies on higher education (Díaz Barriga et al. 2008), we found that the evaluation-funding binomial defines the policies and practices of educational institutions, including curriculum development. In these politics and programs, scholars encounter the neoliberal spirit of the era: individualism and intense competition for funding that has now become the ultimate objective of academic life. This new cult of efficiency ruptures the social fabric of universities as it undermines collaborative or long-term work. Predictably, there is inequality in the distribution of resources, and the most prestigious educational institutions are favored over those located in the poorest states of the country. Finally, there is an imposition of knowledge production dynamics exported from the sciences to the social sciences and humanities, an imposition that ensures students' ignorance of history and social context as well as of the local dynamics of educational institutions. As the power and influence of organizations that accredit study plans and programs continue to grow, dictating which curricular models educators must implement, curriculum decision-making will reside completely in the hands of administrators, functionaries, and evaluating agency bureaucrats external to educational institutions, as resistance from academicians becomes crushed.

For now, residues remain of those social and economic commitments characteristic of previous decades. Among curriculum scholars we find divergent agendas, including interests in theory and history, especially as these enable understanding of curricular processes on local and/or collective levels. Needless to say, these interests conflict with those of administrations who are concerned only with efficient and short-term responses to practical problems. Curriculum research depends not on the priorities of the field's internal intellectual development, but on funding aligned with the accreditation of academic programs. Curriculum scholars in Mexico are confronted not only by these funding priorities but also by regional, national, and international pressures, problems, and politics that accent the restrictions and narrow the possibilities for curriculum research and reform. It is in these present circumstances that we, the curriculum scholars of Mexico, think about our options given the prevailing policies and practices.

References

Arnaz, José. 1981. *Curricular Planning.* Mexico City: Trillas.

Coll, César. 2006. "Every Time That Curricular Change Has Occurred, It Has Been the Result of an Ideological Debate and Not of an Analysis of Evaluations." *Docencia* 29: 30–39.

Commission of New Teaching Methods. 1976. *Programmed Teaching.* Mexico City: CNME/UNAM.

Da Silva, Tomaz Tadeu. 1999. *Identity Documents. An Introduction to Curricular Theories.* Belo Horizonte, Brazil: Autentica Editors.

Díaz Barriga, Ángel, ed. 2003. *Curricular Research in Mexico. The Decade of the Nineties.* Educative Research in Mexico Collection Vol. 5. Mexico City: Mexican Council of Educative Research.

Díaz Barriga, Ángel, Concepción Barrón, Jésus Carlos, and Frida Díaz Barriga. 1995. "Research in the Curricular Field 1982–1992." In *Curricular, Institutional and Organizational Processes*, ed. Ángel Díaz Barriga, 23–172. Mexico City: Mexican Council of Educative Research (COMIE)/General Direction of Superior Education at the SEP, Educative Research in the Eighties Collection, Perspectives for the Nineties.

Díaz Barriga, Ángel, and Teresa Pacheco, eds. 1990. *Five Approximations to the Study of Professions.* Cuadernos Collection of the CESU No. 21. Mexico City: CESU/UNAM.

Díaz Barriga, Ángel, Concepción Barrón, and Frida Díaz Barriga. 2008. *Impact of Evaluations on Mexican Superior Education. A Study of Public State Universities.* Mexico City: ANUIES/IISUE/Plaza and Valdes.

Díaz Barriga, Frida. 2003. "Main Trends of Curriculum Research in Mexico." In *International Handbook of Curriculum Research*, ed. William F. Pinar, 457–469. Mahwah, NJ: Lawrence Erlbaum.

Díaz Barriga, Frida. 2005. "Curriculum Research and Development in Mexico: The Presidential Address, 2004." *Journal of the American Association for the Advancement of Curriculum Studies* 1. Available online at: http://www.uwstout.edu.

Díaz Barriga, Frida, and Elisa Lugo. 2003. "Curriculum Development." In *Curricular Research in Mexico. The Decade of the Nineties*, ed. Ángel Díaz Barriga, 63–123 (Educative Research in Mexico Collection, Vol. 5). Mexico City: Mexican Council of Educative Research.

Gago, Antonio. 1982. *Development of Descriptive Letters.* Mexico City: Trillas.

Glazman, Raquel, and María de Ibarrola. 1976. *Design of Study Plans.* Mexico City: CISE/UNAM.

Hamilton, David. 1999. "The Pedagogical Paradox." *Educative Proposal* 20: 6–13.

Huerta, José. 1981. *Logical Organization of Learning Experiences.* Mexico City: Trillas.

Jackson, Philip, ed. 1992. *Handbook of Research on Curriculum.* New York: McMillan.

Jimenez, Edith. 2000. "The Participation of Scholars in Curricular Design and Study Plans and Programs at the UNAM." Master's thesis. MexMeico City: National Autonomous University of Mexico (UNAM).

Marin, Dora Elena. 1993. *Professional Formation and University Curriculum.* Mexico City: Diana.

Pinar, William, ed. 2003. *International Handbook of Curriculum Research.* Mahwah, NJ: Lawrence Erlbaum.

Pinar, William. 2004. *What is Curriculum Theory?* Mahwah, NJ: Lawrence Erlbaum.

Posner, George. 1998. *Curriculum Analysis.* Santafe de Bogota, Colombia: McGraw Hill.

San Martin, Víctor. 2004. "Formation through Competencies: The Challenge of Superior Education in Latin America." *Latin American Magazine of Education.* Available online at: http://www.rieoei.org.

Schon, Donald. 1992. *The Formation of Reflective Professionals.* Barcelona: Paidos.

Valle, A. 2003. "The Professional Union Organization in Mexico." In *Processes and Practices of University Formation*, ed. Edith Chehaybar and Rocio Amador. Mexico City: CESU/UNAM.

Chapter 4

Curriculum Studies in Mexico: Origins, Evolution, and Current Tendencies

Ángel Díaz Barriga[1]

It was during the 1970s that curriculum studies texts started to circulate in Mexico, all of them translations into Spanish of US publications. During these years Mexico adopted the curriculum concepts of the United States, marked by technical styles that were sometimes very close to behaviorist psychology. In 1982 Mexico lived through one of its great economic crises. In its wake was the ascendancy of the so-called Chicago school, an economic school that extolled the so-called free markets. These historical events mark how Mexico incorporated curriculum theory, first from the United States, then from Latin America, and, most recently, internationally, now installing procedures expressing a homogenizing logic. In this chapter I will offer an interpretation of these historical events and the curricular concepts that followed.

The 1970s and the Utopian Project

To understand why I characterize those curricular projects that emerged in Mexico in the 1970s as utopian, it is necessary to identify the key characteristics of that decade. Central was the student conflict through which Mexican society lived in 1968, which concluded in a massacre of youth in the *Tres Culturas Plaza* (*Tlatelolco*) on October 2 of that year. The Mexican state demonstrated its incapacity to understand that demands for democratization were the social consequence of the economic development policies that it had enacted after World War II. When faced with uprisings in the streets while hosting the Olympic Games, the Mexican state reacted with state repression. To then reconcile itself with the outraged middle class (Labarca 1977), the Mexican State then took on the task of modernizing the educational system, in part by increasing access to higher education for the 19–23-year-old age group.

During the post-World War II period industrial development had been protected by governmental regulation of imports. Rapid industrial growth—there was 8 percent annual growth during the 1970s—demanded training of new workers and professionals. It was in the context of this industrial modernization, then, that the Mexican State imported curriculum theory from the United States. Study plans and programs were rapidly reformatted after guidelines formulated by Benjamin Bloom (1970), Robert Mager (1971), and Ralph Tyler (1971, Hilda Taba (1974), among others. Recall that the original English-language editions of these books were published much earlier: Bloom in 1956, Mager in 1962, Tyler in 1949, and Taba in 1962. The years that I placed in parentheses reference the Spanish-language editions. These years date the political enforcement of technological-behavioral-pragmatist pedagogy that had been developed in the United States during the twentieth century and consolidated after the World War II. Criticism of this pedagogy—evident in Schwab's later assertion that the US field of curriculum was moribund and implied in Philip Jackson's conception of the hidden curriculum and by Pinar's concept of "the Reconceptualization"—did not arrive in Mexico until the end of the 1970s.

The enforced adoption of these technological-behaviorist-pragmatist proposals was not superficial. The Mexican State aligned educational reform with US efforts to contain the Cuban revolution that (the Americans feared) was gaining traction throughout Latin America. Several agencies linked to the United States government, among them the International Agency for Development (USAID), financed the translation into Spanish of more than 20 books on curriculum development. Contracts were issued to several publishers to print between 20,000 and 40,000 copies, distributed for free in libraries throughout the Latin American region. Quickly they reached ministries of education, teacher-training units, pedagogical institutes and schools. These copies have a seal on their last page—"Copy for Free Distribution"—accompanied by the logo of the organization that financed the publication. Curriculum reform in the 1970s was based, then, on behaviorist objectives from which instructional activities were to be derived, then implemented, and then evaluated. School programs were to reflect the programming models that the United States suggested, particularly those by Popham and Baker (1970).[2]

This technological-behaviorist perspective structured the entire Mexican curricular reform; it had a particular impact on higher education. Why? The Mexican educational system was (and remains) highly centralized. Study plans for primary education and for the first three years of secondary education as well as study plans for teacher education and technological education were all dictated by the National Ministry of Education.[3] In contrast, institutions of higher education—public and private universities[4]—enjoyed the prerogative (and obligation) to develop their curricular proposals. This simple fact—centralized control of the K-12 curriculum by the Ministry in Mexico City, academic freedom reserved for higher education only—explains why Mexican curriculum research is directed toward higher education.

At a time when higher education enjoyed significant growth, in terms of the number of both institutions and students,[5] curriculum projects with very different orientations were undertaken. Orientation differed according to the level of the internal organization of institutions (adoption of the departmental model by some institutions, for instance) and even the pedagogical level. While curriculum development of the technical type (Tyler, Bloom, Mager, and Taba) was promoted at several institutions, in other universities different approaches emerged, including (most representatively) problem-solving approaches informed by social ethics and activism.

At the global level there were several influential theoretical developments. From Europe the work of Michel Lobrot, particularly his book *Pedagogía Institucional* (1980) (*Institutional Pedagogy*), was influential, as well as the institutional analyses of Lourau and Lapassade (1974). These coincided with countercultural movements such as those associated with the anti-psychiatry movement. As well we worked with texts such as *Cartas a una profesora/Alumnos de Barbiana* (1972).[6] There was then a strong promotion of Latin American thought, including that of Paulo Freire with his concepts of education as a practice of freedom, his questioning of banking education, and the promise of dialogue. The deschooling theories of Everett Reimer (1971) and Ivan Illich (1972) were influential, as was pedagogical work undertaken by ecclesiastical groups associated with the Second Vatican Council. The creation of the CIDOC[7] (Center for Intercultural Documentation) by Illich in Cuernavaca was a central event. It was at the CIDOC that the first Spanish edition of *Pedagogy as the Practice of Freedom* (1969) was printed on a typewriter[8] and where Dominican priests were psychoanalyzed (resulting in a scandal and a majority of those priests leaving the church). Also in the mix at that time was the Belgian version of Group Dynamics, reconstructed for Latin America by Jésus Andrés Vela (*Técnicas y Prácticas de las Relaciones Humanas* 1972). Indeed, group dynamics became a basic reference. The 1972 reform of study plans in teachers' training schools incorporated for the first (and only time) such "human relations" material into its teacher education topics.

Latin America was also the location for the construction of other types of pedagogical proposals. Breaking structures of vertical authority in classroom organization, precipitated in part by the thought of Paulo Freire, precipitated the formulation of other pedagogical models. There appeared the Didactics movement associated with the National University of Cordoba, Argentina. The work of Susana Barco in "Anti-didactica o Nueva Didáctica," Azucena Rodríguez and Gloria Edelstein in "El Método: Factor Unificador y Definitor de la Instrumentación Didáctica," and Mirtha Antebi and Cristina Carranza in "Evaluación; Una Experiencia Estudiantil-docente"[9] characterized that theory of Didactics elaborated in Latin America for Latin Americans. Didactics remains a regionally variegated discipline in the educational sciences. Other types of educational projects incorporating a social dimension in professional formation were undertaken at this time, among them "popular architecture" and "social medicine," the former of which had been devised in the 1970s under the sponsorship of the Pan-American Association of Health. Both became fundamental references in the literature on the formulation of socially focused curricular modules.

Whereas the technicist model enforced systematization by articulating behaviorist objectives aligned with instructional models and evaluation strategies, this perspective assumed a model of curricular design that was rooted in the diagnosis of social needs. The technicist model had been applied in multiple curricular designs and had been employed in the first national formulations, drawing on models in books entitled *Sistematización de la Enseñanza* (1978), *Diseño de Planes de Estudios* (1978), and *Paquete de Auto-Enseñanza de Evaluación del Aprovechamiento Escolar* (1978).[10] These books were Mexican adaptations of US technicist curriculum theory. They enjoyed an uncontested influence in Mexican curriculum studies during the 1970s and at the beginning of the 1980s.

Starting from the modular curricular design by "objectives of transformation,"[11] professional preparation (or formation) projects were structured by a pedagogical-social orientation. Not only would students learn the basic facts associated with professional preparation, but also these facts would be focused on social problems suffered by marginalized and/or impoverished groups. Transforming social reality became the objective of academic study, thus the concept of "objective of transformation." In each learning module, academic knowledge from different disciplines was integrated with a socioeconomic framework and became the point of reference from which the profession was to be practiced. Examples of such "objectives of transformation" included the following: modules focused on the production of animal meat for human consumption (designed for the preparation of veterinarians); the construction of public housing (designed for students studying to become architects); studies of experience and learning (designed for students preparing to become psychologists). The curriculum of these various professions was not, then, structured by the academic disciplines, but, rather, by social problems, reminiscent of Hilda Taba's conception of an integrated curriculum. Each module represented interdisciplinary knowledge designed to enable students to develop skills to solve professional problems in specific social settings. To demonstrate competence students had to make appropriate interventions in particular communities (see Díaz Barriga-Martínez-Reygadas-Villaseñor 1989).

These study plans determined professional practices. These practices formed the axes of professional education. For a time the determination of transformational objectives replaced behavioral objectives. The labor of learning for students was conducted not only in libraries and classrooms, but in actual communities as well. There they studied first-hand specific social problems. Students participated in the formulation of solutions. Focused on communities, the so-called situated or learning-based curriculum required problem resolution, forcing students to confront social reality not as an abstraction but in its particularity. Students tackled actual problems, presented documentation of specific problems, and researched a range of possible actions that might be undertaken to resolve specific problems. Students had to defend their proposals. Such work was conducted in groups; in recent years such activity has come to be construed as "collaboration."

As enrollment in higher education increased, additional academic staff was required. The number of professors grew rapidly from 25,000 to 70,000, meaning that many very young, recent graduates joined the ranks of the university faculty, more than a few of them with only the bachelor's degree. Faced with this acute shortage of faculty, graduate programs became emphasized in national policy on education. Graduate programs began to offer a wide and diverse range of courses and workshops focused on different educational themes: general didactics, the elaboration of study plans and programs by instructional objectives, group dynamics, the evaluation of learning, the psychology of teaching, among others. While these courses had multiple orientations, many reflected technical conceptions imported from the United States. Others reflected currents of thought that were considered as alternatives to these, currents from Europe and Latin America. In the same institution graduate programs could exhibit contradictory theoretical tendencies, for example, some emphasizing general didactics associated with European humanism, some stressing programming by behavioral objectives, others focused on the evaluation of learning, centered on testing. In some seminars, curriculum content reflected Latin American concerns, among them (1) the student-teacher relationship in the classroom as dialogical; (2) learning as a social process; and (3) the importance of the "whole person" in understanding education. Other seminars reflected US technicist influences, including (1) studies in educational planning, wherein academic content was reduced to observable behaviors; (2) courses in learning commodified as a product; and (3) curriculum comprised of mechanical relationships among objectives, teaching, and assessment.[12]

The establishment of academic research groups responsible for the formulation of study plans and academic programs, including teacher education programs, formed Mexico's first generation of curriculum researchers. These researchers focused on the problems of higher education. Unlike in the United States, curriculum studies in Mexico focused not on K-12 curriculum but on higher education. Alternative proposals—such as the modular system featuring objectives focused on social transformation and utilizing group dynamics in educational work—intensified our questioning of the United States' technicist model. Researchers started formulating proposals to surpass both the formalist/idealist vision of the 1960s and the technicist-behaviorist vision of the 1970s. This critique coincided with a worldwide breakdown of US technicism, precipitated in part by critiques undertaken by Philip Jackson, John Eggleston, and Michael Apple. Jackson's *Life in Classrooms*, first published in English in 1968, was translated into Spanish (1975) and influenced Mexican curricular debates strongly. The US movement known as "reconceptualist" curriculum studies became known in Mexico primarily as a sociological and political critique of curriculum. This critique did not take hold in Mexico as had other imports from the United States (e.g., technicist curriculum theory) or France (e.g., the reproduction theory of Pierre Bourdieu). Instead, the reconceptualist critique was recontextualized, recast in recognition of the social inequality that existed (and exists still) and the significant place in the national imaginary occupied by higher education since the Mexican revolution (Cleaves 1985).

Toward the Formation of Latin American Curricular Concepts

Curricular debate in Mexico started to show a greater number of concepts and developments specific to Mexican national conditions. In 1981, through the National Council of Science and Technology, the first national congress of educational research was held. What distinguished this congress was the invitation of eight scholars to present state-of-the-art addresses assessing the state of research that had been conducted during the 1970s. Eight themes were selected; one of them was curriculum.[13] In this address it became evident that international concepts—especially those imported from the United States—were now coexistent with concepts formulated by Mexican researchers. The main accomplishment of curriculum studies in Mexico was judged to be the development of a social perspective, articulating the complex relationships between higher education and Mexican society. Although the model of "needs diagnosis" privileged the "needs" of economic production and occupational markets, overall the field of curriculum studies in Mexico remained in accord with a nationalist vision inherited from the Mexican revolution and was accorded new meanings by diverse Latin American scholars who had fled to Mexico to escape military *coups d'etat* in Chile, Argentina, and Uruguay.

Education was conceptualized as social action, as moral commitment accepted by those who enjoyed the privilege of access to higher education. This conception required professionals to prioritize marginalized social groups, offering them the skills and knowledge professional preparation had provided them.[14] The modular model was the most advanced design from the Mexican curricular point of view, an example of the concept of integrated curriculum (Taba 1974). At the national level significant developments were underway, among them was the university/factory project of the Autonomous University of Nayarit, as well as similar projects in other democratic, critical, and populist universities. These universities established academic programs that placed students in interdisciplinary assemblages (economists, sociologists, agronomists, doctors, dentists) who then traveled to rural communities, where they offered professional solutions to problems presented to them by the local inhabitants. One example of such professional service to a seaside community was the teaching of marine science in school. Students were also taught varieties of meal preparation and food storage as well as strategies for marketing their fish-catch to the public at affordable prices. Part of the generated income went to the university, which was then regarded not only as an academic institution, but as a socially committed commercial concern as well (Salinas 1977).

A second significant development was the formulation of a nonbehaviorist psychology, derived from several sources, among them (1) Piaget and constructivism; (2) humanistic psychology; and (3) social psychology. These were integrated into different theories of learning. Although the curricular model of plans and programs by objectives enjoyed hegemony throughout the entire educational system, various individuals began to develop didactic strategies with other concepts. This allowed some to start developing a perspective called "lived curriculum" (Furlán 1981).

Two books that were influential (not only in Mexico but throughout Latin America) were *Didáctica y Curriculum: Articulaciones en Los Programas de Estudios* (Díaz Barriga 1984a) (*Didactics and Curriculum: Articulations of Study Programs*) and *Ensayos Sobre la Problemática Curricular* (Díaz Barriga 1984b) (*Essays on the Problem of Curriculum*). Both books not only conducted sustained critiques of technicists from the United States, they also opened paths for the conceptual development of curriculum studies specific to Mexico, drawing upon research conducted throughout Latin America and in Europe. Mexican scholars began to recognize the existence of curriculum communities with distinct traditions, creating forms (after Bourdieu) of "habitus" in their scholarly orientation. One group reiterated technicist positions associated with the United States; a second group searched for alternatives; a third group's research was structured around micro-sociological discourses focused on daily life, supported by ethnography; and fourth was a group that conducted research focused on the hidden curriculum. These two last groups conducted research empirically. The specialization of curriculum history also started to form, analyzing the origins of curricular problems in the United States, specifically those with Tyler (Furlán and Pasillas 1999).

Utopic aspirations for higher education faded. Innovative social projects started to show exhaustion. Prominent among the factors undermining innovation was the economic crisis of 1982, which ended the PRI government that had been in power since the Mexican Revolution. From this year on, another party came into power, this one was associated with the so-called Chicago school. It would impose what would later be called the "Consensus Washington," underwritten with loans from the International Monetary Fund and the World Bank. Neoliberal policies—promoting the primacy of the presumably "free" market—followed. The public sector shrank. The budget assigned to higher education—the state was the sole provider of funds for public universities in Mexico—suffered a drastic decrease.

A second development that contributed to the exhaustion of these projects was the exhaustion of the communities that sustained them. Innovation requires constant effort, and participating academicians suffered not only decreased salaries but also intensified bureaucratization that enforced efficiency over social activism. The proper functioning of the modular system (e.g., integrated curriculum) requires groups of no more than 20 students and the dedication of committed academic personnel. Pro-efficiency bureaucracies began increasing the numbers of students in these groups. The institutional conditions that had enabled these social projects to be undertaken began to dissolve. Despite these new and undermining institutional conditions, the intellectual life of the field still flourished. The state-of the-art address presented at the Second National Congress of Educational Research (Díaz Barriga 1993) disclosed that curriculum studies in Mexico was demarcated by different currents of curriculum thought but that the field was now in a process of consolidation.

Curriculum Studies in an Era of Globalization

The decade of the 1990s was the era of globalization. As a result of the economic crises that affected the Third World in the 1980s (the lost decade, as economists characterized it), several multilateral organizations took it upon themselves to initiate a series of changes in Mexican education policies. The so-called Washington Consensus included an agenda for the Third World, including structural adjustments (e.g., reduction in public finances), strict budget priorities, and the so-called internationalization of the economy (Girón 2008).

International financial organizations such as the World Bank, the Inter-American Bank of Development, and UNESCO orchestrated educational reforms.[15] Emphasizing the discourse of "quality," which the Organisation for Economic Co-operation and Development (OECD) would also employ by the middle of the decade, these entities promoted a series of "reforms" focused on revising the evaluation of education by instituting "performance objectives," the achievement of which became associated with merit pay programs. The World Bank questioned Mexican spending on higher education, insisting that state support was regressive (World Bank 1995). To meet a "need" to diversify the higher education system and thereby encourage "competition," the establishment of private universities was promoted. The state decreed that only those academic programs that were evaluated favorably would receive funding. Evaluation criteria emphasized measurement, including (1) the number of doctorates in the academic faculty; (2) the number of publications; (3) the number of graduating students; (4) the number of volumes in the library; (5) the number of accredited programs; and (6) the number of graduates working in the labor market. Whatever could not be measured was irrelevant.

In Mexico the accreditation of programs had been a recent practice. It began in 1990 with a so-called peer assessment model that evolved by 2002 into the first accrediting agencies. These agencies conducted formal evaluations in terms of numerical criteria, restructuring the curriculum according to percentages (e.g., 25 percent in mathematics and physics).

Higher education institutions had to meet these criteria to achieve the accreditation of their academic programs. Accreditation was important to employers as well as to families and students, and funding from the state depended on it. Rendered irrelevant was the curriculum expert, who was then replaced by an educational engineer responsible for aligning curriculum with accreditation criteria (Díaz Barriga et al. 2008).

The rhetoric of innovation became a key discourse in these evaluation schemes. Curricular debates were marked by new concepts, as policymakers and university administrators were compelled to promote the establishment of "innovative" curricula. The first "innovation" appeared in 1993; it was called curricular "flexibility." Other "new" concepts appeared, among them "innovation logic," "competency," and, of course, the "new technologies" enabling distance or virtual education. Whatever the "innovation," all models were centered not on academic knowledge or on social problems but on "learning," whether that learning was construed as "problem-based" or "collaborative" or "constructivist" and "situated."

With academic knowledge and social reality now rendered irrelevant, scholars began to abandon curriculum research. During the 1990s, research on curricular practices (the so-called lived curriculum) decreased considerably; studies on the hidden curriculum simply disappeared. Researchers who had studied these themes during the 1980s showed interest in studying other problems such as violence and discipline in schools, professional identity, and the curricular "representation" of educational action.

The economistic imperative that has comprised educational reforms since the 1990s has been animated by ongoing pressure to continue to introduce "innovations," most of which have remained rhetorical. What did not remain rhetorical was the quantification of educational experience. Indeed, higher education was reduced to a series of numbers: the number of articles published, the number of PhDs working in the academic "plant" (perhaps only 25 percent of university faculty had a doctoral degree). Productivity was to be quantified as well, indicated by the number of students who had completed their formal studies and the percentage of graduates who then obtained employment. Whatever could not be assigned a number was not relevant as an indicator of quality. More than 3,000 indicators of quality were specified! This amounted to the conversion of the university into a business.

Another "new" concept was "gauge." Curricular innovation became one "gauge" of "quality." Program accreditation became another. These two "gauges" became intertwined in Mexico. One mandate issued by accrediting agencies was that each study plan must be revised every five years; another mandated the percentage of academic content areas each study plan must contain.[16] We moved from an era of socially committed creative curriculum development, requiring specialized professional preparation and academic knowledge, into an era of curriculum engineering. Curricular experts were forced to change accordingly.

These models of curricular "innovation" were widely disseminated. In so doing, a mistake (about which Taba had cautioned) was made: innovation by decree. Although these were decrees, they did not necessarily modify the daily practices of professors and students. Recall that the first concept of "innovation" that had emerged in the 1990s was "curricular flexibility," accented by professional preparation options in the final phases of the bachelor's degree. In the undergraduate psychology curriculum, for instance, concentrations in educational, clinical, social, or labor psychology were available. In addition to these customary options, additional flexibility was provided by offering students the option of obtaining a technical or professional degree, a decision that could be made after completing only 50 percent of the total credits in a program. In the civil engineering curriculum, to provide another example, a student could opt for a technical degree focused on a vocational specialization. Another kind of "flexibility" allowed students to study an optional subject in another university, or in another department within the same university. The truth is that such options had existed since the 1970s, but during this ahistorical era of "innovations" these examples of curricular flexibility were recirculated and renamed as "new."

Others forms of "flexibility" were decreed as "new." After the Bologna agreements, students could, with economic support, study one semester outside Mexico. Student mobility was supported mainly by the Universitas Foundation of the Santander Bank. Internships in businesses were also promoted, formalized by agreements between institutions of higher education and employers. Through such internships students could earn academic credit. But the number of students who enjoyed access to these possibilities was low, not even 1 percent of the total enrollment.

These dynamics of "innovation" and "flexibility" were limited to students. Professors were barred from both, unable to experiment with extant "innovations" and disallowed to make their own. During the 1990s, for example, the innovation known as "competency-based education" appeared. Just like other innovations ("flexibility"), competency-based education was enforced by administrators and policymakers. Unlike internships in business, study plans by competencies were made accessible to all. Unlike behavioral objectives, which by the time of their importation into Mexico had been "tested" in the United States, knowledge about competency-based approaches was, well, minimal. Even its basic definition was unclear: for some it was an ability, for others a skill, and still others thought that it implied competence in unknown situations. The concept of "competencies" was always under development. Moreover, one could be confident that there will always be "new" competencies in demand, requiring new subjects, rendering some experts amateurs as some amateurs suddenly became experts. Perhaps one theme that united all competency-based schemes was an antagonism against knowledge-based teaching. What the world today wants, we were told, is not educated persons, but competent and flexible entrepreneurs filled with skills, able to solve problems. This antagonism amounts to an ancient anti-intellectualism, as debates between knowledge-based and skill-based conceptions of education in Mexico are at least one hundred years old (Perrenoud 2001).

Three persisting problems became associated with competency-based schemes. As noted, one involved definition: some defined them as competencies for life, others construed them as professional; still others offered them as academic and transversal. How to sequence competencies was not obvious and that design issue indicated the second problem, namely, that often competency-based study plans simply reinstalled behavioral objectives. Professional competency, for instance, was divided into multiple sub-competencies following a version of "task analysis." What constitutes evidence for these sub-competencies was never self-evident, and the character of conditions prerequisite to the "execution" of various competencies tended to be similar to that of behavioral objectives, for example, very specific and not necessarily transferable situations.

A third problem concerned the formulation of flexible study plans. Flexibility means offering a range of alternatives that students can elect, but choice does not necessarily bring any change in pedagogical practice. Competency-based education implies that teachers modify their practices, including how they work with students in classrooms and how they evaluate the learning process. A flexible curriculum composed of competencies makes sense only if it is accompanied by pedagogical practices centered on the students, integrating information, focusing on specific problems, and always linking new knowledge with actual problems in real settings. This did not occur. Those who taught by competencies continue to proceed just as they have done using other curricular models. More research is needed, we were told, in order to understand how teaching can be based on problem solving and learning in real settings.

Medical training was sometimes presented as analogous. Consider the phases of such training: first is the study of anatomy, physiology, biochemistry, and other subjects; second comes the clinical cycle, wherein practical studies are carried out in hospitals. In these clinical cases, academic knowledge is now encountered in real life as prospective physicians visit and examine the sick, as they question patients regarding symptoms and then offer diagnoses. Training concludes by returning to the classroom where students reflect on these clinical experiences. Curiously, this medical model of teaching corresponds to the 1970s model of learning (although now discredited) according to social problems (ABP), organized around case analysis involving learning in real settings.

When the "modular study plan by transformational objectives" (Díaz Barriga 1989) was established in Mexico, it was considered that an "objective of transformation" was an actual problem, that it was socially significant and that it could be studied and solved professionally. Although not employed in medical training, this plan structured numerous degree programs: sociology, economy, communications, psychology, medicine, veterinary medicine, deontology, chemistry, pharmacy, biology, nutrition, biology, agronomy, architecture, and design. In each field, the "objective of transformation" was whatever was identified as the central problem to be worked on during the four-month term. The problem identified was different in each of the modules: for example, the production of vaccinated meat for human consumption, or the production of corn, or the construction of single-family homes, or attention to mental health problems in psychiatric patients. Each study plan was comprised of 12 modules, that is, by 12 objectives to be transformed by professional engagement with them. The academic content of each professional degree and each discipline was organized according to the "objective" of each module. In an evaluation of this model, we observed how students demonstrated a greater capacity to confront new situations and devise creative solutions to actual problems. At the same time, however, they did perform less well in written exams wherein order, hierarchy, and memorization were the main markers.

It was, of course, not easy to integrate all the prerequisite academic content for professional engagement with these "objectives of transformation." Workshops were established (on mathematics, on measurement theory, on neurology) so that students could learn whatever academic knowledge was pertinent. In practice, students studied several scientific disciplines at once in order to bring to bear on specific problems the appropriate expertise. This 1970s model combined many of the aspirations that policymakers hoped to achieve by later competencies schemes, learning-based models, and teaching in real settings. One of the greatest merits of the modular system was, in fact, the production of significant shifts in actual pedagogical practices, as modules required different pedagogical practices in classrooms according to the character of specific problems with which students and faculty engaged.

Not only curriculum development but curriculum evaluation also became displaced from the jurisdiction of qualified specialists. Continuous research on curriculum evaluation (based on pedagogical perspectives) had been conducted throughout the 1980s. In each instance, an objective of study was defined as an objective of evaluation; a conceptual perspective was determined wherein the research could be conducted. A methodological strategy would follow. Research results were then communicated to an interested institutional authority, but they were also published so that they could be discussed by the entire academic community.

By the 1990s, however, predetermined forms of evaluation were simply decreed. Organizations evaluated programs more like business investment than as an academic endeavor. Rather than focused on research and its contribution to academic knowledge, understanding, and expertise, evaluation became another cost to be covered by the institutions. The academic demand for expertise disappeared as the majority of the evaluators now obtained their training in 6–12-hour workshops wherein they were taught how to fill out the forms provided. Evaluation became a checklist. Organizations were not required to rationalize the criteria they used, nor did they ground them in the specificity of the problems these presumably evaluated. In this way, evaluation and even program accreditation became activities that were bureaucratic rather than intellectual, a lucrative contract by which "quality" was assessed. Today, what is important is to ensure that all the accreditation requirements are met; missing entirely is evaluation conducted to improve universities' educational mission.

Conclusion

In its enforced incorporation of technicist models from the United States, curriculum studies in Mexico illustrates the globalization we suffer today. Resistance to this enforced importation ensures that such imperialism is not uncontested. In the 1970s, a series of alternatives to US technicist approaches started to form. The most significant of these was the modular system organized according to "objectives of transformation," a socially committed and creative system that remains more advanced than any of the so-called innovations that followed it. The most significant feature of this modular system was its progressive social vision. This social vision was not Anglo-Saxon but Latin American. It demanded that university students attend to the most destitute social sectors of society through their professional actions. I call this period one of utopian reform. This curricular commitment was never institutionalized in the United States or in other "developed" countries: it was a Latin American accomplishment, and a specifically Mexican one at that.

The globalization of educational reform has spelled the homogenization of national educational systems. Logic flying under the flag of "quality" has promoted economistic evaluation schemes. Evaluation prohibits as it permits access to resources; it is not responsive to research feedback. Ostensibly promoting innovation, accreditation requirements formalized the functioning of the bureaucratic system. Despite the appearance of several curricular "innovations" during the 1990s, among them flexibility, competencies, problem-based learning, case studies, they have yet to reach the classroom.

Notes

1. Researcher at the Research Institute about Universities and Education (IISUE). National Autonomous University of Mexico (UNAM). Email: adbc@servidor.unam.mx.
2. The text that had an impact in Mexico was the translation Paidós made in 1972 under the Spanish title *Los maestros y la enseñanza escolar*.
3. Such centralization is distinctive to Mexican education. Even after the federalization (a concept that designated decentralization in the 1990s), study plans and programs remained nationalized.
4. These have several names, among them universities and technological institutes
5. In 1950, the Mexican higher education system enrolled 30,000 students, which meant that for every 100 persons 19 to 23 years of age, only 1.5 had access; in 1970, the number of students enrolled in higher education had increased to 250,000; in 1980 this number had ballooned to 850,000. Still, only 8 of every 100 (so-called) age-appropriate people had access to higher education.
6. Importantly, US texts were known in Latin America only in translation. Thus I refer to the translated document, not the English original. Curriculum studies in Mexico and Latin America generally were (and are) not translated into English. For this reason I retain the references in the original language and I translate its meaning into English only when I consider it necessary.
7. Its acronym in Spanish.
8. The first Spanish edition was published in 1974.
9. These works were published in the journal *Science Education Argentina* between 1972 and 1974. This journal was suppressed during the dictatorship of General Videla in 1976. To our knowledge no English translation exists. Its English titles would be "Anti-Didactic or New-Didactic," (Barco) "The Method: A Unifying Factor and Instrumentation of Teaching" (Rodríguez-Edelstein) and "Evaluation: A Student-Teacher Experience" (Antebi-Carranza). On the one hand, this work promoted a formalist theory of teaching and, on the other, provided a route toward the investigation of teaching as what happens in the classroom.

10. These books were not translated into English, but their titles would be as follows: *Systematization of Teaching; Design of Study Plans; Self-Learning Packages for the Evaluation of Learning.*
11. The concept of "objectives of transformation" synthesized elements of Piagetian and Marxist thought and redirected them toward social change. Specialists who constructed this concept lacked expertise in the field of education. The point was to solve problems in those social sectors with the greatest needs, solutions that were to be studied by students pursuing their university studies. The phrase refers simultaneously to social problems, their solutions, and the academic and practical means by which such interventions occur.
12. Esquivel and colleagues (1987).
13. Subsequently there have been two conferences (in 1993 and 2003) on educational research at which assessments of the state of knowledge in curriculum research were presented. These assessments were later published.
14. This social perspective recalled the Cardenist educative project (1934–1940) when the first medical social service was established in Mexico. (This model was replicated in other fields.) Social service consisted in working (as part of one's academic study) for one year in a community that was in an impoverished area. It was Jésus Díaz Barriga, a member of the Commission of Studies of the Presidency of the Republic of the Government of Lázaro Cardenas, who formulated this "Project of Social Service for Students in Professional Programs" in 1940.
15. These multilateral organizations (World Bank, International Monetary Fund, Inter-American Bank of Development), although involved in the process of development in Latin America over several decades, intensified their involvement in socioeconomic and ideological spheres starting from the 1980s. Their involvement meant the end of interventionist and protectionist policies and politics oriented toward the development of the internal market. Enforced instead was a so-called open economy with presumably open markets and economistic thinking in education (e.g., neoliberalism) (see Orlansky Dora 2006).
16. For example, among the accreditation criteria of agronomy science programs, 20 percent of the credits were to be optional, 35 percent were to be in mathematics, physics, and chemistry (but oriented toward problems of producers), 30 percent in physiology and statistics, 10 percent in philosophy, anthropology, ethics, business, and sociology, 5 percent in information science and English.
17. Book and article titles are translated in brackets at the end of each bibliography.

References

Arnaz, José. 1980. *La Planeación Curricular.* [*Curricular Planning*]. Mexico City: Trillas.[17]
Barco, Susana. 1975. "¿*Antitidáctica o Nueva Didáctica?*" *Crisis de la Didáct. Aportes a la Teoría y Práctica de la Educación* ["*Anti-Didactic or New Didactic?*"

Didactic Crisis. Contributions to the Theory and Practice of Education]. Buenos Aires: Axis.
Bloom, Benjamín. 1970. *Taxonomía de Objetivos. Dominio Cognoscitivo* [*Taxonomy of Objectives. Cognitive Dominion*]. Buenos Aires: Ateneo.
Castañeda, Adelina. 1985. *La Utopía y la Realidad en la Construcción de un Proyectoeducativo. El Currículo del Colegio de Ciencias y Humanidades de la UNAM.* [*Utopia and Reality in the Construction of an Educative Project. The Curriculum from the College of Sciences and Humanities of the UNAM*]. Mexico City: UNAM.
Cleaves, Peter. 1985. *El Estado y Las Profesiones* [*The State and the Professions*]. Mexico City: Colegio de México, Colección Jornadas.
Cartas a Una Profesora ("Alumnos de Barbiana"). 1972, Buenos Aires: Marcha /Schapire.
Díaz-Barriga, Ángel. 1984a. *Didáctica y Curriculum: Articulaciones en los Programas de Estudios* [*Didactic and Curriculum: Articulations in Study Programs*]. Mexico City: Nuevomar.
Díaz-Barriga, Ángel. 1984b. *Ensayos Sobre la Problemática Curricular* [*Essays on Curricular Problems*]. Mexico City: Trillas.
Díaz-Barriga, Ángel, ed. 1995. *Procesos Curriculares, Institucionales y Organizacionales* [*Curricular, Institutional and Organizational Processes*]. Mexico City: Consejo Mexicano de Investigación Educativa.
Díaz-Barriga, Ángel, coord. 2003. *La Investigación Curricular en México. La Década de los Noventa* [*Curricular Research in Mexico. The Decade of the Nineties.*]. Mexico City: Estado del Conocimiento, Secretaría de Educación Pública Consejo Mexicano de Investigación Educativa.
Díaz-Barriga, Ángel, Dolores Martínez, Rafael Reygadas, and Guillermo Villaseñor. 1989. *Práctica Docente y Diseño Curricular. Un Estudio Exploratorio en la UAM-Xochimilco* [*Teaching Practice and Curriculum Design. An Exploratory Study on the UAM-Xochimilco*]. Mexico City: Centro de Estudios sobre la Universidad, UNAM, Universidad Autónoma Metropolitana-Xochimilco.
Díaz-Barriga, Ángel, Frida Díaz-Barriga Arceo, and Concepción Barrón, eds. 2008. *Impacto de la Evaluación en la Educación Superior Mexicana*, [Impact Assessment in Higher Education in Mexico]. Mexico City: IISUE-UNAM-ANUIES.
Díaz Barriga, Jésus. 1981. *Su Pensamiento Sobre la Educación Socialista y la Nutrición Popular* [*Their Thoughts about Socialist Education and Popular Nutrition*]. Morelia, Mexico: Biblioteca de Nicolaitas Notables, Universidad Michoacana de San Nicolás de Hidalgo.
Eggleston, John. 1977. *Sociología del Currículo Escolar*. Buenos Aires: Troquel.
Eggleston, John. 1980.*The Sociology of the School Curriculum*. London: Staples Printing Group.
Esquivel, Juan Eduardo, and Lourdes Chehaibar. 1987. *Profesionalización de la Docencia. Perfil y Determinaciones de una Demanda Universitaria* [*Professionalization of Teaching. Profile and Determinations of a University Demand*]. Mexico City: Centro de Estudios sobre la Universidad, Universidad Nacional Autónoma de México.

Follari, Roberto. 1982. "El Currículo Como Práctica Social" ["Curriculum as Social Practice"]. En *Memorias Encuentro sobre Diseño Curricular [Memories Meeting about Curricular Design]*, ed. Barrón, Concepción; Ángel Díaz Barriga and Blanca Rosa Bautista, 45–69. Mexico City: Escuela Nacional de Estudios Profesionales, Universidad Nacional Autónoma de México.

Furlán, Alfredo, and Miguel Pasillas. 1999. *Ralph Tyler. Lecturas Comprometidas a Cuarenta Años de "Principios Básicos del Currículo"* [*Ralph Tyler. Lectures Committed to Forty Years from "Basic Principles of Curriculum"*]. Ciudad de México: Universidad Nacional Autónoma de México-Universidad Autónoma de Sinaloa.

Glazman, Raquel, and María de Ibarrola. 1978. *Diseño de Planes de Estudios* [*Curriculum Design*]. Mexico City: Universidad Nacional Autónoma de México.

Gagné, Robert, and Leslie Briggs. 1977. *La Planificación de la Enseñanza. Sus Principios*. Mexico City: Trillas.

Gago, Antonio. 1980. *Cartas Descriptivas* [*Descriptive Letters*]. Mexico City: Trillas.

García, Fernando. 1978. *Paquete de Autoenseñanza de Evaluación del Aprovechamiento Escolar* [*Self-teaching Package Evaluation of Learning Achievement*]. Mexico City: Centro de Investigaciones y Servicios Educativos, Universidad Nacional Autónoma de México.

Girón, Alicia. 2008. "International Monetary Fund: From Stability to Instability. The Washington Consensus and Structural Reform in Latin America." In *Globalization and Washington Consensus: Its Influence in Democracy and Development in the South*. Buenos Aires: Gladys Lechini, CLACSO.

Guevara, Gilberto. 1976. *El Diseño Curricular* [*Curricular Design*]. Mexico: Universidad Autónoma Metropolitana-Xochimilco.

Illich, Ivan. 1972. *Deschooling Society*. New York and London: Marion Boyar.

Jackson, Philip. 1968. *Life in Classrooms*. New York: Holt, Rinehart & Winston.

Jackson, Philip. 1975. *La Vida en Las Aulas*. Madrid: Marova.

Labarca, Guillermo. 1980. *Economía Política de la Educación* [*Political Economy of Education*]. Mexico City: Nueva Imagen.

Lappasade, George, and René Lourau. 1974. *Claves de la Sociología* [*Political Economy of Education*]. Barcelona: Laia.

Lobrot, Michel. 1980. *Pedagogía Institucional: La Escuela Hacia la Autogestión* [*Institutional Education: School Toward Self-Management*]. Buenos Aires: Humanitas.

Orlansky Dora. 2006. "El Concepto de *Desarrollo* y las Reformas Estatales: Visiones de los Noventa" ["The Concept of Development and State Reforms: Visions of the Nineties"]. *Revista Documentos y Aportes / FCE-UNL-Universidad Nacional del Litoral* [*Documents and Contributions Magazine*] 6: 41–61.

Perrenoud, Phillipe. 2000. *Construir Competencias Desde la Escuela* [*Building Competencies from the School*]. Santiago, Chile: Dolmen Ediciones.

Pinar, William. 1983. "La Reconceptualización de los Estudios Eobre el Currículo" ["The Reconceptualization of Curriculum Studies"]. In *La Enseñanza su Teoría y su práctica*, ed. Gimeno Sacristán, 231–240. Madrid: Akal.

Popham, James, and Eva Baker. 1970. *Systematic Instruction* [*El Maestro y la Enseñanza Escolar*]. Englewood Cliffs, NJ: Prentice Hall.
Reimer, Everett. 1971. *School Is Dead: Alternatives in Education.* New York: Penguin.
Salinas, Bertha. 1977. "Una Alternativa a la Universidad Tradicional (La Experiencia de la Universidad Autónoma de Nayarit, México)" ["An Alternative to the Traditional University (The Experience of the Autonomous University of Nayarit, Mexico)"]. *Revista del Centro de Estudios Educativos* 7 (2): 79–95.
Serrano, Rafael, and Marisa Ysunza. 1982. *El Diseño Curricular en la Concepción Educativa por Objetos de Transformación* [*Curricular Design in Educative Conception by Objects of Transformation*]. Mexico City: Escuela Nacional de Estudios Profesionales, Universidad Nacional Autónoma de México.
Stenhouse, Lawrence. 1984. *Investigación y Desarrollo del Currículum* [*Curriculum Research and Development*]. Madrid: Morata.
Taba, Hilda. 1974. *Elaboración del Currículo.* [*Curriculum Development. Theory and Practice*]. Buenos Aires: Troquel.
Tyler, Ralph. 1971. *Principios Básicos del Currículo.*[*Basic Principles of Curriculum and Instruction.*] Buenos Aires: Troquel.
Vela, Jésus Andrés. 1972. *Técnicas y Prácticas de las Relaciones Humanas* [*Techniques and Practices of Human Relations*]. Bogotá: Indo-American Service Press.
World Bank. 1994. *Higher Education: Lessons from Experience.* Washington, DC: World Bank.

Chapter 5

Curriculum Studies in Mexico: Key Scholars

Alfredo Furlán

Curriculum studies in Mexico date from the 1970s. Since its inception, the field's scholarly production has been strong. Three state-of-the-art assessments have been conducted under the sponsorship of the Mexican Council for Educative Investigation (COMIE). At the November 2007 meeting, for instante, numerous works were presented. Even though these were irregular in their coverage of the theme, they expressed the ongoing importance of curriculum studies in Mexico. Indeed, in Mexico curriculum studies enjoy an odd popularity. In this chapter I present the key scholars whose original ideas have accorded curriculum studies in Mexico its distinctiveness. These scholars are María de Ibarrola, Eduardo Remedí, Ángel Díaz Barriga, and Alicia de Alba. I am aware that in focussing on these three I am ignoring the contributions of other established scholars, among them Raquel Glazman, Rosa María Torres, Berta Orozco, Concepción Barrón, Monique Landesman, Frida Díaz Barriga, and Miguel Angel Pasillas. As well, I am ignoring the contributions of junior scholars; it is too early to assess their contribution. Although others would add names to my list, who can doubt the quality and pertinence of the four scholars I have chosen? I will present them in the order just listed, quoting extensively from their work so that they speak for themselves.

María de Ibarrola

María de Ibarrola was born in Mexico City in 1945. She took her bachelor's degree in Sociology at the National Autonomous University of

Mexico (UNAM), her masters in Sociology at the University of Montreal, Canada, and her doctorate in Science with a specialization in Educative Investigation and Advanced Studies (CINVESTAV) at the National Polytechnic Institute (IPN). Ibarrola has been a titular professor/investigator of the Department of Educative Investigation since 1977. Since 1985, she has been a national investigator (National Council of Science and Technology: CONACYT is its acronym in Spanish). Serving as a consultant for UNESCO for Latin America, Ibarrola has conducted numerous research projects concerning politics, institutions and their structuring of the relations between education and work in Mexico.

In 1971, Ibarrola served on the Commission of New Methods of Teaching, in the area of the Design of Study Plans, investigating the problems of study plans in superior (higher) education. In 1974 with Raquel Glazman (now Glazman-Nowalski) she published *Design of Study Plans,* a work that established curriculum studies as a key specialization in the broad academic field of education. In the introduction to this text Ibarrola defined a study plan as an "instrumental synthesis" of "socially and culturally valuable professional knowledge, selected, organized and ordered for the purposes of teaching" (Glazman and de Ibarrola 1978, 13). This book proved influential in the actual revison of study plans in professional curricula across Mexico. In 1987, Ibarrola and Glazman published *Study Plans: Institutional Proposals and Curricular Reality,* another widely read text that included a self-critical assessment of the first book. The last chapter, authored by María de Ibarrola, is entitled "Re-thinking the Curriculum." In this provocative and memorable chapter Ibarrola cites new intellectual influences on her conception of study plans and their revision, principal among them is the (then) "new" sociology of education undertaken in the United Kingdom. Particularly, Ibarrola acknowledged theoretical assessments of those social hierarchies typical of industrial societies, studies of symbolic violence (including cultural reproduction and the so-called microphysics of power), the sociology of daily life (which has also influenced curriculum studies in Brazil [editor's note]), and the social construction of reality. From this British influence Ibarrola undertook investigations of the various relations between education and the social class in Mexico, specifically between higher education and structures of economic production, focusing finally on the coordination and administration of research programs in actual institutions.

All of these areas of concern, Ibarolla argued convincingly, required modification, reevaluation, and transformation, an agenda indicated in the title of the chapter: "Rethinking the Curriculum." Also engaging in self-criticism, María de Ibarrola proposed that scholars distinguish between "study plans" and "curricular reality," thereby "opening new, conceptual possibilities toward the understanding of curriculum." She defined study plans broadly to include those "academic-organizational structures" that "facilitate" access to professional knowledge. Through these structures, Ibarolla argued, specific academic and political groups promulgate their conceptions of the field in consideration not only of the field's "historical, political, social, scientific and technical limits" but also of the legitimate "forms" of putting curriculum into "practice." Curricular reality, she continued, includes the "interplay of educative and psychological elements, and of varied and complex social and political sectors that coordinate within the institution." Curricular realities vary because the professors and students who express and inhabit them occupy "distinct social placements" and have distinctive "personal histories." These variegated origins and histories also mean that educational actors work from "diverse concepts about what a profession is" as well as from different notions of how best to access professional knowledge in "specific spaces and times." Coincidences and divergences of these various factors structure academic study differently, from the organization of seminars, round tables, and conferences to these various actors' differing modes of accessing the content and carrying out a program of study. These various unpredictable consequences cannot be anticipated in the composition of study plans (quoted passages from Glazman and Ibarrola 1987, 294–295).

After demonstrating the internal complexity of curricular reality, Ibarrola turned her attention to the crisis that the universities of that era were facing. This crisis, she suggested, reflected a ruptured consensus over the nature and intellectual content of university degrees, even over the very nature of universities' relationship with other political and economic institutions, especially that with the workplace. Any consensus internal to Mexican universities was ruptured as well, in part due to a new generation of students, many of whom represented social classes whose members had never enrolled as students before, persons with different life histories and circumstances and whose commitments to the various professions also differed from those of previous generations of students. When faced with this explosion of difference, universities responded in very diverse ways, including through diverse study plans, whose function was the coordination of difference within institutions and toward other social institutions.

In her recent *Experiences and Reflections Concerning Curricular Design and Evaluation*, María Ibarrola takes up her proposals from the 1980s, adjusting them to the present moment. "Personally," she writes, "for a long time I have insisted on an important conceptual and analytical difference between the three dimensions of the curriculum: (1) study plans and programs of study, (2) the institutional structures of the curriculum, and (3) curricular 'reality.'" Ibarrola reasserts that the study plan is the "fundamental document of every educative institution," as it conveys what knowledge has been chosen as important, as well as the ways it should be taught. In some institutions other documents—such as textbooks or examinations—convey the curriculum. As such, study plans represent an institutional wager: if these aims are set, certain procedures follow. If we follow them, we will obtain certain results. This is an impossible wager, as there are so many actors and other variables that are in play over the entire educative process that what "happens"—that is, what curriculum specialists term the "curricular reality"—inevitably differs from what is proposed (quoted passages from de Ibarrola 2008, 3–6).

Mediating study plans and curricular reality, Ibarrola continues, are the "institutional structures" of the curriculum, "fundamental elements" whose structuration enables students to achieve the desired results. These elements are codified through certain regulations or administrative criteria. Such institutional structures almost certainly involve a budget, which provides for the selection, contracts, and working conditions of professors. Supposedly the scholarly institution employs professors who comply with the requirements that the plan stipulates, in terms of both intellectual and pedagogical expertise. But we have witnessed in national education a failure to fulfill these two basic requirements (quoted passages from de Ibarrola 2008, 6–7). In fact, the failures are several; for example, sometimes teachers who do not have the required preparation are employed. On occasion enrolled students had no teacher; sometimes necessary didactic resources (e.g., a television) were missing, or new technologies were introduced into the classroom without paying sufficient attention to the preparation of the professors who presumably were going to use them. On other occasions the technology that had been made available had not been maintained or updated. Due to these multiple failures, as well as to the presence of multiple variables in play in any curricular reality, curriculum researchers have been challenged to specify what elements cause what results. "The challenge is enormous," Ibarrola continues, "because even though there is a flagrant lack of attention to the aforementioned structures, the actions of the subjects—the directors, the teachers, even the students—overcome these obstacles and obtain favourable results" (de Ibarrola 2008, 12).

Under the concept of institutional structures of the curriculum, Ibarrola places a series of very important factors—factors not always included in concepts of curricular design. Key among these is "curricular reality," which she defines as the "interplay" of those who encounter each other in the educative institutions, at "precise times" and in "specific spaces," those who sometimes share goals and interests but who, at the same time, play different roles, come from different social and cultural backgrounds, with different life histories, varying interests, and specific motivations.

Moreover, within their ongoing and diverse encounters, very different interactions occur, influenced by available resources and differential knowledge. Here Ibarrola is referencing not only prescribed knowledge, but a whole range of knowledge and lived wisdom that comes from very diverse sources. "The curricular reality," Iabarrola concludes, "exceeds and moves away from the foreseen results and widens the potential for a series of results that have not been predicted and sometimes not even imagined in the study plan." Outcomes are thus often "unknown, profound and vast," comprising a complex reality that exceeds even the most ambitious study plans and the formal programs these plans structure. Indeed, this reality exceeds *all* institutional structures. They exceed as well the findings of curriculum research, with its identification of "intentions, interactions and results," including ideology, power, and reproduction. The curriculum reality exceeds familiar concerns, including social exclusion; the daily conditions of work, including what teachers learn while teaching; the situatedness of learning; the transfer of unspoken knowledge; socialization and the influence of peers; and the opportunities and horizons of knowledge itself. Although such topics are, Ibarrola allows, not always characterized as curriculum investigations proper, "they include fundamental elements of them" (quoted passages in de Ibarrola 2008, 12–13).

In addition to complicating our conceptions of curriculum and curriculum research, María de Ibarrola also addresses current social conditions, especially as these inform curricular reality. These conditions include not only technological changes, but broader (and historically specific) ones as well, including the globalization of the economy, the fall of socialism, the resurgence of and demands for recognition by all types of minority groups. Shifts in the economy have eliminated many jobs, and we have witnessed the disappearance of various occupations and professions and the creation of new ones. Whole groups of workers have become unemployed and even complete geographical regions have suffered high unemployment. Among those who now demand recognition are ethnic, religious, cultural, aged, and gendered populations, and all of these various groups have placed strong demands on the educational system. Among these demands is the inclusion in the curriculum of their own cultural identities, histories, and visions of the future as well as their own language. In addition, accelerating technological development confronts those who defend sustainable development and the environment. Designing study plans today means confronting these multiple and intersecting realities; it means making difficult decisions regarding what knowledges are pertinent. According to Moreno (2006, 98), the formulation of study plans focuses students, professors, parents, employers, and interested others on what is important to learn. Constructing hierarchies of knowledge in study plans constitutes "public spaces of debate," inviting ideological confrontations, conflicts of interest, and difficult processes of consensus construction (Moreno 2006, 99; de Ibarrola 2008, 19). Somehow, as Ibarrola points out, various educational actors must come together, despite disagreement, over what is to be studied. Somehow they must achieve consensus.

"Consensus," Ibarrola writes, "is fundamental for the success of the educative proposals." Acknowledging its difficulty, she nonetheless points to its absence as "one of the most serious problems of Mexican education," especially concerning the problems of primary or basic education of the public. Undermining efforts at consensus has been an unprecedented series of "restrictions and obstacles" that preclude "professionalization" (quoted passages in de Ibarrola 2008, 22). "In historic moments like these," Ibarrola concludes, "it is indispensable that we evaluate the fundamental basics of the curriculum." In Mexico, since 1989, proposed curricular changes have become an "open arena," including a wide range of stakeholders. Proposals have forefronted the "decentralization of scholarly management to the state authorities" as well as at the same time (in Ibarrola's elegant prose) the "widening of the obligatory." Researchers know that, in addition to this deprofessionalization and politicization of curriculum change, "none of the foundations of the curriculum offers a safe road" toward curricular consensus. Indeed, curriculum research discloses a complex curricular reality in which consensus is rarely a prominent element. Such reality is simply sidestepped in quantitative schemes of curriculum evaluation, especially those proposed by the Organisation for Economic Co-operation and Development (OECD), enforced through the PISA exams. Public debate over curriculum decisions has been replaced by secret decision-making. Among the consequences is increasing alienation among teachers, who now express their refusal in various ways and through their daily activities in schools (quoted passages in de Ibarrola 2008, 22–23). But María de Ibarrola rarely addresses the curricular problems of basic education, as the theme of the curriculum is principally in reference to superior (higher) education, which is the only level wherein each institution can formulate their own study plans. In basic education all curricular decisions are made by a centralized authority. Unlike in the United Status, curriculum studies in Mexico is focused almost exclusively on the concerns of the universities.

Eduardo Remedí

Eduardo Remedí was born in Cordoba, Argentina, in 1949. He completed his bachelor's degree in Educational Sciences at the National University of Cordoba, his master's degree in Psychoanalytical Studies at the CIEP-Mexico, his doctorate in Sciences with a specialty in Education Investigation at the CINVESTAV and with the support of CONACYT. He completed a postdoctorate in Institutional Analysis at the University of Buenos Aires, Argentina. He emigrated to Mexico for political reasons.

Remedí has been a researcher at the CINVESTAV since 1982. Before that he was a member of the Department of Pedagogy at the ENEP-Iztacala, where he lived through (as he studied) the experience of curricular change. In *Systems of Applied Evaluation of the ENEPI* (1978), Remedí affirms that curriculum evaluation demands acknowledgment of the complexity of curriculum: its planning, programs, activities, teacher-student relations, didactic materials, and assessment instruments, not to mention the overall environment wherein these elements interact among themselves. Only in that complicated and elusive interaction is the nature of the educational experience disclosed. "To understand the curriculum," he continues, is to "visualize" it as a "structure that is developed over time" (1978, 59). To translate "evaluation data into useful interpretations" involves both whoever devised the study plan and "whoever carried it out through teaching" (1978, 60). These two points—that curriculum is a complex reality and that curriculum evaluation cannot be conducted apart from work with the teachers who teach it—remain crucial today.

Psychoanalysis has been a "central reference" in Remedí's work since his time at ENEP Iztacala; this work has been a "constant search for meaning." His "Construction of the Methodological Structure of Bases," a chapter in the book *Contributions to the Didactics of Superior Education* (1978), represents Remedí's "first rupture" with the technicist didactics of that era, centered on the formulation of objectives. It was followed in 1980 by "Continuity and Rupture of the Methodological Approach: Critical Notes for Analysis." One year later Remedí wrote "Ideal Models and Real Practices in Faculty Work" in which he established the main themes for his future research. In another article composed during the same year he acknowledged that the curriculum is no "space of liberation" for the faculty members. Rather, the curriculum becomes the marker of regulation and alienation, chopping organic practice into courses or modules. The teacher becomes alienated by "reproducing" a practice conceived by others, one that is often incongruent with the reality of classroom life (quoted passages in Remedí 1981, 45). He emphasized this point in "Curriculum and Faculty Actions." He wrote, "We should start by understanding the curriculum as a particular space in which the contents are socially systemized, in terms of selection and order" (Remedí 1982, 58). It is through the curriculum that "legitimate and valid knowledge is transmitted and evaluated" (58), and not only formally (in terms of institutional objectives), but also socially, in terms of students' experience. Although the official curriculum declares its interest as fundamentally the presentation of knowledge, the reality is that curriculum is reconstructed according to faculty actions, themselves often in response to students' experiences. Remedí asserts, "To the curricular requirements we must add, in order to comprehend the actions, the expectations and values that come from the social aspects and enrich and redefine the practice of the faculty" (59).

In 1987 Remedí presented an important paper entitled "Theoretical Suppositions: Discourses-Contents-Knowledge in Faculty Work," in which he frankly acknowledged the influences of his psychoanalytical studies. He defined the educational institution as a "configuration of symbolic relations" in which the teacher (in his or her singularity) is inscribed (272). Several consequences follow from this fact. First, he points out that teachers' inscription in a system of symbolic relations legitimizes their work. It is due to their symbolic position in relation to the curriculum that they achieve a "first level of investiture," enabling them to act. Without being inscribed in a field of symbolic relations—structured by academic knowledge—teachers could not act. Thus the curriculum accords teachers legitimacy. Second, teaching is, Remedí writes, "an act of legitimate imposition," as teachers are authorized as agents in/of specific "discourses and specific practices" (quoted passages on p. 273). But this legitimation functions best if ignored, if both teachers and students "fail to acknowledge the meaning of the place that they occupy" (274). Then transmission occurs. Symbolically, Remedí argues (after Freud) that those who are invested with pedagogical authority occupy the place of an archetypal father, as they exploit the affective investment students make in their position through, for example, the transference/counter-transference relations (275).

Eduardo Remedí asserted his opposition to a technocratic vision in "Ralph Tyler: A Notable Meeting." First, Remedí points out that educational practices exhibit a "strong uncertainty," rendering them as never reducible to the conscious intentionality of the subjects who participate in them. Such uncertainty contradicts the very concept of curriculum design, as teaching cannot be reduced to formulas or to fantasies of panaceas. To understand who the faculty are and what they do is to follow them into the solitude of their classrooms, to encounter students with them, and not only in classrooms over assignments but in hallways as well. To understand the faculty is to follow them also into the teachers' room, observing them rushing to finish what they must before the next class. It is to watch them wait as well. One studies the faculty through clues and signs, unintended events that accent the workday. One studies the faculty in their spaces, in their places, and in their times. To understand the faculty is to know their daily lives, what they habitually do and say, noticing their habits and routines.

To understand the faculty is to stand by them where they work, where the urgency of a specific moment transforms the curriculum, accelerating its rhythm, shiftings its references, altering the dynamics of the discussion, the very interaction of those participating in the class. "Evidently," Remedí asserts, with irony, "no one wants to know of 'this.'" It is evidently better, he continues (almost bitterly), to report "empty" and "innocuous" information than to describe "what really happens," to see "without spectacles." To understand the faculty, he insists, one must come close to the complexity of "curricular reality." One must "reconstruct suppressed dialogues" (quoted passages in Remedí 1999, 120–121).

Remedí's rupturing of the social surface is evident too in the title of his 1997 doctoral thesis, *Behind the Murmur: Political-Academic Life in the Autonomous University of Zacatecas, 1959–1977*. In the Introduction, entitled "Frames, Traces and Signs," Remedí states that his "continuous reference is the institution, the place of work," where he identifies a "principle of reality that permits or prohibits," a principle that conveys an entire "cultural system." This symbolic and imaginary reality imprints a "distinctive seal on the body, the work and subjectivity of each." It "gestates a world of internalized norms" that are "not always conscious," but that somehow enable subjects to contest that very world. In this sense, the institution as a whole permits "work, life and love," as it provides the site of a "plot that shakes, exhausts and expresses those who study and teach" there (quoted passages in Remedí 1997, 11). As an expression of academic practices, the curriculum becomes the ground in which the preoccupations of the subjects involved figure, while it risks being reduced to the "range of the decision-making of administrators, directors or experts." This danger derives from restricting the meaning of the curriculum to its "explicit, purposeful face," oversimplifying the concept to study plans, themselves reduced to institutional regulations. In this way study plans appear as only stipulations, enforcing institutional priorities, pretending that once the curriculum has been selected, ordered, and structured, teachers will adopt it predictably, even mechanistically. The fantasy is that students will simply learn it. Such a "false schematization," Remedí makes clear, "distorts and hides the reality of the process." In contrast, he adds, the curriculum must be comprehended as a "practice," appreciating that "all those who participate in it are, in the same way, active subjects in its constitution" (14–15).

It is interesting to appreciate the nuances of concepts that Remedí unravels, depending on the audience he is addressing and the circumstances of his involvement. These are evident in a presentation that he gave in Argentina, entitled "The University Institution and the Construction of Identities." There he reported that in Mexico "we tried, and we were able to, change study plans," and that "we worked hard on faculty formation at the university level," but we found "no change in basic institutional practices." This discovery, he continued, "led us to try to understand what was happening in the institutions," what in particular impeded the changes: "We centered our gaze—strongly—on the university professors." Shifting from study plans to the faculty, Remedí reported, enabled "us to elaborate the concept of the *curriculum as a collection of practices.*" This realization required making distinctions among different moments of this dynamic process. In the first moment we referenced how "*the curriculum specifically stated itself* in the institution," including how it was articulated in study plans and placed into specific programs. In the second moment we studied how the professors "*received the curriculum.*" This moment was, he emphasized, "very important for us," as it enabled us to "observe how the professors situate themselves in their practice." In the third moment we studied how the faculty "*reflected on the curriculum,*" how they interpreted their experience, including in gendered terms. This moment we characterized as the "*reflexive curriculum.*" Finally, we juxtaposed these moments in order to discern the curriculum in its various temporal phases and institutional forms, and this comprehensive view we called the "*restructured curriculum.*" It is this temporal and structural complexity of curriculum that renders reforms impossible. And the central concept of *curriculum as a collection of practices* enables us to see how such an "impossibility" becomes, in fact, an "action"—a "complicated process that exists between the explicit curriculum and the restructured curriculum" (quoted passages in Remedí 2000, 1–2). Within these practices, we noticed, identities are formed. That realization recommends three points. The first, Remedí asserted, is that "we can permit the teachers—as a group—to have more freedom in making decisions in order to benefit the young people with whom the professors work." He emphasizes this point: "This is very central for me." Without more "discretion," he continued, faculty cannot be creative and their work risks becoming "boring." The second point is to encourage a "culture of collaboration," one of "help and of respect" among the faculty. This means, third, that faculty should go further than "just sharing ideas, resources or other practical instruments." Their collaboration should include "critical reflections about the purpose and value of what they teach and about the way that they carry it out." In the realization of these recommendations, the faculty assume a "more radical responsibility," enabling a "horizontal dialogue where they can think about their work and their actions with their peers" (9–10).

One of Remedí's most recent publications is, in my view, of special interest because it defines the nexus between curriculum and the institution. It is the book *Educational Institutions: Subjects, History and*

Identities. In the chapter "The Institution: An Intertwining of Texts," Remedí clarifies that our institutional labor is "intertwined" with "curricular development practices, faculty formation, evaluation processes, didactic proposals, etc." Curriculum as an expression of practices is also embedded in the institution's history, itself "intertwined with various academic and personal trajectories." Our pedagogical labor, then, occurs in institutional spaces that restructure that labor, expressed, in part, through specific enunciations of the project, for example, a collection of interactions. These interactional processes are not necessarily sequential and are often overtaken by institutional routines, themselves structured by "institutional history and culture." Educational actors are not always conscious of their restructurings, which are nonetheless "profound." In this sense, pedagogy and educational action in general amount to a "second degree of articulation," and the "crisis" of the various subjects—centrally the professors—is that this institutionalization of their labor, as routine, ignores their psychic complexity, often resulting in "isolation, urgency, and balkanization" (quoted passages in Remedí 2004, 25–26). Through that psychic complexity, Remedí emphasizes, "we install our presence." He continues: "We sustain our work of intervention and investigation with a *deliberate* attitude that demands more listening and much more time and presence." He underscores "deliberate" as the adjective conveys our obligation to observe and comprehend different points of view, to weigh alternatives, and to establish communication. This *deliberate* attitude of reflection—reflection that is inscribed in our very trajectory as educators—allows us to think about curriculum as our "collection of practices," as "unstable places of identification" that are structured as "intertextuality." Indeed, it is "a pervasive and dynamic intertextuality that our work tackles," Remedí asserts. Structuring that textuality, he explains, is not only the history of the specific institution where the faculty work, but as well its cultural character and "experiential culture," personified in subjects with particular life histories and "expressive practices" (26–27).

Ángel Díaz Barriga

Ángel Díaz Barriga has a doctorate in Pedagogy from the UNAM and has worked in this institution since 1975. Currently he is a titular professor at the Institute of Research on the University and Education (IISUE). Between 1995 and March 2003 he served as the director of the Centre for Studies on the University (CESU) that later was transformed into the

IISUE. He was the coordinator of the state-of-the-art reports "The Field of Curriculum 1982–1992" and "Curriculum Research in Mexico during the 1990s." From the beginning of his career, Ángel Díaz Barriga has been recognized for his critical positions in the curricular field. Early on he dismissed the US discourse as an "invasive epistemology" that displaced the didactic. He was a major participant in the national debate over education in the early 1980s. In 1984 he, published *Essays on the Problem of Curriculum*, wherein he discussed three meanings of the concept:

1. The foundations of a study plan, and the plan and the study programs of an educative institution.
2. An expression of the American pedagogy that looks for a greater articulation between schools and the economic system. This pedagogical expression has displaced the didactic one.
3. The daily actions that teachers and students undertake for the fulfillment of study plans. (1984, 87)

Díaz Barriga advocates constructing curriculum theory derived from the social disciplines, the absence of which he regards as the main deficit of the era. "Curricular theory," he admonished, "cannot be seen as a collection of technical approaches." Nor can it be evaluated according to its "effectiveness" or its capacity for the "improvement" of the educational system. He affirmed the "intrinsic value of theory." Theory enables us to "accept debate on curricular proposals from a social point of view," and it is through such debate that curriculum proposals acquire "meaning and value in the education-society relationship." Rather than disaggregating the curriculum as a "collection of technical steps," Díaz Barriga affirms its social necessity: "Every educative act is a social act" (quoted passages in 1984, 76). For Díaz Barriga, theory is the antidote to the dominance of the technical in the field. The technical is itself a demand of capitalism. First, he points out, the "evolution of capitalism demands, more and more, that education in universities become a technical capability that allows a person to efficiently carry out their work in a certain part of the economic system." Second, he recommends that the "university encourage theory as an element that allows for the fulfilment of its historic function and offers formation to the student, which allows him not only to act in reality, but [also] to extend it and look for its transformation" (1984, 36).

In "The Origins of the Curricular Problem" (1985), Díaz Barriga delves into the historical origins of the technical, specifically its genesis in curriculum studies in the United States. There, he notes, the field emerged in complicity with the processes of industrialization; it advanced a "pedagogy of an industrial society" (1). The transformation of the United States from an agrarian to an industrial society changed all aspects of life, including life in schools. That shift required the formulation of an associated "pedagogical model" with "efficiency" in a "central place" (9). Replacing didactics, then, was "modern curriculum theory," which "articulated the relations between education and the labor that industry requires for its development" (12–13).

In Díaz Barriga's analysis, US schools have been fundamentally vocational in nature. They were institutional forms of what businessmen had promoted earlier, an updated version of manual education. "What they really wanted," Díaz Barriga argues, "was an efficient, technical training that would free them from the growing union regulations" (20). To institutionalize this alignment between public education and private industry, he continues, "curriculum theory had to build a collection of concepts," among which were "needs diagnostics, graduate profiles, and, above all, objectives." Such concepts, Díaz Barriga continued, enabled US curriculum theory to promote a "pedagogy for an industrial society," a pedagogy whose "internal logic" was a curriculum "preoccupied with the development of those technical-professional abilities required for the incorporation of the subject into the labour market, to the detriment of a more ample formation" (quoted passages from Díaz Barriga 1985, 24–27).

Curriculum "control" would be maintained less through the specification of content to be taught, specifically of the "behavior necessary to satisfy vocational requirements." The US curriculum devalued the acquisition of academic knowledge for its own sake as it demanded the "internalization of attitudes of order, obedience and submission." These qualities, Díaz Barriga asserts, comprised the "formation" of the individual in US society. Understanding this history, he concluded, provides Mexicans a "better understanding" of the "emergence of everything curricular and the displacement of didactics." It conveys the "limitations of the structural order" that Mexican curriculum researchers have encountered subsequently in the problem of study plans (29). The origins of the US field remain as traces in the structure of Mexican curricular discourse through frameworks from which it is almost impossible to escape.

In *Curriculum and Scholarly Evaluation* (1990), Díaz Barriga insists on the centrality of these origins of curriculum theory in the United States to the hegemony of practicality in curriculum. Such practicality is a subset of more pervasive demands of US capitalism, wherein the very "value of man" becomes "defined only through his productivity." This is, Díaz Barriga notes, "a one-dimensional vision," as Marcuse elaborated. This reduction of humanity to productivity also creates a "one-dimensional pedagogy that recasts the global meaning of education" as questions of "employment." Díaz Barriga (1990, 20) emphasizes the centrality of origins:

> This is the meaning which contains the genesis of the curricular question. It is not a coincidence that it was an engineer, Franklin Bobbitt, who studied the application of the management systems in schools, who in 1918 elaborated the first systematic text about the curriculum.

In a culture centered on only the "utilitarian," such practical curricular knowledge "cancels the possibility of reflecting about educational problems," replacing reflection with "implementation" (24).

Like his colleagues, Ángel Díaz Barriga shows that the curriculum is also "a part of the institutional space." Referencing Kliebard's historical scholarship associating the history of curriculum development with bureaucratization, Díaz Barriga emphasizes that the "curricular space becomes a scenario where conflicts happen: conflicts of interests, conflicts of conceptions" (26). He forefronts the conflict between faculty and institutional authorities over the curriculum. In fact, Díaz Barriga asserts, "the curriculum becomes a source of tension between that which the teacher (from his formation and experience) considers necessary to be transmitted and what the institution defines as 'obligatory' to be taught" (26). He calls for the curriculum to be a space of expression of the faculty and students through an "ample discussion of its fundamental themes," namely "man, the culture, the history, the meaning of life." Such discussion requires the recognition of a "necessary multiplicity of interests, values, ways of life, and cultural expressions." Such a curriculum exhibits "unique content," and "it is necessary to think in the particular dimensions of the culture, of the students and of the faculty." He asserts, "The curriculum claims to convert itself into a space of expression of the faculty and of the students and not only of the scholarly bureaucracy" (29).

By 2003, Ángel Díaz Barriga had become the most recognized curriculum scholar in Mexico and (Spanish-speaking) Latin America. In that year he wrote "Curriculum: Conceptual Tensions and Practices" with the intention of

> explaining some of the tensions that the curricular field experiences, taking the confirmation of two aspects in its genesis as a reference, at the beginning of the twentieth century, and paying attention to the evolution that these aspects had when this discipline became international in the last third of the past century. (2)

On this occasion Díaz Barriga references John Dewey's *The Child and the Curriculum* (1902) as well as Franklin Bobbitt's *The Curriculum* (1918) as founding events in US curriculum studies. These intersecting and contrasting books instantiated a tensioned complexity that—despite the demands of US capitalism for a vocational education—rendered curriculum studies "unpredictable," due to its "multiplicity of themes," its "series of tensions," including those "between the institutional necessities that gave it origin and the distinct perspectives of investigators and scholars" who followed. These tensions and contradictions, Díaz Barriga continues, have triggered a "process of dissolution as a result of the polysemy that accompanies it." The curriculum is now understood to be at once "occult, formal, lived, procedural." Such definitional multiplicity defies any simple even stable definition of the concept. Such a polysemous state follows the efforts of "those who try to 'define' *everything* [as] curricular" (Díaz Barriga 2003, 3, emphasis added). This "tension"—which extends from planning the curriculum to its evaluation—follows from its "founding rationality (as efficient, behavioral, a concept for management)" and its subsequent "diversity" as an ongoing effort to interpret the "educative act" (3). This is a tension, then, that follows from the field's multiple subjects of investigation, among them

> the selection, organization and distribution of content in some perspectives; the classroom reality; the discontinued fractures that are generated in each scholarly group; the distances between the thought-out curriculum and the one that is taught and lived. Such non-intended but valued learning demands recognition of the existence of a conceptual production that is articulated from a discipline, in relation with it and with the task of realizing it. This discipline is what we call the curricular field. (4).

Díaz Barriga distinguishes between the concept of curriculum and the academic discipline that bears the name, between a present institutional reality and a historically informed effort to align education with the US industrial-democratic society one hundred years ago. The concept of curriculum operates today in service to the "institutional needs of the educative system," to organize the "selection of contents" and the "formation of abilities," not only in terms of institutional, disciplinary, or pedagogical issues, but, more fundamentally and expansively, also as a "problem of the society as a whole." That general problem, which in earlier eras linked the curriculum to social democracy, has now aligned it with transnational capitalism and the vocational demands of the global workplace.

In an earlier era, Díaz Barriga reminds, "the professor was responsible to choose the contents and strategies of teaching," but now, in what he terms "the curricular era," the professor has become responsible for "selecting activities for learning that the specialists recommend" (7). This specification of instructional behavior represents a reinstantiation of much earlier US technicism, several decades after it had been replaced by studies of the occult or hidden curriculum (Jackson 1968). In this latter work scholars had become clear that learning is not always intentional or predictable; it is, inevitably, "a result of experience" (Díaz Barriga 2003, 7). Such scholarship underscored the "limitations" of those study plan models based on behavioral psychology and administrative protocols. It inaugurated a series of studies that were "closer" to interpretive and micro-social theories, and these included developments from micro-sociology and the critical theory of Frankfurt School (7). "From this moment on," Díaz Barriga continues, "a series of studies followed that focused on distinctions between the formal curriculum and lived curriculum, between the official and hidden curriculum, between curriculum as objectives and curriculum as a process" (7). There even appeared, he exclaims, a conception of the "null" curriculum. Such studies reconstructed curriculum studies as a "multidisciplinary" field derived from sociology, history, administration, and economics. "To all of this," Díaz Barriga notes, "epistemological" and other "philosophical" elements were added, "dissolving" the field's "borders" as the topics for research multiplied.

Still, he argues, two points of view have persisted. One concerns the professional discretion individual teachers must exercise when working with study plans, what Díaz Barriga describes as a "level of lesser decisions." We now recognize, he says, that "plans and programs cannot be modeled," that what is key is to "recuperate the riches that are generated in each elaboration or reformulation experience of a study plan or program." The other persisting point of view is the institutional demand to evaluate and revise study plans. "This reality," Díaz Barriga explains, obligates institutional officials to "generate or systemize proposals for the elaboration of study plans," which have led to "flexible curricular organizations" and notions of "competency learning." Through such schema "we try to establish a renovating concept that guides the groups of professors in an institution and invites them to look for ways of innovating their educative work." Study plan specialists, he notes, are "conscious" that the contents established in a study plan cannot be carried out "word for word." In fact, study plan specialists labor to specify a minimum of contents, so that individuals have space to invoke their discretionary judgment. With the blurring of disciplinary borders and the multiplication of topics internal to the field, these base-line problems have been ignored, as contemporary research focuses instead not on "educational experiences in the classroom," but on "what has not been documented" (quoted passages in Díaz Barriga 2003, 9). The consequences for curriculum studies as an academic field, Díaz Barriga judges, "are not the best," as there is a "lack of dialogue" between the two groups. Moreover, in Mexico, the divided field has meant that many researchers have emigrated to other fields. Divided internally, then, curriculum studies in Mexico also suffers the dissolution of its borders, as these blur into philosophies, sociologies, psychologies, micro-social theories, among others (10). Referencing Schwab's conception of deliberation, Díaz Barriga concludes that "in the end education is an act." Achieving the "coordination" of research insights with the imperatives of institutional practice is "a challenge that perhaps the scholars, who tackle these studies, should take more seriously" (11). With the state of the field at the forefront of his preoccupations, Díaz Barriga suggests that the way to the disciplinary dialogue that is necessary can be found in Schwab, whereas in Remedí, also referencing Schwab, there is legitimation of ongoing conversation with faculty if we advance our understanding of the curriculum. In any case, it is a healthy rapprochement.

Alicia de Alba

Alicia de Alba took her bachelor's and master's degrees in Pedagogy from the UNAM, where she works as professor in the Faculty of Philosophy and Liberal Arts. She has a doctorate in Philosophy and Science of Education from the UNED (Madrid, Spain); she conducted her postdoctoral research in Political Philosophy at the University of Essex, England, under the direction of Ernesto Laclau. Her works concerning the curriculum have brought her recognition in Mexico and elsewhere throughout Latin America.

I am going to present two of her most powerful works characterizing the current situation of curriculum studies in Mexico. The first is *Curriculum: Crisis, Myth and Perspectives* (1991). There she defines curriculum as "the synthesis of cultural elements (knowledge, values, customs, beliefs, habits)," but a synthesis that is "driven by diverse groups and social sectors whose interests often conflict." Also referencing Schwab, Alicia de Alba suggests that "we arrive at this synthesis through diverse negotiation and social imposition mechanisms." Study plans must satisfy both "structural-formal and process-practical aspects," as they are analogous to "the general and particular dimensions that interact in the future of curricula." Due to this complexity, the reality of curriculum is "profoundly historical" and never "mechanical or linear." The future and structures of this curricular reality are expressed "through distinct levels of meaning" (quoted passages in de Alba 1991, 38–39). "This synthesis," she adds, "which is contradictory in many occasions, allows us to understand why it is difficult to conceive the curriculum as a congruent and articulated system." It is, de Alba suggests, *time* that enables us to visualize curriculum as a "totality where contradictions, the game of negotiations and impositions are presented in various articulations" (39). She proposes the following conceptualization of "the structural-formal and process-practical aspects of the curriculum," noting that its reduction to the former has been "one of the most important problems concerning the understanding of the curricular field." In its structural-formal reductionism, only the "official dispositions, of study plans and programs, of organization hierarchies in the school, of the legislations that regulate scholarly life," have informed our understanding of the curriculum. But, as de Alba has pointed out on numerous occasions, "the curriculum is not made up exclusively, or in a manner of priority, by the structural-formal aspects; the process-practical development of the curriculum is fundamental to understand its determining constitution and its future in concrete, scholarly institutions" (43). For the sake of a more comprehensive understanding of curriculum, de Alba acknowledges the following dimensions of the reality of curriculum.

- Ample social dimension (cultural, political, social, economical, ideological);
- Institutional dimension;
- Didactic-classroom dimension. (44)

As crucial as these dimensions are to understanding curriculum, they do not exhaust its multifaceted reality.

Structuring that multifaceted reality is the character of the historical moment. At the beginning of the twenty-first century, de Alba (1991, 53) writes, university curricula are faced with several "challenges." It is, she argues, our obligation as curriculum studies scholars to confront these:

- Absence of any vision of social utopia
- Extreme situations: environmental crisis and nuclear threat
- The loss of meaning
- The persistence of poverty: the unjust distribution of wealth in the world
- The impact of the third industrial revolution
- The complexity of communication in our contemporary world
- The ongoing fights for national liberation
- Ethnic minorities in the nations
- The fall of the Berlin wall and the death of real socialism
- The processes of curricular determination

(de Alba 1991, 54–58)

What does she recommend?

De Alba proposes to build Fields of Structural Curricular Arrangement (CCEC). These communities of scholars would be committed to elaborating the reality of the Latin American condition, specifically that of the public universities in the region. In so doing, scholars would become social actors in the determination of curriculum. De Alba proposes four fields of research and action: (1) the epistemological-theoretical, (2) the critical-social, (3) the scientific-technological, and (4) the practical. The practical incorporates "the central elements of professional practices." She draws a map of those authors who influenced her formulation (among them Giroux and McLaren, advocating a "pedagogy of possibility"). She concludes with a reflection about the formation of the pedagogues in Mexico as she characterizes the political circumstances of the era, noting that curricular investigations are sometimes "far away from this preoccupation" (quoted passages in de Alba 1991, 91).

In 2007 Alicia de Alba published *Curriculum-Society: The Weight of Uncertainty, the Force of Imagination*, wherein she draws upon the work of Laclau, Morin, Lyotard, Wittgestein, Lacan, Villoro, Bakhtin, Castoriadis, and others. There is in this text a discernible increase in the complexity of her discourse, as Mario Díaz Villa acknowledges in his prologue, where he praises the work as potentially paradigmatic in the scale of its influence. In the first chapter de Alba presents the theoretical elements that structure subsequent chapters, complicating our understanding of education as

> a constant interchanging of information, of discursive, reconstructive practices; of the constitution of split educative subjects; of the arrangement of educative and social projects, through social imaginaries that are produced in the social canvas, which is made up of multiple tie points and diverse circuits where messages of diverse nature and with different power charges circulate. (de Alba 2007, 89)

Such a complication of education expands the theoretical reach of the field to include, among other domains, "subject constitution, socialization, transmission, adaptation, reproduction (social, cultural, economical and ideological), resistance, message production, transformation, creation and empowerment" (89).

De Alba starts the second chapter with the following question: "Are there ample political and social projects that allow us to work toward the construction of a better world, toward a new figure of the world, and in a particular way, toward the construction of better conditions of life for the Latin American people?" (91). She then focuses on the existing historical blockade to such construction, identifying the tensions between what she terms the generalized structural crisis and globalization. She acknowledges, "we have observed the difficulty of re-establishing the curriculum-society link in present societies due to the absence of political and social projects." This absence occurs in the context of a "generalized social crisis (CEG)" that "urges us" to theorize the complexity of curriculum as incorporating two dimensions: "destructuralization or chaos and organization-structure." The former dimension occurs through social articulation that "breaks the structure-space," precipitating, in effect, a "curricular unravelling," despite "processes of curricular over-determination." The latter incorporates the local, including difference, "in the totality, the universality, the system, the model, the proposal" (144).

Such an understanding, de Alba argues, "confronts the oversimplification of thought" that often dominates the field. It is "time" that is oversimplified in the field, she specifies, either in its elimination or in construing it simplistically, as a "single time, in one single direction," such as in conceptions of "unlimited progress" or in the inevitability of "corruption" in Morin's terms, or "destructuralization" in her terms. "Complex thought faces and assumes not only the question of time," she continues, specifically time's "double direction," at once toward "destructuralization" and/or toward its articulation into "structure." It is time, she asserts, that "signals the generalized structural crisis characterizing the transition from twentieth to twenty-first centuries." This crisis contains, de Alba, continues, the synthesis of contradictory cultural contents that comprise the present. Such synthesis was reached through "fights, negotiations, consensus, and impositions," and it contained and communicated the dissonance between cultural inheritance (historical legacy, selective tradition, and cultural arbitrary) and the "new." It is this synthesis, she observes, that "sustains ... diverse groups and social sectors," as it contains simultaneous processes of "over-determination" as well as processes of "formal structuralization." These tensions become expressed in the "question of identity" and in the "social imaginary" (162–163).

Curriculum reform, Alicia de Alba explains, also contains these contradictory tendencies. Simultaneously it represents the "recuperation" of those "existing structures" it claims to replace as it forces the introduction of "new elements." These derive from "the generalized social crisis," for example, from the "creative, re-meaningful and committed articulation between cultural inheritance and unedited elements." Neither the "new elements" nor the "recuperation" of old ones instantiate actual change. As in the dynamics of "identity," the familiarity of "change" and the newness of "recuperation" result in "conflict and tension" (163–164).

Curriculum that contributes to the Latin American identity has yet to be devised, in part due to these contradictory tendencies. It is these that must be "recombined in a dynamic bond." That "common bond" or "meaningful space" can vary. For instance, it could be the struggle to overcome poverty, or the negotiation of an economic union enabling Latin American countries to compete in the present globalized world. It could take curricular forms of "urgent attention" to the indigenous, and/or the care of the environment. The point, de Alba emphasizes, is for the curriculum to occasion the "social inclusion and constitution of the new social subjects of the twenty-first century" (176–177). For de Alba, then, the question of the globalization-generalized structural crisis is at the heart of the matter, evident in the divide between scholars and the tendency to superimpose globalization upon them as "innovation" and "reform." It is this question, then, that enables scholars to once again elaborate "the curriculum-society link" (215).

Balance

I have sketched the thought of four key scholars, often in their own words and keenly conscious of Díaz Barriga's assessment of the state of the field as polysemous. It is the very polysemy of curriculum studies that disables conceptual development in the field, especially as two uses of the term he identified: one denoting the curriculum in institutions, and the other denoting the academic field that studies the former. The former exhibits situated meanings but the second, through the blurring of its disciplinary borders and its internal fragmentation, risks any meaning at all. Díaz Barriga's strategy of differentiating the term "curriculum" from the "curriculum field" or discipline is, from my point of view, useful. We consider curriculum studies to be a teachable *corpus*, distinguishable from didactics, since its scale is different. It is essential to analyze, inside the *corpus*, the actions of the faculty and the experiences that the students live through under the sponsorship of the institution. Here, the field of curriculum studies is necessarily intersecting with didactics but with different emphases. While didactics take up the tasks of describing, explaining, and guiding the work of teaching and assesses the interventions of the teachers considered individually, curriculum studies remains focused broadly on the range of institutions wherein such teaching takes place. Deep down, curriculum studies as a field implies that the educative power belongs to the institution, especially to the collectivity of faculty working under its aegis. The field of didactics affirms the potential influence of the individual faculty member.

Concerning the concept of curriculum, I think, finally, there is no need to be worried about its polysemy. From my point of view, its modifiers—official, hidden, null—illuminate the concept more than they obscure it. Indeed, they give body to the discipline. In its variegated use also, at least in Mexico, it depicts the lived complexity of the notion, as in *curriculum vitae*. Moreover, polysemy characterizes almost all the concepts that we use in education. The very notion of education is, in fact, polysemic. That is a sign of its vitality.

The juxtaposition of adjectives with the curriculum enables us to elaborate its various realities, and on occasion they produce interesting effects. For example, consider those that Remedí uses: "explicit, received, reflexive, restructured." Each allows for investigations of diverse curricular projects during multiple moments of the subjects' actions (e.g., "practice"). Like other interdisciplinary fields, curriculum studies is accepting of its multi-referentiality. It requires an attitude that is always open and tolerant, wherein uncertainty is accompanied by rigor, requiring careful, sometimes long-term research, always with the "force of imagination," as Alicia de Alba would say. In his "state-of-the-art" curriculum knowledge, Ángel Díaz Barriga reminds us that "in the end we cannot be unaware of the tensions that exist among the actors"—tension and self-enclosure, as there is a tendency to read only like-minded research. In fact, "each author is practically a reference of himself." Consequently, he continues, "we cannot talk of a community of scholars." Although the output in the field is very high, it occurs in silos. What is missing are integrations of these various specializations, syntheses that link new work to old, specifically to the canonical concerns of the field (Díaz Barriga 2003, 258).

Perhaps this fragmentation of the field is reflected in the absence of any recent state-of-the-art assessments, as they occurred in the 1980s and 1990s. Is this apparent incapacity to assess the overall field "due to fatigue," Díaz Barriga asks, "or has the curriculum agenda been hijacked by international agencies?" He recommends that "we need to take up the theme again by promoting the participation of the old speakers and providing a platform where the new producers of discourses converge." That said, Díaz Barriga is optimistic, given that scholars mistake theoretical disagreements for personal attacks. Moreover the institutions where faculty work are less facilitative of this synoptic or integrative research, as they too have specialized and become self-promoting.

Among the four scholars whose ideas I have presented here there is a basic coincidence concerning the configuration of the curricular terrain and the complexity of the curricular reality. In the long term, they seem to agree, the process-practical realities of curriculum are more defining than the specific content of study plans. Nevertheless, an educational institution cannot be conceived without study plans, whether these are prescribed within the institution or by some ministry, whether they are highly explicit or open for reconstruction, whether they constitute a general declaration of principles or a meticulously detailed study plan.

Analyzing the institutional structures of the curriculum, which María de Ibarrola proposes, is very important to understanding curriculum. It also enables us to anticipate many problems in the development of study plans. We can assess, for example, how inflated the objectives are in relation to what is concretely or practically possible within certain institutional structures. Focusing on the institution and on the practices of the subjects teaching, studying, and administering there enables us to understand the complex reality of curriculum. We can open a permanent ear to what the actors think and say. This disposition appears to me as key in consolidating curriculum studies in Mexico. To formulate a deliberate code as a norm and attitude, as Eduardo Remedí and Ángel Díaz Barriga suggest, seems to me a wise move to make. The efforts of Alicia de Alba—according theoretical sophistication to curriculum studies—are praiseworthy, particularly given the crisis that is the present historical moment. The curricular realities that these scholars have unraveled will be altered by the proliferation of distance education programs and the decline of educational institutions. The so-called flexible curriculum—the multiplication of curricular options that leave students more responsible for their education—could prove fatal to our once-proud educational institutions. Under these dire circumstances another state-of-the-art curriculum knowledge must be performed.

In recent months, an unprecedented polemic has arisen around the "Partnership for Quality Education" agreed upon between the government and the National Educational Workers' Union early in 2008. This partnership has been rejected by numerous sectors, including many researchers in the education field. The question of curriculum is considered to remain of primary importance, evident in the text of an open letter signed by members of the Department of Educational Research, including María de Ibarrola and Eduardo Remedí. I conclude by quoting the letter at length:

> Among the serious shortcomings and insufficiencies of management of education required in our country, the Ministry of Public Education (SEP, its initials in Spanish) has given the officers of the National Educational Workers' Union excessive powers, not only to set educational policies but also to establish pedagogical orientations. Any contribution by teachers, specialists, and education researchers has been excluded, giving way to the federal government's current political interests and the union bureaucracy.

The following elements of the agreement topics that are explicated related to the curriculum field are referenced:

- Comprehensive curriculum reform in basic education is to be focused on the adoption of an educational model based on proficiencies. But this model is the object of heated discussion in various parts of the world.

- The signatories express their concern for the fact that in 1993, obligatory basic education through Grade 12 was established through fragmentary constitutional amendments. Developing a comprehensive curriculum reform at three levels (pre-school, primary and secondary) requires more deliberation and the laying of firm foundations, as well as finalizing reforms implemented at various times and their corresponding evaluations, which are essential in order to determine the status of school practices and the knowledge they transmit.

Among other concerns, the letter states:

- A comprehensive reform requires that provision be made for initial and continuing teacher training to ensure the gradual, careful incorporation of the changes needed in the long term. The National System of Continuing Education and Professional Improvement for Teachers must be developed based on a vision that integrates all the organisms and figures involved in this field, staffed with personnel trained to encourage and be involved in the academic development of teachers. The actions planned for that system do not represent real alternatives for realizing the full potential of their services, in the light of the evaluations that are now available.
- No curriculum reform can improve pedagogical practice and its results if it faces obstacles derived from the way the educational system operates. Several factors are a particular cause for concern. Instead of undertaking the necessary transformation of the command structures and the usual, regulated technical/administrative operational rules, the current system has strengthened the union's intervention in those key aspects. Moreover, the focus is on the positive effects of external evaluation systems, without considering that examinations are influencing day-to-day practices in ways that contravene the proposed pedagogical approaches and in the long run lead to deficient learning. The incidence of these and other factors in everyday scholastic conditions constitute an obstacle to the individual and collective efforts of teachers to change the way they work. (Department of Educational Research 2010, 1–7)

Specialists in the curriculum field have become alarmed by the vacillations in the Mexican government's educational policy. However, there will be no "enlightened community" that will take charge of the theoretical discussions and establish a consensus on the paths to follow, because this would involve a qualitative leap that so far has not been taken, for reasons attributable to the uses and customs of academic institutions and their acceptance by intellectuals in the field. Actually, almost all of us who are in the research system act with great caution, giving priority to individual productions. For that reason, the "open letter" signed by the members of the UNAM Department of Education Research is an exceptional event that merits dissemination.

References

de Alba, Alicia. 1991. *Curriculum. Crisis, Myth and Perspectives.* Mexico City: CESU-UNAM.

de Alba, Alicia. 2007. *Curriculum-Society. The Weight of Uncertainty, the Strength of Imagination.* Mexico City: IISUE-UNAM, Plaza y Valdés.

de Ibarrola, María. 2008. "Experiences and Reflections about Curricular Design and Reality." Mexico City: Escuelasenred. Available online at: http://www.escuelasenred.com.

Department of Educational Research. 2010. *Open Letter Concerning the "Partnership for Quality Education."* Mexico City: UNAM. Available online at: http://seccion9cnte.spaces.live.com.

Díaz Barriga, Ángel. 1984. *Essays about Curricular Problems.* Mexico City: Trillas.

Díaz Barriga, Ángel. 1985. *Origins of Curricular Problems. Collection of Essays.* Mexico City: Department of Educative Studies, UNAM.

Díaz Barriga, Ángel. 1990. *Curriculum and Scholarly Evaluation. Rei Notebooks Argentina.* Buenos Aires: S. A. Aique Group Editor.

Díaz Barriga, Ángel. 1995. "Investigation in the Curricular Field, 1982–1992." In *Curricular, Institutional and Organizational Processes: Educative Investigation of the Eighties, Perspectives for the Nineties,* ed. Ángel Díaz Barriga. Mexico City: COMIE.

Díaz Barriga, Ángel. 2003. "Curriculum, Conceptual Tensions and Practices." *Electronic Magazine of Educative Investigation* 5(2). Available online at: http://redie.ens.uabc.mx.

Díaz Barriga, Ángel. 2003. *Curricular Investigation in México. The Decade of the Nineties.* Number 5 of the Collection Educative Investigation in Mexico 1992–2002. Mexico City: COMIE, the SEP and the CESU.

Furlán, Alfredo, and Eduardo Remedí. 1981. "Notes about Faculty Practice: The Pedagogical Reflection and the Normative Proposals." *University Forum* 10: 42–46.

Furlán, Alfredo, and Miguel Pasillas. 1999. *Ralph Tyler. Engaging Lectures Forty Years after "Basic Principles of the Curriculum."* Mexico City: ENEPI-UAS.

Glazman, Raquel, and María de Ibarrola. 1978. *Design of Study Plans.* Mexico City: CISE-UNAM.

Glazman, Raquel, and María de Ibarrola. 1987. *Study Plans. Institutional Proposals and Curricular Reality.* Mexico City: Nueva Imagen.

Remedí, Eduaerdo. 1978. Evaluation Systems Applied in the ENEPI. Paper presented at a symposium entitled Second Days of Teaching and Learning Problems in the Health Area. Mexico City: ENEPI, UNAM.

Remedí, Eduardo. 1978. "Construction of the Methodological Structure of Bases." In *Contributions to Didactic in Superior Education*, ed. Alfredo Furlán, Miguel Angel Campos Hernandez and María Elena Marzolla. Mexico City: ENEPI, UNAM.

Remedí, Eduardo. 1981. *Ideal Models and Real Practices in Faculty Work*. Mexico City: ENEPI-UNAM.

Remedí, Eduardo. 1982. "Curriculum and Faculty Actions." *University Forum*. 25: 57–61.

Remedí, Eduardo. 1988. "Continuity and Rupture of the Methodological Approach: Critical Notes for Your Analysis." In *Curriculum, Teacher and Knowledge: University Themes*, ed. Roberto M. Torres, Eduardo Remedí, Monique Landesmann y Veronica Edwards. Mexico City: Metropolitan Autonomous University.

Remedí, Eduardo. 1989. "Theoretical Suppositions: Discourses-Content-Knowledge in Faculty Work." In *Development of Investigation in the Field of the Curriculum*, ed. Alfredo Furlán, and Miguel Angel Pasillas. Mexico City: ENEPI-UNAM.

Remedí, Eduardo. 1997. "Behind the Murmur. Political-Academic Life in the Autonomous University of Zacatecas, 1959–1977." PhD diss., Department of Educative Investigation, Centre of investigation and of Advanced Studies of the National Polytechnic Institute, Mexico City.

Remedí, Eduardo. 1999. "Ralph Tyler. A Notable Encounter." In *Ralph Tyler. Lectures Committed to Forty Years from "Basic Principles of Curriculum,"* eds. Alfredo Furlán and Mighel Angel Pasillas. Mexico City: ENEPI-UNAM and the Autonomous University of Sinaloa.

Remedí, Eduardo. 2000. "The University Institution and the Construction of Identities. Conference." Paper presented at a seminar entitled "Situations and Institutional Devices of Formation." General Academic Secretariat. President's office. National University of North-East, Argentina. Available online at: http://www.unne.edu.ar.

Remedí, Eduardo. 2004. *Educational Institutions: Subjects, History and Identities*. Mexico City: Plaza y Valdés.

Chapter 6

Acculturation, Hybridity, Cosmopolitanism in Ibero-American Curriculum Studies

José María García Garduño

Ever since Schawb (2004) declared in the late 1960s that the curriculum field was moribund, one has been reading studies signaling a permanent crisis in the field. Indeed, Wraga and Hlebowitsh (2003, 425) declared that curriculum in the "US can be seen as existing in a state of perpetual crisis." Apparently, an inherent characteristic of the curricular field is that of a permanent crisis. If this crisis is a struggle of the old and the established against the new, to a certain extent it seems natural. Certainly education in the modern and postmodern era has been in a state of constant crisis; Coombs (1971), too, cited crisis. In 1978 Pinar stated that areas such as psychology and the natural sciences *regard the curriculum field as in a primitive stage of development* (Pinar 1978). But 25 years later, the outlook was very different. The same author (Pinar, 2003, 27) asserted that "the central question in education is the question of curriculum." This shift is nothing but astonishing. Curriculum started as an instrumental discipline at the beginning of the twentieth century. The explosion of knowledge, due to the scientific progress of that time, demanded a discipline that could select and organize the knowledge to be taught at school (Seguel 1966).

Despite the astounding consolidation of the curriculum discipline, it may be only momentary, as recent analyses state that it is undergoing a stage of internationalization (Pinar 2003). Others, such as the Canadian scholar Smith (2003), are not so optimistic, calling attention instead to the dangers of globalization. Latin American scholars are more specific, referencing *satelitization* (Feeney and Terigi 2003), arguing that the curriculum field in Argentina is not independent but subordinate to the legacies, didactics, and the dictates of educational policy. In the 1980s, the Mexican curricularist Ángel Díaz Barriga (Díaz Barriga 1985, 68), influenced by Martin Carnoy (1977), whose work was widely publicized in Mexico and South America, argued that educational imports from the United States into Mexico was a US strategy to consolidate its ideological hegemony. Such hegemony ensured continued imperialism.

In this regard, Brazilian curricularist Flavio Moreira (1990) pointed out that Carnoy's position was deterministic, assuming that the importers are passive recipients, unable to reconstruct what they now faced. The legacy of internationalization in Mexico is, then, contentious, but what becomes clear is that reproduction theories—implying only imperialism and passivity—do not adequately explain how curriculum studies as an academic discipline has reached its current level of consolidation worldwide. Nor can such theories account for how each country adopts peculiar forms that not only reflect their Anglo-Saxon origin but also display specific characteristics that render curriculum studies in Mexico different both from its counterpart in the United States and in other countries. I suggest that the concepts of internationalization and globalization are insufficient to explain the current development and progress of the curriculum field in Mexico.

In this chapter I will focus not only on Mexico, but on all four fields in Ibero-America—Argentina, Brazil, Spain, and Mexico—accenting how internationalization has helped structure their formation and current state. Study of these four nationally distinctive fields suggests that the evolution of the curriculum field has undergone the two stages of acculturation and hybridity and is currently on the threshold of a third one, cosmopolitanism. My observation derives from but is not limited to reports on the Brazilian field (see Moreira 1990, 2003; Lopes and Macedo 2003; Lopes 2005, 2008). For at least a decade Brazilian scholars have been forefronting the concept of hybridity. Does hybridity characterize each of these Ibero-American fields?

Conceptual Framework

In order to understand the development of curriculum field outside the United States where it originated, the concepts of globalization, internationalization, and imperialistic or hegemonic reproduction are not enough. According to García Canclini (2000), internationalization refers to the geographic expansion of economic activity beyond national boundaries. One example is the maritime trade routes opened between Europe, the Americas, and Asia. Canclini points out that this process was completed through the expansion of the Christian religion. However, Canclini adds that globalization is the culmination of internationalization and transnationalization processes, characterized now by technological development (satellites and computer systems) and the creation of a global financial and economic markets that deterritorialize national boundaries of production. In other words, goods such as cars, designer clothes, and other consumer items are no longer consumed where they originate. Canclini (2003) maintains that the changes in the production systems have brought about a popular international culture that organizes consumers into homogeneous life-styles: clothing, idols, movies, sports heroes, among others.

According to Carnoy (1977), imperialism is the political and economical control of a country by the ruling class of another. Canclini (2000) states that imperialism refers to a time when nations wielded power in a direct, often military, form. Now economy has become transnational; huge corporations establish themselves in different countries. Mexico has not been free of imperialistic domination; the United States seized half of its territory in the middle of the nineteenth century. Only since the twentieth century has Mexico enjoyed a relative independence from the United States. Although Mexico is the United States' third commercial partner— around 80 percent of its exports go to the United States—it would be very difficult to talk about economic imperialism. What we should talk about is codependency and dependency in certain areas. In countries such as Argentina and Brazil, the dependency on the United States is less. Nowadays, the biggest investor in Argentina is not the United States but Spain (García Canclini 2003).

Acculturation

This concept derives from cultural anthropology and its founding fathers: Franz Boas, Ralph Linton, and Melville Herskovits. Gonzalo Aguirre Beltrán, a Mexican anthropologist and a former disciple of those celebrated anthropologists, carried out one of the most important investigative works on acculturation process. I draw upon his work for the theoretical development of the concept. Despite the significance of the work, acculturation has been used infrequently in recent years. Aguirre Beltrán (1970) rejects the word "transculturation" as a translation for "acculturation." If this word existed in Latin, Beltrán observes, it would be "acculturation," which means culture-contact. Inspired by his former professor Herskovits, Beltrán (1970, 11) defines acculturation as "those phenomena that happen when groups of people from different cultures come into continuous and first-hand contact, resulting in changes in the cultural patterns of both groups."

Beltrán points out that the concept must be distinguished from the broader notion of cultural change. Likewise, it must be distinguished from assimilation, which is one stage of acculturation. The process of assimilation, Beltrán (1970, 127) suggests, "implies the total incorporation and, therefore, the complete participation of the person in the culture that receives him/her within its womb." The concept of acculturation differs from that of education, which, as a broader concept, refers to the transmission of a cultural heritage from one generation to another. Herskovits called this process endoculturation.

Beltrán (1970) draws six contrasts in his analysis of the acculturation process. The first is past versus present, as the past is incorporated into the present. The second is compulsion versus volition. Acculturation can be voluntary or forced, as with the indigenous peoples in the Americas. Third is collective versus individual, as acculturation occurs with (and within) groups and/or with isolated individuals. When the individual breaks free from a mother culture and accepts another, we talk about assimilation; if he or she continues to have bonds with the mother culture and acts as an agent of his own original group, we call it acculturation. Fourth is continuity versus alternation. Not all acculturation processes are continuous. One example is Mexicans who work in the United States; many travel frequently to Mexico to visit their families and remain in Mexico for some time. An example of continuity can be the presence of the United States in Puerto Rico; ever since the end of the nineteenth century when the United States occupied the island, a continuous process of acculturation has been underway.

The fifth contrast is induced versus spontaneous. Beltrán notes that acculturation processes can be deliberate or induced by the dominating group. An example is the "English only" policy that several states within the southwestern United States have tried unsuccessfully to enforce. Not all induced processes are negative for a cultural group; likewise, not all spontaneous processes are positive. Beltrán's example of spontaneous acculturation is what occurred in Mexico in the nineteenth century when the liberal governments of the time implemented laissez faire reforms that negatively affected indigenous populations. The lack of direct support resulted not only in indigenous peoples' impoverishment, but also in the loss of their traditional forms of communal organization.

The last contrast Beltrán draws occurs within sociocultural integration. From this process of cultural dissonance, a new culture can emerge. In the case of Latin America it was a hybrid culture (*cultura mestiza*). In countries such as the United States, a country of immigrants, immigrant ethnic groups—Mexicans, Indians, Chinese, Japanese, and Cubans (to name only a few)—have retained elements of their native cultures while devising new elements, all different from the mainstream. Acculturation contains conflicts and resistance. Trueba (2000) describes such conflicts (exploitation, discrimination, resistance, and integration) within a second generation of Mexican women farm workers in California. The sociocultural integration process named by Beltrán creates a *mestizaje*. The group is no longer the original one but preserves part of the old culture as it incorporates part of the new one. However, the concept of cultural integration does not seem adequate to explain the processes of *mestizaje* or fusion that the curriculum field has undergone in Ibero-America.

Hybridity

Néstor García Canclini, an Argentinean anthropologist living in Mexico, coined a concept that can help us understand this *mestizaje* or fusion that the curriculum field has undergone since the 1973 Spanish translation of Tyler's *Basic Principles of Curriculum and Instruction*. García Canclini understands by hybridity all "sociocultural processes where discrete structures or practices that existed separately combine themselves to generate new structures, objects and practices" (2000, 8). This category is common in cultural studies. An example Canclini provides is "Spanglish," which was born in the United States within the Spanish-speaking communities. Spanish itself is a hybrid language, derived from Latin but with words from Arabic added. Latin America is a living example of hybridity. The mixture of Spanish and Portuguese colonizers, followed by the English and Africans (later by Germans and Italians in South America), has made the *mestizaje* a foundational process in these nations.

García Canclini (2003, 3) proposes shifting the object of the identity that we study to heterogeneity and intercultural hybridity. He argues that globalization is one more reason to emphasize the concepts of *mestizaje* and hybridity. The concept of identity is static, but modern and postmodern cultures are in constant change. Globalization produces not only *mestizajes*, Canclini (2005, 1) notes, but also inequalities:

> Hybridity implies reconciliation among adverse cultures; it is a notion that tries to picture the condition of the contemporary cultures in which there are several mixes between the educated and the popular, the traditional and

the modern, the national and the foreign. These mixes, moreover, can happen in several manners.

Nevertheless, as Canclini (1995, 1997) has argued, hybridism occurs within contradictions and inequalities. It is not a matter of "a relationship of mere dependency, but rather a more complex circulation of ideas, albeit not devoid of its own hierarchies and exclusions" (Kokotovic, 2000, 289). As Lopes (2008) points out, the attempt to build consensus tends to mask conflicts in the struggle for new hegemonies.

Cosmopolitanism

"I am a man; I consider nothing human is alien to me." This sentence of Terence, born in Cartago, is well known in Mexico. Being cosmopolitan goes beyond dressing fashionably, or speaking several languages, or appreciating exotic foods and feeling at home in a foreign city. It also means that there is more than one home, and that one feels at home in the world (Hannerz, 2006). For Hannerz (1990, 239), "cosmopolitanism in a strict sense includes a stance toward diversity itself, toward the coexistence of cultures in the individual experience. A more genuine cosmopolitanism is first of all an orientation, a willingness to engage with the Other." In order to be cosmopolitan, living in a big city or being highly educated is not necessary. Ferguson (cited in Hannerz 2006) has found cosmopolitanism in Zambia's mining zone, where people have not traveled frequently.

According to Hannerz (2006, 16), the United States and Europe "have increasingly lost their cosmopolitanism because of a concept of cosmopolitanism that considers Western culture to be definitionally universal and therefore automatically cosmopolitan." Cosmopolitanism means the opening of human beings, boundaries, and states. As the German sociologist Ulrich Beck (2008, 6) states,

> We require a cosmopolitan point of view in order to be able to perceive the reality of the interweaving of people and cities all over the world; the common conceptual denominator of our dense world is "cosmopolitanism," that is: the erosion of clear frontiers that separate markets, states, civilizations, cultures and, last but not least, the human being's vital environments.

There are several kinds of cosmopolitanism, then: cultural, political, moral, and economic. Cultural cosmopolitanism is related to "the ability to make one's way into other cultures and the appreciative openness to divergent cultural experiences" (Hannerz, 2006, 13). Cosmopolitanism that is political "has to do with global government and governance, with world citizenship and responsibility toward humanity" (Hannerz 2006, 14). Moral cosmopolitanism can be defined as commitment to helping human beings regardless of social or political affiliation (Kleingeld and Brown 2006).

Perhaps the oldest antecedent of cosmopolitanism found in the curriculum literature is Moreira and Macedo's work (2000). Moreira's later works have been more oriented toward multiculturalism (Moreira 2001). According to David Hansen (2008, 294), cosmopolitanism goes beyond multiculturalism and educational pluralism; cosmopolitanism "does not privilege already formed communities. It seeks to defend emerging spaces for new cultural and social configurations reflective of the intensifying intermingling of people, ideas, and activities the world over." For Hansen (2010) a cosmopolitan education must strike a balance between the local and the global world; it presupposes a local socialization into language, values, and ways of moving about the world. Such education supports multicultural education projects as well as liberal education projects that allow detachment from local traditions and legacies. It also favors the formation of local and universal values along with critical openness and tolerance to the heterogeneity of human life. Hansen (2010) demonstrates such education through analyses of various educational projects in the United States and England.

The teacher in a cosmopolitan curriculum, Hansen (2008) suggests, underlines the quest for meaning within any school subject. This search transcends the search for knowledge in an instrumental manner. The teacher, Hansen continues, will conceive the curriculum as providing students with knowledge of both the local and larger worlds. He quotes Dewey's observation that "learning from all the contacts of life does not imply dispersing self or community" (Hansen 2010, 13). For Hansen (2010) several of the educators of our time have been cosmopolitan, among them were Maria Montessori and Dewey himself. The name of Paulo Freire could also be added to the list.

Acculturation and Hybridity before the Birth of the Curriculum Field (1800–1950)

It must be emphasized that the Latin American countries share a similar cultural legacy: they were Spanish or Portuguese colonies. The countries from the Iberian Peninsula southward were colonies in what became known as Ibero-America. Under the domain of Spain and Portugal, a compulsive, collective, induced, and continuous acculturation occurred. The colonial governments exported their educational system to the colonies in order to educate the elite. Indians had little access to education. Not until the twentieth century did the Spanish colonies became independent. The new countries still looked to Europe in order to organize the curriculum.

Historical instances of curricular acculturation are numerous. Recall, for instance, that the Jesuits' curriculum not only prevailed in Spain but was also transplanted in Brazil and Mexico (Monés 1999; Moreira 1990; Meneses 1983). Moving in the other direction, the wealthy classes of Latin America sent their children to Europe (especially France) to be educated. Later, European models were again imported, as in Latin American governments' adoption of the Lacasterian (or "mutual learning") method. In this method, outstanding students taught the less gifted. Invented by the Spanish Jesuit Lorenzo Ortiz in the seventeenth century, the concept was adopted in France by Harbault (1747), practiced by the religious order of Escolapios in Madrid (1780), improved by Andrew Bell in India, and then transferred to England (1789), where it was finally perfected by Joseph Lacanster, after whom it was named (Meneses 1983).

Another example of curricular acculturation was the importation of the ideas of Herbert Spencer and Auguste Comte. Gabino Barreda, the Mexican philosopher and educator, was a disciple of Comte (Larroyo 1970). At the end of the nineteenth century and beginning of the twentieth century, the educational ideas of Herbart, Froebel, and Johann Heinrich Pestalozzi were also imported. Also at this time, in both Spain and Latin America, another curricular movement known as *escuela nueva* (new school) was imported (Monés 1999; Moreira 1990; Meneses 1998). Other educational concepts brought to Mexico included those formulated by Ovide Decroly, Celestine Freinet, María Montessori, and particularly John Dewey.

Contrary to common belief, Dewey did not became known in Latin America through the United States, but through Spain, which remains one of the most important channels through which Latin America becomes acquainted with the educational innovations produced in Europe and the United States. After Japan, Spain was the second country to translate Dewey's *My Pedagogic Creed*. Part of this work was translated to Catalan in 1899 shortly after its English edition; then it was translated to Spanish. Dewey had a profound influence on the innovations proposed by the great Mexican philosopher and educator José Vasconcelos, organizer of the Mexican public education in the early twentieth century (Nubiola and Sierra 2001).

The Spanish Civil War (1936–1939) caused the diaspora of Spanish pedagogues working on the renowned *Institución Libre de Eseñanza* (Free

Learning Institution), who were forced into exile in Mexico, Costa Rica, and Argentina. These pedagogues in exile also influenced other countries in the region, such as Colombia, Venezuela, and Chile. The ideas of *Institución Libre de Eseñanza* were inspired by Dewey, Freinet, Decroly, Montessori, and the German philosophers Georg Wilhelm Frederich Hegel and Karl Christian Friedrich Krause (Negrín 1999). In Mexico, the ideas from the new school in the institutions created by the Spanish pedagogues tended to use Freinet's pedagogy more than that of any other pedagogue from the new school. The educational platform of Patricio Redondo and Ramón Costa Jou, two of the pedagogues from this institution who immigrated to Mexico, was inspired mainly in its use of the Freinet method (Costa Jou 1974). In Brazil, the new school movement was established by Fernando de Azevedo, Anísio Teixeira, and Lourenço Filho (Moreira 1990), educated in Brazil, Europe, and the United States.

One remarkable example of the circulation of pedagogical ideas among Latin American countries recalls the foundation of the Regional Center for Basic Education for Latin America (CREFAL) at the end of the 1950s. At the suggestion from UNESCO, this institution was dedicated to adult education. The institution's pedagogical creed was a product of the prominent Latin American pedagogues. These pedagogues had been influenced, Rivas (2003) points out, by the works of Erich Kahler, Clyde Kluckhohn, Karl Mannheim, José Ortega y Gasset, John Dewey, and Max Weber. From this hybridity process, a fusion resulted: Latin American adult education.

Another example is the influence of Brazil's educational ideas on the consolidation of the Argentinian school movement through the educator Lourenço Filho. His book *Introduction to the Study of the New School* was published in Argentina two years after it had been published in Brazil. It was so well accepted that Argentineans considered it one of the fundamental works in Latin American pedagogy (Jafella 2002). Filho's work was also influential in Mexico and other Latin American countries. Since the early 1960s, the ABC Lourenço Filho test has been used to measure the readiness for writing and reading in school children.

Summarizing, processes of acculturation and hybridity in Ibero-America were (1) the result of the intermingling of the pedagogical ideas or curriculum theories from Spain and other European countries; which followed (2) the mixture of the Spanish pedagogical ideas with those from the United States; which precipitated (3) a mixing of Spanish pedagogical ideas with those already circulating in Latin American countries; which encouraged (4) an exchange of these ideas among Latin American countries; which has resulted in (5) a hybridity of pedagogical ideas circulating among Latin America, Spain, and Portugal.

The Curriculum Field in Ibero-America

Acculturation

The initial acculturation of Anglo-Saxon curriculum studies into Ibero-America took place in a context of modernization and renewal (Appadurai 1996). Brazil was the first country to establish cultural contact with the Tylerian curriculum tradition in the United States. This contact was coincident with the modernization process of the 1950s led by President Getúlio Vargas. Argentina was the second country in the curriculum acculturation process, which began at the end of the 1960s. In Mexico, after the student movement of 1968 was crushed by paramilitary and military forces, killing hundreds of students, the new administration headed by President Luis Echeverría made an unprecedented effort toward democratization and educational renewal. The establishment of new universities accompanied comprehensive educational reform. It was in this context that the curriculum acculturation process took place.

Although there is a general agreement regarding the stages the development of the curriculum field has undergone—(1) adoption of the technical-rational Tylerian model; (2) incorporation of critical theory; and (3) the consolidation of the field—these stages were not homogeneous in each country. For instance, the Spanish acculturation did not coincide with the translation of Tyler and Hilda Taba (who never had much influence in Spain), but, rather, with the arrival of the critical theory that overlaps the end of the Franquist dictatorship and the beginning of the democratic phase, causing Moreno (1998) to assert that curriculum studies entered Spain through the back door.

Moreover, acculturation occurred sometimes through individuals, and sometimes through collectivities. In Brazil, for instance, it was during the government of President Juscelino Kubitschek that the Program of American Brazilian Assistance to Elementary Education was created, training Brazilian teachers in curriculum planning and design. In 1955 the first Brazilian book on curriculum was published, Roberto Moreira's *Introducao ao estudo da escola primária* (Introduction to the Study of Primary School). As a UNESCO consultant, Hilda Tabla lectured throughout Brazil at the end of 1950s (Moreira 1990; Krull 2003). Brazil was the only Ibero-American country to be visited by this author of Estonian descent and disciple of Tyler (Moreira 2003).

In the case of Argentina, the curriculum field was started through the Alliance for Progress, President John F. Kennedy's initiative for US cooperation with Latin America in the early 1960s. Working with the Organization of American States, UNESCO and other agencies promoted the translation into Spanish and Portuguese of US works and the establishment of national centers for curriculum development (Palamidessi and Feldmann 2003). Mexico was part of these cooperation agreements through which Mexican publishing houses translated several books. Curiously, translations of Tyler's and Taba's works, the most influential in Ibero-America at that time, were not on the list of books promoted by the US government (Furlán 1998). Argentinian publishers (Troquel) undertook their translation in 1973 and 1976, respectively. During the 1960s and 1970s, Argentina was the largest producer of educational books in Ibero-America. Production in Spain was still limited. Now, roles have been reversed: Spain is the largest exporter to Spanish-speaking countries.

Hybridity

Moreira (1990) introduced the topic of hybridity, pointing out that the curriculum field in Brazil had been established under the influence of the United States. He characterized this process as educational borrowing, which he understood to be the movement of ideas and institutional models and practices from one country to another. Later, Moreira (2003) and Lopes and Macedo (2003), inspired by García Cancilini's ideas, called this process curricular hybridity. Lopes (2005, 2008) has made the most important contributions to the understanding of this process. Lopes (2005, 2) states that hybridity occurred through the association of the Neo-Marxist, phenomenologist, and interactionist-based criticism theories linked to the postmodern, post-structural, and postcolonial discourses. In her pioneer analysis of hybridity in the educational reforms, Lopes (2005) documents contradictions and inequalities that took place during the Brazilian curriculum reform that established curriculum standards for secondary education.

Another example of hybridity concerns the very adoption of the term "curriculum." The concept was not introduced through Latin (where it originated) but, rather, through the Anglo-Saxon literature (Moreno 1998). In Mexico curriculum has meant the *course of study* (*plano de estudios*). While in Brazil the term "curriculum" circulates now in everyday language (Pedra 1997), in Argentina the term remains more specialized (Palamidessi and Feldman 2003). In Spain, the concept was imported from Latin America (Moreno 1998), presumably through the first translations published in Argentina.

In Mexico, the curriculum field was focused not on elementary or secondary education, as has been the case in many countries, but rather on higher education. Ángel Díaz Barriga (2003) maintains that this followed from the centralization of control of the elementary-secondary school curriculum. Higher education in Mexico, however, has historically enjoyed relative autonomy. It was this intellectual autonomy—the opportunity to compose curriculum—that focused curriculum studies in Mexico.

The first influential work of curriculum studies in Mexico was written by Glazman and De Ibarrola (1978), published for the first time in 1974. Without a doubt, this was the most influential work of the 1970s. No orthodox adaptation of the Tylerian or Taba model, this work is hybrid, bearing more resemblance to the conceptual-empiricist approach described by Pinar (1975) than to the traditional Tylerian model. Glazman and de Ibarrola forefronted behavioral objectives in the systemic planning of teaching, employing content analysis in curriculum planning and development, and emphasizing evaluation. In Mexico, according to Tylerian tenets, evaluation was considered a sub-discipline integrated into curriculum planning. This phenomenon may indicate that in this country educational evaluation had not yet established itself as an independent field.

In the 1980s critical theory flourished, as the region experienced the worst economic crisis in its recent history. Brazil and Argentina suffered four-digit inflation rates while in Mexico it reached three digits. Latin America had a huge foreign debt, indeed considered to be impossible to pay. Several countries, including Argentina and Brazil, declared default. In Latin America the 1980s is known as the lost decade. But not in curriculum studies.

The first critical questioning of the technical-rational approach in Ibero-America occurred in Argentina. Azucena Rodríguez, one of the academics who migrated to Mexico during the dictatorship, published the first text questioning the Tyler Rationale in 1972, only two years after Kliebard (1970) conducted what became one of the first and most influential criticisms of the Tyler Rationale. Due to the military coup, the development of critical curriculum theory was interrupted and it was resumed only after halfway into the 1980s when a democratic government was established (Palamidessi and Feldman 2003). There is no question that the development of the curriculum field was connected with the development of democracy. The exile of curriculum experts delayed the process of creation of the curriculum field in Argentina. After several years in Mexico, several scholars returned to Argentina, among them Roberto Follari. Others, such as Alfredo Furlán, live in Mexico, while maintaining close contact with their native country.

The incorporation of critical theory into the Brazilian curriculum field occurred in the 1970s. Freire was the inspiration of this trend (Moreira 1990, 2003). However, it was the 1980s that saw a tremendous increase in foreign influence, mainly from European scholars and, secondarily, from North Americans (Lopes 2003). The acculturation process was not collective or induced; rather, it was composed of individual actions by curriculum experts. Despite Freire's impact on Brazilian critical theory in the 1970s, over the long term it would seem that his work has been more influential outside Brazil (judging by how frequently his work is cited in the Brazilian curriculum literature). For example, Moreira (1990) cited two of Freire's works; in contrast, Giroux cited Freire ten times.

Moreira's (1990) *Currículos e programas no Brasil* was a best-seller; it has had 15 printings, the last one was in 2008. Paulo Coelho, the famous Brazilian writer, would be envious of Moreira; his book has not been translated into Spanish. With the exception of Argentina, in the Hispanic world there is little familiarity with Brazil's curriculum studies. That is the case despite the fact that Hispanic America knows more about and is more influenced by Brazil than is Brazil by its Spanish-speaking neighbors. Language is one barrier. Although there exists a certain similarity between the two languages, some Portuguese speakers consider Spanish a badly spoken Portuguese, and some Spanish speakers have similar views on Portuguese. It is easier for Portuguese speakers to learn Spanish than it is for Spanish speakers to learn Portuguese.

Besides soccer and music, Spanish-speaking Latin America has been influenced by two renowned Brazilian pedagogues whose works have been translated into Spanish—Lourenco Filho and Paulo Freire. More recently, another notable influence in Mexico (although not of the same magnitude as that of Freire) has been Giomar Namo de Mello (1998). His work, whose original title is *Administrative Models for the Satisfaction of Learning's Basic Needs*, was translated by Mexico's Public Education Ministry in cooperation with UNESCO and the Organization of American States. A million copies were printed for distribution to elementary school teachers. Brazil is becoming an increasingly important presence throughout Latin America; more and more Brazilian scholars publish in Spanish language educational journals and are invited to serve as keynote speakers at educational conferences.

In Mexico, at the beginning of the 1980s, the technical-rationalistic curriculum model began to be criticized (Aristi and Furlán 1982; Díaz Barriga, A. 1982; Remedí 1982). As noted, a number of young exiled Argentinean scholars found positions at Mexican institutions, particularly at Mexico's National Autonomous University. It was they—Azucena Rodríguez, Alfredo Furlán, Eduardo Remedí, and Roberto Follari—together with the Mexican Ángel Díaz Barriga, who started to question the technical-rational curriculum model. The best-known critique of the model was made by Ángel Díaz Barriga, expressed in his most important and famous work in Ibero-America, *Didactica y Curriculum* (1984a). He questions the Tyler Rationale and proposes alternative conceptions of curriculum development; the book is well-known and widely cited in Spain and Argentina. Díaz Barriga was a passionate critic of the Tyler Rationale and of educational technology, especially of US industrial or efficiency pedagogy. He wrote,

> Enough North-American pedagogy! Let our intellectuals commit themselves to studying our educational problems using categories that can allow them to explain their real meaning; they don't need to go on reading the latest from the Educational Technology Service in order to translate and summarize them in Spanish. This is not research because it does not produce knowledge, yet, on the other hand, it constitutes a dangerous cultural penetration. (Díaz Barriga 1984b, 7)

Ángel Díaz Barriga acknowledged the contribution to his work made by his Argentinean colleagues. Unlike in Spain, where it arrived from Great Britain and North America, critical curriculum theory had came to Mexico through the Argentinean academics in exile. They had been influenced by the readings of Gramsci and the Neo-Marxist pedagogues such as the Frenchman George Snyders and the Italian Mario Manacorda. They were also influenced by Latin American sociologists' (Brazilian, Argentinean, and Chilean) dependency theory in which the developed countries were positioned at the center and Latin America at the periphery. Later those academics, together with Ángel Díaz Barriga and Alicia de Alba, incorporated into their views contributions from the Frankfurt School and other neo-Marxist authors.

In the mid-1980s ideas from North American critical theory (e.g., Apple, Giroux, McLaren, and Pinar) were incorporated; Alicia de Alba's work is an example of this (De Alba 1986). The most hybrid work incorporating French, British, and North American authors is certainly Alfredo Furlán's doctoral thesis that he defended at the University of Paris V, Rene Descartes, in 1986 (Furlán 1998). In this work Furlán made a severe criticism of the Tyler Rationale and the ideology of curriculum discourses. Furlán's work makes the first Mexican reference to Pinar's edited book (1975) *Curriculum Theorizing: The Reconceptualists*. At first Furlán's work was little known outside specialized academic circles, but another more widely read edition was published eight years later (Furlán 1988). Furlán's original dissertation in French is cited by Moreira (1990).

In Spain, the political situation gave rise to the adoption of the critical curriculum theory. The country was undergoing a process of change in all of its political, social, economic, and educational structures after the death of the dictator Francisco Franco in 1976. In less than a decade, the curriculum field in Spain managed to produce original scholarship that became widely known throughout Ibero-America. Moreno (1998) calls this period the rising years. According to Bolívar (1998), Gimeno Sacristán's book (1982), wherein he criticizes behavioral objectives, marks the end of the technical-rationalistic curriculum era in Spain, an end that has yet to happen in Mexico. Sacristán's work was inspired by Raymond Callahan's (1962) classic work. Sacristán maintains that the behavioral objectives express a cult of efficiency. A clear instance of hybridity, Gimeno's work incorporates references from US and UK scholarship, among them is the American Michael Apple's *Ideology and Curriculum*. Gimeno Sacristán also played an important role in translating British curriculum scholars.

Teoría y Desarrollo del Currículo (*Curriculum Theory and Development*), the first major Spanish book on curriculum, was also written by Gimeno Sacristán and published one year before his decisive critique of behavior objectives. In it Sacristán (1981) questions the technical-rational theory, referencing British, American, and French scholars, as well as translations made in Argentina and Mexico. Sacristán's (1988) most important book is, however, *El Currículum: Una Reflexión Sobre la Práctica* (*The Curriculum: A Reflection on its Practice*). In it the references cited are mainly to UK and US scholarship. This is the best known and most popular book on curriculum in Spanish. It is frequently cited in Spain and in Latin America, from Mexico to Patagonia, including Brazil. It is an example of hybridity between Tylerian traditionalism and critical theory. It has become a true best-seller (eight printings so far).

The arrival of the curriculum critical theory in Spain shows that hybridity does not always occur in logical and organized ways. Through Spain, Hispanic America became acquainted with texts from Adorno, Habermas, and Foucault. Yet, as Bolívar (1998) acknowledges, it was through *American* scholars that critical theory was incorporated in Spain. Hybridity processes are obviously not linear. The ideas of one scholar sometimes goes unnoticed; sometimes it takes an outside agent to demonstrate their value. Freire is the most outstanding case. Mexican and Spanish publishing houses had translated Freire's work since the beginning of the 1970s, but it was through Henry Giroux that Spanish curriculum scholars discovered him (Bolívar 1998). Hybridity may happen haphazardly. Henry Giroux (2007, 141) describes how he met Freire:

> I met Paulo in the early 1980s, right after I was fired by John Silber, the Rector of Boston University. Paulo was at the University of Massachusetts lecturing and I invited him over for dinner at my house. His modesty did not at all match his reputation, and I remember that he greeted me with so much warmth and sincerity that I immediately felt at ease with him. We talked for a long time about his exile, my dismissal, about what it meant to be different and at the end of the evening a strong friendship had developed

between the two of us; a friendship that would last until his death, 15 years later. At that time I felt very depressed at having been fired and I had no idea what the future might hold for me. I am sure that, had it not been for Paulo and Donaldo Macedo, another friend of Paulo's, I would not have remained in the education field.

How would the development of the critical theory have been affected if Giroux had left the education field? We cannot know, but the critical theory of our time would not have been the same. Maybe the discovery of Freirean theory by the Anglo-Saxon world and by Spain would have taken a while longer.

At the end of the 1980s and beginning of the 1990s, postmodern and post-structuralist theory emerged in Brazil and Mexico and their most visible representatives are Tomaz Tadeus da Silva and Alicia de Alba, respectively. In Mexico, if to a lesser degree, has occurred what Lopes (2003, 10) observed in Brazil: "one of the main traits of current Brazilian curricular thought is the blending of postmodernist discourses with the focus of politics characterized by critical theorization." This has been the most recent phase of hybridity of the Ibero-American curriculum field.

On the Emergence of Cosmopolitanism

In the case of Ibero-America, there are indications that processes of cosmopolitanism are underway. However, they are not completely clear. The most outstanding trait of cosmopolitanism is an openness to other trends and scholarship, the acceptance of different points of view without losing one's own. Curriculum journals that exist in Brazil and in Spain publish articles from both Latin American and Anglo-Saxon scholars. An attitude of cooperation among Ibero-American curriculum experts can be seen. The Spaniards seem to be the most cosmopolitan: they travel frequently to Mexico and other countries in the region to give courses and conferences; they have also established cooperation networks with academics from Mexico and other Latin American countries. Spanish curriculum experts, mainly César Coll and Gimeno Sacristán, have assisted in curriculum reforms in Brazil, Chile, and Argentina (Rigo, F. Díaz Barriga, and Hernández 2005; Lopez 2008). César Coll keeps close contact with academics from the UNAM (National Autonomous University of Mexico). Argentinean publishing houses have published Ángel Díaz Barriga. Apparently, without fear of losing their locality, the Ibero-American curriculum experts are beginning to show some signs of cosmopolitanism.

There is still a much work to do, but the way is being paved. The traits of cosmopolitanism seem clearer on an international level. It could be said that they started to formally manifest themselves with the establishment of the International Association for the Advancement of Curriculum Studies (IAACS), an initiative of William Pinar. When the subject turns one century old, after the formal establishment of the first curriculum university course in 1912 by John Franklin Bobbitt, IAACS will meet in South America, and its progress toward curriculum cosmopolitanism will continue. IAACS is a cosmopolitan organization, as its mission indicates:

> The International Association for the Advancement of Curriculum Studies is established to support a worldwide—but not uniform—field of curriculum studies. At this historical moment and for the foreseeable future, curriculum inquiry occurs within national borders, often informed by governmental policies and priorities, responsive to national situations. Curriculum study is, therefore, nationally distinctive. The founders of the IAACS do not dream of a worldwide field of curriculum studies mirroring the standardization and uniformity the larger phenomenon of globalization threatens. Nor are we unaware of the dangers of narrow nationalisms. Our hope, in establishing this organization, is to provide support for scholarly conversations within and across national and regional borders about the content, context, and process of education, the organizational and intellectual center of which is the curriculum.

As evident in this language, the IAACS mission is to cosmopolitize the curriculum field by learning from all the contacts of life, as Dewey used to say. The IAACS mission matches one marker of educational cosmopolitanism: it does not privilege already formed communities (Hansen 2010, 294). It seeks to clear emerging spaces for new cultural and social configurations reflective of the intensifying intermingling of people, ideas, and activities worldwide. IAACS encourages openness to other points of view, cultures, and frontiers.

The Institutionalization of the Curriculum Field in Ibero-America

The consolidation of the curriculum field in Ibero-America can be assessed by the degree of institutionalization of the field. According to Khun (1962), the institutionalization of a field of knowledge takes place by way of two basic processes in constant interaction: the adoption of one or more paradigms and the creation of a scientific community dedicated to the cultivation (through research and scholarship) of present and emerging paradigms. The adoption of a paradigm and the creation of a scientific community require certain practices, conditions, and artifacts that promote the interaction of its members in and outside the community. These processes can be summarized as the field's *institutionalization*. In this section I will explore the institutionalization level of the curriculum field in Ibero-America by means of three basic indicators: (1) training of new members of curriculum community; (2) the presence of professional associations and research networks providing opportunities for the communication of published research; and (3) international exchange with other curriculum communities.

The formulation of a paradigm requires educating new members of the curriculum community. In the curriculum field, as in any other discipline, the education (or formation) of new members takes place mainly through doctoral programs. The older and more numerous the programs dedicated to the formation of new researchers and professors in the field, the higher the level of institutionalization. Internationally, the United States has the highest level of institutionalization: the first doctoral programs in education were founded at Teachers College at the end of the nineteenth century; the first curriculum course was taught by Franklin Bobbitt in the University of Chicago in 1912; also, around this time, the first doctoral dissertations on curriculum appeared. By the 1940s, curriculum courses were commonplace in the education schools of North American universities (Seguel 1966).

In the case of Ibero-America, the level of institutionalization can be appraised by analyzing how old doctoral programs dedicated to education (especially to curriculum) are, as well as by the number of doctoral programs accredited by national agencies. There are few doctoral programs specializing in curriculum. Brazil boasts the highest degree of institutionalization in training new members of the scientific curriculum community. In 1975 the first master's degree program in curriculum studies in South America was created in the Pontifícia Universidade Católica de Sao Paulo (PUC-SP). This institution also created Brazil's first doctoral program in 1990. Brazil has 45 doctoral programs accredited by Coordenação de Aperfeiçoamento de Pessoal de Nível Superior (CAPES 2009); CAPES is the oldest Ibero-American accreditation agency founded in the early 1950s.

After Brazil, the second highest degree of institutionalization is found in Spain. Although this country has less than a third of the doctoral programs accredited (14) by the *Ministerio de Ciencia e Innovación* (2008), recently the program *Curriculum, Faculty and Educational Institutions* offered by the University of Granada was accredited. Other accredited doctorate educational programs such as the ones from Córdoba and Málaga have research lines focused on curriculum. However, in neither of these two countries do independent curriculum departments exist. Often in Brazil as in Spain doctoral programs are located within Didactics departments, the equivalent of the designation (Department of Curriculum and Instruction) used by the education schools in the United States. In Chile and Costa Rica some university departments have adopted this US designation.

Mexico and Argentina have lower levels of institutionalization than Spain and Brazil. Although Argentina has a larger number of programs accredited (12) by the *Comisión de Evaluación y Acreditación Universitaria* (CONEAU 2008) than those approved by the *Consejo Nacional de Ciencia y Tecnología de México* (7) (CONACYT 2008), the accreditation of Mexican graduate programs seems to be stricter, bearing more resemblance to the rigor of accreditation in Brazil and Spain. The pedagogy doctoral program at the UNAM is the only program that has showed a consistent research line focused on curriculum studies. As early as the 1970s, María de Ibarrola and Raquel Glazman gave seminars focused on curriculum at the UNAM. In 1972 the *Associación Nacional de Universidades e Institutos de Enseñanza Superior* (ANUIES)—National Association of Universities and Institutes of Higher Education—opened a course on curriculum planning for teachers (Ángel Díaz Barriga, personal communication July 2009). In Mexico, unlike in Brazil and Spain, curriculum institutionalization has been associated with higher educations reforms. The influence of curriculum experts on K-12 education reforms in Mexico is not very significant.

Research in education is associated with doctoral programs. Brazil is the largest producer of curriculum research. During the 1996–2006 period its programs produced 92 curriculum doctoral dissertations in elementary education alone (Lopes and Macedo 2007). Spain comes in second: during the same period at least 80 doctoral theses focused on curriculum were produced (Ministry of Education 2009). In Mexico and Argentina the production of doctoral theses on the topic is limited, but no comprehensive databases on educational doctoral theses are available, confirming that Brazil and Spain are ahead on the level of institutionalization of research on curriculum.

Despite the fact that the number of doctoral theses is one indicator of the degree of institutionalization of the curriculum research, research conducted by scholars and by students associated with doctoral programs and its publication (through indexed journals, books, and professional meetings) reveals even more clearly the degree of institutionalization of the field. Again Brazil exhibits the highest degree of institutionalization; it has three journals, all released in the current decade and all dedicated to publishing research in curriculum studies: *Curriculum sem Fronteiras* (*Curriculum without Borders*), *E-curriculum*, and the recently created *Espaço do Currículum* (*The Curriculum Corner*). Non-specialized education journals regularly publish curriculum research, among them: *Educacao e Sociedade*, (*Education and Society*), *Revista Brasileira de Educacao*, (*Brazilian Education Review*), *Educação e Realidade* (*Education and Reality*) (Lopes, personal communication, July 2009). Several of these journals are indexed.

After Brazil, Spain presents the highest degree of institutionalization. The University of Granada has been publishing the *Revista de Curriculum y Formación del Profesorado* (*Curriculum and Faculty Development Review*) since 1997. In 1998 the journal *Estudios de Curriculum* (*Curriculum Studies*) was created, but it ceased publication in the year 2000. *Revista Iberoamericana de Educación* (*Iberoamerican Review of Education*), sponsored by the Organization of Ibero-American States and RELIEVE, specializing in evaluation and featuring a 93 percent rejection rate (possibly the highest among the educational journals in Ibero-America and comparable with the most prestigious education journals in the United States and England), also publishes articles on curriculum.

In Mexico and Argentina there are no journals specializing in curriculum. In Mexico there are indexed research journals that publish curriculum research, among them *Revista Electrónica de Investigación Educativa* (*Electronic Review of Educational Research*), one of the most visited e-journals, as well as the *Revista Mexicana de Investigación Educativa* (*Mexican Review of Educational Research*). Unlike in Brazil and Spain, where curriculum research is mainly focused on elementary and secondary education, 71 percent of Mexico's research on curriculum is concentrated on higher education (Díaz Barriga, F. 2005). During the 1990–2002 period, 652 studies about curriculum were carried out, but only 16 percent of these qualify as research; one-third reports on projects of curriculum development (Díaz Barriga, F. 2005). Argentina appears to have the lowest degree of institutionalization; research in curriculum studies in that country is not very significant. Feeney and Teregi (2003) state that between 1983 and 1998, 29 books and only 25 articles were published. The military dictatorships of the 1970s can be blamed for the underdevelopment of the field (Palamidessi and Feldman 2003).

Another indicator of the field's institutionalization is the establishment of professional associations and other specialized research groups to report and publish research results. Going by this indicator, Brazil has the highest level of institutionalization. As early as 1986 Brazilian scholars formed research groups for the study of curriculum. Prominent among these are *Grupo de Trabahlo de Currículo da Associação de Pós-graduação e Pesquisa em Educação* (ANPEd), *Núcleo de Estudos de Currículo* (NEC) of the Federal University of Rio de Janeiro (UFRJ), and *Laboratório de Educação e Imagem* and *Currículo Sujeitos, Conhecimento e Cultura* (led by Alice Casimiro Lopes and Elizabeth Macedo). There are several regional research groups also dedicated to curriculum studies (Lopes, personal communication, October 10, 2009).

Mexico might feature the second highest level of institutionalization in curriculum research. Government agencies in Mexico, like those in Spain and Brazil, finance educational research. Curriculum-related research groups started in 1981 with the organization of the first National Conference on Educational Research where, for the first time, a review of the state of research of the existing knowledge on the curriculum field was presented. In 1993 the Mexican Council for Educational Research (similar to the American Educational Research Association [AERA]) was founded; it organizes the National Seminar on Education Research every two years. One of the sections of this seminar is dedicated to the presentation of research on curriculum and evaluation.

Although Spain might have the highest institutionalization level in relation to educational research as a whole, formal curriculum research groups are few. Among those agencies that finance research, *el Centro de Investigación y Documentación Educativa* (CIDE) is a part of the Ministry of Education and Culture that stimulates and publishes research conducted at different institutions of higher education. In the mid-1980s, a national award honoring the best educational research was created, followed in the 1990s by an award honoring the best doctoral dissertation research in education. Interculturality, inequality, and values are among recurring curriculum themes in Spain. As Moreira (2001) suggests, there remains a lack of consensus concerning what is distinctively research in curriculum. In Argentina no formal groups or associations dedicated to funding and publishing curriculum research exist.

The last indicator of curriculum institutionalization I will consider is contact between national associations and their international peers. In this category, Brazil and Spain feature the highest degree of institutionalization. British, Spanish, North American, and Portuguese scholars frequently write in their respective curriculum journals and speak at their respective conferences. Spanish curriculum experts and, more recently, Brazilian scholars are regularly invited to the National Seminar on Educational Research that takes place in Mexico every two years.

More and more Brazilian curriculum scholars publish in journals written in Spanish, while several of their Spanish counterparts publish articles in Brazilian and Mexican journals. Concerning international exchange of curriculum experts with their peers, Mexico comes in second. In an initiative by Ángel Díaz Barriga, the Ibero-American Network of Curriculum Researchers, which assembles researchers from several countries of the region, was created. Although Argentina enjoys a certain international presence, it seems to present a lower institutionalization level in this area.

In general it can be seen that Brazil features the highest level of institutionalization in the curriculum field, followed by Spain and Mexico; Argentina features the lowest institutionalization level.

Conclusion

The purpose of this study was to analyze the institutionalization of the curriculum field in Argentina, Brazil, Spain, and Mexico. Even though the study is exploratory, it is possible to say that the development of the curriculum field in Ibero-America has already undergone two phases (acculturation and hybridity) and is currently undergoing a third one (cosmopolitanism).

The analyzed countries have experienced acculturation and hybridity processes that are somewhat similar. In the pre-Tylerian period, the "new school movement" was strongly influenced by Dewey. Brazil was the first country to enter the Tylerian or technical-rationalistic era, followed by Argentina and, later, Mexico. In the case of Spain, the date of entrance into this era is not very clear, as in the 1970s (when Tyler was imported into Brazil and Mexico) Spain embraced critical curriculum theory. The translation of British and North American curriculum experts influenced this phenomenon. Curiously enough, Argentina had embraced critical curriculum theory before any of the other analyzed countries. It was a local event, free of influence from the Anglo-Saxon curricularists. Argentinean critical curriculum theory arrived in Mexico by way of the exiled Argentinean scholars fleeing the military dictatorship. Later, this Mexican-Argentinean work mixed with the critical theory from North America and Great Britain. In this regard, it is curious that Freire's influence came through Anglo-Saxon critical theory, although he had already been translated into Spanish since the early 1970s. The cosmopolitanism moment is recent, and its signs are just now becoming visible. One of the first important signs was the establishment of the Internationalization Association for the Advancement of Curriculum Studies (IAACS).

References

Aguirre Beltrán, Gonzalo. 1970. *El Proceso de Aculturación y Cambio Cultural en México*. Mexico City: Universidad Iberoamericana.
Appadurai, Arjun. 1996. *Modernity at Large*. Minneapolis: University of Minnesota Press.
Aristi, Patricia, and Alfredo Furlán. 1982. "Razón, Técnica y Currículum." *Foro Universitario* 25: 62–67.
Beck, Ulrich. 2008. "Un Nuevo Cosmopolitismo Está en el Aire." *Armas y Letras* 62. Available online at: http://www.armasyletras.uanl.
Bolívar, Antonio. 1998. "Tiempo y Contexto del Discurso Curricular en Espáña." *Revista de Currículum y Formación del Profesorado* 2(2). Available online at: http://www.ugr.es.
Carnoy, Martin. 1977. *La Educación Como Imperialismo Cultural*. Mexico City: Siglo XXI.
CONACYT. 2008. *Programa Nacional dePosgrados de Calidad (PNPC)*. Consejo Nacional de Ciencia y Tecnología: Benito Juárez. Available online at: http://www.conacyt.gob.
CONEAU. 2009. *Posgrados Acreditados*. Ministerio de Educación: Ciudad de Buenos. Available online at: http://www.coneau.gov.ar.
Coordenação de Aperfeiçoamento de Pessoal de Nível Superior. 2009. Relação de Cursos Recomendados e Reconhecidos *Mestrados/Doutorados Reconhecidos*. Brasilia: Commission for the Development of Higher Education Personnel. Available online at: http://www.capes.gov.br.
Coombs, Philip H. 1971. *La Crisis Mundial de la Educación*. Barcelona: Ediciones Península.
Costa Jou, Ramón. 1974. *Patricio Redondo y la Técnica Freinet*. Mexico City: Sepsetentas.
de Alba, Alicia. 1986. "Del Discurso Crítico al Mito del Currículum." In *Desarrollo de la Investigación en el Campo del Currículum*, ed. Alfredo Furlán and Miguel Pasillas, 13–33. Mexico City: UNAM-ENEPI.
Díaz-Barriga, Ángel. 1982. "Contradicciones en la Teoría Curricular." *Foro Universitario* 8: 46–52.
Díaz-Barriga, Ángel. 1984a. *Didáctica y Curriculum*. Mexico City: Ediciones Nuevo Mar.
Díaz-Barriga, Ángel. 1984b. *Ensayos Sobre la Problemática Curricular*. Mexico City: Trillas.
Díaz-Barriga, Ángel. 1985. "La Evolución del Discurso Curricular en México 1970–1982." *Revista Latinoaméricana de Estudios Educativos* 15 (2): 67–79.
Díaz-Barriga, Ángel. 2003. "Curriculum Research: Evolution and Outlook in Mexico." In *The International Handbook of Curriculum Research*, ed. William F. Pinar, 443–456. Mahwah, NJ: Lawrence Erlbaum Associates.
Díaz Barriga, Frida. 2005. "Desarrollo Del Currículo e Innovación: Modelos e Investigación en Los 90." *Perfiles Educativos* 27 (107): 57–84.

Feeney, Silvina, and Flavia. 2003. "Curriculum Studies in Argentina: Documenting the Constitution of a Field." In *International Handbook of Curriculum Research,* ed. William F. Pinar, 101–108. Mahwah, NJ: Lawrence Erlbaum Associates.

Furlán, Alfredo. 1998. *Ideología Del Discurso Curricular.* Culiacán, Mexico City: Universidad Autónoma de Sinaloa/ ENEPI UNAM.

García Canclini, Néstor. 1995. *Hybrid Cultures: Strategies for Entering and Leaving Modernity.* Minneapolis: University of Minnesota Press.

García Canclini, Néstor. 1997. "Culturas híbridas y estrategias comunicacionales." *Estudios Sobre Culturas Contemporáneas 3* (5): 109–128. Available online at: http://redalyc.uaemex.mx.

García Canclini, Néstor. 2000. *La Globalización: ¿Productora de Culturas Híbridas?* Actas

Del III Congreso Latinoamericano de la Asociación Internacional para el Estudio de la Música Popular, Bogota, agosto. Instituto de Historia, Pontificia Universidad Católica de Chile: Santiago. Available online at: http://www.hist.puc.cl.

García Canclini, Néstor. 2003. "Noticias Recientes Sobre la Hibridación." *Revista Transcultural de Música* 7. Available online at: http://www.sibetrans.com/trans/trans7/canclini.htm.

García Canclini, Néstor. 2005. "En Defensa de Las Lenguas. La Vigencia de la Culturas Híbridas." *Entrevista.* Available online at: http://www.aulaintercultural.org.

Gimeno Sacristán, José.1981. *Teoría y Desarrollo Del Currículo.* Madrid: Ediciones Anaya.

Gimeno Sacristán, José.1982. *La Pedagogía Por Objetivos: Obsesión Por la Eficiencia.* Madrid: Morata.

Gimeno Sacristán, José. 1988. *El Currículo una Reflexión Sobre la Práctica.* Madrid: Morata.

Glazman, Raquel, y María De Ibarrola. 1978. *Diseño de Planes de Estudio.* Mexico City: UNAM- CISE.

Hannerz, Ulf. 1990. "Cosmopolitans and Locals in World Culture." *Theory, Culture and Society* 7: 237–251.

Hannerz, Ulf. 2006. *Two Faces of Cosmopolitanism: Culture and Politics.* Barcelona: CIDOB Edicions.

Hansen, David. 2008. "Curriculum and the Idea of a Cosmopolitan Inheritance." *Journal of Curriculum Studies* 4 (3): 389–312.

Hansen, David. 2010. "Cosmopolitanism and Education: A View from the Ground." *Teachers College Record* 112 (1): 1–30.

Internacional Association for the Advancement of Curriculum Studies 2008. "Mission." International Association for the Advancement of Curriculum Studies. Available online at: http://iaacs.org.

Jafella Sara. 2002. "Escuela Nueva en Argentina y Brasil: Retrospectiva de un Ideario Pedagógico en la Formación Docente." *Revista de Pedagogía* 23 (67): 333–344. Available online at: http://www.scielo.org.ve.

Khun, Thomas. 1962. *The Structure of Scientific Revolutions.* Chicago: University of Chicago Press.

Kliebard, Herbert. 1970. "Reappraisal. The Tyler Rationale." *The School Review* 78 (2): 259–272.
Kleingeld, Pauline, and Eric Brown. 2006. "Cosmopolitanism." In *The Stanford Encyclopedia of Philosophy*. Available online at: http://plato.stanford.edu.
Kokotovic, Misha. 2000. "Hibridez y Desigualdad: García Canclini Ante el Neoliberalismo." *Revista Crítica Literaria Latinoamericana* 25 (52): 289–300.
Krull, Edgar. 2003. "Hilda Taba (1902–1967)." *Prospects* 23 (4): 481–491.
Larroyo, Franscisco. 1970. *Historia Comparada de la Educación en México*. 9th ed. México: Editorial Porrúa.
Lopes, Alice Casimiro. 2005. "Política de currículo: Recontextualização e Hibridismo." *Currículo sem Fronteiras* 5 (2): 50–64.
Lopes, Alice Casimiro. 2008. "Articulaciones en Las Pólíticas Del Currículo." *Perfiles Educativos* (120): 63–74. Available online at: http://www.scielo.org.mx.
Lopes, Alice Casimiro, and Elizabeth Fernández de Macedo. 2003. "The Curriculum Field in Brazil in the 1990s." In *The International Handbook of Curriculum Research*, ed. William F. Pinar, 185–203. Mahwah, NJ: Lawrence Erlbaum Associates.
Lopes, Alice Casimiro, and Elizabeth Macedo. 2007. *Currículo da Educação Básica*. Brasília: Ministerio da Educação, Instituto Nacional de Estudos e Pesquisas Educacionais Anísio Teixeira. Available online at: http://www.publicacoes.inep.gov.br.
Lopez, Georgia Carmena, Angel Ariza Cobos, and Eugenia Bujanda Bujanda. 2008. *El Sistema de Investigación Educativa en España*. Madrid: CIDE. Available online at: http://www.educacion.es.
Meneses Morales, Ernesto. 1983. *Tendencias Educativas Oficiales en México 1821–1911*. Mexico City: Editorial Porrúa.
Meneses Morales, Ernesto. 1986. *Tendencias Educativas Oficiales en México 1911–1934*. Mexico City: Centro de Estudios Educativos, Universidad Iberoamericana.
Ministerio de Educación. 2009. *Consulta de la Base de Tesis Doctorales (TESEO)*. Ministerio de Educación: Madrid. Available online at: https://www.micinn.es.
Ministerio de Ciencia e Innovación. 2008. *Estudios de Doctorado a Los Que se Concede la Mención de Calidad Para el Curso 2008–2009*. Available online at: http://web.micinn.es.
Monés, Jordi. 1999. "La Innovación Pedagógica. Marco Español e Influencia Internacional." *Cuadernos de Pedagogía* 286: 27–33.
Moreira, Antoni Flavio.1990. *Currículos e Programas no Brasil*. Sao Paulo: Papirus Editora.
Moreira, Antoni Flavio. 2001. "O Campo do Currículo no Brasil: Os Anos Noventa." *Currículo sem Fronteiras* 1: 35–49.
Moreira. Antoni Flavio. 2003. "The Curriculum Field in Brazil: Emergence and Consolidation." In *The International Handbook of Curriculum Research*, ed. William F. Pinar, 171–184. Mahwah, NJ: Lawrence Erlbaum Associates.

Moreira, Antoni Flavio, and Elizabeth Fernández de Macedo. 2000. *Multiculturalismo e o Campo do Curríoculono Brasil* (Projeto de Pesquisa). Faculdade de Educação, Universidade do Rio do Janeiro. Available online at: http://www.curriculouerj.pro.br.

Moreno, Juan. Manuel. 1998. "Notas Para Una Genealogía de Los Estudios Curriculares en España." *Revista de Currículum y Formación del Profesorado* 2 (2). Available online at: http://www.ugr.es.

Negrín, Olegario. 1999. *La Influencia Pedagógica Española en Ibero América: Estudios Sobre Historia de la Educación Contemporánea.* Madrid: Universidad Nacional de Educación a Distancia.

Namo de Mello, Guiomar. 1998. *Nuevas Propuestas Para la Gestion Educativa.* Mexico City: Secretaría de Educación Pública.

Nubiola, Jaime, and Beatriz Sierra. 2001. "La Recepción de Dewey en España y Latinoamérica." *Utopía y Praxis Latinoamericana* 6 (13): 107–119. Available online at: http://www.unav.es.

Palamidessi, Mariano, and Daniel Feldman. 2003. "The Development of Curriculum Thought in Argentina." In *The International Handbook of Curriculum Research*, ed. William F. Pinar, 109–121. Mahwah, NJ: Lawrence Erlbaum Associates.

Pedra, José Alberto. 1997. *Currículo, Conhecimento e Suas Representações.* Sao Paulo: Papirus Editora.

Pinar, William. 1978. "Notes on the Curriculum Field 1978." *Educational Researcher* 7 (8): 5–12.

Pinar, William. 2003. "The Internationalization of Curriculum Studies." Paper presented at the Annual Meeting of the Mexican Council of Education, Guadalajara, November 17, 2003.

PUC-SP. 2009. *Programa de pós-graduação em educação: Currículo.* Rua Ministro de Godoi: Sao Paulo. Available online at: http://www.ced.pucsp.br.

Remedí, Eduardo. 1982. Currículum y Accionar Docente. *Foro Universitario* 25: 57–61.

Rigo, Marco Antonio, Díaz Barriga, Frida, y Hermández Rojas, Gerado. 2005. "La Psicología de la Educación Como Disciplina y Profesión. Entrevista con César Coll." *Revista Electrónica de Investigación Educativa* 7 (1). Available online at: http://redie.uabc.mx.

Rivas, Jorge 2003. "¿Volver a la Educación Fundamental? Notas Para Una Arqueología de Los Mandatos Fundacionales Del CREFAL. Primera Parte." *Revista Interamericana de Educación de Adultos* 25 (1).

Schwab, Joseph. 2004. "The Practical: A Language for Curriculum". In *The Curriculum Studies Reader*, ed. David Flinders and Stephen Thornton,102–117. New York and London: RoutledgeFalmer.

Seguel, Mary Louise. 1966. *The Curriculum Field: Its Formative Years.* New York: Teachers College Press.

Smith, David Geoffrey. 2003. "Curriculum and Teaching Face Globalization." In *The International Handbook of Curriculum Research*, ed. William Pinar, 35–51. Mahwah, NJ: Lawrence Erlbaum Associates.

Trueba, Enrique. 2000. "Las Voces de Las Mujeres Mexicanas Inmigrantes en California Central: Etnografía Crítica y 'Apoderamiento'." *Estudios sobre Culturas Contemporáneas* 6 (11): 89–111.

Wraga, William, and Hlebowitsh, Peter. 2003. "Toward a Renaissance in Curriculum Theory and Development in the USA." *Journal of Curriculum Studies* 35 (4): 425–437.

Chapter 7

Revisiting Curriculum Studies

Raquel Glazman-Nowalski

Introduction

Approaching a research topic implies assuming ideological elements that represent the location and identity of the researcher, defined from her[1] social, psychological, and historical situation. These elements become evident through various expressions throughout her lifelong relationship with knowledge and constitute what Morin, based on Lorenz's work, characterizes as *imprinting*.[2] Linking ourselves to a work theme presupposes, as well, accepting that our constructions are the result of readings, monologues, and dialogues; together with public and private, individual and collective reflections that obey internal interests and external demands materialized in writings that are often insufficient for expressing our initial intentions. Often the work is being constructed through following a personal story; it is the result of questions that have arisen during previous reflections that have awakened the need to stop at points of special concern. This work is also one's answer to others' perceptions that have seemed erroneous or false to us, and that may have a multiplicity of origins. All this is a crucial part of the intellectual history of the field and of the individual scholar.

In Mexico, for various reasons, among which the search for a delimitation of educational fields is prominent, since 1980 there have been developing "state-of-the-art" reports, balance sheets, critiques, and other publications. In every case these constitute compilations and studies by one or more scholars who come together to present their points of view on criteria and idiosyncrasies; revisions of the results of works on educational problems; and in the case we are addressing, the much-debated theme of the curriculum. These represent an interesting source for tracking segments, texts, scholars, and approaches—obviously full of the views of those who write them—on the subject of how curriculum is treated in Mexico.

Naturally, the authors of these studies define and establish categories that afford systematic access to the work produced. In this process each person traces his appraisal of the writings or statements through conscious or unconscious choices; these choices are based on the need to reduce and systematize the existing material for the purposes of analysis and saving time. Based on his own particular "imprinting," he selects certain aspects for his own interpretations. The categories exclude as they include the original work, and in many cases, disregard it—with the result that evidence stamped with that particular imprinting gets created for the category defined and the classification applied. Thus, it happens that out of one or various texts written at a certain moment in national educational history, there emerges a chain of interpretations based on someone's original, specific interpretation, which is later repeated and revised by others.

In Latin America today, most educational research is deeply rooted in reading. The scholar's analysis is thus established in a basic work source. This gives us ideas about theories and methods regarding the way to approach certain facts, phenomena, or problems of social reality; to affirm or deny positions; to glimpse, illustrate, inform, develop, predict. It is hard to imagine a researcher who would not rely on others in the development of her work. In any case it would be impossible or unreliable that due to the struggle for originality at all costs, she should fail to do so. In Mexico, educational researchers have been nourished on the scholarship from the United States, England, France, Spain, Argentina, Colombia, and other nations. Texts from these and other countries, as well as those produced within Mexico, have been imprinted with what is distinctive about curriculum studies in Mexico.

Curriculum Design (Glazman and Ibarrola 1980) was well-suited to the time and the particular needs of the 1970s. This book approached readings considered valid at the time and related them with curriculum design, social needs, the world student situation (specifically the 1968 university movement in Mexico), the structure of knowledge, creativity, the role of the universities, the field of education, the development of knowledge, humanism and education or scholastic planning. Referenced was the work of George Beauchamp, Arno Bellack, Benjamin Bloom, Noam Chomsky, Arthur Coombs, John Dewey, Emile Durkheim, Gonzalez Casanova

H., Henriquez Ureña, Robert Mager, McGrath, Muñoz Izquierdo, Jean Piaget, Galen Saylor and William Alexander, Israel Scheffler, Hilda Taba, Tierno Galvan, and Ralph Tyler (see Glazman and de Ibarrola 1980, 525–536, and Glazman [n.d.]). Then as now, the vastness of the subject and, above all, the location of the curricular problem in the historical moment impeded the acceptance of the work. Also impeded was its packaging, in terms of representing its technical rationality—a classification that was repeated several times in critical analyses. Despite its widespread dissemination, *Curriculum Design* never saw a second edition, due to unidentified political reasons. That acknowledged, I now turn my attention to Mexico's "history of curriculum production" from the standpoint of my own saga—my particular approach.

The Beginning

I begin with a curriculum study that began around 1969 in the National Autonomous University of Mexico (UNAM), and its Commission for New Teaching Methods (CNME). The primary purposes of that commission were to promote educational research, advance the training of university teachers, and disseminate new forms, methods, and educational procedures related to curriculum, the organization of teaching, and the evaluation of student learning and educational communication. The CNME appeared alongside a considerable number of new universities, high schools, and public technical schools in the various Mexican states and the Federal District. At that time President Echeverria was attempting to curry favor with the younger generation that had suffered the brunt of unprecedented violence in Mexican university life during the second half of 1968; he was using the promotion of education as a means to that political end.

Inside the UNAM itself, and considering demographic growth of the youth population, new schools were created, and new ways of teaching were devised to deal with a constantly unsatisfied demand for training. Now, 40 years later, higher education still reaches a low percentage (25.2 percent) of all those young people eligible to receive it.[3] Created to support the new high schools and universities, the CNME was comprised of an interdisciplinary group of researchers from various university programs in educational psychology, communication, sociology, engineering, and law and was devoted chiefly to investigating different forms of teaching. Based on different topics of research, several work teams were formed, each having one or two leaders. After two years of work the teams made available the results of their research. These texts functioned as a basis for the preparation of countless courses for university teachers.

Each team worked autonomously, each with its own budgets and purposes. The teams shared, however, the idea that, given the latest facts, it was imperative to systematize teaching in what seemed a situation of considerable chaos. Indeed, the lack of any systematic approach to the treatment of educational problems became more serious through widespread institutional disorganization. Together, these two conditions spelled a situation in which little or no attention was given to the problems of teaching and learning. Some of these work groups, mainly composed of educational psychologists, showed a certain behaviorist tendency in their work. In the case of the curriculum design group, it was quite evident that their early training had taken place in sociology and communication studies.

In the projects mentioned above, preference was given to members of the UNAM. Later, principals of schools located outside Mexico City attended as did, later still, teachers from private schools. Eventually this training was directed toward teachers working at every level of the nation's educational system, always with a majority of university students. Many individuals trained in the CNME went on to become directors of colleges and of their own universities. By the mid-1970s, the CNME was recognized as the national leader in research, teaching, and educational outreach. Its courses included research based on the work of the teachers themselves, producing publications enriched by concrete experience.

In terms of commitments to curriculum research and its impact on practice and national educational policy, the situation today may be understood in terms of globalization, as indicated by Pinar (2004, 2). Referring to the United States in a manner that also corresponds to the Mexican national educational situation, he states:

> In this interest in, and commitment to the study of educational experience, curriculum theory is critical of contemporary school "reform." Indeed, "educational experience" seems precisely what politicians do not want, as they insist we focus on test scores as the "bottom line." By linking the curriculum to student performance on standardized examinations, politicians have, in effect, taken control of what is taught: the curriculum. Examination-driven curricula demote teachers from scholars and intellectuals to technicians in service to the state.

This is very much the case in Mexico today, but it was not always so, certainly not in the 1970s.

The Work Demanded

The work conducted in the CNME arose from Mexican educational institutions' intentions to design their own curriculums. Thus, a curriculum design team was formed with the idea of promoting the creation of UNAM curricula, most of which were based on copies of curricula from the US or European universities. This need was framed during a historical moment when the UNAM, especially at the middle and upper levels,[4] was ready to initiate a series of reforms concerning its educational processes and their management, within a context of promoting public university education. Given the origin, composition, and characteristics of the team itself, as well as the requirements of the task requested by the UNAM, the work was focused on defining study plans considered synonymous with curricula.

Our work on the curriculum design was geared toward proposing a planning method for university studies that would lead to the mastery of a profession. Frida Díaz Barriga and Elisa Lugo (2003, 64) give an operative definition of a model: it is

> a theoretical construct or form of representation of some object or process (in this case the area of the curriculum) that describes and allows one to explain and to become involved in it. This includes the selection of elements or components considered more important, as well as their relationships and manners of operation. It represents an ideal or prototype which serves as an example to imitate or reproduce, for which reason, it is both descriptive and prescriptive. A curriculum model is a potential strategy for developing the curriculum, and given its relatively generic character, can be applied and given new meaning in a more or less wide range of specific curricular proposals allowing its specificity and location in context.

The task of the group was, therefore, directed primarily toward the search for a viable way to accord the academic personnel of an institution the size of the UNAM professional autonomy, what in our country is known as "academic freedom." We would specify those elements that comprise its enabling conditions, among them is the clarification of educational aims these academicians would pursue in the training of their students. Also researched were ways to translate these intentions or expressed goals into operational expressions or guidelines by which to organize the university curriculum.

Mexico in the early 1970s was characterized by governmental authoritarianism. In such a period we were authorized to attend to the demands of higher education. But we did so by reflecting on those social needs that demanded the attention of public university[5] graduates in Mexico. This conception would take into account conditions relating to professional labor in specific settings as well as social participation of all sectors. Thus conceived, the curriculum could be considered a jointly owned property in which the voices of all the different members of a university community would be heard.

The Proposal

In the specific case of the curriculum study group, two types of studies were developed. One was basically intended to formulate curriculum guidelines and organizational forms for directors and academics from colleges and universities. The other was primarily aimed at clarifying the social components of any curriculum proposal whose positive elements would today be conspicuous in three ways: First, the concept of the curriculum would be understood as a way of leading the student to a mastery of the requirements, contents, and capabilities of a profession (Glazman and de Ibarrola 1980, 28).

The second element concerned the idea of analyzing four elements as the basis for each of the curricula. Developed by María de Ibarrola, these basic principles, with their plans and expressions, would become evident in the training and informational content of the profession itself, emphasizing the social, political, cultural, and economic context, and in the professional obligations of both the educational institution and the student.

Each of these fundamentals was configured into a set of contents comprising the curriculum. The institution would formulate a curriculum that cast teaching as a sociopolitical but specifically professional academic endeavor. This basic concept and its components were to be addressed at three levels: the conceptual, the normative, and the authentic situational (Ibid., 127). In the research on the fundamentals, a prominent place was accorded to social needs that the profession could embrace. The third would contain, remarkable at that time, the development of a concept for student participation in curriculum decisions.[6] This idea of participation, understood in a specific sociohistorical context, promoted the need for a democratic organization including the interests of students in everything related to their own training. The university authorities and administrators "would provide all the support necessary for the students' curricular development" while the students, teachers, and researchers, based on their own requirements, would contribute to the clarification of curricular needs.

Basic Ideas

As a consequence of several courses taught, the advice given to several university schools, and the progress of the research work, principles of curriculum development and change were identified by Glazman (1979, 711–721). These included:

- The student of any university study program should be familiar with the social, political, and economic development of Mexico in order to contextualize his/her professional training.
- The university graduate should have the ability to analyze the social needs of his specialty, with emphasis on the problems of the disadvantaged classes.
- It is advisable that before graduation, the student should have an overview of what professional practice in her field implies, concerning both the individual and the collective, as well as her potential for finding solutions for problems related to it, whether through her intervention in her disciplinary field or by means of her involvement in multidisciplinary teams.
- The need to increase critical thinking throughout the curriculum: critical thinking as an attitude that questions, explores, and investigates both current knowledge in her profession, and the conditions that may affect social change.
- The sense of addressing the demands that the curriculum expresses regarding its own technology.
- The need to ensure, at the professional level, the forms of teaching that include the promotion of research.
- The integration of theory and practice in the university curriculum as an expression of the fundamental dialectical relations constituent of education.
- The recognition and curriculum integration of other disciplinary fields that affect solving the problems of a particular profession.
- The scientific and technological advancement of a field as the basis of professional progress and of the curriculum itself; this should be submitted to review and characterized by constant innovation.

- An integration of the didactic elements that come together in the curriculum proposal, so as to facilitate access both to a knowledge of the field and to the sociocultural needs of the student.
- The curriculum's emphasis on the need for graduates' continuing education.
- The requirement for a coherent curricular organization of courses, rooted in objective criteria based on the order of learning of the contents.

Despite the intellectual authority and current validity of these principles 30 years after their initial formation, their distance from the educational reality surrounding us today converts them into educational utopias. How did such a shift occur? Due to the demands of international resource providers, ideological and economic resources for higher education have been reallocated away from social and professional development toward the development of science and technology.

Due to the use of objectives and the methodological structure of the curricular design, these principles of curriculum development were criticized as expressing the technical-rationalistic rationale. The text was located in a category that, despite our insistence, has prevailed in the works of different scholars both at the time and later (Glazman and de Ibarrola 1980). From the beginning, we have maintained that the curriculum is a reflection of an intricate set of social, political, educational, legal, economic, psychological, and epistemological mechanisms. To these, in each case, there would have to be added those belonging to the interplay of the curricular proposal and didactic specificity. Such curriculum development would be readily understood as a complex task. Instead, these principles were a casualty of simplistic criticism locating them in a technical-rationalistic tradition.

Current Work on Curriculum in Mexico

Conspicuous in the state-of-the-art assessment of curriculum studies for the period 1993–1995, prepared for the Mexican Council for Educational Research (COMIE) by Ángel Díaz Barriga, was the wide range of studies and the difficulty of delimiting the area, due to the multiple definitions of curriculum employed for basic research in this area at that time. Thus, in the research of that period there can be seen approaches on various levels; a plurality in theoretical references that results in a multiplicity of contextual and referential frameworks; and a certain variety in research methods.

Also demonstrable is the fact that national curriculum reforms have emphasized their formal systematic structures, as opposed to reflections on the particular conditions of each school, and ignored the recommendations of educational specialists concerning curriculum and educational processes (CFRE. A. Díaz Barriga 1997, 17–30]). Meanwhile, Frida Díaz Barriga (2003, 453–469)[7] in Pinar's *International Handbook of Curriculum Research* organizes curriculum production in Mexico into five categories: (1) technological-systematic; (2) reconceptualist critique; (3) pedagogical; (4) training and practice; and (5) interpretative. Each trend represents a line/scope of curricular production that in most cases conforms to a theoretical, historical, or institutional imperative.

By 2008, national education was managed and manipulated based on neoliberalism. Curricular reform proceeded without public debate, thereby demonstrating a decontextualized character, a lack of consensus, and little or no consultation with curriculum specialists, as already pointed out by Ángel Díaz Barriga. How did we reach this dismal point? I summarize the main markers of this devolution as follows:

1. *Methodological curriculum design.* In the 1970s the majority of schools and colleges of Mexican public universities were governed by plans and curriculums coming from other universities. Taking as representative of that era the particular case cited by Ibarrola and Glazman (de Ibarrola and Glazman 1980), research was guided by the need to find ways of defining the national curricula for higher education.
2. *Critique of the initial curriculum design, development of a strong theoretical work supported by current psychoanalytic currents of a different type, with few methodological proposals.* Between 1980 and 2000 various national scholars wrote texts/critiques and varied proposals emerging from their own centers of learning, with specific intents and various influences. There were, at this time, searches for curricular proposals that would emphasize Latin American conditions, and more particularly the national or institutional conditions. At the time there were great struggles against dictatorships in South America, and Mexico enjoyed the support of education specialists from Chile and Argentina. These scholars in exile influenced the development of curriculum work through widespread publications or counseling for educational centers from elementary to upper level.
3. *The influence of neoliberalism and a return to behavioristic positions promoted by education's economic and administrative constituencies, advanced by government agencies and based on various decrees.* The

measures had the support of private universities that accepted the ideological influence of the movements favoring NAFTA and the inevitability of the education-productivity link. Beginning in the second half of the 1990s there was a radicalization of evaluations, harangues regarding "quality" and "excellence," the structuring of training "by competencies," and the casting of instruction not as the transmission of knowledge but a means to efficiency and efficacy. This linking of the curriculum with the socioeconomic reality predominated.

4. *A strong criticism of neoliberalism, particularly from the academic sector.* However, there emerged evaluation as the main driver of innovation, including proposals for the so-called flexible curriculum, teacher training (both at the universities and in teaching practice itself), an emphasis on graduate degrees, and an insistence on precise educational research concepts.

5. *Works that analyze the distance between the proposed curricula and the institutional reality.* Beginning in the late 1970s and the early 1980s, identification of gaps between proposals and everyday reality, between theory and practice, predominated. Since that time, a stream of testimony has sought to "locate the text in the context" with jobs that contribute to clarification and alignment between policy and practice, recasting teacher preparation (formation), the ideological function of research within colleges and universities, the actions of the various managements, and the very conception of curriculum change (Furlán 1989, 1992, 1997; de Alba 1993, 2002; Casarini 1997; F. Díaz Barriga 2003; Angulo and Orozco 2007). At this point in time it is not possible to describe conditions of national education and the particular themes such as curriculum or evaluation, without acknowledging the triumph of neoliberalism and its campaigns of distraction (such as the demeaning of teaching and teachers). The consequence is the deterioration of public schools.

The state of the nation may be the key influence in the state of curriculum studies, but there is a throughline of subjective interest as well. Debates over curriculum concentrate the interests of each researcher that have been explored and expressed earlier in her previous research, all the while incorporating new knowledge. Such knowledge is born out of the uncertainties experienced during previous journeys, rereading the situations addressed earlier, structured by dialogues and scholarly discussions and, of course, by other specialists' reviews.[8] But overshadowing subjectivity is social reality, evident in the predominance of evaluation in Mexican curriculum reform.

Evaluation

During the rectorship of Jorge Carpizo (1985–1989) there began at the UNAM the promotion of "departmental reviews"—that is, joint assessments designed by teams of teachers from the various departments. These assessment would be applied in all the courses of a given area, field, or department to regulate the accreditation of each university degree program. Supporters of this scheme alluded to concepts familiar to curriculum specialists: educational evaluations would be conducted so as to gather useful information for improving and adjusting the processes of education. These tests, applied throughout the departments, would document the failures and successes of the teaching, and they would standardize curriculum content with the student in mind. To these familiar rationales for evaluation were added arguments with an administrative stamp.

Meanwhile, as experience has demonstrated, the risk that certain professional functions would be imposed according to the demands of these departmental examinations was not improbable. These constituted an indirect attack on "academic freedom," a concern particularly in the public universities, especially in the areas of social science, philosophy, and humanities.[9] Together with the "proposal" of the theme of departmental reviews, there would be a standardization of curricular processes, including ways of teaching and organizing, replacing existing academic content. Deep down, departmental reviews represented a threat of regression concerning the democratization of higher education, as well as the free expression of knowledge. What was at stake, then, was the indirect regulation of teaching, a conclusion I reached after years of research (Glazman 2001, 2005).[10] What I came to understand was that the increased emphasis on evaluation—presumably a means to educational betterment—was a means of administrative control of the university curriculum.

In Mexico today, there is criticism of evaluation as the most important element of education, recognizing its function as control of every form of expression in education. Evaluation has become the administrative means to standardize subjects, processes, and forms of knowledge, rendering them no longer creative but routine processes, quantified and controlled by select groups. This arrangement affects the decisions of educational practice as it intrudes into the personal lives of researchers, teachers, and students, as wages too are based on the results of evaluations. Evaluation has also become the key driver of proposals and educational reforms and has intensified as financial support for education has been reduced. Evaluation justifies the exclusion of teachers, researchers, and students from educational decision-making. Indeed, the number, variety, and impact of evaluation has proliferated to include the following:

1. Accreditation is now determined by assessment. The National Income Examinations (EXANI) are academic aptitude tests that certify basic skills and specific disciplinary knowledge acquired in or out of school. Assessment determines the allocation of scholarships locally or internationally; admission tests now rationalize the inadequacy of access to higher education made more acute by reduction in public funding. Since assessment are now compared internationally, Mexico's global competitiveness is deemed worrisome, as measures of educational achievement—especially in mathematics and literacy—remain low (see various PISA results).
2. Institutional assessment in higher education has increased, guided by the Secretariat of Public Education at the national level, and by administrators in the universities themselves. Such assessment is quantitative, never qualitative, and among its effects is the expansion of bureaucracy and administrative control. While accountability has been popular politically, it has been a catastrophe academically, as public universities today find their budgets controlled by assessments by non-academic functionaries. By these assessments the UNAM is now ranked as comparable to other prestigious universities in North America.
3. Teachers and researchers have become subjects of rigorous and sustained evaluations through "merit pay," regarding which productivity is one of the most important criteria. Such assessment has become more complex and stringent, and it increases depending on economic constraints. Faculty salaries have enjoyed no general increases in recent years; we are subjected to assessment for any significant increases. Many criticize the arbitrariness of assessment criteria.

Unsurprisingly, then, there exists a major debate between the advocates and the enemies of evaluation. Advocates claim that accurate assessment improves all aspects of education: there is now an increase in the percentages of postgraduates and doctorates among university faculty, a higher registration of students in public universities, and a relative decrease in dropouts. Advocates insist that educational management is monitored more strictly, and that academic "production" is emphasized. They assure us that efficiency has increased, despite the fact that employment opportunities in Mexico have not increased, and university graduates travel to other countries to look for work.

In the last Congress of Educational Research scholars analyzed these problems[11] including the lack of clarity in the assessment criteria for both research and teaching. Assessment must be linked to the curriculum, specifically to study plans, not externally generated and thereby arbitrary. Assessment is expensive, draining funds that would otherwise go into the classroom and sponsor research. Besides administrators and politicians, the primary beneficiaries of increased assessment are evaluation specialists.

Critical Capability

Despite increased assessment, I have found increased weakness in the analytical ability, critical thinking, and argumentation skills of my students. This finding directs my research and teaching. As data, I include assessment-driven university training, supplemented by the speeches and debates of the candidates, the campaigns of the mass media, and the limited participation of civil society in the country's most recent presidential elections. To this I add a conviction regarding the foundational role of critique as an engine of research. This intellectual concern, the agenda of research, and my present productivity are all focused on the formation of a critical capacity in the Mexican university student. I have used critical capacity in oblique forms to study questions relative to the complex character of education as a field of teaching and research, the criteria used for evaluation in general and the assessment of educational research in particular, the curriculum in relation to the Mexican university students' own writing ability and reading comprehension, and the hidden curriculum. The formation of critical thinking must be cultivated, by which I mean the formation of political consciousness, the capacity for understanding and analysis, the mastery of debate, expertise in dialogue as a method of teaching, sharpness in the analysis of ideology and other things that have their own content and specific intellectual skills. Despite current conditions in Mexico, the UNAM remains deeply committed to the autonomy of knowledge, and my research on critique will continue.

Notes

1. Before the advent of the feminist movement, speakers of English used the masculine pronoun in constructions covering both genders. Now, however, this usage is considered sexist, and for that reason we shall sometimes use the feminine pronoun, and sometimes the masculine.
2. "Cultural imprinting marks human beings from birth, first with the seal of the family culture, then with that of the school, and then with the university or professional performance. Thus the sociological and cultural selection of ideas rarely reflects the truth, or conversely, can be unforgiving in the pursuit of truth" (Morin 1999, 10).
3. *In Observatorio Ciudadano A.C.,* and using data from the Second 2005 Census of the National Population Council (CONAPO) Marisol Silva observed: "Mexico has a population of 9,773,000 young people of an age suitable for enrollment in higher education for the 2007–2008 school year." However, only 2,461,000, or 25.2 percent, were studying in BA or BS programs, or in upper-level technical degree programs. Officially, the figure is 26.8 percent, which undoubtedly includes the postgraduate population.
4. UNAM includes three levels: university, vocational training, and postgraduate studies. The latter have been the object of increased attention during the last ten years.
5. In Mexico the prevailing conception of the academic mission varies significantly between public and private universities. In the latter, research and cultural diffusion are not commonly understood as fundamental goals.
6. Glazman R. *Los estudiantes y el plan de estudios Deslinde.* Cuadernos de Cultura Política Universitaria, UNAM, México. No source.
7. In this handbook, both Frida Díaz Barriga and Ángel Díaz Barriga made systematic reviews of Mexican curriculum research in recent years.
8. Debated even today, the presumed link between research and teaching dates back to the 1980s. The inadequate discussion of its complexity produced my work on curriculum integration.
9. In summary, academic freedom depends on the capacity of teachers to teach and the institutional elasticity enabling professors to teach what and how they deem appropriate. Today, in Mexico, this is no longer regarded as a professional prerequisite, but as a contentious claim.
10. As a result of work begun in 1996, there will be works published regarding the content of point D, mentioned above. The first, by a single author, locates evaluation in the context of the neoliberal policies applied in Mexican education, particularly in universities. The second, the product of a cooperative effort, compiles the writings of colleagues and students who approach different aspects of assessment in Mexico.
11. Phillips, Denis. Nov. 2007. Is this piece of research rigorous and scientific? Is it the wrong question? *Respuestas de Alba Alicia y Glazman Raquel. Diálogos del IX Congreso de Investigación Educativa.* Mérida, Yucatán, México.

References

de Alba, Alicia. 1993. "El Currículum Universitario de Cara al Nuevo Milenio." In *University Curriculum Faced with the New Millennium*, 29–45. Mexico City: CESU-UNAM; Plaza y Valdés.

de Alba, Alicia. 2002. *Curriculum Universitario. Académicos y Futuro*. Mexico City: Plaza y Valdés.

Angulo, Rita, and Bertha Orozco, eds. 2007. "Alternativas Metodológicas De Intervención Curricular En Educación Superior." Colección Educación, Debates e Imaginario Social. Serie Curriculum y Siglo XXI. Mexico City: Coedición CONACyT/Universidad Autónoma de Guerrero/Seminario Currículum y Siglo XXI del IISUE-UNAM/Universidad Autónoma de San Luis Potosí/Universidad Autónoma Chapingo/Plaza y Valdés.

Phillips, D.C., Alicia de Alba, and Raquel Glazman. 2007. "Diálogos Sobre Investigación Educativa." IX Congreso de Investigación Educativa, Yucatán México, November 17, 2007.

Casarini, Ratto Martha.1997. *Teoría y diseño curricular*. Mexico City: Trillas.

Díaz-Barriga, Ángel. ed. 1997. *Curriculum, Evaluación y Planeación Educativas*. Mexico City: COMIE, CESU ENEP Iztacala.

Díaz Barriga, Frida. 2003. "Main Trends of Curriculum Research in Mexico." In *International Handbook of Curriculum Research*, ed. William F. Pinar, 457–469. Mahwah, NJ: Lawrence Erlbaum.

Díaz Barriga, Frida, Ma. De Lourdes Lule, Pacheco Pinzón Diana, Rojas-Drumond Silvia, and Saad Dayan Elisa 1992. *Metodología de Diseño Curricular Para Educación Superior*. Mexico City: Trillas.

Díaz Barriga, Frida and Elisa Lugo. 2003. "Desarrollo Del Curriculo." En *La Investigación Curricular en México. La Década de Los Noventa*, ed. Ángel Díaz Barriga, 63–93. Mexico City: COMIE, SEP CESU.

ENEP-Iztacala. 1982. "Jornadas VII Aniversario." Mexico City: UNAM. Furlán, Alfredo, Ortega Pérez Faustino, Remedí Vicente Eduardo, Campos.

Furlán, Alfredo, and Miguel Pasillas. 1989. *Desarrollo de la investigación en el campo del currículo*. Mexico City: ENEP-I. UNAM.

Furlán, Alfredo. 1997. *Ideología del discurso curricular*. Mexico City: UAS.

Glazman, Raquel.1979. "Trece Principios que Deben Considerarse en el Cambio de la Educación Superior." *Revista de la Unión de Universidades de América Latina* 77: 711–721.

Glazman, Raquel. 1975. "Los Estudiantes y el Plan de Estudios." Deslinde. Serie Nuevos Métodos de Enseñanza. Comisión Nuevos Métodos de Enseñanza. Dirección General de Difusión Cultural. Departamento de Humanidades. Mexico City: UNAM.

Glazman, Raquel. 1990. *La Universidad Pública: La Ideología en el Vínculo Investigación-Docencia*. Mexico City: Editorial El Caballito.

Glazman, Raquel. 2001. *Evaluación y Exclusión en la Enseñanza Superior*. Mexico City: Editorial Paidós Mexicana.

Glazman, Raquel. 2005. *Coordinadora y Editora. Las Caras de la Evaluación*. Mexico City: FFL and DGAPA Publicada.

Glazman, Raquel, and de Ibarrola, María. 1987. *Planes de Estudios Propuestas Institucionales y Realidad Curricular*. Mexico City: Nueva Imagen.

Glazman, Raquel, and de Ibarrola, María. 1980. *Diseño de Planes de Estudios*. Mexico City: CISE-UNAM.

Morin, Edgar Los. 1999. *Siete Saberes Necesarios Para la Educación Del Futuro*. Paris: UNESCO.

Pinar, William, William Reynolds, Patrick Slattery, and Peter Taubman.1995. *Understanding Curriculum*. New York: Peter Lang.

Pinar, William, ed. 2003. *International Handbook of Curriculum Research*. Mahwah, NJ, London: Lawrence Erlbaum Associates Publishers.

Pinar, William. 2004. *What is Curriculum Theory?* Mahwah, NJ, London: Lawrence Erlbaum Associates Publishers.

Chapter 8

Professional Education in Mexico at the Beginning of the Twenty-First Century

María Concepción Barrón Tirado

The process of transition from higher education to employment has become longer and more complex and this is coupled with a growing imbalance around the world in the demand in some fields of study for graduates with certain profiles. Due to this, there is an increasing trend toward devoting more attention to questions related to the vocational relevance of higher education.

The question of institutionalizing these connections is among the key issues in the debate about the challenges faced by higher education; they were discussed throughout the 1990s by international organizations such as the Organization for Economic Cooperation and Development (OECD) (1997), the World Bank (1995), the International Labour Organization (ILO) (1997), and UNESCO (1997). The intensity of interest in this subject had diminished during the previous decade, when it was seen that neither the high hopes of the 1960s for increased investment in higher education nor the profound sensation of social crisis felt in the 1970s could be maintained. Now, however, this topic is again on the discussion agenda since, on the one hand, higher education institutions (HEIs) are showing a willingness to respond to changing demands, and on the other, a deep concern has been generated by the heavy pressures being put on higher education to give preference to serving practical purposes.

In the 1990s, the relation between higher education and employment became one of the key recurring topics on every educational agenda, whether for orienting research, shaping public policies, or designing the various educational intervention processes. This link again became the center of the debate from the moment when universities began to be questioned about inefficiencies; enrollment saturation; a decline in the quality of the education offered; loss of economic, cultural, social, and political status; and disparities regarding the kinds of knowledge, skills, and attitudes demanded by the labor market. In short, the questioning began because of a visible deterioration in their value as seen by society.

It has become common to see words coined in the areas of management and organizational theory being transferred to academic and administrative management of educational institutions, especially to their professional training programs. Concepts such as efficiency, performance, evaluation, and planning, among the ones used most often, have acquired legitimacy in educational speeches and activities (Torres 1994). Subsequently another concept was transferred from management vocabularies, one that is now a pillar of any educational project: quality. Terms such as "differentiation" have come from organizational analysis of the neo-functionalist type in the style of Burton Clark. And, more recently, although it has its origin in neoclassical economic theory, the concept of flexibility has been incorporated (Barrón and Gómez 1999).

Labor Flexibility

Flexibility is an inclusive phenomenon within a wider process: economic restructuring. This process has been encouraged, at least in Latin America, by the so-called opening up of economies, particularly from the period when the nations began to apply a set of adjustment policies and structural reforms to their economies (De la Garza Toledo 1996, 1997). In the 1970s, flexibility of the labor force was identified as a necessity for economies, particularly in developed countries, arising from the combination of specific factors such as the pressure to achieve competitiveness, technological change, the need to reduce production costs, and trends in population growth and distribution (European Training Foundation 1997).

As De la Garza notes, labor flexibility is a polysemous concept with several meanings and contents, depending on the theory that sustains it, so one can speak of flexibility according to the neoclassical theory, according to post-Fordism theories (the Regulation School, Flexible Specialization, and neo-Schumpeterianism), and according to the new wave of management

(De la Garza Toledo 1997). In this chapter the focus is on post-Fordism theories and management theories that endorse work flexibility. Post-Fordism assumes that the paradigm of mass or large-scale production has reached its end and that a new production paradigm is now arriving characterized by strategies of flexibility and quality that make it possible to have levels of productivity and competitiveness with which to cope with global market liberalization.

Defenders of the flexible specialization theory believe that with the hyper-development of technologies, especially those that contribute to programmable automatization of production processes, conditions are favorable to shift from an economy of scale to an economy that offers the customer a wider variety of quality products. The worker in such an economy of variety must demonstrate a greater capacity for adaptation and rotation, and overall, for flexibility in various jobs and duties, which in economistic jargon is called polyvalence. At the same time, an economy of variety requires higher qualifications in order to handle automated processes efficiently. In contrast, workers employed in mass production are assigned exclusively to jobs, routines, and fixed tasks with few qualification requirements. Therefore, a company that offers a wider variety of products or services needs to restructure its organization to provide organizational, technological, and labor flexibility (Mertens 1988).

According to the principles of flexible specialization, job content would be modified within this new production paradigm, since the technological base and administrative management of a variety economy must demonstrate great versatility and labor mobility. This means redefining the professional profile of the worker required in this era of economic reconversion and internationalization (Palomares and Mertens 1987, 1989, 1991). In addition, the management doctrine of work organization emphasizes that the new paradigm pressures companies to be productive within the framework of competitiveness, not only within domestic markets but especially across international markets. For this purpose, the new forms of work organization and management in scenarios of competitiveness need to have processes and products that are oriented toward total quality and according to schedule (Carrillo 1995).

For decades industrialization worldwide has been linked to processes of industrial reconversion. These processes, taken as a whole, have as their overarching goal ever-increasing flexibility, this being understood as a capacity for rapid adaptation to the oscillations of the market by reshuffling machines and workers in different combinations so as to be able to cope with changes in demand for products and services. In turn, this flexibility demands change in the patterns of industrial work organization to enable mobility of workers among various jobs, depending on the volumes of products required and the ever-shifting delivery schedules. In addition, this flexibility must demonstrate the ability to respond to the unexpected while maintaining the quality of processes and products (Regini and Sabel 1989).

Despite the rhetoric, at present job flexibility exists more in intentions than in realities. Flexibility has not become established or generalized, even in those countries where presumably there has been a restructuring of work across a broad spectrum of industries, such as Japan and Germany. Evidently there are even empirical studies that indicate that total flexibility in companies is a hindrance to their operations; what is more common is a coexistence of actions of a flexible nature and work organizations of the Fordist type. Trends toward flexibility have not yet realized in practice to support the claim, as the post-Fordists do, that we are seeing the emergence of a new production paradigm (De la Garza Toledo 1997 and 1998).

A phenomenon within the global process of economic reconversion in the logic of globalization, flexibility has become a key strategy for the achievement of that process. So it is not possible to visualize it independently of the general framework in which it is applied. The coinciding of process and content is evident in the transfer of this strategy of flexibility to higher education. Just as labor flexibility demands different professional profiles and new job descriptions, its application to education, particularly in the curriculum field, incorporates the need for new graduate profiles where versatility is emphasized in order to face the demands of the employment world: "We note (...), at least a first sight, a surprising degree of consensus about the major curriculum trends that are desirable in higher education. Obviously, the voices that speak most frankly say that graduates should acquire general proficiencies, cultivate social and communication abilities, be prepared for entrepreneurship, and finally, they should be *flexible*" (Teichler 1998, 15; emphasis added).

Education and Globalization

Since the beginning of the 1990s, international organizations have promoted new priorities for higher education, in view of the problems of democratization, globalization, regionalization, polarization, marginalization, and fragmentation that characterize contemporary society (Barrón and Ysunza 2003). In the industrialized countries, debates about industrial reorganization and competitiveness have focused on human resource training. In 1989, an OECD report highlighted among its conclusions that it is not possible to realize the full technical or economic potential of the new technologies without introducing necessary changes in the institutional and social sphere; this is of particular importance in the educational system because companies are tending to develop more flexible types of work organization, with polyvalent jobs and a marked emphasis on communication and problem-solving skills and workers' entrepreneurial aptitudes (ECLAC-UNESCO 1992). According to the Economic Commission for Latin America and the Caribbean-United Nations Educational, Scientific, and Cultural Organization's (ECLAC-UNESCO) 1992 study, certain common changes can be identified, which, in spite of differences among countries and the specificity of domestic problems, characterize the current state of education, among them (1) longer duration of schooling and the growing demand by society for education; (2) the search for alternative sources of funds to finance education; and (3) the efforts made by many countries in the 1990s to bring education closer to the economy (Barrón and Ysunza 2003).

Midway through the decade UNESCO proposed a set of principles to institutionalize processes of change and development in higher education, including criteria for relevance, derived from the presumably new role of higher education in society, specifying its teaching, research, and service functions, all orchestrated according to "its connections to the employment world in a broad sense, to the State and public financing, and its interactions with other levels and forms of education" (UNESCO 1995, 8). According to UNESCO, the need for relevance in higher education "has acquired new dimensions and greater urgency as society's economic activities require graduates capable of constantly updating their knowledge and acquiring new knowledge that will allow them not only to find employment, but also create jobs in a constantly changing market" (8).

Professional Training and the Market

The origin of the professions was linked to industrialization processes, and professional knowledge and practices exist in specific political-cultural settings. Professional training can be said to have been born and to have grown in parallel with the demands generated by historic, economic, and social development. Historically, for instance, the need for professional training that would meet the demands of society's development was linked to the guilds of the Middle Ages, with their system of apprentices, journeymen, and master craftsmen (Lipsmeier et al. 1975, 12). This system followed the same apprenticeship principle as did other medieval professionals, such as the squire and the knight, the student and the professor, and the novice and the monk.

Starting with the industrial revolution at the beginning of the nineteenth century, the apprenticeship relationship was replaced by standardized professional training to produce highly qualified workers and technicians. During that century, a system of professional education was organized. Lipsmeier and colleagues (1975, 14) point out that "professional teaching in Germany, which was born at the beginning of the last century and did not take long to become differentiated, from the first moment had to face up to the demands of the pedagogical theory derived from neo-humanism." On the one hand, there was a demand for training that would provide a broad, general culture to aspiring professionals, regardless of their scholastic level, and, on the other, there was a demand for students to acquire specific expertise relevant to the work they intended to do. Subsequently, a global reorganization, associated with the American and French Revolutions and the Napoleonic conquests, created a network of economic, political, and cultural links among the various countries and continents, through the construction of nationalism, industrialization, and capitalism. There were efforts to make the political community coincide with the nation or cultural community, based on a linguistic, historical, ethnical, and sometimes religious affinity. Industrialization was characterized by the utilization of mechanical production methods and the exploitation of new energy sources.

It is paradoxical that these broad changes were not accompanied immediately by a conception of the world in accordance with them. Several decades passed before there was greater integration between the development of the forces of economic production and the political and cultural superstructure. The requirements of a society in constant change led countries such as Germany and France to differentiate humanistic studies from technical and professional studies and to emphasize scientific research. In both countries, the education of professionals has been a responsibility of the State, in contrast with England where, during that same period, private schools specialized in the arts and crafts for lathe operators, mechanics, and others. It is clear, then, that the process of industrialization marked a fundamental shift with regard to the concept of education. Education acquired a different meaning, linking professionalization with economic development.

Starting in the twentieth century, then, "educational activity began to be visualized as a system of investment and economic costs, in which results should be measured in terms of efficiency and productivity" (Díaz Barriga 2003). By mid-century, education was considered to be the driving force for any country's economic and social development, a relationship that was accentuated with the incorporation of technology as a key factor of production. With the theory of human capital, this conception saw its consolidation wherein education is considered a synonym for schooling and a key factor in production and productivity—in other words, as just another production input that can be measured in terms of the costs of the subjects' schooling. The nature of the investment can be analyzed at two levels: at the level of the whole production system, as an input, just one more investment; and at the individual level, where it is regarded as an investment for the future, since a higher level of schooling portends higher income, associated with greater social mobility.

Human capital theory was derived from classical and neoclassical theories of the economy in which it was believed that "all income can be capitalized, including human beings, which gives as a result the economic value of a person" (Dettmer and Esteinou 1993, 58). Each job calls for certain qualifications, and training for these is the responsibility of the educational system. As requirements for jobs increase, it becomes necessary to maintain closer links between training and jobs, and consequently schools must align coursework with the specific demands of the job market. Human capital theory assumes that

> a country's economic development depends on the degree of development of its educational system, and that the relationship between education and the economy is of a technical nature. A country's productive capacity, that is, the volume and quality of the goods and services that it produces, depends not only on its natural resources, infrastructure, facilities, machinery, etc., but also [on] the educational level of its labor force, so the educational system is assigned the role of a provider of an important production factor: the human resource. (Gómez and Espitia 1988, 128)

Human capital theory postulates that it is necessary to qualify the labor force for every job in the production system and that there is a correspondence between the requisites for the job and its requirements. As technological advances occur, job complexity increases. Finally there is a homogeneous, objective, neutral job market that offers opportunities to everyone as a function of their educational profile. From this perspective, the disparity between education and employment occurs in correspondence with weaknesses in the training offered by the educational institutions and not with the dynamics of the country's economy.

Another theoretical line proposes a different way of conceiving the relationship between education and employment (see Gómez and Espitia 1981; Dettmer and Esteinou 1983; Reynaga 1983). This alternative takes historical materialism as the basis for its analysis. Its initial premise derives from the fact that the characteristics assumed by the relations between education and the economy are expressions of a historical process in which the social relationships of production have been developed. Of particular note in this theoretical vein are essays that criticize liberal notions about the job market and propose concepts such as a dual structure (Gordon, Reich and Edward 1973), segmented markets (Carnoy 1982), and heterogeneous structure. This proposal is based on the following elements: (1) the production system is determined by specific social relations that define how production occurs, what is produced, for whom the production is intended, and how production is distributed socially. These decisions are made as a function of profit-making criteria; (2) the nature of production's social relationships determines the technical and organizational options; (3) the job market is the necessary institution for the purchase and sale of a heterogeneous labor force; on this market depends the distribution of labor in the various occupations and crafts; (4) educational disaccreditation plays an important role as a selection and exclusion criterion for the different occupations; (5) the differences between most occupations and industrial crafts refer to the status, power, autonomy, compensation, and quality of the job, notions that are derived from the arbitrary classification made by the owners of the means of production; (6) the selection of the labor force is, at the same time, a process of selection and social differentiation; and (7) there is no corresponding relation between the educational level and the possibilities for well-paid employment, nor does an increase in educational level guarantee job advancement (Ibarrola and Reynaga 1983).

As society becomes more complex, the roles of professionals become more varied and, therefore, a range of specialties and subspecialties increases: "In the context of modern society, the predominance of the corporate model is established based on the occupational restrictions of the market as an alternative figure for reshaping the demand for professional services" (Pacheco 1990, 30). This corporate model increasingly calls for more specialization, differentiation of roles, bureaucratization, and the professional's identification with the organization.

The history of the professions in Mexico is different from that of the United States and the United Kingdom, due to the fact that consolidation of the Mexican State occurred prior to the development of the professions, in contrast to those countries where the professions enjoyed autonomy from the State (Cleaves 1985). Professionals in Mexico have not had any involvement in the State's decisions and the various associations have no authority to validate the competence level of their colleagues directly. They do so through the educational institutions when the latter modify their curricula and consider it relevant to take the occupation or association into account.[1] Despite this fact, the origin and evolution of the professions in Mexico are linked to various political-cultural projects of the State. In summary, it could be said that the significance of a profession—that is, its intrinsic legitimatization, its validity, and its function—is determined by the historical characteristics of the society in which it appears and develops. Thus, its specific forms of training, reproduction, exclusion, certification, and evaluation depend on the conditions in which they arise, the interests of those promoting it, and the political power of its members. This means, therefore, that no degree program is fully explained by the objective needs for the development of knowledge, or by its application to finding solution to a given problem (Gómez and Tenti 1989, 63).

From this perspective, several considerations can be presented regarding professional training as a set of social processes for preparing the subject for specific purposes leading to a subsequent performance in the employment field that is based on pursuing, mastering, and using a body of theoretical and instrumental knowledge (differentiated learning) about a given field of knowledge, science, activity, or discipline. Depending on its complexity, education is linked to two basic points of reference: the field of knowledge and that of employment.

It is pertinent to mention that every profession, depending on its nature, gives preference to specific meanings of knowledge (reflection) and work (application). On its part, training takes place within an educational framework under institutional prescriptions that regulate the activities that are considered to be necessary and pertinent and that provide endorsement of the preparation offered by various curricular models through the awarding of certificates and professional degrees. The current job market calls for professionals with different characteristics than in the immediate past. The preference for eminently theoretical training or even practical training is replaced by demands for the acquisition of job-specific skills.

Research conducted during the last decade in Mexico on the relationship between profession-professional training and the job market examined the knowledge, explanation, characterization, and diagnosis of the modes of interaction between these spheres. The research focused on the following items: (1) studies of a specific profession; (2) studies analyzing the influence that the new industrialization processes and production restructuring have on professionals' employability; (3) studies analyzing employers; and (4) analytical studies that discuss and conceptualize institutional, economic, and educational factors (Reynaga and Ruiz 2003). Other studies were conducted at the same time whose objective was to characterize the effects of educational level on employment from an economic standpoint, using principally census information about the behavior of the economically active population and to a lesser degree data from the 1993 National Education, Training and Employment Survey (Reynaga and Ruiz 2003).

Curricular Models and Professional Training[2]

Early in the 1990s, proposals appeared for structural reforms in higher education focused on their study plans and curricula as well as on teaching and learning methodologies. Their rationale rested on the requirements of globalization and training of professionals. There was acknowledgment of the university's traditional critical function in society. Among the topics discussed during the decade were the following: improving the quality of educational processes and outcomes; replacing the model of schooling that occurs in a specific place and with a separate time for studying and learning with a model involving learning as a permanent process; more flexibility in school organization, supported by the new information technologies; development of students' intellectual skills for handling technological, economic, and cultural change; and a closer link between students and actual work scenarios.

The 1990s was marked by large-scale projects for curriculum reform and by a search for or the adaptation of academic models that would respond to certain job market demands. To a large extent, these projects were framed by educational policies that arose in the context of the globalization of economy, treaties for international cooperation and trade, the search for certification and uniformity of educational programs and professions (or definition of national and international standards for professional training and practice), and decentralization of the national educational system (Díaz Barriga Arceo et al. 2003).

Curriculum models were developed to meet these requirements. Among these were models of flexibility. Others were based on proficiencies. There were tutorial systems, models guaranteeing total quality, education reengineering, strategic curriculum planning, and more, all of which emphasized efficiency, quality, and excellence in educating human resources to be highly competent and competitive. These concepts were, presumably, associated with standards of certification and evaluation guaranteeing professional quality, requiring uniformity of curricula not only across various institutions, but even across countries.

Present conditions in the production sector and the job market require, then, qualification models that are different from the classic models for training professionals. Such qualifications would allow professionals to adapt more dynamically to new job market conditions. From this analysis emerges a need for polyvalent training, which means the development of basic proficiencies that allow individuals to cope with changes that occur and to have a capacity for adaptation and an attitude toward constant change. The three elements "polyvalence, flexibility and constant change" are hallmarks of educational policies that have been gradually incorporated into educational institutions, their curricula, the structure of academic cycles, and administrative management models.

The question of curriculum flexibility in schools, particularly in higher education, has thus become a part of the obligatory discourse in international forums where public policies are discussed (UNESCO, World Bank, OECD, ECLAC) and in the various academic units engaged in research, intervention, and management. In Latin America, curriculum flexibility has been presented to us as a new concept that can give specific answers to the problems of higher education, particularly in this era of economic liberalization, rapid mutations of technologies, new forms of work organization, and population pressures (specifically the one having to do with transition)—that is, transformations that are occurring in practically all orders of society.

However, the concept of flexibility is not all that new, since the scheme suggested for institutions of higher learning (HEIs) in our regions had already been designed, developed, evaluated, and rethought in the educational systems of several European countries (principally in France, Germany, and England) and the United States. The combination of short- and long-term training, progressive cycle structures, final graduations with the awarding of diplomas that give recognition to proficiencies with different degrees of complexity and specialization: these are schemes that have already existed for a number of years in those educational systems. For that reason, it is necessary to open a debate around curriculum flexibility in order to examine its possibilities and its organizational, political, cultural, and social implications in order to understand the application contexts and conditions for its operation in various specific countries.

At present, flexibility is directed toward the spheres of curriculum and administration, since that is where there is space for training for excellence, where knowledge of the disciplines, sciences, and professions is selected, organized, distributed, and controlled. In addition, it is in the terrain of curriculum in higher education establishments where standards, symbols, and the set of subjectivities that contribute to social and cultural reproduction are disseminated. HEIs must organize their curricula based on a series of specific objectives, such as developing problem-solving skills, orientating toward practical experience, promoting interdisciplinary learning, and learning how to develop humanistic sensitivity and international proficiencies in the framework of a flexible curriculum organization.

Just as there are different approaches to job flexibility, curriculum flexibility also presents a range of possibilities. Díaz Barriga Arceo and her colleagues (2003) point out that there are both academic and administrative characteristics in all the proposals for flexible curricula. The academic features include the following: a trend toward reorientation and diversification of academic offerings, the creation of adaptable curricula that allow for continuous renovation of their structure (UAG 1995), and meeting social and scientific educational needs while also contributing to the individual and social growth of the subject (UABC 1993); an open curriculum that offers the student opportunities to choose among all the courses offered by the university (BUAP, Proyecto Fénix 1994); a form of organization of university studies that permits their maximum adaptation to the aptitudes and interests of the students, always oriented as a function of the demands of the professional field and technical and scientific advances of knowledge (Poder Ejecutivo Federal 1995); and learning activities that are selected considering both the requirements of the program and the student's characteristics. From the *administrative standpoint*, this means facilitating interdisciplinary work (UAG 1995) and promoting the flow of interaction and utilization of resources (UABC 1993), thereby increasing the range of possibilities offered in the university academic structure.

Perspective of Proficiency-Based Training

Education in proficiencies constituted another of the bases for the debate on curricula of that period. What underlies the phrase "proficiency-based training" is clear. In her analysis of the ILO, Barrón (2000) identifies three foundations of education based on proficiencies: (1) it permits the centralization of economic growth and social development of the human being; (2) it makes possible the creation of better jobs where the determining factor is the employability of each person; and (3) it focuses on the need for change. In Mexico, the phrase fused economic and social development, evident in the National Development Plan 1995–2000, which established as one of its main objectives "laying the foundation for overcoming social imbalances between geographic regions, social groups and production sectors, as well as overcoming the contrasts between individual opportunities for training, employment, and income" (25).

The programs designed to achieve these aims were the Educational Development Program 1995–2000 and the Employment, Training and Defense of Labor Rights Program 1995–2000. In addition, in the document entitled "Project for the Development and Implementation of the National System for Training for Work, First Phase (based on proficiencies)," developed by the Ministry of Public Education (SEP, its acronym in Spanish) and the World Bank (1994), a specific proposal is presented for developing and establishing the National System for Training for Work (SNCT, its acronym in Spanish). It is asserted that comparing and standardizing the systems of proficiencies would benefit the integration provisions included in the framework of North American Free Trade Agreement (NAFTA) and internally the system would give flexibility and a larger opening in educational training institutions with regard to social demands, influencing the entire national educational system by accrediting and certifying knowledge and work proficiencies. The Ministry of Public Education and the Ministry of Labor and Social Welfare jointly designed and currently operate the Project for Modernization of Technical Education and Training (PMETYC, its acronym in Spanish), the framework within which the Council for Standardization and Certification of Labor Proficiency (CONOCER, its acronym in Spanish) was created.

During the period 1988–1994, the transformation of the national educational system was given impetus by the so-called Educational Modernization Program. CONALEP was the Spanish acronym for the pilot project for technical education financed by the World Bank for the purpose of institutionalizing the program. Again, this model was proposed as a means of establishing closer links to the production sector (Thierry 1998). In the case of the National Polytechnic Institute (IPN, its acronym in Spanish), Gómez (1997) asserts that this model was adopted because it allows the student to take employment or be self-employed, depending on the skills acquired. For higher education, Valle (1996) insists that the persistent deficiencies shown by university graduates in applying the training received to the requirements of professional practice demand a training model that trains the students in certain proficiencies. The various education proposals based on proficiencies assume that there will be curricular unification or harmonization in professional training in order to meet quality standards, obtain accreditation of graduates, and facilitate their placement in the versatile national and international labor context, faced with the urgency for professional recognition or equivalence in a field framed by market globalization, free professional movement, and the recommendations of international organizations.

Tutorial Models

Based on recommendations of international organizations such as the UNESCO and the Regional Center for Higher Education in Latin America and the Caribbean (CRESAL, its initials in Spanish) for the creation of a teacher-tutor model that would link student development with national educational policies as well, educational institutions were instructed to design an institutional tutorial system.

In this system, the role of the professor in higher education is to be transformed from a transmitter of knowledge to that of tutor or adviser to the student, so as to provide an education that will prepare the student for development in keeping with his or her life project. It could be seen as an instrument for change that could strengthen programs' support of students' academic, cultural, and human development, in the effort to achieve the ideal of individualized attention in the educational process.

The use of models that focus on the student and that are oriented toward learning through academic tutoring requires training and collaboration on the part of the various university players. Tutoring is also a form of educational attention where the professor instructs a student or a group of students systematically with structured objectives, programs by areas, and other teaching techniques that are appropriate for groups formed in accordance with certain criteria and monitoring and control mechanisms, among others (Alcántara 1990). The tutorial model fosters a different pedagogical relationship from that established by teaching to large groups. In this case, the professor assumes the role of a counselor or "big brother"; the exercise of authority is softened almost to the point of disappearing and the environment is much more relaxed and friendly (Latapí 1990).

At the undergraduate level, *Asociación Nacional de Universidades e Instituciones de Educación Superior* (ANUIES) proposes that the institutional tutorial system should be considered as "a set of actions to provide individual attention for the student ... deployed throughout the training process" (ANUIES 2000, 43). Finally, it is pertinent to include other types of support, such as health care and psychology units, continuing education and university extension programs, vocational counseling, and financial support programs for students. It emerges as a possibility for solving problems of dropping out, failure to advance, and low graduation percentages among students. The institutional tutorial proposal is also conceived as a process of accompanying the student during the educational process through personalized attention or attention to small groups of students by competent academics trained for this role. It differs from but at the same time complements the method of teaching to a large group. According to Sánchez Puentes and Martínez (2000), one of the main difficulties regarding the tutorial concept is related to the diversity of meanings involved, linked to a broad, dense conceptual field that makes reference to other models different from the tutorial model and, therefore, from its functions and practices.

At present, a number of doctoral programs depend more on the quality of their academic tutors than on the curriculum structure itself. As well, students can obtain support from tutors in disciplines other than their own, thus serving the purpose of enriching their education (Barrón and Gutiérrez 2002). Several public universities—such as the University of

Baja California, the University of Hidalgo, the University of Nuevo León, the University of Colima, and the University of Puebla, among others—have adopted the tutorial model, linking it to changes in their curricula and thus emphasizing flexibility. Private institutions, such as the Anahuac University, the Ibero-American University, and the Monterrey Institute of Technology and Higher Education (ITESM, for its initials in Spanish), provide students with personalized tutorial service.

Practical Experience or the In-Service Model

This model is also derived from the demand to transfer knowledge from the world of learning, science, and erudition to the world of professional labor and has to do with the complex relationship between learning and work requiring specialized knowledge and complex cognitive tasks. Higher education oriented toward practical experience attempts to approach the complexity of real phenomena in intellectual terms. The expectation is that higher education will ensure a systematic confrontation between thinking and solving problems by academic theories on the one hand, and professional ways of thinking and solving problems on the other. This objective involves the organization of learning spaces that create environments in which students are engaged in autonomous, significant learning in actual work scenarios as well as in diverse types of work studied in the classroom through workshops, seminars, and laboratories. To achieve this objective, the in-service model includes internships and other practical opportunities, requiring professionals to participate in teaching and other academic activities (Barrón and Ysunza 2003).

Learning Based on Problem Solving

This trend is also based on the concern that general knowledge and general proficiencies are not necessarily applicable *per se* to the working world, so graduates must find the means to transfer these academic proficiencies to the everyday world of employment. Learning-based problem solving (LBP) is conceived as an educational strategy that has the student as its axis and organizes both the curriculum and the teaching-learning process. Gutiérrez (2003) considers that learning based on problem solving is one of the teaching-learning methods that has been most accepted in higher education institutions in recent years. It was first applied in the 1960s in the Medical School of Case Western Reserve University in the United States and in McMaster University in Canada.

The purpose for which this methodology was developed was to improve the quality of medical education, changing the orientation from a curriculum based on a collection of disciplinary subjects presented by faculty to a curriculum organized around problems of real life, wherein the different areas of academic knowledge were put into play in solving problems. Learning-based problem solving has now been incorporated into higher education through some educational models such as that of the National Polytechnic Institute (IPN, for its acronym in Spanish), the Monterrey Institute of Technology and Higher Education, and the undergraduate programs in medicine, psychology, and engineering in the National University of Mexico (UNAM, for its acronym in Spanish).

LBP is promoted as a teaching-learning strategy in which both the acquisition of knowledge and the development of skills and attitudes are important. Gutiérrez (2003) identifies the following characteristics of LBP:

- It is an active work method in which students participate constantly in knowledge acquisition.
- The method is oriented toward solving problems selected or designed for learning certain knowledge objectives.
- Learning focuses on the student and not on the professor or only on the content.
- It is a method that encourages collaborative work in various disciplines and takes place in small groups.
- Courses with this work model are opened up to various disciplines.
- The teacher becomes a facilitator or tutor in the learning process.

From this perspective, the role of the professor is to provide the bases for the student's reasoning about a specific, previously selected problem, whose solution requires the student to review the theoretical and practical knowledge that the course, or a part of it, is intended to teach. The teacher ensures that the proposed problems or projects are motivating and effective. These criteria are met if problems are taken from daily life or the professional sphere.

While solving a problem, the members of the group may discover the areas in which their collective knowledge is weak. By recognizing weakness, they can deal with it as a learning opportunity, that is, as an issue that requires study that will be done outside the tutorial meeting. Teaching through problem solving is intended to train individuals to cultivate independent judgment and the ability for self-teaching so that they can direct their own efforts. It provides students with aptitudes and skills that offer them skills to advance in their careers as it fosters the acquisition of proficiencies in solving problems, exercising creativity, and developing effective communication, all prerequisites for adapting to the ever-changing conditions of modern society. Problem-solving curriculum ensures that students will develop those skills that are needed to evaluate their own comprehension systematically and become reflective professionals (Barrón and Ysunza 2003).

Modular Models

This approach, developed in the 1970s, is considered an alternative to curriculum structures that fragmented knowledge and reality. The professional practice category became a structural axis around which the new curriculum was designed. This model recognizes the historicity of social and economic demands for professionals by specifying social problems around which teaching units were prepared. These problems are conceptualized as transformational objectives whose achievement would change social reality. Subsequent analysis of this curriculum design disclosed innumerable problems, including (1) teachers' lack of understanding of the educational project (2) rapid changes in the economic, political, and social conditions upon which the various curricula were constructed; and (3) resistance to having all curricular contents organized by transformational objectives, especially from certain politicians and businessmen.

In the 1990s, UNESCO surveyed European uses of teaching modules, particularly in the field of technical training, whose general structure accents acquisition of work proficiencies. This model is currently in evidence in Mexico in several modalities in institutions such as UAM-Xochimilco, FES-Zaragoza, and the School of Theater Arts (Barron and Ysunza 2003).

Transdisciplinary Learning

Of course, experts differ with regard to what knowledge is of most worth in coping with the future challenges of the employment world. Some see a continuing need for specialized knowledge, while others advocate a more general education. Still others emphasize so-called transdisciplinary knowledge, produced in contexts of application. Transdisciplinarity is characterized by curricular structures directed toward the solution of problems, including both theoretical and empirical components, disseminating results during the production process itself and converting concrete solutions into a point of departure for subsequent development (Gibbons 1997).

As the name implies, transdisciplinarity means going beyond the disciplines, which tend to compartmentalize knowledge, segmenting it artificially, a situation that does not correspond to the everyday world and its problems. Transdisciplinarity asserts a closer link between academic knowledge and actual work scenarios and to government and business policies. In contemporary societies there is increased emphasis on the development of new theories of innovation and the production of knowledge, on new trends at the national and international levels in designing policies for science, technology, and innovation, attentive to the specific characteristics of the scientific and technological systems of each country, with new linkages configured among these sectors. In theories of innovation and production of knowledge, notions of national and regional innovation systems emphasize relations among economic, political, and academic institutions, focusing attention on the scientific and technological capacities of nations and regions. Likewise, the identification of new interactive (non-lineal) models for knowledge production has been important: the so-called Mode 2 (Gibbons et al. 1997) as well as the triple helix model (Etzkowitz and Leydesdorff 1998), both of which emphasize the interaction among research, educational organizations, businesses, and government.

Casas and Luna (2000) argued that in the 1990s major changes were made in government, in universities, and in businesses, all emphasizing the importance of knowledge to support the production sectors, changes that led to a reorganization of the relations among these sectors. This situation precipitated a high volume of research production by university specialists in an attempt to understand this phenomenon and its repercussions. This research appeared in essays on training for engineers (Covarrubias 1995; González 1997; Barrón and Gómez 2004), as well as in the projects institutionalizing linkage between higher education research centers (CINVESTAV, IPN) and businesses through institutional agreements.

Training Reflective Professionals

In the concept of the reflective professional, three components can be distinguished: knowledge in action, reflection in action, and reflection about action and about reflection in action. According to this orientation, students learn principally through action with the help of a tutor; their *practicum* is reflective in two senses: students self-reflect on their actions and engage in reciprocal reflection through dialogue with tutors (Schön 1992). Based on this perspective, there are training models for teachers and professional training for architects, as well as an analysis of the system of practical experiences in the UNAM's School of Psychology (Barrón and Ysunza 2003).

Transverse Topics and Values

Another concern regarding the closer relationship between higher education and life is that the former should include in its teachings ethical aspects that guarantee the integral development of the person. This presents a new challenge for educational institutions, which usually place more emphasis on the intellectual dimension to the detriment of the ethical function, which should be recovered. Transversals play a fundamental role as "an important and valuable cultural content that is necessary for life and coexistence, that form especially the type of citizen demanded by each society through an education in values that allows students to become sensitized to and to position themselves with regard to problems, to judge them critically and to act with a freely-assumed commitment" (Martínez 1995, 12). These transversal cultural contents should be approached from all areas around axes that organize the teaching-learning process (Barrón and Ysunza 2003).

These ideas are evident in educational reforms in countries such as Spain, Canada, Chile, and Argentina, which (with some nuances of difference) share the same curricular approach of transversality, with the intention of reconstructing and reformulating a new integrating, interdisciplinary curriculum. "Transversality is without question one of the most innovative elements of the current educational reforms and the basic element of what is known as Global Education sustained by four axes: cultural globalization, integral education of the person, democratic organization of schools, and commitment by education to socio-natural problems" (Yus 1997, 158). For Monclus and Sabán (1999), transverse topics are stated as curricular content that make reference to current conflicts and problems regarding which students assume an ethical position. By articulating values and ethical attitudes in specific contexts, presumably students will consciously make judgments and develop attitudes. The transverse topics model cannot be limited to passive learning of concepts; they must be approached with active, participative methodologies, by means of which students feel that they are protagonists, make interventions, express opinions, criticize, work in groups, and collectively build their values.

The most significant feature of sociocultural contents is their "transversality," since they traverse and thereby permeate the whole curriculum, from the most general objectives to the most concrete activities. They should be present in all concrete actions undertaken and in all situations that are created in every educational setting. They do not have any precise curricular location, either in space (assignments or specific areas) or in time (courses or determined educational levels). They serve as the basis for organizing disciplinary contents and infuse curriculum areas with valuable aspects of social life. They are open, flexible topics that permit the subsequent incorporation of contents related to new problems that may arise in the future. They are associated with the purposes of education, since they refer to the most fundamental aspirations of education. An outstanding feature of these topics is the evaluative and attitudinal elements that underlie them. An education in values occurs through dealing with these, which contributes especially to the person's ethical development and moral personality, enabling him or her to participate responsibly in building a better world (Barrón and Ysunza 2003).

Yus (2001) and González (1994) have argued that transversality is not acceptable as a set of unconnected topics; knowledge about transverse topics has to be organized around a common interpretative framework that acknowledges the complexity of reality. They also insist on the need to interrelate the transverse topics so that they can be complementary, interdependent, and mutually clarifying. Among the topics suggested are the following: education about the environment; education about consumption; education for health; education for peace, moral, and civic education; traffic education; education about equality between the sexes; education for leisure; education about the communications media; education for music; and education for tolerance.

Final Reflections

Globalization has become a keyword for analyzing a complex conflicted world. In no way isolated from globalization, educational institutions, in addition to playing their traditional roles as centers for research and scholarship, must now provide their students with the conceptual and attitudinal tools that enable them to situate themselves in the world with the ability to act and influence it consciously and critically. In view of the needs and demands for training professionals in a globalized economy, Mexican higher education has been reorganized to address multiple developments, among them are (1) the heterogeneity imposed by disciplinary diversity, including the marks and signals that characterize the academic disciplines as scientific, technological, and humanistic fields, and (2) the complicated and vexed demands of government and other power structures, especially the economic sector, that the university become an agent of change. To address thoughtfully these new and changing realities, curriculum studies in Mexico must remember deeply rooted classic educational ideals models. In aligning curriculum to the market politicians contradict the cultural and social mission of educational institutions.

Demands for cooperation between business and educational institutions are hardly new. Ongoing questioning of the intentions and purposes of such "cooperation" is imperative if we are to avoid the subordination of the academic enterprise to the business enterprise. Academic and economic organizations are different from each other. They exhibit different temporalities (short-term versus long-term), rhythms (thoughtfulness versus action now), and organizational structures (democratic versus autocratic) and autonomies (knowledge production versus product production), and such distinctions should not disappear into the universality of entrepreneurial culture, thereby effacing the localisms of the traditional scientific communities and humanistic cultures.

In particular, I believe that maintaining the national relevance of educational institutions, which includes strengthening their commitment toward the whole of society and not only to some of its sectors, continues to be of great importance. Due to this, the strategy of flexibility for educational systems cannot necessarily be generalized, neither for all institutions nor for all professional training. Its inclusion, in any case, would have to take into account the heterogeneity and diversity of higher education institutions (HEIs) and the missions they represent.

In addition, we need to acknowledge an obstacle to the implementation of any strategy for curriculum innovation in the HEIs. I refer to the centralization of decision-making processes; In addition to this absence of democratic governance, academic administrations, entrapped in a logic of institutional rationality, are structured more by tradition and custom than by needs for change. Likewise, in the framework of present institutional and curricular practices, it is necessary to analyze the processes of participation, negotiation, and decision-making regarding pedagogical and curriculum management, for example, "the aspects of institutional management directly linked to the functioning of educational activity (pedagogical management) and the project for teaching the cultural segment selected for this purpose (curriculum management)" (Furlán 1995, 331).

Academic administrative changes involve a different type of curriculum and institutional management that goes from new forms of knowledge production, based on the multidisciplinary, interdisciplinary, and principally transdisciplinary structures, to the creation of hybrid degree programs, as well as a system of credits with possibilities of inter- and intra-curriculum and institutional mobility, which requires the creation of a well-structured system of equivalencies. Similarly, each curriculum proposal requires training teachers differently, so that they can not only interpret and apply a curriculum but also recreate and reconstruct it. It should not be forgotten that the teacher is fundamental in understanding the existing culture and its social problems.

Finally, it must be noted that models for professional education need not deal exclusively with technical issues, since multiple actions and meanings are at stake whatever the level of educational institution. Management and administration are not the only factors relevant to the scholastic, cultural, and political processes and practices of the various subjects involved in educational action. The difficulty in designing and developing professional education models, such as the tutorial model or learning based on problem solving or on transverse topics, is that they require a consensus around which to define them conceptually, methodologically, and operationally. In no case can they be presented as abstract elements disconnected from the social reality and the historical moment in which they are inserted.

Various models, trends, and curricular orientations for professional education attempt to transcend the fragmentary vision of knowledge, rigidity and disconnection from reality, and mechanical and repetitive teaching and learning methodologies. But there is an imperative need to establish a process of collaboration among the various scientific and entrepreneurial areas if these models are to have any chance of understanding the complexity of the problems of today's world and enable students to seek alternative viable solutions.

Although in the 1990s HEIs undertook the task of shaping their own educational models, incorporating in many cases one or more of the models described above, the analysis still pending must explore to what degree these "models" institutionalize the ideals they claim. Do they provide solid conceptual and methodological bases and clear curriculum development strategies? Rather than models in such a full sense, we are facing "a very peculiar form in which each institution organizes its professional education programs." Without adequate models with which to work, various local educational projects are left to develop as they can, attempting to be relevant to the educational context of origin. We are faced with continued analyses and evaluation of these models and proposals that elucidate their actual meaning and real significance for the players involved.

Notes

1. As is the case of the associations of accountants (ANFECA) and nurses (ANFEO), and the engineers' and architects' societies, among others. It should be noted that these occupations are more solidly established. It would be difficult to find other associations at the same level in professions that have less political weight.

2. A first version of this section was prepared with Marisa Ysunza. The final version of this document is the responsibility of the author.

References

Alcántara, Armando. 1990. "Considerations about Tutorship in University Faculty." *Educative Profiles Magazine* 2: 49–50.
ANUIES. 2000. "Institutional Programs of Tutorship." An ANUIES proposal for the Organization and Functioning of Institutions of Superior Education. Mexico City: ANUIES, Superior Education Library.
Barrón, Concepcón, and Gómez, José. 2003. "The Flexibility of Courses, the Only Alternative for University Professional Formation?" In *Education Regarding Internationalization-Globalization*, ed. Patricia Ducoing. Mexico City: AFIRSE-CESU-UNAM.
Barrón, Concepcón. 2000. "Competency Based Education in the Framework of the Processes of Globalization". In *Competency Formation and Professional Certification*, ed. Angeles Valle, 1–44. Mexico City: CESU-UNAM.
Barrón, Concepcón, and Gutiérrez Norma. 2002. "La formation des tuteurs pour la recherché en sciences sociaux dans le Mexique d'aujourd'hui: Analyse des strategies." In Congress de l'AFIRSE, 1–15. Mexico City: COMIE.
Barrónn, Concepcón, and Marisa Ysunza. 2003. "Curriculum and Professional Formation." In *Curricular Research in Mexico. The Decade of the Nineties* |(1992–2002), ed. Ángel Díaz Barriga, 125–164. Mexico City: COMIE, Educative Research in Mexico.
Barrón, Concepcón, and José Gómez. 2004. "The New Professions in Institutions of Superior Education." In *Professions in Mexico Faced with the Work Market. The Challenges of Formation*, ed. Angeles Valle. Prensaq: Col. University Thought.
Benemerita Autonomous University of Puebla. 1994. *Fenix Project*. Puebla: the Vice-Presidency of Faculty, BUAP.
Carnoy, Martin. 1982. "Education, Economy and the State." In *Cultural and Economic Contradictions in Education: Essays on Class, Ideology and the State*, ed. Michael Apple. New York, London: Routledge and Keagan.
Carrillo, Jorge. 1995. "The Latin American Experience of Just in Time and Total Quality Control." *Latin American Magazine of Work Studies* (1): 193–210.
Casas, Rosalba, and Luna, Matilde. 2000. *Government, Academy and Businesses: Toward a New Configuration of Relationships*. Mexico City: IIS. UNAM / Plaza and Valdes.
Cleaves, Peters. 1985. "Las profesiones y el estado: el caso de México." México, *El Colegio de México* 107: 244.
Covarrubias, José Manuel. 1995. "Engineering and Society." *Civil Engineering*, 210. Mexico City: Faculty of Engineering, UNAM.

de Ibarrola, María, and Sonia Reynaga. 1983. "Estructura de Producción, Mercado de Trabajo y Escolaridad en México." *Revista Latinoamericana de Estudios Educativo* 13 (3): 11–81.

De la Garza Toledo, Enrique. 1996. "The Restructuration of Production in Mexico: Extension and Limitations." *El Cotidiano. Magazine of Current Reality in Mexico* 9–17. Mexico City: Autonomous Metropolitan University-Azcapotzalco (UAM).

De la Garza Toledo, Enrique. 1997. "Flexibility of Work in Latin America." In *Latin American Magazine of Work Studies* 3 (5): 129–157.

De la Garza Toledo, Enrique. 1998 (November 19). "The End of Work or Nonstop Work?" Paper presented at the II National Congress of Work Sociology, Jalapa, Veracruz, Mexico.

Dettmer, Jorge Esteinou. 1983. *Enfoques Predominantes en la Economía de la Educación*. Cuadernos del TICOM, 27. Mexico City: UAM-Xochimilco.

Díaz Barriga, Ángel, ed. 2003. *Curricular Research in Mexico. The Decade of the Nineties*. Educative Research in Mexico Collection, 1992–2002. Mexico City: Mexican Council of Educative Research (COMIE).

Díaz Barriga Arceo, Frida, and Elisa Lugo. 2003. "Curriculum Development." In *Curricular Research in Mexico. The Decade of the Nineties*. Educative Research in Mexico, 1992–2002, ed. Ángel Díaz Barriga, 63–123. Mexico City: COMIE.

Etzkowitz, Henry, and Leot Leydesdorff. 1998. "The Triple Helix as a Model of Innovation Studies." *Science and Public Policy* 25 (3): 195–203.

European Training Foundation. 1997. *Glossary of Labor Market Terms and Standard and Curriculum Development Terms*. Turin: ETF.

Furlán, Alfredo. 1995. "The Probable Evolution of Curricular Management in Our Universities." *Iberoamericana University (UIA) and Union of Latin American Universities (UDUAL). Latin American Universities faced with the new scenarios of the region*, 330–342. Mexico City: UIA-UDUAL.

Garcia Guadilla, Carmen. 1996. *Knowledge, Superior Education and Society in Latin America*. Caracas, Venezuela: Center for Development Studies (CENDES) and New Society Publishing.

Limoges, Camille, Simon Schwartzman, Helga Nowtony, Martin Trow, and Peter Scott. 1997. *New Production of Knowledge. The Dynamics of Science and Research in Contemporary Societies*. Barcelona: Pomares-Corredor Editions.

González Lucini, Fernando. 1994. *Temas Transversales y Areas Curriculares*. Madrid: Alauda/Anaya.

Gómez, Campo, and Jorge Víctor Manuel Munguía Espitia. 1988. "Educación y Estructura Económica. Marco Teórico y Estado del Arte de la Investigación en México." *Congreso Nacional de Investigación Educativa. Documentos Base* 1: 47–85.

Gómez, Campo, and Emilio Tenti Fanfani. 1989. *Universidad y Profesiones. Crisis y Alternativas*. Buenos Aires: Miño y Dávila Editores

Gómez Campo, and Jorge Munguía Espitia. 1995. "Institutional and Curricular Diversification: Condition of Productive Transformation with Equality." In *Iberoamericana University (UIA) and Union of Latin America Universities*

(UDUAL). Latin American Universities Faced with the Scenarios of the Region. Mexico City: UIA-UDUAL.

Gómez, Rosa Amalia. 1997. *Curricular Innovation in Institutions of Superior Education.* Mexico City: ANUIES-UAS.

González, Daniel. 1997. "The Profile of an Industrial Engineer Faced with the XXI Century." *Academy* 11: 49–55.

Gordon, David, Richard Edwards, and Michael Reich. 1973. "A Theory of Labor Market Segmentation." *American Economy Review* 63 (2): 359–365.

Gutiérrez Puertos, Patricia. 2003. "Problem Based Learning (ABP), a Methodological Proposal for the Creative Development of Interdisciplinary Groups." PhD diss. Faculty of Humanities and Social Sciences, La Salle University, Mexico.

International Labour Organization (ILO). 1997. "International Labor Organization." In *Summary of Proceedings. Enterprise Forum Geneva, 8–9 November 1996.* Geneva: ILO.

Latapí, Pablo. 1988. "Tutorial Teaching: Elements for a Proposal Oriented toward Elevating Quality." *Magazine of Superior Education* 68: 5–19.

Lipsmeier, Antonius, Helmut Nölker, and Eberhad Schoenfeldt. 1975. *Pedagogía de la Formación Profesional.* Mexico City: Roca.

Pacheco, Teresa. 1990. "La Institucionalización Del Mundo Profesional." In *Cinco aproximaciones al estudio de las profesiones,* ed. Ángel Díaz Barriga and Teresa Pacheco. Mexico City: Cuadernos del CESU-UNAM.

Luna Serrano, Edna. 1997. "Benefits and Requirements of Flexible Plans in Universities." In *Educative Curriculum, Evaluation and Planning.* Vol. 1, ed. Ángel Díaz Barriga. Mexico City: COMIE, Study center about universities (CESU), and National School of Professional Studies, Iztacala of UNAM.

Martínez, María José. 1995. *Transversal Themes.* Buenos Aires, Argentina: Magisterium of Rio de Plata.

Mertens, Leonard. 1988. "The Workers Movement and the Need for Training Faced with Productive Reconversion. Reconversion of Training?" In *The Workers Movement Faced with Productive Reconversion,* ed. Leonard Mertens. Mexico City: Confederation of Workers of Mexico (CTM), International Work Organization (OIT) and Friedrich Stiftung Foundation.

Monclus, Antonio, and Saban Carmen. 1999. *Education for Peace.* Madrid: GRAO.

Organization for Econonomic Co-operation and Development (OECD). 1997. *Thematic Review of the First Tears of Tertiary Education: Comparative Report.* Paris: OECD.

Palomares, Laura, and Leonard Mertens. 1987. "The Uprising of a New Type of Worker in the High Technology Industry: The Case of Electronics." *Economic Analysis* 11: 31–53.

Palomares, Laura, and Leonard Mertens. 1989. "Programmable Automation and New Work Content. Experiences in the Electric, Metal-Mechanic and Secondary Petro-Chemical Industries in Mexico." *Development Problems* 20 (76): 111–132.

Palomares, Laura, and Leonard Mertens. 1991. "Businesses and Workers Faced with Programmable Automation." In *Mexico Faced with New Technologies*, ed. Corona Leonel. Mexico City: Center for Interdisciplinary Research in Humanities (CIIH), UNAM; Miguel Angel Porrua.

Poder Ejecutivo Federal. 1995. *Plan Nacional de Desarrollo 1995*. Mexico City: Secretaria de Programación and Presupuesto.

Regini, Mario, and Charles Sabel. 1989. "Processes of Industrial Restructuration in Italy in the Eighties." *Work Sociology: New Era* 6: 3–20.

Sánchez Puentes, Ricardo, and María de la Paz Santa María Martínez. 2000. "The Tutorship Process and Practices." In *Postgraduate in Social Sciences and Humanities. Academic Life and Terminal Efficiency*, ed. Ricardo Sanchez Puentes and Martiniano Arredondo Galvan. Mexico City: CESU-UNAM.

Schon, Donald. 1992. *The Formation of Reflective Professionals: Toward a New Design of Teaching and Learning Professions*. Barcelona: Paidos.

CEPAL-UNESCO. 1992. *Education and Knowledge. Axis of Productive Transformation with Equality*. Santiago, Chile: CEPAL-UNESCO.

Teichler, Ulrich. 1998. "Demands in the World of Work." Paper presented at the Global Conference about Superior. Paris, France, August 27.

Thierry, David Rene. 1998. "Labor Competency for Teaching in Programs of Formation and Development." In *Scenarios of Superior Education to 2005*, ed. Axel Didriksson. Mexico City: CESU-UNAM.

Torres, Jurjo. 1994. *Globalization and Interdisciplinarity: The Integrated Curriculum*. Madrid: Spain, Morata Editions.

UNESCO. 1988. *The Modular Focus in Technical Teaching*. Santiago, Chile: OREALC-UNESCO.

UNESCO. 1995. *Document of Politics for Change and Development in Superior Education*. Paris: UNESCO.

University of Guadalajara. 1994. University Network Project of Jalisco, Guadalajara, Jalisco: University of Guadalajara.

University (Autonomous) of Baja California. 1991. *Methodological Considerations for the Restructuration of Study Plans of the Degrees at UABC*. Baja California: UABC.

World Bank. 1995. *Superior Education. Lessons Derived From Experience*. Washington, DC: BIRF/BM.

Valle, Angeles. 1996. "The University-Industry Link through Opinion Studies About the Formation of University Graduate in National Industry." *El Cotidiano* 13 (79): 44–48.

Yus Ramos, Rafael. 1996. *Transversal Themes and Global Education. A New School for Global Humanism. Classroom and Educative Innovation* V(51): 5–12.

Yus Ramos, Rafael. 1997. *Toward a Global Education Through Transversality*. Madrid: Alauda/Anaya.

Chapter 9

Curriculum Studies in Mexico: The Exchanges, the Concepts, the Practices

William F. Pinar

As in my study of curriculum studies in South Africa (Pinar 2010) and Brazil (Pinar 2011), I summarize the exchanges between the participating scholars and international panel members. From this summary I derive concepts and practices characteristic of curriculum studies in Mexico. These emerged not only through the exchanges—accented by the individuality of the participants and panel members—and the preceding chapters but through my ongoing preoccupations as well. These preoccupations—disciplinarity, life history, dialogue—have structured the study.[1] Before going to press, I shared my summary of the exchanges and my identification of key concepts and practices with the participants, asking them to correct any errors and register their disagreements in the epilogue, the "final word."

I have organized the exchanges into two broad categories reflected in the subtitle of the book. In the first, I summarize those exchanges that focused on the history of curriculum studies in Mexico. The systematic study of a discipline's history is prerequisite to understanding its present, a history that is at once internal (e.g., its history of concepts and practices that, in fact, define the field as an academic specialization) and external (e.g., the political and economic history of not only the nation wherein the discipline unfolds). It is the nation that curriculum studies as a field addresses and serves, although not uncritically, as this collection testifies.

As in South Africa, the field's external history seemed especially imprinting. The violent crushing of the 1968 student movement, the government's subsequent efforts at reparation that were themselves crushed by the 1982 economic crisis, which in Mexico reopened the door to international infiltration of not only its economy but also its educational policy, culminating in NGO-driven neoliberal reform: these calamitous events have proved decisive in determining the intellectual course of curriculum studies in Mexico.

There is an imprinting internal history as well. The forced importation of Ralph Tyler's principles of curriculum and instruction and other US technicist models (Benjamin Bloom, Robert Gagné) during the early 1970s, although countered almost immediately by Latin American (including Argentinean, but also Italian) scholarship, set the stage for the forced installation of neoliberal concepts such as "flexibility" and "competency" by the 1990s. The hegemony of these concepts structures the field's present circumstances. During the last four decades a series of individuals—several of whom are participants in this project—have featured prominently in these events, publishing important works and engaging in pivotal debates, if finally marginalized by the government's complicity in international directives. Their intellectual centrality to curriculum studies in Mexico has not changed despite changing circumstances.

Laboring to understand the Mexican field's intellectual history and present circumstances, international panel members Professor Alice Casimiro Lopes of Brazil and Professor Yuzhen Xu of China asked a series of important questions. Sometimes they asked for explanations of concepts, sometimes for clarification of events, and sometimes for comparisons with concepts and developments in other countries. On occasion they simply asked for more information. It was a free-ranging and protracted exchange, often lasting weeks, even months, but always conducted diplomatically and professionally. Although questions concerning the history of field were posed throughout the exchanges, I will (as noted) sequester these in part I. Questions concerning the present circumstances of the field I restrict to part II. In exchanges over the field's present circumstances four concerns kept surfacing, and these I discuss in four subsections within part II: (a) the theory-practice relationship, (b) the changing character of teaching, (c) the effects of globalization, and (d) the history and promise of internationalization. In the final section I discuss the concepts and practices that characterize curriculum studies in Mexico.

I: Intellectual Histories

Understanding is possible not because we stand above history, but because we do not.

David D. Roberts (1995, 35)

In reply to Alice Casimiro Lopes' question, Ángel Díaz Barriga provided a prehistory of curriculum studies in Mexico. He identified four features. First was "a significant influence from European pedagogical thinking," in particular Herbartian pedagogy, reflected in the work of Francisco Larroyo, whose books (*La Ciencia de la Educación, Didáctica General*, and *Historia de la Educación*) were required reading during three decades of teacher education in Mexico. A second influence was the 1968 student protests in Paris, especially as these comprised a pedagogical and self-managed social movement. Third was Latin American educational thought (especially that of Paulo Freire, Susana Barco, Gloria Edelstein, and Azucena Rodríguez) and its incorporation of European approaches associated with Montessori and Freinet. Fourth was US test theory: Ángel Díaz Barriga emphasizes that until recently tests were confined to examining what students had learned. Only now have they become curriculum-detached certifications of general intellectual or vocational "competency."

As a formal field, curriculum studies was inaugurated in Mexico in the forced importation of US technicist models, preeminently those of Ralph Tyler, Hilda Taba, Benjamin Bloom, James Popham, and Eva Baker, as well as that of Robert Gagné. Tens of thousands of copies of their translated works were distributed free of charge, including to the Ministry of Public Education, the National Education Council, the Pedagogical Research Institute, and the Didactics Center of the National University of Mexico (UNAM). This subsidized and forced importation, Ángel Díaz Barriga reminds us (in his reply to questions from Lopes and Xu), "formed part of U.S. expansion and ideological domination ... confront[ing] the Cuban revolution by using a curricular theory that would make it possible to 'Americanize' Latin-American educational thought." In the name of "modernizing educational systems," these models

> eliminated approaches focused on philosophical topics linked to the broad education of the human being, with the aim of overcoming Platonic educational perspectives (endowing human beings with all the perfection that can be aspired to) or Herbartian perspectives (man as a preeminently

educable being), in order to incorporate a pragmatic vision of scholastic work governed by results; and on the economic level, to form the cadres needed by U.S. companies and corporations in their projects of expansion throughout the region.

The United States tried to disguise this ideological intervention, Ángel Díaz Barriga continues, by using "various international agencies to disseminate the U.S. pedagogical doctrine," among them the Organization of American States (OAS), the Department of Education and Culture, and the Agency for International Development, among others.

The most recent history of curriculum studies in Mexico, Alicia de Alba explained, exhibits a "strong tension" between "forces of globalization" and internal developments. The "functionalist and structuralist trend" that she associates with the forced importation of the work of Tyler, Taba, and, later, Bloom was, she notes, contested during the 1980s by "a persistent critical position" theorizing the broad relationship between school and society. Before that moment in the intellectual history of the field, functional-structuralism was supplemented, de Alba suggests, by the "transfer of educational technology" project, yet another instance of US efforts to influence Mexican—indeed, Latin American—education. Such ideological imperialism was contested by the 1968 student movement. After crushing it, the Mexican government made efforts at reparation. In reply to Yuzhen Xu's question concerning the significance of the 1968 "movement," Raquel Glazman-Nowalski also acknowledged this post-1968 sequence of events: (1) "the expansion of higher education in the country," (2) "the democratization of universities," and (3) "the search for greater student participation in the educative processes at the university level."

In other exchanges between scholar-participants and panel members the question of US influence surfaced again and again. Alice Casimiro Lopes asked Alfredo Furlán whether there are similarities between Tyler's *Basic Principles of Curriculum and Instruction* and Glazman's[2] *Diseño de Planes de Estudio* [*Designing Study Plans*]. Does, she asked, Glazman's sociological training surface in this work? In reply, Furlán pointed to differences between the Glazman-Ibarrola text and the Tyler text, characterizing his colleagues' book "an original work ... even though the central proposal is the formulation of objectives and systematic evaluation." Replying to Lopes' question concerning Glazman's sociological disposition, Furlán judged that it surfaced through a certain sensitivity to students in the study plans she devised. Citing quoted passages in Furlán's chapter, Lopes alleges a certain instrumentalism in Ibarrola's approach. Furlán agrees that "at certain times it can sound like a prescriptive discourse." In her other books, Furlán continues, one finds "a more comprehensive critical focus."

Speaking more generally but to this same point, Ángel Díaz Barriga concludes that Mexican scholars "hybridized the technicist curriculum perspective that came from the United States to form a position more specific for the country."

Yuzhen Xu asked how "non-technicist curriculum perspectives" had become incorporated in "study plans" for Mexican universities. Raquel Glazman-Nowalski referenced her earlier publications (with María de Ibarrola); these, she explained, expressed concern for the "integration" of "study plans" with "course programs." Although she acknowledged that this work was later criticized due to its "technical rationality," Glazman-Nowalski insists that the work was always contextualized (e.g., addressed to nationally and regionally distinctive issues).

One significant example of such regional contextualization was evident in 1970s *"objetos de transformación"* [objects of transformation], as Ángel Díaz Barriga explained. As an example he pointed to the UNAM Architecture program, whose curriculum (at that time) prepared students for various regional destinations:

> One curriculum was oriented towards monumental architecture, towards modern, industrial Mexico, and towards the members of society who can pay a high price for their housing where they want to have every possible comfort. Another curriculum was oriented towards architecture for low-cost housing, e.g., houses or buildings for poor people, emphasizing lower costs, and respecting the idiosyncrasies of those who would live in low-cost housing.

A similar regional structuring of the Medical School curriculum occurred during the 1970s. In the curriculum of these various programs, Ángel Díaz Barriga summarized, "students were given a problem (in general, directly connected to a community) and were expected to find a solution to it."

In another question concerning this powerful moment in the history of the field, Xu asked de Alba to elaborate upon her characterization of Mexican universities in the 1970s as exhibiting a "clear socialist orientation." Referencing the Mexican Constitution, amended during the presidency of Lázaro Cardenas (1934–1940) to guarantee a socialist education for all citizens, de Alba affirmed the continuity of Marxist-Socialist currents in Mexican political life in general, resulting in conceptions of "popular, critical and democratic universities."

In his reply to Lopes and Xu, Ángel Díaz Barriga also acknowledged that in the early 1970s universities experienced an especially intense period of "socialist education," led by leftist faculty (who had been influenced by the varieties of Marxism) who devised projects to "prepare professionals to deal with social problems and to be the basis for the 'social revolution.'" He employed the word "excess" to characterize this period when, in his words, "the political project replaced the academic project." As an example, he recalled a movement at the Autonomous University of Sinaloa known as *Los Enfermos* (1972), the stated purpose of which was "to develop a model of a university-factory." He also recalled a project at the Autonomous University of Guerrero for a "People's University," featuring a university radio station that provided legal assistance to residents of the local community, who were to be taught to read and write by undergraduate students. Ángel Díaz Barriga concludes, "Everything was in ferment."

In reply to Lopes' question concerning the theoretical emphases of Eduardo Remedí's 1978 book, Alfredo Furlán replied that Remedí's *Constribuciones a la Didáctica de la Educación Superior* [*Contributions to the Didactics of Higher Education*] "represented the first rupture with the technological emphasis, wherein instructional objectives had replaced questions of intellectual content." Although Remedí's (and Furlán's) intellectual formation in Argentina had been Marxist, Marxism was not, Furlán tells us, a strong influence in this text. It was, Furlán recalls, "Gustavo Vainstein who gave us a course in 'Analysis of the Discourse of Educational Technology' that was based on … the Frankfurt School (1979)." Furlán adds,

> The Gramscian influence came through Mario Manacorda…. Years later we invited the Italians Antonio Santoni Rugiu and Angello Brocoli to come to Mexico to give courses to us, e.g., the pedagogues who comprised the faculty of the Department of Pedagogy. Through Henry Giroux—but above all through the work of Alicia de Alba—the thinking of Paulo Freire became significant to us. While Freire is never mentioned in de Alba, it is possible to trace the Freirean inspiration in her texts.

Here we glimpse the international—indeed, cosmopolitan, in José María García Garduño's characterization—character of curriculum studies in Mexico.

Lopes wondered whether theoretical differences among major curriculum scholars had caused open conflict, or did a "mixture (or hybridization)" occur? There have been few open debates, Furlán replies. This reply recalls the relative absence of dialogue cited in the South African (Pinar 2010a, 232) field. Lack of conflict may also signal solidarity, especially in the face of US ideological imperialism. The critique of US technicist models was a Latin American undertaking supplemented by the voluntary importation of critical theory from the United Kingdom, Italy, and (paradoxically[3]) the United States. In her second round of comments and questions, Lopes asked that Furlán's rationale for his list of key curriculum scholars in Mexico be included in a footnote.[4]

As in the exchanges in the South African and Brazilian projects, there were during these exchanges moments of "situating-the-self." Citing Furlán's identification of key figures in Mexico, Lopes referenced the research she has undertaken in Brazil with Elizabeth Macedo and Edil Pavia; in it they used "analogous criteria—participation of researchers in congresses [e.g., conferences], periodicals, and development agencies—for choosing those researchers [who serve] as representatives of Brazilian curricular production." Citing Furlán's acknowledgment of Italian intellectual influences, Lopes remarked that (aside from Antonio Gramsci) there have been few Italian influences in curriculum studies in Brazil. She wonders to what extent this is a function of scholars' second language—in Brazil it is English, Spanish, and French but infrequently Italian—and of the lack of availability of translations. Finally, referencing Furlán's report that "structuralist-poststructuralist" debates have not proved pivotal in curriculum studies in Mexico, Lopes registers the centrality of such debates in Brazil and the continuing influence of Marx even in post-Marxist scholarship.

In his reply to Lopes' question, Ángel Díaz Barriga confirmed Furlán's judgment of poststructuralism's marginality in Mexican scholarship. But he goes even further, criticizing poststructuralism as restricted to "a very abstract plane," and thereby exhibiting "a linguistic code that only they [its practitioners] can understand." He recalled Herbart's 1806 caution against pedagogy's subsumption in philosophy. "In my opinion," he asserts, "that is what post-structuralist discourse is, a conquest of the curriculum that does not necessarily help to establish clearer intervention strategies in the scholastic sphere."

In another question concerning key concepts and intellectual traditions in Mexican curriculum studies, Xu asked Glazman-Nowalski about the history of scholarly attention to social class in curriculum studies. Glazman-Nowalski replied that social class has not functioned as an abstract concept but, more typically, had been grounded in the specificity of place or "zone." She provided Xu with an example:

> If we were working on the curriculum for a veterinarian, and if his professional practice was located in a region of Jalisco (a state in Mexico), we would emphasize the need for the veterinarian to know the sociopolitical and economic conditions of that particular region so that his veterinary work would be based on actual knowledge of the resources available, and thereby the concrete possibilities for working toward his goals.

Glazman-Nowalski underscored that curriculum problems were (in the 1970s) linked with "the conditions of the place, time, possibilities, resources, and limitations of the place where we were working." The fundamental curricular question—*what knowledge is of most worth?*—was answered according to concrete and thereby variable circumstances, circumstances that included not only the practicalities of the specific situation, but also the ethical convictions and political commitments of the students and faculty.

II: Present Circumstances

If the real message is the medium, the real content is the context.

Mel Watkins (2007, 164)

In reply to Lopes' question concerning Tyler's influence (specifically in the important book Glazman-Nowalski composed with Ibarrola), Glazman-Nowalski replied that although "of course Tyler had been an influence," he had not been the sole influence. More influential were "reviews of the current curricular situation in our universities and attempts to insist on the elaboration of study plans for superior [higher] education in the country." Lopes wondered whether the reappearance of "behaviorism" in contemporary "curriculum by competencies" schemes has been modified—"hybridized"—by "constructivist forces." Glazman-Nowalski affirmed that "curriculum-by-competencies is one of the current trends of contemporary curricular thought," adding: "I am afraid that the prevailing conception of this trend leads to the dominance of 'abilities' and 'skills'." Although worried that "theoretical discourse" is often "incomprehensible" to practitioners, Glazman-Nowalski admitted that the traditional emphasis upon "practical work" in curriculum studies has been "very limiting to educative processes because they [practice-oriented scholars] forget the human, moral, axiological, social and psychological dimensions of a complete education." Agreeing that (as in Brazil) "we tend toward hybrid products," Glazman-Nowalski believes that contemporary "conceptions of competencies has remixed ideas from the 1960s and 1970s," and "a touch of constructivism brings them up to date."

In a second round of questions, Lopes again asked Glazman-Nowalski about the current influence of Tyler, especially in the sphere of evaluation, including its centralization by the federal government. Lopes questioned the utility of any one concept of "neoliberalism" given that, in Brazil, it had been a leftwing government that centralized evaluation and curriculum development under the rubric of "quality." What, she asks, has been the situation in Mexico? Is the centralization of evaluation alleged to be in the service of democratization?

In reply, Glazman-Nowalski worried that "teachers limit their tasks of teaching to what is going to be evaluated" and that university students start their studies not by asking "what are we going to analyze or study here, but how will we be evaluated?" She continued,

> I agree with you that this vision [of evaluation] privileges certain conceptions of "knowledge" and I would like to add that it must be interpreted as it functions in the social and cultural conditions of different environments and countries. In this sense, I need to point out that certain cultural conditions in our country, in my opinion, have significantly distorted some good intentions of evaluations and even the evaluators, leading to extreme situations and strong critiques of our specialists.

The implication here is that abstractions—like "neoliberalism"—become concrete only when contextualized in specific nations at specific historical conjunctures and at specific political moments. Even *within* nations, then, concepts and practices (such as those summarized by the concept of "evaluation") shift in meaning and significance according to shifts in power and consequent shifts in political rhetoric and policy. The distortion Glazman-Nowalski references above has, then, a double meaning: There is what we might call a sophistic misappropriation of scholarly concepts by self-aggrandizing politicians (resulting in scapegoating, as implied above, very much the case in the United States: Pinar 2004, 9) and the inevitable recontextualization of abstraction that occurs in any concrete circumstance.

Lopes complained that the primacy of "evaluation" enables "public control of what is being developed in the University," including the privileging of "scientific production," especially in curriculum research. Evaluation translates, then, into "greater socialization ... and democratization ... of what is done." Although evaluation "contributes to ... 'shared' control ... and a greater visibility" of all that transpires, Glazman-Nowalski agreed that "evaluation" also functions politically, preferring "certain groups and sectors" over others. Confirming Lopes' observation concerning "scientific production," she adds that there is now a "very accentuated tendency toward quantification," and "philosophical works ... and other types of research ... are often denied ... status." This tendency toward quantification is also evident in the United States (see, for instance, Taubman 2009) and (but less so) in Canada (Chambers 2003).

Concerning Lopes' question on the interrelation between graduate programs and "increased research into curriculum," Frida Díaz Barriga Arceo replied (my words, not hers) "not necessarily." Various influences factor in program development and the curriculum research it supports, especially (she noted) "politics and international agencies." These favor programmatic standardization,[5] a development that Díaz Barriga Arceo also found "worrisome," especially as it "effaces the specificity of national contexts and disciplinary knowledge." Curriculum research is, then, prompted by variable, and not always intellectual factors, Díaz Barriga Arceo emphasized. These can be not only extracurricular but also "overlapping" phenomena, such as the effects of increased student enrollments during times of budgetary constriction. These have also contributed to curricular standardization.

Such "overlapping" became evident in Yuzhen Xu's question concerning "student overcrowding." Díaz Barriga Arceo resisted that term, preferring "massification" to denote the "large expansion of enrollment." She explained, "In Mexico, it is common to find classrooms where only one professor attends to 50–60 students (and even more), a situation that occurs frequently as well in primary and middle level public education, but also in ... high schools." One consequence, she suggested, is depersonalization, including teachers' incapacity to attend to individual differences. Despite this reality, there has been the promotion of "constructivist" models of teaching, models that, by their very nature, require smaller groups of students.

Frida Díaz Barriga Arceo referenced the Argentinean researcher Emilio Tenti Fanfani who, she reports, found that throughout Latin America "massification" meant a decrease in educational quality. Decreased rates of retention and increased rates of school failure follow from the unequal distribution of educational services. This observation has been substantiated by a series of studies conducted by the National Institution of Educational Evaluation (INEE is its acronym in Spanish). As has been the case in the United States, the key correlative of differential educational achievement remains socioeconomic status.[6] Such differential achievement is reflected in the so-called pyramid effect, with enrollments decreasing as students move through elementary schools onto high schools and universities.

In reply to Xu's question concerning the genesis of standardized evaluation in Mexico, Díaz Barriga Arceo cited the research of Rosa Aurora Padilla Magaña, who traced the practice to France (and to the Binet's psychological measurement of intelligence) and to the United States, where it began both in public schooling and in the US army during World War I. Standardized evaluation began in Mexico in the 1960s at the UNAM, where standardized examinations were then used in the admission of new students. By the 1980s, such examinations had proliferated in number, encouraged by the secretary of public education. They were used to measure various abilities as well as the acquisition of academic knowledge. It was during the 1990s that the National Evaluative system was established, mandating national examinations. Now Mexico is enduring (in Díaz Barriga Arceo's phrase) an "era of reports and accountability." Díaz Barriga Arceo points out that "despite the proliferation of evaluations," there has been no "improvement in educational quality," in part because the emphasis upon evaluation has not been accompanied by improvement in the material conditions in which education occurs. As in the United States (see, for instance, Dillon 2010, A15), teachers' salary hikes are increasingly aligned with the test scores of their students.

The Theory-Practice Relationship

A canonical concern for curriculum scholars (Pinar and Grumet 1981), the tension between theory and practice was, in these exchanges, associated with critical theory. Lopes cited Brazilian scholarship that suggests that prescriptions of practice derived from critical theory contradicted its "comprehensive focus." That comprehensiveness had in itself signaled a move away from "the pragmatic focus." What, Lopes asked Díaz Barriga Arceo, has been the situation in Mexico? Díaz Barriga Arceo replied that the situation is similar, for example, that critical theory has been rendered superficial, "even contradictory," by efforts to render it "practical." "Conveying this discourse into technical-practical proposals is ... not really viable," she reports. Educators "concluded that it is not possible to transform education and therefore they assumed a stance of immobility ... favoring the status quo." The "resistance" that critical theory promised has, then, ensured only "reproduction," a defeat not limited to the world of *Realpolitik* but embedded in the scholarship itself (Pinar 2009a).

Rather than deepening our knowledge, Díaz Barriga Arceo continued, "people have tried to restrict the curriculum field to the technical area, [dictating] what educators should know and do." She adds, "This is, in my judgment, a great mistake." Especially during this time of "attack" in which educators are positioned as targets of governmental policies, "I consider that it is indispensable to look for a way to recuperate the subjectivity and intersubjectivity of curriculum actors in the direction of generating proposals and actions for educative transformation." In this statement the tension between theory and practice dissolves as the two domains become conjoined for the sake of educational transformation.

Also traversing the theory-practice divide, Lopes asked about "the psycho-pedagogical approximation to the curriculum" that Díaz Barriga Arceo suggested represents "a crossroads between curriculum studies and those studies dedicated to ... teaching and specific didactics." Are there tensions, Lopes asked, between "psycho-pedagogical" and "critical" perspectives? Are there efforts to combine the two traditions? There has been "antagonism" between critical and psycho-pedagogical perspectives, Díaz Barriga Arceo acknowledges, in part due to the difference between their scales of focus: the social for the former, the individual for the latter. Indeed, she continued, each discourse can deteriorate into reductionism: for example, sociologism and psychologism. Moreover, educational psychology has "an intention to prescribe," Díaz Barriga Arceo notes. There remains a tendency to dissociate the two categories that, she suggests, "should be integrated in a congruent explanation."

Díaz Barriga Arceo points out that "psychological and learning processes do not happen in an isolated way or in the same way when faced with different socio-cultural contexts." In order to "understand" and "intervene," then, "we need to recognize the complexity of this relation of reciprocal influence between one and the other." Because there are no "natural" or "ideal" means of learning, the influence of context is crucial. Moreover, Díaz Barriga Arceo continued, "the actual role of curricular content has been reconsidered as knowledge or cultural construction with specific dynamics." She adds, "In this way, the theme of specific didactics has been articulated with a socio-constructivist vision of knowledge. I can not assure you that it is not all harmonious and congruent, but at least there is an agreement on some fundamental approaches." Here is underlined the concept of "approximation"—not as mimesis but as agency—in construing teaching as a "psycho-pedagogical approximation to the curriculum."

To illustrate this point, Díaz Barriga Arceo mentions the sciences (specifically STS: Science-Technology-Society), foreign language (the teaching of which now emphasizes communication in contrast to grammar), and mathematics (inspired by the emphasis of the French School on problem-solving). What these curricula have in common, she notes, is the centrality of "competencies ... focused on experiences of real contexts (project methods, learning based on problems and cases, learning in community service, etc.)." In tension with the curriculum logic of academic disciplines (a logic that, Díaz Barriga Arceo notes, "offers identity," and not only for the organization of the faculty in distinctive departments), the emphasis upon "competencies has been derived, in its most restrictive version, from a behavioral approach centered on the analysis of discrete tasks." Once again politicians and bureaucrats recirculate earlier discourses as "innovations," as Ángel Díaz Barriga reminds in his chapter.

In a second round of questions, Lopes again asks Díaz Barriga Arceo about "theory and practice in the field of curriculum." For Lopes, the problem with "theory" is not that it is by its very nature "complex" and "not always accessible to teachers," but that it is invoked to direct practice. This, she judges, is "limited view." Although she believes that "teachers should be theoretically well trained," Lopes also believes that theoretical questions arise from daily practice, and that only those who work in schools can reflect theoretically on specific solutions to specific problems. Moreover, it is practitioners who must take the lead in fighting politically for solutions to practical problems, a position that Madeleine Grumet (2009) also has endorsed in the United States. "We university-based researchers," Lopes continued, "have a commitment to theoretical production, but that production cannot prescribe daily practice. We can be in dialogue with practitioners, but not specify their conduct." Lopes sees this problem of prescription as a "crucial tension" in the field. Lopes wonders whether the "theory-practice" relationship in Mexican curriculum studies is expressed in the "conflict between pragmatic interest and the interest for knowledge"? In Latin America—but not in Mexico?—Lopes senses an interest in the production of theory unconstrained by practical demands.

The Changing Character of Teaching

The theory-practice tension is evident in changing conceptions of teaching. To Lopes' question concerning the association of curricular "flexibility" with instrumentalism, rendering the curriculum subordinated to the demands of "knowing-how-to-do," María Concepción Barrón Tirado replied by referencing "an element constitutive of the curricular project regarding flexibility," for example, "flexible didactics." Because "new professions" have emerged from "scientific advances and new technology" (e.g., biomedicine and biotechnology)—the role of the instructor must be "rethought" to include promotion of "self-learning." Curricula linked to these new professions require "new" teacher training, as now instructors must demonstrate "the capacity to not only interpret and apply a curriculum, but also to recreate it and construct it." Concepción Barrón Tirado adds a key cautionary note: "We must not forget that the instructor is one of the fundamental actors to preserve the comprehension of the current culture and socially problematic issues."

In this important reminder I hear an echo of those 1970s "*objetos de transformación*" that Ángel Díaz Barriga commemorates. Even the most technical and vocational preparation was then attuned to culture, society, and the historical moment. But the "exterior" in contemporary vocationally oriented curricula is articulated not by the socially engaged intellectual but, as Tirado notes, by the appearance of the "guest instructor." These visitors arrive from the various businesses that are now said to represent the destination of education. Such didactical "flexibility" reflects intensified administrative control of various study plans, "facilitating" (my term, not Concepción Barrón Tirado's, and used here cynically) shifts in curricular emphasis, including specific course requirements and program duration, institutionalized through evaluation and accreditation. One casualty in this regime, Concepción Barrón Tirado adds, is that there is no sharp sense of "generations," as students of variable ages in various programs with multiple destinations—what she terms the "great heterogeneity of study plans"—cannot cultivate a sense of shared experience.

Lopes dwells on these discourses of flexibility, noting that "many of them are associated with the integrated curriculum," citing "traversal themes" and "curriculum by competencies" as examples. In Brazil, she points out, these have influenced teacher training as well, as institutions attempt to prepare prospective teachers for "new professional careers" accented by flexibility. Lopes asked Concepción Barrón Tirado, "Is the same happening in Mexico? What do you think about it?" In Mexico, Barrón replied, "career paths" can be "personalized," requiring continual "diversification" of curricular options. As a consequence, "no recommended sequence exists in the courses, nor rigid time limits, only accumulation of credits."

Standardization allows students to take equivalent courses in different institutions, even in different countries, as long as they satisfy his or her own career trajectory. The truth is more complex, Concepción Barrón Tirado cautions, noting that curriculum flexibility is not so straightforward, as different curricula demonstrate different internal demands. For instance, in certain curricula the specifications of the job market are primary, whereas in others the internal demands of the profession predominate. For the former, apprenticeships in "real-world" settings are primary, but in the latter more theoretical concerns—including questions of "cultural formation"—are forefronted. Add to these curricular complexities questions of national (and regional) specificity, and the discourse of "flexibility" fractures. Given the consumerism implied by personalized career trajectories, there is no democracy here, as "flexibility" itself is administratively installed and controlled. "Due to multiple reasons and necessities," Concepción Barrón Tirado points out, "it is important to conceive the university as a complex system where knowledge, academic power and labor are interlaced." That interlacing has been forced by globalization.

The Effects of Globalization

Like teaching, allusions to "globalization" traversed the exchanges. Indeed, it became clear that to a considerable extent globalization structures contemporary curriculum studies in Mexico. In Alice Casimiro Lopes' theoretical question, posed to Alicia de Alba, we discern how globalization (however local and mutable its forms) functions as structuration: "Would it be possible to discuss the constitution of equivalents that hegemonize a certain conception of curriculum, nowadays, in Mexico? In such case, is it possible to identify what antagonism sustains the constitution of those chains of equivalents?" Alicia de Alba answered emphatically:

> I consider that at this historic moment there is a strong tendency to follow the guidelines of international organizations in the politics of university curriculum (and in other levels of education) in Mexico. In this way, the empty meanings that try to hegemonize the curriculum field come from the discourses of these organizations. During the last fifteen years the most important ones have been quality, flexibility and competencies.

Alicia de Alba was not alone in underscoring the influence of international organizations—the institutional form of globalization—in Mexican educational policy.

Like Frida Díaz Barriga Arceo, Lopes linked colonization with "satellization"[7] but Lopes emphasized the (former) colony's resignification of unequal power relations. She asked whether Mexican implementation of neoliberal policies has also involved such resignification. Díaz Barriga Arceo replied that reproduction theory has missed "local reconstruction," for example, "processes of rejection, resistance and the elaboration of counter-proposals." The technocratic model remains hegemonic, as Díaz Barriga Arceo acknowledged: "We have not been able to work from the understanding that every curricular project implies an important transformation of structures, processes and practices, of actors and institutions. Nor have we been able to achieve, in my judgment, this holistic or ecological view of community or social group." Even recent "constructivist" policies are "deep down... revisited versions of business type projects that we have seen before."

Lopes prefaced her question to Concepción Barrón Tirado by referencing the situation in Brazil where, Lopes acknowledged, there is "a recovery... of instrumental forces associated with social engineering." This pervasive instrumentalism is "no longer envisaging an efficiency that attends to society as a whole," but it is specifically "transposed to educative processes." "These transpositions," Lopes continued,

> envisage the efficiency of the self-regulated individual, supposedly capable of being translated into an efficiency of the system. That conception, very often, is associated with curriculum by competencies, in its more instrumental foci. I would like to know up to what point you consider that that reasoning makes sense for curricular discussions in Mexico. Up to what

point is an unsubordinated relationship between professional training and education not still a Utopia to be conquered?

Given the totalizing character of the phenomena Concepción Barrón Tirado describes in her chapter, I was surprised by the force of her answer: "I consider that the subordination of higher education to the exclusive criteria of the labor market is not possible for the following reasons." What might mitigate the subordination of higher education to market forces?

Although it is true that in general higher education has been harnessed to the labor market,[8] Concepción Barrón Tirado points out that students' actual destinations cannot be known in advance: "graduates do not know what company they are going to go to and the specific requirements that they will be asked to fulfill." Even if these were known years in advance (and somehow did not change over the interim), "formation [education] in any ample sense considers incorporating not only knowledge and developing skills and abilities, but also appropriating the culture of the period, the values and the commitment to society for the development of a country." Here Concepción Barrón Tirado underscores that not only education but the overall economy occurs within (as well as across) nations, and that even vocational education requires acknowledgment of the specificity (the multiplicity) of the nation. The competency demands made by international agencies, Concepción Barrón Tirado added, tend to be abstracted, and in terms of individual self-formation, these tend to be "intangible values such as respect for life, convenience and honesty, among others." These curricular traversals imply a universality of knowledge to be "applied and demonstrated in different fields." In the US context, this insight becomes an argument for the liberal arts.[9]

Among these different fields are specific areas of professional specialization. Lopes references Díaz Barriga Arceo's discussion of "curricular studies on the formation and social practice of professionals," asking whether this category includes "critical perspectives." The category is structured by "purpose and educative level," Díaz Barriga Arceo replied, not by "theoretical or methodological approach." It is what professionals do that informs the academic content of professional preparation. A separate line of research focuses on "identities" and "practices"—conducted from "sociological, social psychological, historical perspectives"—that also inform academic content or professional preparation. Díaz Barriga Arceo judges that both of these categories of research "are relevant and valuable."

In Mexico, Concepción Barrón Tirado offered, curriculum researchers have designed study plans to produce specific skills, aligned with the most sophisticated educational technology and informed by constructivist perspectives. Others have questioned the instrumentalism of such plans and the very meaning of such "skills."[10] Overall, she summarizes, a "reductionist and technical vision...proliferates nowadays." Moreover, "there seems to be an absence of theoretical debate about this perspective." Concepción Barrón Tirado declines to characterize professional preparation (e.g., formation) as "technical and technological education...as a curricular model." An import from "Anglo-Saxon countries," such miseducation is indeed "problematic." Despite its national specificity, such education is now distributed globally, linked to that "new economic order based on the development of the technologies of information and communication," and specified in various documents issued by UNESCO and the World Bank. She summarizes, curriculum conceived in terms of "efficiency, quality, evaluation, financing, pertinence and relevance are now present in all of the different levels of the national educational system." We live now in a so-called society of knowledge.

What we live in is a society of standardization, as the requirements and demands of globalization—accented by the concepts listed above, enshrined in policy documents from the aforementioned organizations—become aligned with economic agreements, especially with Free Trade Agreements (TLC).[11] That has meant the establishment of what Concepción Barrón Tirado terms "equivalent professional evaluation mechanisms to provide guarantees of the quality of the international trade of professional services." The consequence is that Mexico no longer controls the educational system by means of which its professionals are prepared. The "world of work" now controls professional preparation, informed by two "parallel tendencies." The first involves "the mental training of masses" as the globalization of the economy requires more graduates to constitute an "intelligent work force." The second involves "the permanent [ongoing] transformation of the world of work," obligating workers "to update their knowledge and acquire ever new and specialized knowledge." These tendencies require higher education "to offer diversified and flexible options" aligned with a job market that is always transforming itself and wherein "the specified knowledge students acquired during their initial formation is quickly no longer current" (all quoted passages are Concepción Barrón Tirado's).

The inability of higher education to anticipate what specific skills and information will be required for competence in specific workplaces—due in part to the ever-shifting character of the workplace itself—suggests that universities are well-advised to emphasize the knowledge students need to understand these phenomena, knowledge now marginalized as non-vocational and associated with the "liberal arts." Concepción Barrón Tirado recommends that the curricular "priority" now be "the development of the intellectual capacities of the students to adapt to the rapid economic and cultural changes and ever new technologies ... and develop qualities such as the spirit of initiative and an enterprising spirit or the capacity to adapt." By emphasizing creativity and human development in general, higher education might help its students face an unpredictable and often dehumanizing world of work.

The History and Promise of Internationalization

In these exchanges "globalization" denotes standardization achieved through the alignment of Mexican policies with neoliberal policies promoted especially (and aggressively) by global institutions. In contrast, "internationalization" referenced intellectual exchanges among scholars sharing concern over the effects of globalization on the curriculum. The exchanges between participants and international panel members are but one brief example, as it is clear that Mexican scholars have long been engaged with their colleagues worldwide, especially those working across Latin America.

In reply to Yuzhen Xu's question concerning foreign influences on the intellectual formation of Mexican scholars, Raquel Glazman-Nowalski replied that "much of the curriculum research done in our country is based on scholarship from other countries, and that many of us have applied perceptions, theories, and concepts [from this scholarship] in terms of our own national conditions." Glazman-Nowalski emphasized that foreign "concepts have been extrapolated or adapted to the curriculum conditions in Mexico and to the particular characteristics of the problem being dealt with in accordance with specific curriculum problems, with the educational conditions in the country at the moment, and with the problems of the educational institution where the work is being done. Moreover, these [foreign] concepts are often evident in the efforts of curriculum researchers to address these problems." Here Glazman-Nowalski is accenting the processes of translation and recontextualization.[12]

Alicia de Alba pointed out (to Lopes) that the internationalization of Mexican curriculum studies has not been unidirectional, that Mexican scholarship has been exported as well: "In my travel ... [through] Argentina, Costa Rica and Columbia—principally—and in ... Spain, United States, England, Australia and Germany, I have been able to perceive the impact of some of the scholars of the curriculum field in Mexico." De Alba provided documentation[13] of Mexican scholars' international influence, especially in Spanish-speaking countries. Stressing the significance of dialogue, she reported that

1. There has been a "strong dialogue" among scholars who speak Spanish regarding the curriculum field in general and in the curriculum field in Mexico in particular: "internal strengths of dialogue."
2. Due to the "internal strengths of dialogue," we, the practitioners of the curriculum field in Mexico, have been able to maintain for more than two decades a constant and growing production[14] in Spanish and since the end of the 1990s we have started to publish in other languages, including English. Due to the role that the English language plays in the international academic field and specifically in curriculum studies, the thought and work of Mexican authors in this field have been relatively unknown in countries where Spanish is not spoken.
3. The "internal strength of dialogue" among scholars who speak Spanish has favored a certain degree of internationalization of curriculum studies in Spanish-speaking countries, particularly the Latin American countries, although there is some dialogue between Latin American countries and Spain.
4. The "internal strength of dialogue" among Spanish-speaking scholars, combined with the scarce knowledge of the production of Spanish-speaking scholars in non-Spanish-speaking parts of the world, has acted and continues to act as an obstacle to participating more fully in the internationalization of curriculum studies.

I hope the present volume contributes to a weakening of this "obstacle."

Curriculum Studies Today

Efficiency, productivity, quality, and achievement indicators form the logic that prevails at present in the Mexican educational system.

Ángel Díaz Barriga (2010)

Despite the effects of globalization on the logic of Mexican education, curriculum studies in Mexico is an intellectually vibrant field animated by pressing and important concerns. One mapping of the contemporary field is evident in Alica de Alba's reply to Lopes' request for additional information regarding the key texts in Mexican curriculum studies. De Alba distinguished between two types of scholarly production: (1) curriculum research, including "theoretical, methodological and technical contributions," and (2) "curriculum design, politics, and evaluation, a broad category that includes policy-makers and developers." Alba then summarized the "themes" and "concepts and debates" characteristic of curriculum research in Mexico.

- Study plans and curriculum
- Curricular design
- Didactics and curriculum
- Curriculum-society relationship and the social function of universities
- Faculty formation [e.g., faculty development, professional preparation]
- Curricular planning, management and evaluation
- Research about the curriculum
- Transversals: education for peace, environmental education, human rights, gender, citizenship, values.
- Intercultural aspects and curriculum
- Debate about the curriculum concept itself
- Curriculum design and evaluation
- Critical thought (from Latin America, from Michael F. D. Young and the British New Sociology of Education, from the Reconceptualist Movement in the USA)
- Modular system of the Autonomous Metropolitan University (UAM)
- Interdisciplines
- Quality
- Flexibility
- Competencies
- Subject, subjectivity
- Curricular over-determination
- Curriculum-society link
- Multiculturalism, interculturalism, cultural contact
- Environment, environmental education, sustainability, and curriculum

The module system of *Universidad Autónoma Metropolitana* (UAM), José María García Garduño points out, is regarded as "a stepping stone on the development of curriculum field." Garduño associates the UAM system with US curricular integration as formulated by Harold Rugg. In his reply to the panel, Ángel Díaz Barriga reports that "there was a certain disillusionment with the study of topics that have little impact on the community," as well as "a certain enthusiasm for the discovery of new issues," among them "school discipline, professional identity, etc."

Official occasions for such mappings have been the state-of-the-art assessments authorized by the Mexican Council for Educative Research (COMIE). In reply to Yuzhen Xu's questions concerning these, Raquel Glazman-Nowalski affirmed their importance, as did Frida Díaz Barriga Arceo, who explained that these "systematic and evaluative analyses of scientific output generated around a field of educational research and development [over] a determined period of time" are usually conducted every ten years. These systematic assessments enable the "identification of objects or themes that are being studied, the main theoretical focuses and research methodologies, the type and impact of output and its beneficiaries, as well as the conditions or restrictions that research communities face." The "effects of disciplinary politics"—for instance, the "absence of pertinent themes or even prejudices in presentation"—can also be identified (all quoted passages from Díaz Barriga Arceo). Systematic reviews of the state of learning theory, Didactics, educational history, as well as curriculum studies have been authorized by COMIE. Díaz Barriga Arceo noted that references for previous reviews of curriculum studies are available on COMIE's website.[15]

In these state-of-the-art assessments, Díaz Barriga Arceo continued, curriculum studies was declared to be "one of the most important specialties in education in Mexico," judged by the volume of scholarly production (including postgraduate theses and dissertations) and by the "conceptual centrality of curriculum to all educational practice." During the last decade, Díaz Barriga Arceo continued, curriculum studies in Mexico has emphasized theory, history, development, processes and practices, professional formation, and evaluation. Although a polysemous term (especially theoretically), curriculum continues to denote the content of courses and programs, and that definition is reflected in a strong and continuing interest in applied studies, including (in Díaz Barriga Arceo's words) the "instrumentation and solution of concrete problems."

For some, Lopes pointed out, the "eternal crisis" of curriculum studies is associated with its porous boundaries and "diffuse limits," a point also made elsewhere by Ángel Díaz Barriga (2003, 445). But such "hybridism," Lopes asserts, is, in fact, an intellectual strength of the field. Lopes asked José María García Garduño whether such hybridity is protected in graduate programs in Mexico. Garduño answered affirmatively, citing the incorporation of US, Spanish, and Argentinean ideas in curriculum studies in Mexico. Hybridity, he suggested, has for decades characterized the field, including the academic preparation of its practitioners. Ángel Díaz Barriga agreed, offering as an example "my first book, *Didáctica y Curriculum* (1984), wherein curricular thinking is enriched by connecting it to subjects that come from the field of didactics." That book, he notes, included influences from French Didactics as well as from Brazilian (especially from Freire, who, as noted in the introduction, was in Mexico during the 1970s) and Argentinean sources.

Discussing distinctions drawn and boundaries blurred between structuralism and poststructuralism, Lopes again invoked the concept of "hybridism"—so important in curriculum studies in Brazil (see Pinar 2011)—to denote the distinctiveness of curriculum scholars' appropriation of these dissonant traditions. Alicia de Alba reported that she prefers "to work on the notion of articulation logic rather than that of hybridization." She explained that "articulation logic allows us to understand the conformation of equivalents. In an equivalent, elements from distinct differences are retaken (differences from and in discursive dissemination) and become overdetermined in an equivalent (differences as a constitutive part of the equivalency, the identities and the processes of *subjectivation*)." This more nuanced depiction allows us, de Alba suggested, to discern traces of presumably contrary discourses embedded in each other. "Far from tracing an irreconcilable line between positions," de Alba continued,

> I consider that anti-essentialist, post-fundamental and poststructuralist positions allow and favor the articulation among differences, a matter that is difficult to conceive from other aspects. This is one of the main reasons why I have positioned myself in these perspectives for quite some time now.[16]

Are the processes of subjectivation that produce the "I" also a "conformation" of "distinct differences"?

In reply to Lopes' question concerning the isolation of Brazil's field within Latin America and, in particular, its relative invisibility in Mexico, Garduño pointed to language differences. Although differences between Spanish and Portuguese do constitute a language barrier, there are, he suggested, "border crossings." Freire is cited more often in Mexico than in Brazil, Garduño pointed out, and "Lourenço Filho—the pioneer of the new school movement in Brazil—has been one of the most influential educators in Latin America." Implying that Brazil's isolation may also be somewhat self-legislated, Garduño speculated that Brazil has tended to look to Europe and the United States more than it has to Spanish-speaking countries. Regarding Lopes' question concerning hybridity—specifically the danger of its uncritical acclaim—Garduño offered that "hybridism occurs within a framework of contradictions and inequities. It is not only a relationship of dependence." This seems to me a crucial point, as translation implies not only mimesis but reconstruction.[17]

Replying to Lopes' question concerning "interpretive studies," Díaz Barriga Arceo distinguished between studies focused on "social and economical structures" and those that emphasize "intersubjectivity, identity construction, and the discourse of actors from the perspective of local culture." She referenced the scholarship of the Brazilian theorist Tomaz Tadeu da Silva[18] and her Mexican colleague Alicia de Alba, who "recovers" Derrida and Laclau, as well as Berger and Luckmann, Schutz, and Moscovici.

Replying to Xu's question regarding her reference (in her chapter) to "formative investigations," de Alba explained that these projects occurred in Mexico, Argentina, Ecuador, Columbia, Costa Rica, and Spain. These interchanges continue today under the general theme "Education Debates, and the Social Imaginary," one seminar of which is "Curriculum and the Twenty-First Century." Animating this Latin American project, de Alba suggested, is the absence of utopian horizons in contemporary educational research, in part due to the over-determination of the curriculum by political forces associated with neoliberalism, resulting in a situation wherein university faculty are unable to undertake critical theory development.

Despite the unfavorable circumstances globalizing neoliberal policies create, Alicia de Alba judges that important theoretical progress has been made as a consequence of these cooperative ventures with colleagues in various Spanish-speaking nations. She endorses such "formative research," wherein researchers (in groups or teams, working with students and colleagues at other institutions) revise their inquiries as the research proceeds, "in the measure that they continue to be strengthened and enriched." The research group or team assumes responsibility for management of the project and may offer additional training to members during the process. For some, it is this "formative dimension" that is the "key ... and constitutive element of the research process itself," namely those formulations and discoveries that are not planned and occasioned by courses, seminars, workshops, and colloquia.

"The results obtained have been satisfactory," de Alba reports, "to the extent that some of the researchers who have participated in these projects have achieved recognition, autonomy and leadership in their institutions and regions." She observes that although these teams are hierarchical, organized according to the academic authority of the participants, at the same time they remain "formative and open," enabling some mobility in status and in the academic labor of specific participants. Credit as a participant is conferred according to the results achieved and "independent of their scholarly level and experience." There is, as this description implies and de Alba accents, "relative autonomy" among participants, somewhat irrespective of status and authority. Moreover, she reports that "human relations" among research team participants are considered important, that is, working relationships are "direct, personal, friendly and respectful ... in such a way that it is always possible to resolve different types of problems." Academic rigor has been no casualty of this collaborative undertaking.[19]

To Yuzhen Xu's question concerning internationalization, de Alba replied by underlining Mexican participation in Latin America and Europe, especially in Spain. There are in Mexico research centers focused on *"social outlines*, linked with ideas like those of the world figure." She credits the "social outlines" category with helping Mexican scholars "to get out of the straightjacket ... of 'right' and 'left,' incorporating a radical opening in our analytic thought ... with the intent of recognizing the work of new generations ... and [attending] to the limitations of our own generation." De Alba continued:

> This line of thought and research in the curriculum field has moved from a critical analysis that allowed for the deconstruction and comprehension of a complex situation, of a historical and social block in academics at public universities in the decade of the 1990s, toward a radical opening that assumes the challenge of thinking of "world-worlds" and of contributing to its improvement in different terms and recognizing the importance and need of building new theoretical, epistemic and ontological categories to achieve a better articulation between curriculum and social, political, cultural and economic reality.

Such intellectual labor requires "cultural contact," a concept on which de Alba is now working.

III: The Concepts, The Practices

Historical understanding is itself historically situated.

David D. Roberts (1995, 35)

Despite the vocationalism and instrumentalism that have accompanied globalization, curriculum studies in Mexico is not only a "practical" field, as it remains committed to—in Glazman-Nowalski's terms—"the human, moral, axiological, social and psychological dimensions of a complete education." Díaz Barriga Arceo shares this view, as she laments efforts to limit curriculum studies to a "technical area" dictating "what educators should think and do." For her, curriculum studies in Mexico concerns curriculum development as well as efforts at understanding curriculum. Reflecting this wide spectrum of research—from the theoretical to the practical—it is not only concepts but also practices (interrelated as the two terms are) that are prominent in curriculum studies in Mexico. Indeed, in at least one instance theory and practice fuse, as in the case of "study plans." Although derived from Jesuit (e.g., the *Ratio Studiorum*) and German (the tradition of *Lehrplan*) conceptions, these distinctly Mexican instances of curriculum development register key concepts (including "activity" and "formation") as they plot education in a range of specialized and professional fields.

Study Plans

Study plans specify what must be learned to achieve competency[20] in specific fields. Mexican curriculum scholars have devised study plans for a wide range of fields (including the various professions), combining different curriculum theories to design study plans that speak simultaneously to the internal demands of academic fields and to the social and economic problems those fields must practically, politically, and ethically address. In curriculum terms, study plans traverse the theory-practice divide, restating theory in practical terms, restructuring theory according to practical everyday realities that are sometimes regionally specific. However comprehensive these study plans may have been, they assumed the presence of teachers not only to ensure that students fulfilled the obligations that the study plans specified but also to encourage students to reflect on their studies, connecting these to the everyday world of those they intend to serve.

Such teaching—a "psycho-pedagogical approximation to the curriculum," as Díaz Barriga Arceo characterizes it—represents "a crossroads between curriculum studies and those studies dedicated to ... teaching and specific didactics." Because there is no one "natural" or "ideal" means of learning, she notes, the influence of context is crucial. She summarizes: "the actual role of curricular content has been reconsidered, as knowledge or cultural construction but with specific dynamics." She adds: "In this way, the theme of specific didactics has been articulated with a socioconstructivist vision of knowledge."

The sequencing of study plans amounts to a program of study, as Glazman-Nowalski implied, expressing concern for the "integration" between "study plans" and "course programs." Study plans adapted to the 1990s demand for "flexibility." Concepción Barrón Tirado reminded us that curriculum researchers did not always design study plans to produce specific skills, aligned with the most sophisticated educational technology and informed by constructivist perspectives. They have also questioned the instrumentalism of such plans as well as the very meaning of such "skills."

Indeed, in the 1970s—this decade would seem to have been the heyday of curriculum studies in Mexico[21]—study plans were structured by *objetos de transformación*. These replaced the "behavioral objectives" that had been forcibly imported from the United States. In these transformational study plans—in a wide range of fields, not just teacher education—the "labor of learning" was conducted not only in libraries and classrooms, but also in actual communities, where, as Ángel Díaz Barriga recounts, "they studied first-hand specific social problems." Students not only studied social problems, they also participated in the formulation of solutions. In study plans structured by *objetos de transformación* students confronted social reality not only as an abstraction but as a particularity, structured by the specificities of place. "If we were working on the curriculum for a veterinarian and if his professional practice was located in a region of Jalisco (a state in Mexico)," Glazman-Nowalski explained,

> we would emphasize the need for the veterinarian to know the sociopolitical and economic conditions of that particular region so that his veterinary work would be based on actual knowledge of the resources available, and thereby the concrete possibilities for working towards his goals.

Glazman-Nowalski affirmed that it was during the late 1970s that curriculum problems were linked with "the conditions of the place, time, possibilities, resources, and limitations of the place where he was working." This model of curriculum development, then, acknowledged the "historicity of social and economic demands for professionals by specifying social problems around which teaching units were prepared. These problems are conceptualized as *objetos de transformación* whose achievement would change social reality" (Chapter 8). Concepción Barrón Tirado tells us that this historically attuned and socially situated conception of study plans met strong resistance, not only from politicians and businessmen,[22] but also from teachers whose understanding of the concept was evidently inadequate.

Now, Concepción Barrón Tirado notes, it is curricular flexibility, not social engagement or the historical moment, that structures study plans. ("Flexible didactics" is a term Alice de Alba employed to denote the alignment of teaching to curricula that are themselves aligned with the workplace). Presumably because "new professions" have emerged from "scientific advances and new technology" (including biomedicine, biotechnology), the role of instructor must be "rethought," Concepción Barrón Tirado explained, to include a provision for "self-learning." The 1970s remain as a trace in Barrón's caution: "We must not forget that the instructor is one of the fundamental actors to preserve the comprehension of the current culture and socially problematic issues." Especially when structured by *objetos de transformación*, study plans conveyed this sophisticated conception of curriculum and teaching.

Globalization (Again)

Although there is what Alicia de Alba termed a "strong tension" between "forces of globalization" and the internal intellectual history of curriculum studies in Mexico, it seems from these exchanges that globalization has triumphed and will continue to do so at least in the foreseeable future. The first wave of enforced importation of concepts from elsewhere was the "functionalist and structuralist trend" that de Alba associates with Tyler, Taba, and, later, Bloom. Although contested in the 1980s by "a persistent critical position" focused on the "broad relation between school and society," this "first wave" has returned in revised form in present-day demands for curricula with "flexibility" and "competency."

Tyler, Taba, and Bloom: such a selective importation of US concepts! It could have been Dewey, Counts, and Brameld, or Schwab. It was not incidental that US technicist models were the ones selected (evidently by the US government) to be forcibly imported during an era of student rebellion and communist insurgency throughout the region. The authoritarianism of these models (and the conditions of their installation in Mexico) brought the school curriculum under sharp focus of broader US political efforts at containment of the communist movement. Although Tyler's original formulation was in service of socially progressive experimentation in the United States (The Eight-Year Study), once detached from that study, it functioned in reactionary ways, and not only in Mexico but in the United States as well (Pinar 2010b).

As it had in the Eight-Year Study, Tyler's "principles" of curriculum and instruction—once reformulated in Mexico—also spoke to the issues of the day. This recontextualization is implied in Furlán's characterization (to Lopes) of the Glazman-Ibarrola adaptation to Tyler as "original" and in Glazman-Nowalski's assertion (in reply to Xu) that her early work, however "technicist" it was later judged to be, did address specific Mexican concerns. Although usually associated with capitalism where it becomes even more intensified, instrumentalism is also associated with socialism, which, evidently, characterized curriculum studies during the 1970s, specifically in study plans structured by *objetos de transformación*.

In the present era, however, programmatic standardization predominates. This development, as Díaz Barriga Arceo pointed out, effaces "the specificity of national contexts and fields of disciplinary knowledge." Recall that she underscored that curriculum research is prompted by variable, and not always intellectual, factors. Prominent among these non-intellectual factors have been the aggressive tactics of international organizations in dictating Mexican educational policies and practices. Recall that Alicia de Alba charges that "the empty meanings that try to hegemonize the curriculum field come from the discourses of these organizations." These "empty" meanings are "quality, flexibility and competencies." The technocratic model remains hegemonic, Frida Díaz Barriga Arceo concurs.

Concepción Barrón Tirado, too, acknowledged that Mexican education is now linked to the so-called "new economic order, based on the development of the technologies of information and communication," and specified in various documents issued by UNESCO and the World Bank. Curriculum is conceived, she emphasized, in terms of "efficiency, quality, evaluation, financing, pertinence and relevance; these terms are now present in all of the different levels of the national educational system." What seems missing is academic knowledge. Indeed, Ángel Díaz Barriga confirms that it was "prior to the 1970s [that] the educational system functioned on the basis of curricula." Now it functions on the basis of business. Recall that the absence of "utopian" aspirations, as Alicia de Alba notes, becomes a pressing problem now collectively addressed by scholars throughout Latin America.

While globalization emphasizes standardization, achieved through alignment of Mexican policies with neoliberal practices promoted especially by global institutions, internationalization references intellectual exchanges among scholars. In these terms, then, the involuntary importation of Tyler foreshadowed the forceful restructuring that globalization guaranteed decades later. Since scholarship challenging Tyler's technicist model was voluntarily imported and occurred through free exchanges among Mexican and foreign scholars, that exchange denotes an instance of internationalization. In his critique of US ideological imperialism, Ángel Díaz Barriga cited the US scholar Martin Carnoy. Furlán acknowledged Argentinean challenges[23] to "the technological emphasis" (Remedí, Vainsten, Manacorda, and Furlán himself led the charge, followed by the Italian scholars Antonio Santoni Rugiu and Angello Brocoli). Recall that Freire came to Mexico through Henry Giroux and was recontextualized by Alicia de Alba: these are all, it seems to me, instances of internationalization.

There are others as well. In reply to Yuzhen Xu's question concerning Mexican participation in the internationalization of curriculum studies, de Alba pointed to Mexican participation in ongoing dialogues across Latin America and Europe (especially in Spain). De Alba also pointed out (to Lopes) that the internationalization of Mexican curriculum studies has been a matter not only of imports but of exports as well. And José María García Garduño's chapter extols the cosmopolitanism of curriculum studies in Mexico. Garduño's account underscores that the two phenomena—internationalization and cosmopolitanism—are interrelated.

The glimpse of curriculum studies in Mexico we are afforded here is simultaneously sobering and inspiring. Sobering are the testimonies wherein national and local commitments to social justice are eviscerated by the force of globalization, allegedly in the interest of economic development. Avoided in this economistic calculation are not only political questions associated with economic and social injustice, but also fundamental questions of the nation: its histories, its cultures, its futures.[24] A curriculum that addressed these would incorporate, in Concepción Barrón Tirado's terms, "not only knowledge and developing skills and abilities, but also the culture of the period, the values and the commitment to society for the development of a country." What we face instead is a curricular reinstallation of the *ancien régime*, wherein disparities between the rich and the poor, the powerful and the powerless, are affirmed, even extended, but not contested. It is the *régime* that Adam Smith criticized, the same Adam Smith whom "free market" advocates invoke as the philosophical father of the "free market." Smith disclaimed the "disposition to admire, and almost to worship, the rich and the powerful, and to despise, or, at least, to neglect persons of poor and mean conditions." Such neglect is, he continued, "the great and most universal cause of the corruption of our moral sentiments" (quoted passages in Judt 2009, 88). Tony Judt points out that it was Adam Smith who realized that the greatest peril of a commercialized culture was its moral effect. As Judt (2009, 88) and these chapters testify, this peril "is now upon us."

In the midst of this nightmare I discern "heroic individuals" dedicated to keeping us "awake" by contesting what is enforced, laboring to explicate its genesis, articulate its contours, and discern its effects. By "heroic individuals"—I reference not the fabrications of Hollywood or CNN but the participants in this project—who, against the odds, continue to speak truth to power, to testify to the unrealized promise of the past, and to search for local passages through globalization.[25] (Fate has been no kinder to curriculum studies in the United States, as the "next moment" devolves into identity politics [Pinar 2009b] and public pedagogy [Pinar 2010c]). I take heart from my Mexican colleagues' fidelity to the actuality of history,[26] from their lucid analyses of the present and its hypocrisies, and from their ongoing commitments to scholarly exchange and dialogue, with colleagues elsewhere in Latin America and Spain. Such structures of disciplinarity are also, in this terrible time, modes of political engagement.

Despite adverse institutional conditions—governmental imposition of international agencies' globalization agenda, incessant demands for "innovation" and accountability,[27] and the danger of intellectual manipulation through research funding priorities[28]—it is clear from this collection that neither intellectual independence nor insight has been sacrificed. The cause of curriculum is in Mexico "a great cause,"[29] as it incorporates the socialist traditions and historic aspirations of the Mexican nation, a nation that in 2010 celebrated its 200th anniversary. It is this scale of cause I find ennobling.

Notes

1. For my linking of disciplinarity with intellectual advancement, see Pinar (2007). Because I have defined curriculum as complicated conversation—classroom exchanges structured by the academic disciplines, addressed to society, history, and culture—dialogue has been a key category (Pinar 2004). These concepts converge in this ongoing project: studying curriculum studies in South Africa, Brazil, China, India, and, as this present volume testifies, Mexico.
2. Glazman and Glazman-Nowalski name the same person.
3. The paradox is only apparent, as the instrumentalism of the Tyler Rationale has been contested in the United States at least since Herbert Kliebard's (2000) definitive critique, first published in 1970. In his reply to Lopes and Xu, Ángel Díaz Barriga points out that when "critical theory" arrived in Mexico from the United States and the United Kingdom, Mexican critique was already well underway, having been already intensified by the arrival of academic exiles from Argentina, Chile, and Uruguay.
4. Furlán explains: "I chose María de Ibarrola because of her career path and because she recently wrote on this topic, once again occupying an active place in the field, with respect to what is understood to form part of the 'current circumstances' of the curriculum field. I chose Eduardo Remedí in part because he works in the DIE (Department of Educational Research), one of the institutions that contributes the most to the development of the field. Remedí has been one of the most prominent—and polemical—participants in the field. Ángel Díaz Barriga and Alicia de Alba are part of the IISUE (Institute of Research on the

University and Education) of the UNAM; it is another institution that supports curricular debate in Mexico. Ángel Díaz Barriga is the most famous and prolific member of the quartet and is the scholar who remains the most identified with the field, coordinating the state-of-art assessments of curriculum knowledge conducted each decade by the Mexican Council of Educational Research (COMIE). In addition, he organized an international congress on curriculum, the first held in the decade, which was convened in November 2009 in Tlaxcala (the State that is next to the Federal District). Alicia de Alba has also been active in the field with the recent publication of her book *Curriculum-Society: The Weight of Uncertainty, the Strength of the Imagination*. This work has provoked much interest, including in Argentina, and it has achieved a more general international visibility. Mexican influence in Argentina is also registered there" (see Feeney and Terigi 2003, 102; Palamidessi and Feldman 2003, 111

5. Lopes expressed concern over the Bologna Treaty and its promise of curricular homogeneity, asking Frida Díaz Barriga Arceo whether she shared Lopes' sense that this is a "problem"? Ought we as field, Lopes wondered, "question this movement"?

6. This acknowledgment—that socioeconomic status and academic achievement are positively correlated—has been inverted by US politicians now displacing their responsibility onto teachers who are now held responsible for student test scores (which are presumed to predict students' socioeconomic mobility. In the United States, the shift in emphasis from "inputs" to "outputs" has been catastrophic for the intellectual quality of the curriculum, as even school "deform" apologist Diane Ravitch (2010) now admits.

7. I am reminded of the Canadian philosopher George Grant's characterization of Canada as a "branch-plant satellite" (2005b, 85) of the "American Empire" (2005a, lxix).

8. In Mexico, Concepción Barrón Tirado pointed out, small- and medium-sized businesses (the so-called PYME or "pipymes") dominate the economy, both in terms of employment and GNP. These small- and medium-sized concerns exhibit, she notes, "distinctive characteristics," due in part to certain occupational and financial limits prefixed by the states or regions. Moreover, these businesses exhibit specific logistics, cultures, interests, and senses of enterprise. The 4 million small and medium companies that exist in Mexico offer 73 percent of the total employment and contribute 52 percent of the Gross Internal Product (PIB). Concepción Barrón Tirado emphasized that not all of the PYMES are governed by the same production model, nor do their variable production processes copy those of the large and transnational companies. Moreover, she added, not all of the professions can be incorporated into these types of organization.

9. Such argument was made recently by David Brooks, the well-respected journalist and commentator on The News Hour (on PBS or Public Television) in the United States. Pointing out that there has been a nearly 50 percent drop in the liberal arts majors at US universities in recent decades, Brooks presented three reasons for even students of business to study the humanities: such study (1)

improves one's capacity to read and write, (2) increases familiarity with the representation of emotion, and (3) provides a "wealth of analogies" (2010, A23), enabling one to bridge various and apparently separate domains. Brooks points out that over the past century researchers have constructed elaborate conceptual systems to help us understand human behavior, among them (the list is his) economics, political science, game theory, and evolutionary psychology. Although "useful in many circumstances," Brooks (2010, A23) allows, these fail to "completely explain behavior because deep down people have passions and drives that don't lend themselves to systemic modeling. They have yearnings and fears that reside in an inner beast you could call The Big Shaggy." This latter term is Brooks' folksy phrase for the unconscious. If in an instrumentalist logic, Brooks nonetheless provides additional rationale for Concepción Barrón Tirado's assertions.

10. I, too, have questioned the very meaning of "skills," especially when these are deracinated, split-off from academic knowledge (Pinar 2004, 2012).

11. "Perhaps the original flaw of Globalization," John Ralston Saul (2005, 32) has suggested, "lies in its overstatement of the success of nineteenth-century free trade, along with an overstatement of the determinism of technology and the superiority of rational management systems." Not only then but even today "free trade" can cost dearly, especially in the wages and benefits of workers, the quality of products, and the ecological balance of impoverished trade partners.

12. Encoding recontextualization, translation was one of the key concepts in curriculum studies in South Africa, perhaps in part due to the influence of Basil Bernstein there. As Muller (2000, 63) points out: "Knowledge passes through the educational system via series of reinterpretations which Bernstein calls recontextualizations." In the United States, the term derives from Richard Rorty who used it to designate the narrativism cultural critics employ. The concept and practice of recontextualization substitute for the pragmatic method of "inquiry," enabling the critic to devise the ground rules for engagement (Hall 1994, 5). The term acknowledges worldliness, as implied in Rorty's critique of Derrida (Rorty 1991, 112).

13. **Table 9.1** Referencing Internationalization

Year of edition. Author(s). Title of the book or article (specified)	Number of times cited on Academic Google in Spanish	Observations, commentaries
1978, Glazman, Raquel and María de Ibarrola, *Diseño de Planes de Estudio*. Book.	13	Cited 12 times in Spanish publications and once in an English publication

Continued

Table 9.1 Continued

Year of edition. Author(s). Title of the book or article (specified)	Number of times cited on Academic Google in Spanish	Observations, commentaries
1979, Furlán, Alfredo, Eduardo Remedí, and others, *Constribuciones a la Didáctica de la Educación Superior*. Book/ Notebook. Internal edition of the National School of Superior Studies Iztacala (ENEP-I) of the National Autonomous University of Mexico.	20	Chapter by Alfredo Furlán cited 19 times and 1 citation of the book in the design of a Masters Program on Faculty and Educative Innovation. All citations in Spanish.
1979, Furlán, Alfredo, "Metodología de la Enseñanza," in Furlán, Alfredo, Eduardo Remedí, and others, *Constribuciones a la Didáctica de la Educación Superior*. Book/Notebook. Internal edition of the National School of Superior Studies Iztacala (ENEP-I) of the National Autonomous University of Mexico.	19	All citations in Spanish
1984, Díaz Barriga, Ángel, *Didáctica y Curriculum*, Nuevomar Edition, 1985, Díaz Barriga, Ángel, *Didáctica y Curriculum*, Nuevomar Edition, 1997, Díaz Barriga, Ángel, *Didáctica y Curriculum* (revised edition), Paidos Edition.	63	61 citations in Spanish, 2 citations in English (in another two citations the publications in Spanish had an abstract in English)
1985, De Alba, Alicia et al., *Tecnología Educativa*	5	Chapters cited: Eufrosina Rodriguez and Oscar A. Zapata's 3 times and Alfredo Kuri and Roberto Follari's twice

Continued

Table 9.1 Continued

Year of edition. Author(s). Title of the book or article (specified)	Number of times cited on Academic Google in Spanish	Observations, commentaries
1991, De Alba, Alicia, Ángel Díaz Barriga, and Edgar González Gaudiano. *El Campo del Currículo, Anthology* (Volumes I and II)	8	Cited 7 times in Spanish publications and once in English
1991, De Alba, Alicia, *Curriculum, Mito y Perspectiva*. Book.	127	123 citations in Spanish, 3 citations in English, 2 abstracts in Portuguese, and 2 abstracts in English
1996, Furlán, Alfredo, *Curriculum e Institución*. Book.	17	
2000, García Garduño, José María, "Las dimensiones de efectividad, la validez y fiabilidad de los cuestionarios de evaluación de la docencia: síntesis de la investigación internacional," in Mario Rueda and Frida Díaz Barriga (compilers), *L'evaluación de la Docencia*, Chapter of Book.	4	All citations in Spanish
2002, Concepción Barrón Tirado, "Educación basada en competencias en el marco de los procesos de globalización," in María de los Angeles Valle Flores (coordinator), *Formation in Competencies and Professional Certification*. Book, in Spanish.	20	19 citations in Spanish and 1 citation in English

Continued

Table 9.1 Continued

Year of edition. Author(s). Title of the book or article (specified)	Number of times cited on Academic Google in Spanish	Observations, commentaries
2001, 1st Edition, Arceo, Frida Díaz Barriga and Gerardo Hernandez Rojas, "Constructivismo y aprendizaje significativo" (Chapter 2), in *Faculty Strategies for Significant Learning. A Constructivist Interpretation*. Mexico, McGraw-Hill.	56	All citations in Spanish
2002, 2nd Edition, Arceo, Frida Díaz Barriga and Gerado Hernandez Rojas, "Constructivism and Significant Learning" (Chapter 2), in *Estrategias para el Aprendizaje Significativo. Una Interpretación Constructivista*. Mexico, McGraw-Hill.	292	282 citations in Spanish, 8 citations in English, 1 citation in German, and 1 citation in Portuguese
2003, Glazman, Raquel, *Evaluación y Exclusion en la Enseñanza Universitaria*, City of Mexico, Paidos Educator.	16	All citations in Spanish

Table 9.2 Referencing Internationalization

Year of edition. Author(s). Title of the book or article (specified)	Number of times cited on Academic Google in Spanish	Observations, commentaries
1999, de Alba, Alicia, "Curriculum and Society: Rethinking the Link," in *International Review of Education*. Netherlands.	1	1 citation in English
2000, de Alba, Alicia, Edgar González Gaudiano, Colin Lankshear, and Michael Peters, *Curriculum in the Postmodern Condition*, Peter Lang.	21	17 citations in English, 2 citations in Spanish, 1 citation in Chinese, and 1 citation in German
2003, Díaz Barriga, Ángel, "Curriculum Research: Evolution and Outlook in Mexico," in *International Handbook of Curriculum Research*.	1	1 citation in English
2003, Díaz Barriga, Arceo, Frida, "Main Trends of Curriculum Research in Mexico," in *International Handbook of Curriculum Research*.	1	1 citation in English
2004, Díaz-Barriga, Ángel and Concepción Barrón, "Curriculum, labor market and professional training," American Association for the Advancement of Curriculum Studies. April 10, 2004. Third annual meeting.	Without citations	
2009, Díaz-Barriga, Ángel, "Assessment in Mexican education. An excess of programmes and absence of the pedagogical dimension in Sisifo," *Educational Sciences Journal*, No. 9, May-Aug 2009, ISSN 1645-6500.	Without citations	

14. "Production" means published books, chapters of books, articles, as well as papers presented at different national and international events and the influence of these on study plans and graduate programs and related areas.
15. Visit the COMIE website at http://www.comie.org.mx/v1/sitio/portal.php.

16. Lopes wondered whether poststructuralism has been more influential in curriculum studies in Brazil than in Mexico. De Alba confirmed that structuralism is "still dominant" in Mexican curriculum studies, an unsurprising fact given its influence among Mexican intellectuals in general. As Cusset (2008, 299) points out:

    Mexico was the first Spanish-speaking country to begin spreading French structuralism, long before Spain (where Franco was still in power), and even ten years before the United States. On this occasion, the great importer was the publisher Arnaldo Orfila, who was married to a French anthropologist and … published the works of Foucault, Althusser, and Lévi-Strauss just one or two years after their release in France.

    Recall that Foucault's later works deemphasized the structuralism of his earlier period (Ransom 1997; Paras 2006).

17. I link "reconstruction" to research and the discovery or formulation of "new" academic knowledge, suggesting that its contrasting term—"reorganization"—risks reshuffling what we know already (Pinar 2010, 304). No coldly cognitive affair, reconstruction is animated by passion. As Viano (1993, 321 n. 34) notes in another (but related) context: "Passion … shapes the manner in which individuals respond to historical situations and allows the translation of philosophy into deed, of thought into action." In this sense, reconstruction affirms agency.

18. The work of Tomaz Tadeu de Silva is well known not only in Brazil (see Lopes and Macedo 2003, 190–194; Moreira 2003, 171), but also in the United States (see Baker 2001, 60 n. 44), Argentina (see Feeney and Terigi 2003, 104), and Mexico (see F. Díaz Barriga 2003, 465).

19. In the United States as well collaboration has become a keyword (see Gershon 2010). Evidently I am out of sync as I discern only its downside (Pinar 2009c, ix).

20. Although, as Frida Díaz Barriga Arceo points out, the current emphasis upon "competencies has been derived, in its most restrictive version, from a behavioral approach centered on the analysis of discrete tasks," that was not always the case. Social problems animated conceptions of competence in the late 1970s, as in *objetos de transformación*.

21. "That is why I say that in the seventies," Ángel Díaz Barriga tells Lopes and Xu, "the curricular perspective in Mexico had some signs of utopia: seeking the possible good and seeking to solve the ancient problems of Mexican society. The best experiences were canceled abruptly or withered away due to national politics, particularly policies that were implemented after the crisis of 1982." He adds:

    "President Miguel de la Madrid (1982) began his mandate by establishing what would become a set of neo-liberal policies agreed upon directly with the IMF…. The presidency was later occupied by Carlos Salinas de Gortari and Ernesto Zedillo Ponce de León, both of whom were economists trained in the United States in the economic rules of the neo-liberal school. The Chicago

School is a term that was established to indicate people who were trained in the theses of the U.S. economist, Milton Friedman."

Such "free-market" economics resulted in the world financial crisis of 2008. Ángel Díaz Barriga suggests that this catastrophic event may spell the end of "consensus" regarding this conception of economic growth. One can only hope.

22. Resistance came not only from large business concerns (as one might guess), but also from small businesses, as Ángel Díaz Barriga explained in his illustration (in reply to Xu and Lopes) of transformational projects at the Autonomous University of Nayarit (UAN, to which he also alludes in his chapter):

> The basis for a university education was service to the community, aiming at financial self-sufficiency for the university. The School of Oceanographic Sciences began to produce fish, and also to process the by-products (fish meal). In addition to training students, it promoted the sale of its products at very low prices. In this rural setting, it achieved what the UAN had not been able to bring off, e.g. forming student brigades (sociologists, lawyers, doctors, veterinarians, livestock specialists) working with the members of the community to promote integrated solutions to the problems faced by marginalized groups of society. The university also promoted processing sugar cane to make brown sugar ... [so] that the farmers would have another form of their product to sell to the sugar mills that processed the sugar. The local business people objected to these university practices; the university was taken over by the army, its authorities were removed, and the project was canceled. (emphasis added)

Resistance from local business would probably be sufficient in itself to close a community-based university project; add military force and all educational "transformation" ceases.

23. Argentinean influences have not been limited to challenging technological rationality. Frida Díaz Barriga Arceo references the Argentinean researcher Emilio Tenti Fanfani who, she reports, found that throughout Latin America "massification" meant a decrease in educational quality.

24. As Anthony Grafton (2010, 32) has warned, "Accept the short term as your standard—support only what students want to study right now and outside agencies want to fund right now—and you lose the future. The subjects and methods that will matter most in twenty years are often the ones that nobody values very much right now."

25. It is not incidental that a central and imprinting event of the imported "technical-functionalist trend" was technology, including a specific "transfer of technology" project cited by Alicia de Alba, Frida Díaz Barriga Arceo, José María García Garduño, and María Concepción Barrón Tirado. Technology is the medium of globalization; its frenetic development and aggressive exportation have been central to US efforts at global ideological hegemony. George Grant appreciated that such technological development amounted to nothing less than a struggle "between the American Empire and its peripheries in

Québec, Mexico and English-Canada" (Kroker 1984, 35) over the very forms that life in North America can take.
26. Recall that for Walter Benjamin, imagining the future does not consist in representing and striving for an utopian moment or place but occurs instead through remembrance (see Rauch 2000, 50). Historicity, then, replaces instrumentalism in the subjective and social reconstruction of the present.
27. Ángel Díaz Barriga tells Xu and Lopes that "the logic [of innovation] is that a reform should be followed by another one in a period of 5 years." Such incessant "innovation" precludes, as do the demands of "accountability," the long-term contemplation that social critique and serious scholarship require. Documenting past events as well as future intentions is time-consuming. Noting how elaborate curriculum plans have become, for example, Ángel Díaz Barriga recalled Professor Santiago Hernández Ruíz's humorous recollection: "I can bear personal witness to the fact that in Spain in the 1920s the program for a school course could fit on a cigarette paper." Ángel Díaz Barriga comments, "That was also the situation in Mexico… then. Now curricula can be documents that are more than a hundred pages long."
28. In Mexico, Ángel Díaz Barriga reports, "university professors receive a much lower salary than other professionals, but they are offered many compensating bonuses through lectures and published research. Their contracts with the university make up 30 percent of their salaries, and the other 70 percent has to be earned in annual or biennial evaluations showing research results." To the extent funding agencies stipulate topics of research, the danger to academic freedom (e.g., intellectual independence) increases. As ominous as the Mexican situation is, it is worse in the United Kingdom (Nussbaum 2010, 128–130).
29. In their review of curriculum studies in China, Zhang and Zhong (2003, 254) report that
    in ancient China, "temple" did not only mean a kind of architecture, but it also symbolized "great cause," "great contribution." So curriculum (ke-cheng) originally pointed to "temple," signifying "great cause," "great contribution." In the Tang Dynasty, curriculum was not limited to school curriculum, it included all the great undertakings in the society.
It is this scale of cause that distinguishes curriculum studies in Mexico as well.

References

Baker, Bernadette M. 2001. *In Perpetual Motion: Theories of Power, Educational History, and the Child*. New York: Peter Lang.
Brooks, David. 2010, June 8. "History for Dollars." *The New York Times*, June 8, A23.

Chambers, Cynthia. 2003. "'As Canadian as Possible Under the Circumstances': A View of Contemporary Curriculum Discourses in Canada." In *International Handbook of Curriculum Research*, ed. William F. Pinar, 221–252. Mahwah, NJ: Lawrence Erlbaum.

de Alba, Alicia, Edgar González Gaudiano, Colin Lankshear, and Michael Peters. 2000. *Curriculum in the Postmodern Condition*. New York: Peter Lang.

Díaz Barriga, Ángel. 2003. "Curriculum Research: Evolution and Outlook in Mexico." In *International Handbook of Curriculum Research*, ed. William F. Pinar, 443–456. Mahwah, NJ: Lawrence Erlbaum.

Díaz Barriga, Ángel. 2010. Email Communication with the author, from Vancouver, Canada to Mexico City, May 22, 2010.

Díaz Barriga, Frida. 2003. "Main Trends of Curriculum Research in Mexico." In *International Handbook of Curriculum Research*, ed. William F. Pinar, 457–469. Mahwah, NJ: Lawrence Erlbaum.

Dillon, Sam. 2010. "A Tentative Contract Deal for Washington Teachers." *The New York Times*, April 8, A14.

Feeney, Silvina, and Flavia Terigi. 2003. "Curriculum Studies in Argentina: Documenting the Constitution of the Field." In *International Handbook of Curriculum Research*, ed. William F. Pinar, 101–108. Mahwah, NJ: Lawrence Erlbaum.

Gershon, Walter, ed. 2010. *The Collaborative Turn: Working Together in Qualitative Research*. Rotterdam and Taipei: Sense Publishers.

Grafton, Anthony T. 2010. "Britain: The Disgrace of the Universities." *The New York Review of Books* LVII (6): 32.

Grant, George. 2005a. "Introduction to the Carleton Library Edition of *Lament for a Nation* (lxix–lxxvi)." Montreal and Kingston: McGill-Queen's University Press.

Grant, George. 2005b. *Lament for a Nation*. 40th Anniversary Edition. Montreal and Kingston: McGill-Queen's University Press.

Grumet, Madeleine R. 2009. "The Public Expression of Citizen Teachers." *Journal of Teacher Education*: XXX: 1–11.

Hall, David L.1994. *Richard Rorty: Prophet and Poet of the New Pragmatism*. Albany: State University of New York Press.

Judt, Tony. 2009. "What Is Living and What Is Dead in Social Democracy?" *The New York Review of Books* LVI (20): 86–88, 92, 94, 96.

Kliebard, Herbert M. 2000. "Reappraisal: The Tyler Rationale." *School Review* (1970), 259–272. Reprinted in *Curriculum Theorizing: The Reconceptualization*, ed. William F. Pinar, 70–83. Troy, NY: Educator's International Press.

Kroker, Arthur. 1984. *Technology and the Canadian Mind: Innis/McLuhan/Grant*. Montreal: New World Perspectives.

Malewski, Erik, ed. 2009. *Curriculum Studies Handbook: The Next Moment*. New York: Routledge.

Moreira, Antonio Flavio Barbosa. 2003. "The Curriculum Field in Brazil: Emergence and Consolidation." In *International Handbook of Curriculum Research*, ed. William F. Pinar, 171–184. Mahwah, NJ: Lawrence Erlbaum.

Muller, Johan. 2000. *Reclaiming Knowledge: Social Theory, Curriculum and Education Policy*. London: Routledge.
Nussbaum, Martha C. 2010. *Not for Profit: Why Democracy Needs the Humanities*. Princeton, NJ: Princeton University Press.
Palamidessi, Mariano, and Daniel Feldman. 2003. "The Development of Curriculum Thought in Argentina." In *International Handbook of Curriculum Research*, ed. William F. Pinar, 109–122. Mahwah, NJ: Lawrence Erlbaum.
Paras, Eric. 2006. *Foucault 2.0: Beyond Power and Knowledge*. New York: Other Press.
Pinar, William F. 2004. *What Is Curriculum Theory?* Mahwah, NJ: Lawrence Erlbaum.
Pinar, William F. 2007. *Intellectual Advancement through Disciplinarity: Verticality and Horizontality in Curriculum Studies*. Rotterdam and Taipei: Sense Publishers.
Pinar, W. F. 2009b. "The Unaddressed 'I' of Ideology Critique." *Power and Education* 1 (2): 189–200. Available online at: http://www.wwwords.co.uk.
Pinar, William F. 2009b. "The Next Moment." In *Curriculum Studies Handbook: The Next Moment*, ed. Erik Malewski, 528–533. New York: Routledge.
Pinar, William F. 2009c. *The Worldliness of a Cosmopolitan Education: Passionate Lives in Public Service*. New York: Routledge.
Pinar, William F., ed. 2010a. *Curriculum Studies in South Africa*. New York: Palgrave Macmillan.
Pinar, William F. 2010b. "The Eight-Year Study." *Curriculum Inquiry* 40 (2): 295–316.
Pinar, William F. 2010c. "Foreword." In *Handbook of Public Pedagogy*, ed. Jennifer A. Sandlin, Brian Schultz and Steven Burdick, xv–xix. New York: Routledge.
Pinar, William F., ed., 2011. *Curriculum Studies in Brazil*. New York: Palgrave Macmillan.
Pinar, William F. 2012. *What Is Curriculum Theory?* 2nd ed. New York: Routledge.
Pinar, William F., and Madeleine R. Grumet. 1981. In *Rethinking Curriculum Studies*, ed. Martin Lawn and Len Barton, 20–42. London: Croom Helm.
Ransom, John S. 1997. *Foucault's Discipline: The Politics of Subjectivity*. Durham, NC: Duke University Press.
Rauch, Angelika. 2000. *The Hieroglyph of Tradition: Freud, Benjamin, Gadamer, Novalis, Kant*. Madison, NJ: Fairleigh Dickinson University Press.
Ravitch, Diane. 2010. *The Death and Life of the Great American School System: How Testing and Choice Are Undermining Education*. New York: Basic Books.
Roberts, David D. 1995. *Nothing but History: Reconstruction and Extremity after Metaphysics*. Berkeley and Los Angeles: University of California Press.
Rorty, Richard. 1991. *Essays on Heidegger and Others*. Philosophical Papers. Vol. 2. Cambridge: Cambridge University Press.
Saul, John Ralston. 2005. *The Collapse of Globalism: And the Reinvention of the World*. Toronto: Viking Canada.
Taubman, Peter M. 2009. *Teaching by Numbers: Deconstructing the Discourse of Standards and Accountability in Education*. New York: Routledge.

Viano, Maurizio. 1993. *A Certain Realism: Making Use of Pasolini's Film Theory and Practice*. Berkeley: University of California Press.

Watkins, Mel. 2007. "Reflections on Being Born in a Group of Seven Canvas That Is Magically Transformed into a Sensuous Eleanor Bond Painting." In *Beyond Wilderness: The Group of Seven, Canadian Identity, and Contemporary Art*, ed. John O'Brian and Peter White, 161–165. Montreal and Kingston: McGill-Queen's University Press.

Epilogue: The Final Word
Alicia de Alba

I consider very important to recognize the research that has been conducted by William Pinar about the curriculum field in Mexico, because we need to have the *conversation*—as he said—in this special and conflictive historical moment that we are living in. The category of *conversation* opens an interesting path amongst scholars and researchers because it implies different forms of hearing others and commenting on and discussing ideas, values, concepts, conflicts, and different kinds of possible solutions about problems related to the curriculum field.

In the context of Pinar's research *conversation* is a philosophical category that implies, at the same time, the possibility to take part in a very formal research as an object/subject of study and to be a protagonist in the research and in its conclusions and results.

I am going to highlight several points.

1. The conception of this study is in the avant-garde of the field of educational research. It has been a key productive experience. Regarding this type of experiences it is important to say that we can see the capacity and possibility to articulate different and diverse methodological strategies and techniques, for instance the autobiographic narrative and the essay.
2. It is also important that we not only acknowledge that Pinar's methodology required the difficult task of inviting a group of scholars to participate in his research as authors, but also discuss the different positions of their colleagues in the same country.
3. The methodology implies a complex articulation[1] that comes from the conception of what it means to conduct research in the educational field in the twenty-first century. We are in a historical period in which it is necessary to learn, mainly, to set up new questions and to hear each other all the time about all kinds of subjects

and objects. In this project, William Pinar has made a study that is very professional, careful, and rigorous, in academic and intellectual terms, but above all with a strong social, political, cultural, and educational commitment. We are in a world that is facing some problems that are one hundred percent new, like the environmental crisis or the nuclear threat, as well as old problems such as social injustice, inequality, and poverty. In this kind of context of social research (particularly educational research), most try to understand the role of education from the smallest scale (e.g., the community) to the world dimension. Of course, it is necessary to pay attention to educational national problems but not in a closed way, instead it is important to place this kind of problems in an international context, in the context of the world as it is today. And because this is a type of historical imperative, the *conversation* became a kind of historical research imperative.
4. The dialogue with the Mexican colleagues and with Alice Casimiro Lopes and Yuzhen Xu implied a serious and productive way of encounter, discussion, and debate and of getting new ideas and concepts. One part of the research was by Mexican scholars—researchers from important universities and research centers and institutes. Another part consisted in submitting essays to Alice Casimiro Lopes and Yuzhen Xu. Both of them read the essays and asked some questions to the Mexican authors. This was another important part of the *conversation*.
5. The category of conversation worked by William Pinar is the nodal point—in my opinion—that permits and moves the entire project to achieve its goals. In the book different chapters recuperate and show the different parts of this nodal point of Pinar's research.
6. The idea of internationalization of the curriculum is a germinal notion and—from my perspective—must be conceptualized, developed, and taken as a tool to investigate the interrelations amongst the different kinds of curriculum proposals. Trying to work in the possibility of curriculum internationalization implies facing many challenges. It seems to me that one of the most important challenges refers to cultural contact and I would like to work internationalization of the curriculum from the theoretical position of cultural contact.

I am convinced that this way of conducting research must be promoted and supported into our countries and regions and in international projects.

Frida Díaz Barriga Arceo

William Pinar has established a fruitful intercultural dialogue with a group of Mexican academics who for several decades have been doing research in the field of curriculum studies. Writing the chapters in this current volume has allowed the authors not only to relate our own intellectual history on this subject but also to engage in deep reflection, both retrospective and prospective. The questions put by Yuzhen Xu and Alice Casimiro Lopes have also contributed to discovering new angles of the problems stated, and also to rethinking some concepts, thanks to the mediation of a view from outside. The intellectual concerns and research agenda of the Mexican academics who participated in this project have many points in common, but at the same time they present major differences. Simply put, it should be remembered that, as Pinar says, "curriculum is a complicated conversation," and in Mexico this has been the case since its beginnings as a field for research and intervention. It is evident in the chapters that there are different conceptions of curriculum studies (hence the polysemy of the term, which is recognized by all the authors) that are based on a diversity of theoretical references and study objectives. At the same time, there is a coincidence in the basic concerns and in recognition of the existence of different research traditions that converge in curriculum studies.

In my case, in the chapter "Curriculum Studies in Mexico: Transformations and Current Circumstances," I attempt to identify the main trends in research and curricular development in my country in recent decades. I agree with some of my Mexican colleagues that there are major tensions between research activities (the agenda of university academics specializing in curriculum) and intervention or curriculum development activities (the agenda of educational institutions and school authorities). The practice of curriculum design is not always consistent with the theoretical or methodological approaches it attempts to incorporate, and nowadays it is subject to policies emanating from various national and international agencies. As a reflection of the universality of neoliberal policies, new forms of production and regulation of knowledge now prevail, and this includes the curriculum studies field. In the big curriculum reforms made starting in the 1990s and continuing today, what prevails is a vision that is too pragmatic and the conviction that it is necessary to introduce quality control, accountability, and incentive systems similar to those used in business. Although we speak of an increasing participation by teachers in curriculum development, the reality is that the logic of a generic curriculum designed by experts continues to prevail, which cannot give an appropriate response to the problems of such diverse educational communities. In synthesis, although there are enriching and encouraging experiences in the field of curriculum development in Mexico, the reality is that the so-called technical rationality continues to prevail in the process that leads to the generation of new educational models and study plans. Concern for an understanding of educational reality, for theoretical construction and reflection on curriculum as a field of knowledge, and, even more, interest in participation by teachers, students, or society in general in curricular issues that affect them continues to be found only in the bosom of communities of researchers and academics interested in curriculum studies. I understand that similar situations occur not only in other countries in the Latin American region, but also in industrialized Western countries. In the *International Handbook of Curriculum Research* (2003), edited by Pinar, it is clear that the impact of global curriculum trends is important in many countries throughout the world, but at the same time there are very interesting local contributions. This is the case of Mexico, which receives important external influences and imports educational modalities from other countries, but at the same time has generated a curriculum studies field with its own physiognomy, as the fruit of contributions by its academics.

José María García Garduño

> What is curriculum theory? The short answer is that curriculum theory is the interdisciplinary study of educational experience. Not every interdisciplinary study of educational experience is curriculum theory, of course, nor is every instance of curriculum theory interdisciplinary. Curriculum theory is a distinctive field of study, with a unique history, a complex present, an uncertain future. Discernible in this field are influences from disciplines across the humanities and the arts and, to lesser extent, from the social sciences (primarily social theory). William Pinar (2004, 2)

The above quotation serves as a departing point, not to bring a closure, as it commonly occurs in epilogues, but to unveil a little the complex theoretical framework that lies behind this book and what it represents to the current development of curriculum field. Pinar's work on curriculum theory spans almost 40 years since his first publication in a major journal (1972), "Working from Within" (Pinar, 1994), in which he parallels how he was teaching existentialism to secondary-school students like Jackson Pollock, the American icon of the abstract expressionism movement, created a painting: without a conceived plan. In that work Pinar announced, perhaps without being fully aware of it, his poststructuralist stage of curriculum theory several years prior to the formal inception of the movement.

After the Tylerian era, curriculum theory has experienced three main stages: *reconceptualization, postmodern or poststructuralist,* and a new stage that emerged in this decade, the *cosmopolitan*. Although the reconceptualization stage did not have a clear head, Pinar is considered to be the catalyst of this movement (Pacheco 2009). He played a key role in the Rochester Conference in 1973; his edited volume *Curriculum Theorizing: The Reconceptualists* (1975a) marked, to a great extent, *the* formal initiation of the reconceptualization stage. Reconceptualization meant a transformation of the field "from essentially non-theoretical, pseudo-pragmatic (i.e., narrowly technical) area into theoretically potent, conceptually autonomous field which inquires systematically into a multi-dimensional reality, in ways to transform both" (Pinar 1994, 71). As reconceptualization reached its pinnacle during the 1970s and mid-1980s, Postmodern curriculum or postreconceptualization came to the fore. For Slattery (1997) postmodernism has articulated concepts such as "the death of the subject, the repudiation of depth models of reality, the rejection of grand narratives or universal explanations of history, the illusion of the transparency of language, the impossibility of any final meaning, the effects of power on the objects it represents, the failure of pure reason to understand the world, the de-centering of the Western logos and with it the dethroning of the 'first world,' the end of a belief in progress as a natural and neutral panacea, and a celebration of difference and multiplicity." Under this umbrella curriculum has several meanings and discourses; it is understood as political, racial, phenomenological, gender, aesthetic, deconstructed, theological, autobiographical, and international.

Early in the current decade the de-centering of the *Western logos* and the *first world* as well as the approach to curriculum as international discourse, both paved the way to the inception of the current stage of curriculum theory: cosmopolitanism or internationalization as Pinar has called the movement, that is, "the emergence of worldwide curriculum studies field with a vocabulary, and intellectual agenda that incorporates and expresses both national and international curriculum questions and concepts" (Pinar 2010, 1). However, cosmopolitanism might reflect better the meaning of this movement. According to Hansen (2008, 294) cosmopolitanism goes beyond multiculturalism and educational pluralism; cosmopolitanism "does not privilege already formed communities. It seeks to defend emerging spaces for new cultural and social configurations reflective of the intensifying intermingling of people, ideas, and activities the world over."

Pinar has led the postmodern curriculum to another more advanced stage: the cosmopolitan. The main facts of this new stage are the founding of the *International Association for the Advancement of Curriculum Studies* in 2001, and the editing of the *International Handbook of Curriculum Research* (Pinar 2003) in which curricularists of 29 countries from all continents analyzed the creation and development of curriculum field. The next step into the cosmopolitanism of curriculum is underway. Under Pinar's initiative, curricularists of South Africa, Brazil, Mexico, China, and India are analyzing the state of the field in their own countries. If we consider the scholars and countries that collaborated in *International Handbook of Curriculum Research* and books dedicated to the in-depth study of curriculum field, Pinar has already surveyed the state of curriculum field that affects at least two-thirds of the world's population. Pinar believes that curriculum is embedded in national cultures (Pinar 2004).

The Mexican book was created and recreated through the *currere* or autobiographical method, envisioned by Pinar in his early years. Pinar transformed the noun "curriculum" into a verb. The *currere* method was inspired by the works of Sartre (1943) and Laing and Cooper (1971). The aim of the method is to reconceptualize the meaning of curriculum by using "oneself and one's existential experience as data source, contributors built a multidimensional biography based in preconceptual and conceptual experiences" (Pinar 1975b, 1). The method consists of four steps: regressive, progressive, analytical, and synthetical. Pinar's introduction to this volume shows how past and present personal experiences are intermingled with curriculum theoretical positions. Some of the contributors to this volume have either participated in the 1968 Mexican student revolt or had been harassed or threatened by the Argentinean military in the mid-1970s; thus their experiences have influenced their critical and postmodern views. Besides, one might understand why Mexican curriculum has been highly preoccupied by development and innovation as means of breaking the status quo of the realm of higher education. "Pinar suggests that curriculum development is not procedural or bureaucratic as Tyler had stipulated it to be" (Pacheco 2009, 40). The curriculum histories told in this volume confirm such assertion.

Pinar asserts that curriculum is a complicated conversation. Since the beginning, in the early 1970s, the main end of Pinar scholarship has been to understand such complicated conversation with, as he points out, *a complex present and an uncertain future*. Pinar's Dad told him that everything was about understanding. Perhaps that is why Pinar *currere* displays the broadest erudition on the curriculum field. As Shirley Steinberg points out in the introduction to *Autobiography, Politics and Sexuality* (Pinar 1992), "No one writes like Bill Pinar."

Note

1. Complex articulation in an ontological, epistemological, theoretical, semiotic, methodological, technique, political, cultural and educational way.

References

Hansen, David. 2008. "Curriculum and the Idea of a Cosmopolitan Inheritance." *Journal of Curriculum Studies* 4 (3): 389–312.
Laing, Ronald David, and David Graham Cooper. 1971. *Reason and Violence: A Decade of Sartre's Philosophy, 1950–1960*. Galway Ireland: M. W. Books.
Pinar, William. 1975a. *Curriculum Theorizing: The Reconceptualists*. Berkeley, CA: McCutchan.
Pinar, William. 1975b. "The Method of "Currere."" Paper presented at *the Annual Meeting of the American Research Association*, Washington, DC , April 1975.
Pinar, William. 1994. "Working from Within." In *Autobiography, Politics and Sexuality*, ed. William Pinar, 7–12. New York: Peter Lang.
Pinar, William. 2003. *The International Handbook of Curriculum Research*. Mahwah, NJ: Lawrence Erlbaum Associates.
Pinar, William. 2004. *What is Curriculum Theory?* New York: Routledge.
Pinar, William. 2010. "Curriculum Studies in China and India." University of British Columbia. Available online at: http://csics.educ.ubc.ca.
Pacheco, José Augusto. 2009. *Whole, Bright, Deep with Understanding*. Rotterdam: Sense Publishers.
Slattery, Patrick. 1997. "Postmodern Curriculum Research and Alternative Forms of Data Presentation." Public Seminar/Occasional paper presented to The Curriculum and Pedagogy Institute of the University of Alberta. Available online at: http://www.quasar.ualberta.ca.

Contributors

Ashwani Kumar is a PhD candidate at the University of British Columbia where he has studied curriculum studies in South Africa, Brazil, and Mexico. He has published in *Journal of the American Association for the Advancement of Curriculum Studies, Education Review,* and *Journal of Critical Education Policy Studies* and presented his research at meetings of American Association for the Advancement of Curriculum Studies, American Educational Research Association, Canadian Society for the Study of Education, and National Council for the Social Studies. His dissertation research focuses upon developing the concept of *Curriculum as Awareness* based on his study of the works of Jiddu Krishnamurti and James Macdonald.

Alicia de Alba teaches Curriculum Theory and Philosophy and Education at National University Autonomous of Mexico. She belongs to the National System of Researchers (Sistema Nacional de Investigadores SNI) and Mexican Academy of Sciences (Academia Mexicana de Ciencias). The Director of the editorial collection *Educacion, debates e imaginario social*, de Alba is the author of *Curriculum in the Postmodern Condition* (with Edgar González Gaudiano, Colin Lankshear, and Michael Peters 2000), *Der Kultural Kontak* (Transcript, Bielefeld, Germany, 2006), *Curriculumsociedad* (2007, UNAM–Mexico), and *Que dice la investigacion educativa?* (coedited with Raquel Glazman, COMIE–México, 2009). Two projects—Curriculum, culture, identity and horizons of future; Analysis, revision and instrumentation of the curriculum of six Military Educative institutions from the gendered perspective—are now underway.

Frida Díaz Barriga Arceo serves as researcher and teacher at the Faculty of Psychology of the National Autonomous University of Mexico. She holds a master's degree in Educational Psychology (Faculty of Psychology) and a PhD in Education (Faculty of Arts). She is the author or coauthor of *Teaching Assessment* (*Evaluación de la docencia, Paidós*, 2001); *Teaching Strategies for a Meaningful Learning: A Constructivist Approach* (*Estrategias* *docentes para un aprendizaje significativo: Una interpretación constructivista*) (McGraw Hill, 2002; 2010); *Situated Teaching* (*Enseñanza situada. Vínculo entre la escuela y la vida*, McGraw Hill, 2006); *Impact of Higher Education Evaluation Programs in Mexico* (*Impacto de la evaluación en la educación superior mexicana*, ANUIES, 2008).

Ángel Díaz Barriga earned the PhD degree in the Faculty of Philosophy and Letters of the UNAM. He joined the UNAM as Associate Professor in 1975 and is currently a Researcher Emeritus. He is the author of *Didáctica y Curriculum* (1984) *Ensayos sobre la problemática curricular* (1984), *Empleadores y egresados universitarios* (1995). He is the editor of *La Investigación curricular en México, La década de los ochenta* (1993), *La investigación curricular en México, La década de los noventa* (2003), and *Impacto de la evaluación en la educación superior* (2008).

Alfredo Furlán took his PhD in Education Sciences from René Descartes University (Paris V) (France, 1986). At present he is a full-time Professor in the Interdisciplinary Unit for Research in Health and Education Sciences at the Iztacala Faculty of High Studies (FESI, for its initials in Spanish), a satellite campus of the National University of Mexico (UNAM), where he is developing a line of research on *Pedagogical Management in Schools: The Problems of Coexistence and Discipline*. He is also an advisor to doctoral students in the FESI's postgraduate psychology programs and in postgraduate programs in pedagogy at the UNAM's Faculty of Philosophy and Literature. He has published articles and books on pedagogical and didactic theory, curriculum and student management and discipline. He coordinated preparation of the status of knowledge, *Discipline and Coexistence in Schools: The Problems of Lack of Discipline, Incivilities and Violence* (2003), published by the Mexican Council on Educational Research. He is a member of the National Researcher System, Level 2.

José María García Garduño obtained a master's degree in Educational Administration from SUNY Albany and a PhD in Education from Ohio University. He is a Professor at the Universidad Autónoma de la Ciudad de México. His research interests are related to curriculum theory and educational leadership. He published with Graciela Cordero *Tyler's Curriculum Rationale and the Reconceptualists. Interview with Ralph W. Tyler (1902–1994)* in *Revista Electrónica de Investigación Educativa* (2004).

Raquel Glazman Nowalski studied Philosophy in the National University of Costa Rica, Communication and Journalism in the Political Sciences School of the National Autonomous University of México, her master's degree and her PhD in Pedagogy in the same University (UNAM) where she teaches and is developing a line of research around how to develop a critical capacity in Mexican university students. Having published widely in scholarly journals, monographs, and newspapers, she has been an advisor to doctoral students of many universities and is a member of the National Researcher System, Level 2.

María Concepción Barrón Tirado is a researcher in the National University of Mexico's Institute for Research on the University and Education. She is a Professor of undergraduate and graduate courses on pedagogy in that university (UNAM), a member of the National Researcher System, Level 2, and coordinator of the graduate program in pedagogy in the UNAM. Barrón Tirado is a member of the Ibero-American Curriculum Network and of the Mexican Section of the French-Speaking International Association for Research in the Educational Sciences (AFIRSE), and the Mexican Educational Research Council (COMIE), where she served as General Secretary from 2007 to 2009. Her research lines and publications are in the field of didactics, curriculum, and professional training.

William F. Pinar teaches at the University of British Columbia, where he holds a Canada Research Chair. He is the editor of the *International Handbook of Curriculum Research* (2003, Lawrence Erlbaum) and, most recently, of *Curriculum Studies in South Africa* (2010, Palgrave Macmillan), and *Curriculum Studies in Brazil* (2011, Palgrave Macmillan).

Index

Academic
   Freedom, 55, 93, 169, 175, 178, 236, 245
   Knowledge, 37, 42, 55, 79, 94, 100–104, 118, 123, 196, 198, 216, 234, 238, 243
Accountability, 42, 46, 47, 77, 83, 84, 176, 217, 236, 245, 251
Accreditation, 29, 42, 43, 45–47, 83, 88, 89, 99, 100, 104–106, 154, 155, 175, 176, 193, 220
   Disaccreditation, 188
Acculturation, 137–140, 143–146, 148, 158
   see also Transculturation
Activity, 3, 4, 6, 20, 231
Adorno, Theodor, 151
Advising, 193
Aesthetics, 253
   Aesthetic education, 24
Agency, 6, 218, 243
Alba, Alicia de, 6–8, 34, 35, 37, 40, 41, 49, 54, 56, 57, 69, 79, 111, 127–133, 150, 152, 210–212, 220, 221, 224–226, 228–230, 233–237, 239, 240, 242–244, 249
Alexander, William, 36, 57, 167
Alignment, 83, 123, 174, 224, 233, 234
Althusser, Louis, 3, 12, 36, 57, 79, 243
Amorim, Antonio, 22
Antebi, Mirtha, 32, 94

Anti-intellectualism, 102
Aoki, Ted, 15, 21
Apple, Michael, 36, 53, 79, 96, 150
Arceo, Frida Díaz-Barriga, 6–12, 23, 30, 31, 34, 41, 56, 75, 169, 173, 191, 215–218, 221, 222, 227, 229, 231, 234, 237, 240, 242–244, 251
Archeology, 4–6
Arcos, Enrique Moreno de los, 55
Argentina, 12, 15, 35, 36, 52, 57, 97, 116, 117, 119, 138, 139, 145–148, 150–152, 156, 158, 166, 173, 199, 208, 212, 216, 224, 227–229, 234, 236, 237, 243, 244, 254
Arnaz, José, 78
Artaud, Antonin, 21, 22
Assessment, 33, 46, 47, 96, 117, 175–178, 237, 242, 257
   Disciplinary, 56, 58, 76, 87, 106, 111, 131, 132, 172, 227
   Peer, 99
   Self-critical, 112
   Theoretical, 112
Australia, 51, 224
Ausubel, David, 36, 39, 57, 81
Authoritarianism, 19, 39, 54, 82, 87, 169, 233
   Anti-authoritarianism, 9
Autobiography, 4, 49, 51, 249, 253, 254
Auto-ethnography, 40, 82
Autonomous Metropolitan University of Xochimilco, 13, 37, 79

Autonomous University of Guerrero, 212
Autonomous University of Nayarit (UAN), 13, 97, 244
Autonomous University of Sinaloa, 212
Autonomous University of Zacatecas, 119
Autonomy, 12, 45, 46, 88, 148, 168, 177, 188, 195, 229, 230, 253
   Intellectual, 148
   Professional, 169
Azevedo, Fernando de, 145

Baker, Eva, 12, 30, 93, 209
Barco, Susana, 32, 36, 57, 94, 209
Barreda, Gabino, 144
Barriga, Ángel Díaz, 2, 6, 8, 9, 12–14, 16, 17, 20, 22, 23, 30, 31, 34, 35, 37, 40, 41, 52, 53, 55–57, 68, 76, 78, 85, 86, 91, 121–127, 131–133, 138, 147, 149, 150, 152, 158, 172, 173, 209–213, 218, 219, 225, 227, 228, 232, 234, 236, 237, 239, 240, 242–245
Bauldelot, Christian, 36, 79
Beauchamp, George, 166
Beck, Ulrich, 142
Behaviorism, 9, 10, 30, 78, 91, 168, 173, 214
   Behavioral (or behaviorist) objectives, 30, 92, 94
   Non-behaviorist, 97
   Technicist-behaviorist, 33, 96
   Technological-behaviorist, 31, 92, 93
Bellack, Arno, 166
Beltrán, Gonzalo Aguirre, 139–141
Benjamin, Walter, 245
Bernstein, Basil, 36, 57, 238
Bildung, 4
Binet, Alfred, 216
Bishop, Father Jordan, 21

Bloom, Benjamin, 12, 13, 17, 20, 30, 31, 53, 92, 93, 166, 209, 210, 233
Boas, Franz, 139
Bobbitt, Franklin, 3, 22, 35, 36, 40, 52, 56, 57, 124, 125, 153
Bolívar, Antonio, 151
Bologna agreements, 44, 101, 237
Bourdieu, Pierre, 12, 36, 57, 79, 98
Brameld, Theodore, 233
Brazil, 3, 6, 12, 16, 22, 112, 138, 139, 144–146, 148–152, 154–158, 207, 213, 214, 220, 221, 228, 229, 236, 243, 254
Brooks, David, 237, 238
Bruner, Jerome, 17, 36, 39, 57, 81
Bureaucratization, 38, 98, 104, 105, 124, 188, 254
Bureaucracy, 98, 124, 133, 176
Bureaucrats, 13, 34, 38, 46, 78, 88, 218
Business, 13, 44, 46, 88, 101, 104, 106, 198, 201, 219, 221, 234, 237, 244, 251
   Men, 123, 197, 232
   Schools as, 16, 24
   Thought, 11, 12, 84
   University as, 100

Callahan, Raymond, 151
Canada, 21, 23, 41, 51, 83, 112, 137, 195, 199, 215, 245
Canclini, Néstor García, 139, 141, 142, 147
Capitalism, 64, 122, 186, 234
   Global, 38, 41–43
   Transnational, 125
   US, 123, 125
Caraveo, Luz Maria Nieto, 53
Cardenas, Lázaro, 106, 211
Carnoy, Martin, 138, 139, 234
Carranza, Cristina, 32, 94
Casas, Rosalba, 198
Castaneda, Carlos, 21

Castoriadis, Cornelius, 36, 58, 129
Center for Intercultural
    Documentation (CIDOC), 2, 21,
    32, 47, 93
Cerdá, Michel, 41, 56
Certification, 10, 11, 42, 43, 47, 77,
    83, 84, 88, 176, 189, 190, 193,
    209, 240
Charters, W. W., 3, 45
Chase, Stuart, 2
Chicago School, 13, 38, 91, 98, 244
Chile, 12, 97, 145, 150, 152, 155, 173,
    199, 236
China, 7, 236, 245, 254
Chomsky, Noam, 166
Clark, Burton, 182
Classroom(s), 14, 33, 38–40, 43,
    76, 77, 82, 85–87, 94–96,
    102, 103, 105, 114, 117, 118,
    125, 126, 128, 177, 195, 216,
    232, 236
Coelho, Paulo, 149
Cognitive psychology, 9, 10, 39, 78, 81
Coll, César, 14, 39, 81, 152
Collaboration, 39, 81, 95, 120, 191,
    202, 243
Colombia, 53, 145, 166, 224, 229
Colonization, 31, 47, 78, 138, 221
    see also Satellitization
Communication(s), 59, 60, 65, 66,
    103, 121, 128, 154, 167, 185,
    197, 218, 258
  Abilities, 184
  Cyber, 50
  Educational, 167
  Intercultural, 87
  Media, 200
  Proficiencies, 43
  Studies, 168
  Technologies, 43, 87, 223, 234
  Theorist, 23
Communism, 233
  Communist Party, 7

Cuban, 31
Italian, 23
Competency, 10, 11, 15, 22,
    43–47, 76, 77, 84, 86–88,
    95, 100, 102, 103, 105, 174,
    188, 190, 208, 214, 218,
    220–223, 226, 231, 233,
    234, 240, 243
  -based, 14, 44, 45, 101, 102
  learning, 126
  Vocational, 209
Competitiveness, 9, 11, 42, 43, 85, 88,
    99, 176, 182–184, 190
Comte, Auguste, 144
Conscience, 9
Constructivism, 9–11, 14, 15, 29, 36,
    39, 40, 45, 81, 86, 87, 97, 100,
    214, 216, 218, 221, 223, 231,
    232, 241, 257, 258
Consumerism, 220
Consumption, 200
Contemplation, 5, 245
Conversation, 3, 59, 71, 127, 153, 236,
    249–251, 254
Cooper, David, 254
Cosmopolitanism, 11, 137, 138, 142,
    143, 152, 153, 158, 212, 235,
    253, 254
Costa Rica, 53, 145, 155, 224,
    229, 258
Counts, George, 233
Creativity, 166, 197, 224
Critical pedagogy, 9, 10, 79, 80
Critical theory, 29, 36, 37, 78, 126,
    146, 148–152, 158, 212, 217,
    229, 236
    see also Frankfurt School
Critical thinking, 9, 171, 177
Cuba, 12, 19, 31, 92, 141
Cuernavaca, 2, 22, 32, 93
Cultural contact, 59, 64–66, 69, 71,
    140, 230, 250
Currere, 4, 6, 254

INDEX

Curriculum (the), 3, 4, 10, 11, 14–18, 22, 23, 33–37, 40–45, 52, 53, 55, 57, 59, 60, 63, 75–88, 95–100, 112–120, 122–133, 137, 141, 144, 147, 149–151, 153–157, 166–174, 177, 191, 192, 195–197, 199–201, 208–211, 213–215, 217–221, 223, 224, 226–237, 239, 240, 242, 245, 250, 251, 253, 254
  Administrators, 46
  Composition, 46, 148
  Concepts, 3, 4, 91, 231, 253
  Construction, 22
  Cosmopolitan, 143, 153, 254
  Decision-making, 46, 88, 116, 170
  Deliberation, 16
  Departments, 155
  Design, 31, 32, 54, 75, 81, 86, 118, 146, 166–169, 173, 197, 226, 251
  Designers, 46, 88
  Development, 11, 13, 16, 18, 30, 35, 39, 46, 75, 77, 79, 81, 85–88, 92, 93, 101, 103, 124, 148, 150, 156, 170, 172, 202, 214, 231, 232, 251, 252, 254
  Discourses, 11, 150, 253
  Engineering, 43, 101
  Evaluation, 32, 52, 54, 103, 116, 117, 125, 226
  Expert(s) (specialists), 41, 43, 58, 59, 75, 100, 114, 148, 149, 152, 155, 157, 158, 173, 175
  Field, 8, 11, 34, 35, 49–51, 55, 56, 59, 60, 68, 84, 92, 122, 131, 133, 134, 137, 138, 141, 143, 146–148, 150, 152–154, 157, 184, 217, 218, 221, 224–226, 230, 234, 236, 249, 252, 254
  Flexibility, 44, 102, 133, 174, 191, 220
  Guidelines, 170
  Hidden, 47, 76, 92, 98, 100, 126, 177
  History, 16, 17, 35, 40, 51, 56, 76, 84, 85, 98, 254
  Implementation, 39
  Inquiry, 153
  Integration, 38, 95, 97, 98, 171, 178, 220
  Issues, 16
  Journals, 152, 156, 157
  Knowledge, 41, 46, 56, 77, 87, 132, 133, 237
  Lived, 4, 15, 47, 98, 100, 125, 126
  Logic, 218
  Management, 201
  Model(s), 18, 33, 35, 37, 149, 169, 190
  Organization, 191, 196
  Planning, 39, 81, 117, 125, 146, 148, 190, 245
  Policies, 31, 84
  Practice(s), 34, 113, 120, 121
  Projects, 35, 54, 93
  Questions, 11
  Reality, 113, 115, 128, 132, 133
  Reconceptualization of, 33
  Reform(s), 8, 43, 76, 77, 84, 85, 92, 130, 133, 134, 147, 152, 173, 175, 190, 251
  Research, 2, 9, 10, 13, 16, 17, 30, 39, 45–48, 52, 75, 76, 78, 81, 84, 85, 89, 93, 100, 106, 115, 116, 122, 155–157, 168, 173, 177, 215, 216, 222, 224, 226, 234, 242, 252, 254
  Researcher(s), 33, 39, 56, 81, 84, 85, 96, 114, 123, 224, 232
  Scholars, 17, 34, 36, 40, 45–48, 57, 76, 88, 89, 128, 151, 212, 217, 228, 231
  Scholarship, 2, 16, 45
  School, 37, 79, 93, 96, 233, 245
  Standards, 147
  Structure(s), 194, 197

Index

Studies, 1–6, 8–11, 13–15, 17, 20–22, 24, 29, 31, 34, 35, 38, 40, 41, 45–47, 49–55, 58, 59, 64, 67, 75–79, 81, 84, 85, 87, 91, 94, 96–99, 104, 105, 111, 112, 116, 122, 125–127, 131–133, 137, 138, 146, 148, 149, 153–158, 165, 166, 172, 174, 200, 207–210, 212–214, 217, 219, 220, 224–228, 230–236, 238, 242, 243, 245, 251–254
Teacher education, 15
Theory, 12, 13, 16, 17, 21, 29, 34, 37, 76, 78, 80, 84, 85, 91, 92, 94, 96, 122, 123, 145, 148, 150, 151, 158, 168, 231, 252, 253
Thought, 18, 33, 99
Trends, 184, 252
Understanding, 11, 21, 35, 76, 85, 113, 117, 127, 128, 133, 231
University, 12, 19, 52, 80, 169, 171, 175, 191, 221
Cusset, François, 243

Daowz, Patricio, 16
Darder, Antonia, 53
Deconstruction, 61, 69, 230, 253
Decroly, Ovide, 144, 145
Deleuze, Gilles, 22, 23, 36, 57
Democratization, 33, 92, 175, 184, 210, 215
Derrida, Jacques, 21, 22, 36, 57, 229, 238
Deschooling, 32, 93
De Veaux, Alexis, 2
Dewey, John, 22, 24, 36, 40, 56, 57, 125, 143–145, 153, 158, 166, 233
Dialogue(s), 5, 7, 23, 93, 119, 120, 127, 165, 174, 177, 207, 212, 219, 225, 235, 236, 250, 251
Didactics, 12, 14, 18, 32, 55, 76, 94–96, 98, 105, 117, 123, 128, 131, 149, 212, 217, 219, 226–228, 231, 233

Didaktik, 4
Dienstag, Joshua, 5, 21
Disciplinarity, 4, 197, 207, 236
Discourse Analysis, 40, 82
Dislocation, 62, 65, 66, 70
Displacement(s), 13, 65, 66, 103, 122, 123
Distance education, 100, 133
  see also Virtual education
Diversity, 8, 56, 78, 84, 85, 125, 142, 194, 200, 201, 251
Durkheim, Emile, 36, 57, 166

Economic Crisis (1982), 38, 91, 98, 208
Economism, 20, 47
Ecuador, 229
Edelstein, Gloria, 32, 94, 209
Efficiency, 9, 11, 35, 38, 83, 88, 98, 123, 150, 151, 174, 177, 182, 186, 190, 221, 223, 225, 234
  Social, 3, 22
Eggleston, John, 96
Eight-Year Study, 233
Engels, Friedrich, 36, 57
Environmental, 59
  Crisis, 60, 128, 250
  Education, 85, 87, 226
Equality, 83
Establet, Roger, 36, 79
Ethics, 11, 87, 93, 106
Ethnography, 14, 98
Evaluation, 8, 10, 11, 13, 14, 16, 19, 20, 22, 29, 32–35, 37, 42, 43, 45–47, 52, 54, 57, 60, 75, 77–80, 84–86, 88, 94–96, 99, 100, 103–106, 112, 113, 116, 117, 121, 123, 125, 134, 148, 156, 157, 167, 174–178, 182, 189, 190, 202, 210, 214–217, 220, 223, 226, 227, 234, 245
Excellence, 11, 43, 86, 174, 190, 191
Exile, 2, 15, 36, 54, 68, 145, 148–151, 158, 173, 236

Experience, 3, 6, 8, 9, 11, 21, 38, 40, 51, 52, 59, 67, 68, 82, 87, 95, 105, 113, 117, 120, 124, 126, 131, 168, 175, 218, 230, 243, 249, 252, 254
   Clinical, 103
   Cultural, 142
   Curricular, 82
   Educational, 22, 78, 86, 100, 118, 126, 168, 252
   Existential, 254
   Field, 124
   Individual, 142
   Learning, 81
   Lived, 4, 5, 23
   Practical, 191, 195, 198
   Shared, 220
   Student, 118

Fanfani, Emilio Tenti, 215, 244
Federal University of Rio de Janeiro (UFRJ), 157
Feeney, Silvina, 156
Fellini, Federico, 23
Feminism, 178
   Feminist pedagogy, 82
Filho, Lourenço, 145, 149, 228
Flexibility, 11, 42–44, 86, 87, 100–102, 105, 182–184, 190, 191, 193, 195, 201, 208, 219–221, 232–234
   Labor, 182
Follari, Roberto, 35, 37, 52, 54, 56, 79, 148, 149, 239
Formation, 3, 4, 6, 17, 20, 40, 52, 77, 80, 87, 96, 123–125, 129, 154, 174, 177, 220, 222, 231
   Faculty, 120, 121, 226
   Intellectual, 15, 16
   Professional, 19, 32, 40, 43, 76, 86, 94, 222, 227
   Self-, 9
   Students, 19

Foucault, Michel, 5, 36, 57, 151, 243
France, 7, 16, 44, 50, 51, 96, 144, 150, 151, 166, 186, 191, 216, 228, 243
Frankfurt School, 18, 19, 126, 150, 212
Freinet, Celestine, 144, 145, 209
Freire, Paulo, 2, 12, 18, 21, 32, 36, 79, 93, 94, 143, 149, 151, 152, 158, 209, 212, 235
Freud, Sigmund, 18, 36, 57, 118
Friedman, Milton, 38, 244
Froebel, Friedrich, 144
Fromm, Erich, 2, 19
Fuentes, Bertha Orozco, 53, 58
Furlán, Alfredo, 6, 14–16, 35, 37, 41, 54, 56, 57, 79, 111, 148–150, 210–213, 233, 234, 236, 239, 240

Gadamer, Hans-Georg, 36, 57, 71
Gagné, Robert, 30, 78, 208, 209
Garduño, José María García, 6, 16, 23, 30, 137, 212, 226–228, 235, 240, 244, 252
Gaudiano, Edgar González, 8, 32, 40, 41, 54–57, 240, 242
Gender, 40, 59, 76, 82, 87, 115, 120, 178, 226, 253, 257
Genealogy, 4–6, 20, 22, 23, 61
Germany, 44, 184, 186, 191, 224
Gestalt psychology, 18
Giral, Galán, 41, 56
Giroux, Henry, 36, 40, 53, 55–57, 79, 129, 149–152, 212, 235
Glazman-Nowalski, Raquel, 6, 8, 17, 18, 31, 35, 41, 53, 55–58, 78, 111, 112, 148, 155, 165, 171, 173, 210, 211, 213–215, 224, 227, 230, 232–234, 236, 238, 240
Globalization, 6, 11, 12, 15, 20, 23, 29, 41, 48, 59–63, 77, 83, 85, 99, 104, 105, 115, 130, 131, 138, 139, 141, 153, 168, 184, 190, 193, 199,

200, 208, 210, 220, 221, 223,
    224, 230, 233–236, 238, 244
Gómez, Rosa Amalia, 193
González Lucini, Fernando, 200
Grafton, Anthony, 244
Gramsci, Antonio, 36, 57, 70, 150,
    212, 213
Grant, George, 237, 244
Great Britain, *see* United Kingdom
Greene, Maxine, 24
Group Dynamics, 94–96
Grumet, Madeleine R., 219
Guevara, Ché, 2
Gutiérrez, Gustavo, 21
Gutiérrez Puertos, Patricia, 196

Habermas, Jürgen, 57, 151
Hamilton, David, 36, 57, 85
Hannerz, Ulf, 142
Hansen, David, 143, 253
Hegel, Georg W. F., 36, 57, 145
Hegemony, 10, 11, 23, 30, 31, 37, 47,
    79, 84, 97, 123, 138, 244
Heidegger, Martin, 36, 57
Herbart, Johann Friedrich, 144,
    209, 213
Hermeneutics, 40, 82
Herskovits, Melville, 139, 140
Higher education, 34, 35, 38, 42–44,
    46, 55, 78, 83, 88, 92, 93,
    95–101, 105, 112, 147, 155–157,
    167, 169, 172, 173, 175, 176, 178,
    181, 182, 184, 185, 190, 191, 193,
    195, 196, 198–201, 210, 212,
    222–224, 254, 258
    see also Superior education
Historical, 4, 5, 8, 20, 21, 23, 35, 47,
    57, 59, 62–65, 79, 85, 91, 113,
    115, 122, 124, 125, 127, 129,
    130, 144, 148, 170, 173, 185–
    187, 189, 222, 230, 232, 250
    Ahistorical, 101
    Conjectures, 215

Knowledge, 20
Materialism, 187
Moment, 128, 133, 153, 167, 169,
    202, 219, 233, 249
Situation, 165, 243
Understanding, 230
Historicity, 4–6, 197, 232, 245
History, 5, 12, 18, 20, 21–23, 46, 50,
    65, 75, 88, 121, 124, 126, 187,
    207, 209, 224, 236
    Academic, 51
    Intellectual, 6, 49, 50, 58, 61, 67,
        165, 208–210, 233, 251
    Life, 61, 82, 113, 121
    Mexican national, 6
    Professional, 10
    US-Mexico, 1
Hlebowitsh, Peter, 137
Holt, John, 21
Hughes, Langston, 22
Human capital, 11, 19, 186
    Theory, 187
Humanism, 10, 22, 96, 166, 186
Humanities, 9, 52, 67, 68, 88, 175,
    237, 252
Human rights, 23, 87, 226
Husserl, Edmund, 36, 57
Hybridism, 142, 227, 228
Hybridity, 137, 138, 141–143, 145,
    147, 148, 150–152, 158, 211, 212,
    224, 227, 228
    see also Hybridism

Ibarrola, María de, 8, 17, 31, 35, 37,
    41, 53, 55–58, 78, 111–116, 133,
    148, 155, 170, 173, 210, 211,
    236, 238
Identity, 8, 21, 55–57, 59, 64, 65, 70,
    82, 83, 85, 100, 115, 119, 121,
    130, 141, 218, 222, 227, 228
    Politics, 64
Ideology, 36, 47, 84, 115, 147, 151, 177
Illich, Ivan, 2, 21, 32, 93

Imagination (the), 1, 3, 23, 24, 40, 58, 59, 129, 132, 237
Imperialism, 30, 47, 104, 138, 139, 210, 212, 234
Imprinting, 165, 166, 178, 208, 244
India, 236, 254
Indigenous, 50, 131, 140, 144
Industrialization, 33, 122, 183, 185, 186, 189
Inequality, 14, 19, 46, 76, 88, 157, 200, 250
  Economic, 77
  Social, 33, 76, 77, 96
Information, 45, 67, 102, 119, 129, 170, 175, 189, 208, 223, 226
  Age, 83
  Science, 106
  Society, 12, 63
  Technology, 42, 43, 60, 83, 87, 190, 223, 234
Informationalism, 11
Innis, Harold, 23
Innovation(s), 5, 17, 29, 42–45, 48, 83, 86, 87, 100, 101, 104, 105, 131, 198, 201, 218, 236, 245, 254
Institutionalization, 37, 42, 79, 121, 153–158
Instrumentalism, 210, 219, 221, 222, 230, 232, 234, 236, 245
Inter-American Bank of Development, 14, 41, 83, 99, 106
International Association for the Advancement of Curriculum Studies (IAACS), 153, 158, 254
International Handbook of Curriculum Research, 2, 84, 173, 242, 252, 254
Internationalization, 5, 22, 58, 59, 138, 139, 183, 208, 224, 234, 235, 250, 253
  Of curriculum studies, 63, 64, 67, 137, 225
International Monetary Fund (IMF), 38, 98, 106, 243

Internet (the), 49, 60, 69, 72
Interpellation, 3, 66
Interpretive studies, 40, 82, 229
Intertextuality, 121
Irwin, Rita L., 21
Italy, 150, 208, 212, 213

Jackson, Philip, 36, 57, 85, 92, 96
Japan, 141, 144
Jay, Martin, 5
Jesuit(s), 15, 16, 144, 231
Jou, Ramón Costa, 145
Judt, Tony, 235
Juxtaposition, 4, 18, 65, 120, 132

Kahler, Erich, 145
Kant, Immanuel, 36, 57
Karier, Clarence, 21
Katra, Lyle Figueroa de, 53
Kemmis, Stephen, 36, 57
Kliebard, Herbert, 124, 148, 236
Kluckhohn, Clyde, 145
Kögler, Hans-Herbert, 6
Krause, Karl Christian Friedrich, 145
Kroker, Arthur, 23
Kuhn, Thomas, 153
Kumar, Ashwani, 6, 29

Labra, Herrera, 56
Lacan, Jacques, 36, 57, 129
Laclau, Ernesto, 36, 57, 67, 69, 70, 127, 129, 229
Laing, R. D., 254
Lancaster, Joseph, 144
Landesman, Monique, 111
Lankshear, Colin, 53, 242
Larroyo, Francisco, 209
Latapí, Pablo, 17
Latin America, 9, 10, 12, 13, 16, 17, 31–37, 44, 47, 51, 54, 55, 57, 60, 62, 68, 76, 78, 79, 81, 83, 91–98, 104–106, 112, 124, 127, 129–131, 138, 141, 143–152,

166, 173, 182, 185, 191, 193, 208–210, 216, 219, 224–226, 228–230, 234–236, 244, 252
see also South America
Learning, 10, 11, 17, 33, 35, 53, 76, 77, 79, 81, 86, 95, 96, 100, 102, 103, 106, 125, 126, 134, 143–145, 149, 153, 168, 172, 173, 189, 191, 192, 194–196, 199, 202, 218, 231, 232, 241, 257
  By competencies, 46, 88, 126
  Evaluation of, 32, 33, 96
  Experiential, 43
  Higher, 44, 191
  Methodologies, 190, 202
  Module, 94
  Problem-based, 43, 86, 105, 195, 196, 218
  Problems, 13
  Self-, 32, 106, 229, 233
  Situatedness of, 115
  Student, 80, 167
  Theory, 15, 97, 227
  Transdisciplinary, 197
Lévi-Strauss, Claude, 36, 57, 243
Liberation Theology, 18, 21, 36
Libraries, 31, 38, 43, 92, 95, 99, 232
Linton, Ralph, 139
Lipsmeier, Antonius, 186
Lobrot, Michel, 12, 32, 93
Lopes, Alice Casimiro, 6, 20, 22, 23, 142, 147, 157, 208–215, 217–221, 224, 225, 227–229, 233, 236, 237, 243–245, 250, 251
Lora, María Esther Aguirre, 8, 41
Lorde, Audre, 2, 22
Lugo, Elisa, 86, 169
Lyotard, Jean-François, 36, 57, 129

Macedo, Donaldo, 53, 152
Macedo, Elizabeth, 147, 157, 213
Magaña, Rosa Aurora Padilla, 216
Mager, Robert, 12, 13, 92, 93, 167

Manacorda, Mario, 36, 55, 150, 212, 234
Mannheim, Karl, 145
Marcuse, Herbert, 19, 123
Martínez, María de la Paz Santa María, 194
Marx, Karl, 36, 57, 213
Marxism, 23, 60, 61, 69, 106, 211, 212
  Neo-Marxism, 147, 150
  Post-Marxism, 61, 213
Matus, Don Juan, 21
McLaren, Peter, 36, 49, 79, 129, 150
Meaning(s), 23, 40, 43, 44, 60, 61, 63–67, 69, 70, 76, 82, 85, 87, 95, 97, 105, 117–119, 122, 124, 127, 131, 143, 150, 169, 182, 186, 189, 194, 202, 215, 221, 223, 232, 234, 238, 253, 254
  Intersubjective, 82
  Loss of, 128
  Subjective, 11, 40, 82
Mello, Giomar Namo de, 149
Méndez, Marín, 56
Mercado, Bravo, 56
Mestizaje, 141
Mexican Counsel of Educative Investigation (COMIE), 9, 15, 41, 56, 69, 76–78, 111, 157, 172, 227, 237, 242
Monclus, Antonio, 199
Montessori, Maria, 143–145, 209
Moral, 214, 231, 235
  Commitment, 97
  Cosmopolitanism, 142, 143
  Education, 200
  Personality, 200
Morality, 5
Moran, Porfirio, 37, 79
Moreira, Antonio Flavio Barbosa, 138, 147, 149, 150, 157
Moreira, Roberto, 146
Moreno, Juan, 115, 146, 150
Morin, Edgar Los, 129, 130, 162, 178

Mouffe, Chantal, 69
Muller, Johan, 238
Mullin, Molly, 2
Multiculturalism, 40, 49, 59, 64, 71, 76, 82, 83, 85, 143, 253
Music, 149, 200

Narcissism, 2
National Autonomous University of Mexico (UNAM), 7, 8, 18, 20, 23, 35, 51–55, 57, 67, 68, 105, 112, 121, 127, 135, 149, 152, 155, 167–169, 175, 176, 178, 196, 198, 209, 211, 216, 226, 237
Nationalism(s), 153, 186
Neoliberalism, 10–13, 15, 17, 29, 38, 41, 42, 45–47, 63, 77, 84, 88, 98, 106, 173, 174, 178, 214, 215, 221, 224, 229, 234, 251
Niebla, Guevara, 54, 56
Nietzsche, Friedrich, 4–6, 18, 23, 36, 57
North American Free Trade Agreement (NAFTA), 174, 193
Novak, Joseph, 81

Objectives of transformation or *objetos de transformación*, 211, 219, 232–234, 243
see also Transformational Objectives
Organization for Economic Co-operation and Development (OECD), 99, 116, 181, 184, 191
Organization of American States (OAS), 30, 146, 149, 210
Originality, 166
Ortega y Gasset, José, 145
Ortiz, Lorenzo, 144
Owen, David, 4, 6

Pansza, Margarita, 37, 41, 79
Pasolini, Pier Paolo, 14, 23
Passeron, Jean-Claude, 36, 79

Passion(s), 150, 238, 243
Pasternak, Boris, 23
Pavia, Edil, 213
Paz, Octavio, 67
Penna, Anthony, 36, 53, 55, 57
Performance, 22, 77, 182, 189
  Assessment of, 47
  Evaluation of, 84
  Objectives, 99
  Professional, 178
  Student, 168
Perrenoud, Phillipe, 81
Pestalozzi, Johann Heinrich, 144
Peters, Michael, 53, 242
Phenomenology, 40, 85, 147, 253
Phillips, D. C., 178
Piaget, Jean, 18, 39, 81, 97, 106, 167
Pinar, William, 31, 36, 49, 53, 55, 57, 58, 61, 68, 79, 85, 92, 148, 150, 153, 168, 173, 207, 249–254
PISA, 116, 176
Place, 16, 38, 96, 118, 119, 121, 123, 170, 190, 213, 232, 245
  Emplacement, 58
  Nonplace, 5
Pluralism, 64, 143, 253
Polysemy, 40, 75, 125, 131, 132, 182, 227, 251
Popham, James, 12, 13, 30, 93, 209
Popkewitz, Thomas, 53
Portugal, 144, 145, 157
Posner, George, 81
Post-critical, 82
Post-Fordism, 182–184
Postmodernism, 137, 141, 147, 152, 242, 253, 254
Poststructuralism, 61, 82, 152, 213, 228, 243, 252, 253
Poulantzas, Nicos, 36, 58
Poverty, 128, 131, 250
Power, 5, 14, 46, 88, 112, 115, 129, 131, 133, 188, 189, 200, 215, 220, 221, 235, 253

Practicality, 75, 123
Practice(s), 5, 9, 12, 13, 32, 34, 36, 39, 44, 46, 56, 57, 64, 66, 71, 78, 80–82, 85, 86, 88, 89, 93, 95, 99, 102, 113, 117–121, 124, 132, 133, 141, 151, 154, 168, 173, 174, 184, 185, 190, 194, 202, 207, 214, 215, 217, 218, 221, 222, 227, 230, 231, 234, 238, 251
   Academic, 119
   Cultural, 50, 67
   Curricular, 8, 15, 47, 55, 100, 121, 201
   Daily, 84, 101, 134, 219
   Educational, 39, 40, 52, 82, 86, 87, 118, 175, 227
   Expressive, 121
   Institutional, 120, 127, 147
   Neoliberal, 234
   Pedagogical, 39, 55, 85, 102, 103, 134
   Political, 3
   Professional, 95, 129, 171, 193, 197, 213, 232
   Reconstructive, 129
   School, 134
   Social, 3, 6, 80, 222
   Teaching, 174
   Theory and, 34, 78, 86, 171, 174, 208, 217–219, 231
   University, 244
Presence, 114, 121, 149, 154, 231
Program(s), 9, 14, 19, 22, 34, 46, 75, 78, 92, 96, 115, 120, 122, 126, 216, 220, 232, 242, 245
Psychoanalysis, 5, 18, 40, 93, 117, 118, 173
Psycho-pedagogical, 10, 11, 40, 80, 81, 86, 87, 217, 218, 231
Puiggros, Adriana, 8

Quality, 11, 12, 15, 42, 43, 76, 77, 81, 83, 84, 86, 99, 100, 104, 105, 111, 133, 174, 182–184, 187, 188, 190, 194, 196, 214, 216, 221, 223, 225, 226, 234, 238
   Assurance, 47, 77, 84
   Control, 42, 83, 251
   Educational, 217, 244
   Intellectual, 237
   Of life, 77
   Professional, 190
   Standards, 193
Québec, 245

Race, 82, 253
Ransom, John S., 4, 5
Ravitch, Diane, 237
Reconstruction, 3, 6, 64, 118, 119, 126, 129, 132, 138, 199, 201, 221, 229, 243
   Social, 20, 37, 80, 245
   Subjective, 22
Recontextualization, 1, 3, 12, 32, 96, 215, 224, 233, 238
Redondo, Patricio, 145
Reductionism, 35, 78, 128, 218, 223
Reimer, Everett, 32, 93
Remedí, Eduardo, 16, 35, 37, 41, 54, 57, 79, 111, 116–121, 133, 149, 212, 234, 236
Remembrance, 245
Reproduction theory, 33, 96, 221
Rivas, Jorge, 145
Rivera, Diego, 2
Roberts, David D., 4, 7, 20, 23, 209
Rodríguez, Azucena, 32, 35, 52, 94, 148, 149, 209
Rorty, Richard, 238
Rugg, Harold, 226
Ruíz, Santiago Hernández, 245

Sacristán, Gimeno, 151, 152
Sánchez Puentes, Ricardo, 194
Sartre, Jean-Paul, 254

Satelitization, 31, 47, 78, 85, 221, 237
  see also Colonization
Saul, John Ralston, 238
Saylor, Galen, 167
Scheffler, Israel, 167
Schon, Donald, 39, 80
Schwab, Joseph, 36, 57, 92, 127, 137, 233
Science(s), 19, 34, 51, 67, 68, 72, 88, 97, 106, 112, 117, 127, 172, 189, 191, 195, 198, 218
  Agronomy, 106
  Education, 105
  Educational, 15, 22, 94, 116, 242
  Experimental, 86
  Health, 86
  Information, 106
  Marine, 97
  Natural, 9, 137
  Oceanographic, 244
  Political, 238
  Social, 8, 9, 18, 67, 68, 88, 175, 252
  STS, 218
  Teaching, 55
Seo, Bong, 61
Silva, Marisol, 178
Silva, Tomaz Tadeu da, 16, 35, 40, 51, 56, 76, 80, 82, 229, 243
Skill(s), 45, 95, 97, 101, 102, 177, 182, 193, 196, 197, 214, 222, 223, 232, 235, 238
  Basic, 176
  Intellectual, 42, 177, 190
  Job-specific, 189
  Problem-solving, 185, 191
Skinner, B. F., 18
Slattery, Patrick, 253
Smith, Adam, 235
Smith, David G., 138
Snyders, George, 36, 150
Social action, 38, 97
Socialism, 19, 36, 52, 60, 67, 68, 115, 128, 211, 234, 236

Sorel, Georges, 23
South Africa, 3, 207, 208, 212, 213, 236, 238
South America, 18, 21, 54, 138, 141, 153, 154, 173
  see also Latin America
Spain, 51, 52, 138, 139, 144, 145, 147, 151, 152, 154–158, 166, 224, 227, 229, 230, 235, 236, 243, 245
Spencer, Herbert, 144
Spring, Joel, 2, 21
Standardization, 10, 22, 42, 153, 175, 192, 193, 216, 220, 223, 224, 234
  see also Uniformity
Standardized
  Curriculum, 175
  Educational programs, 42, 83
  Evaluation(s), 47, 77, 84, 216
  Exams, 14, 168, 216
  Professional training, 186
Structuralism, 33, 210, 213, 228, 243
Student Movement (1968), 7, 12, 19, 23, 30, 31, 36, 50, 60, 68, 91, 146, 166, 208–210, 254
Study, 133, 190
Study plan(s), 13, 14, 18–20, 22, 23, 30, 31, 34, 44, 46, 53, 55, 75, 77, 78, 92–96, 100, 102, 105, 106, 112–114, 119, 120, 122, 126, 127, 132, 133, 177, 190, 210, 211, 219, 220, 222, 226, 231–233, 242
  Modular, 32, 37, 97, 103, 104, 226
Subject (school or curricular), 82, 121, 143, 189
Subject (the human), 21, 64, 82, 114, 118, 119, 121, 123, 129, 131–133, 187, 189, 192, 202, 226, 253
Subjectivation, 228
Subjectivity, 3–6, 11, 20, 22, 40, 57, 59, 64–67, 76, 82, 119, 174, 175, 191, 217, 226, 245
  Intersubjectivity, 40, 82, 217, 229

Index

Superior education, 19, 83, 88, 112, 116, 117, 194, 212, 214, 239, 258
see also Higher education
Sustainability, 12, 43, 87, 115, 226

Taba, Hilda, 12, 17, 18, 30, 31, 36, 38, 40, 56, 78, 92, 93, 95, 101, 146–148, 167, 209, 210, 233
Task analysis, 45
Teacher education, 15, 31, 33, 93, 96, 134, 174, 209, 232
Teachers College, Columbia University, 154
Teaching, 10–12, 16–18, 21, 24, 33, 40, 42, 75, 76, 78, 80, 81, 86, 87, 95–97, 102, 103, 105, 106, 115, 117, 118, 125, 131, 133, 148, 168, 170, 171, 174, 175, 177, 178, 185, 186, 194–196, 199, 201, 202, 208, 215–220, 231, 233, 252, 257, 258
  Classroom, 87
  Knowledge-based, 45, 102
  Methods, 32, 78, 112, 167, 190, 194
  Modules, 197
  Programmed, 32
  Science, 55
  Units, 197, 232
Technical rationality, 167
Technological rationality, 30, 35, 47, 78, 79, 84, 87, 252
see also Technical rationality
Technology, 34, 54, 60, 62, 67, 97, 112, 114, 171, 172, 186, 195, 196, 198, 212, 218, 233, 238, 244
  Biotechnology, 219, 233
  Educational, 18, 30, 35, 54, 55, 78, 150, 223, 232
  see also Information, Technology
Teixeira, Anísio, 145
Temporality, 70

Terigi, Flavia, 156
Tirado, María Concepción Barrón, 6, 8, 18–20, 41, 181, 192, 219–224, 232–235, 237, 238, 240, 242, 244
Tomkins, George, 21
Transculturation, 139
Transdisciplinarity, 198
Transfer of Technology Project, 54, 57, 210, 244
Transformational Objectives, 32, 37, 38, 47, 80, 94, 95, 103, 104, 106, 197, 219, 232–234, 243
see also Objectives of transformation or *objetos de transformación*
Translation, 22, 139, 224, 229, 238, 243
Transversal, 86, 102, 199, 200, 202, 226
Transversality, 199, 200
Trotsky, Leon, 36, 57
Trueba, Enrique, 141
Tutoring, 43, 86, 190, 193–196, 198, 202
see also Advising, Tutorship
Tutorship, 43, 86
Tyler, Ralph, 12, 17, 18, 30, 31, 35, 36, 40, 55, 57, 78, 92, 93, 98, 118, 141, 146–150, 158, 167, 185, 208–210, 214, 233, 234, 236, 252, 254

Understanding, 7, 11, 16, 20–22, 35, 39, 40, 46, 59–61, 63, 66, 71, 76, 79, 82, 85, 87, 89, 96, 104, 113, 117, 123, 127–130, 133, 147, 177, 197, 201, 202, 207, 209, 221, 230–232, 252, 254
UNESCO, 41, 42, 83, 99, 112, 145, 146, 149, 191, 193, 197, 223, 234
Uniformity, 43, 47, 85, 153, 190
see also Standardization

United Kingdom, 13, 16, 36, 69, 79, 112, 118, 150, 158, 212, 236, 245
  England, 44, 49, 51, 53, 59, 67, 69, 127, 143, 144, 156, 166, 186, 191, 224
University of Chicago, 154
University of Granada, 155
University of Paris, 15, 150, 258
Uruguay, 97, 236

Vasconcelos, José, 144
Vela, Jesus Andres, 32, 94
Venezuela, 12, 145
Viano, Maurizio, 243
Villa, Mario Diaz, 53, 129
Villanueva, Rita Angulo, 53
Villasenor, Guillermo, 54
Violas, Paul, 21
Violence, 1, 14–16, 77, 100, 167, 258
  Symbolic, 112
Virtual education, 100
Vocationalism, 22, 29, 123, 125, 178, 181, 219, 222, 230
Vygotsky, Lev, 39, 81

Watkins, Mel, 214
Weber, Max, 145
Wilfred, Carr, 36, 57
Willis, Paul, 36, 57
Wittgenstein, Ludwig, 70, 71, 129
Workplace, 20, 42, 113, 125, 223, 233
World Bank, 14, 38, 41, 83, 98, 99, 106, 181, 191–193, 223, 234
Worldliness, 6, 238
World-worlds, 50, 61, 67, 230
Wraga, William, 137

Xu, Yuzhen, 6, 20, 22, 23, 208–211, 213, 216, 224, 227, 229, 230, 234–236, 243–245, 250, 251

Young, Michael F. D., 36, 53, 55, 57, 79, 226
Ysunza, Marisa, 53, 56, 203
Yus Ramos, Rafael, 200

Zhang, Hua, 245
Zhong, Ququan, 245
Zizek, Slavoj, 36, 57, 64

GPSR Compliance

The European Union's (EU) General Product Safety Regulation (GPSR) is a set of rules that requires consumer products to be safe and our obligations to ensure this.

If you have any concerns about our products, you can contact us on

ProductSafety@springernature.com

In case Publisher is established outside the EU, the EU authorized representative is:

Springer Nature Customer Service Center GmbH
Europaplatz 3
69115 Heidelberg, Germany

www.ingramcontent.com/pod-product-compliance
Lightning Source LLC
LaVergne TN
LVHW021653060526
838200LV00050B/2339